M000235776

My Clients...

My Teachers

Scottie, May this help you decide if you choose the noble profession of Mental Health Counseling! Enjoy & Learn

Jennie Gable

My Clients. . .My Teachers

Elefante Publishing
www.JenniferGoble.com

Library of Congress Control Number: 2014931341

ISBN: 978-0-9914717-0-6

1. Psychotherapy / Counseling
2. Self-Help / Motivational & Inspirational
3. Mental Health

Interior design by Andrea Costantine

QUANTITY PURCHASES: Companies, professional groups, clubs, and other organizations may qualify for special terms when ordering quantities of this title. For information e-mail info@ElefantePublishing.com

This book is published in the United States of America.

My Clients…
My Teachers

The Noble Process of Psychotherapy

Jennifer J. Goble, Ph. D.

Dedication

This book is dedicated to my clients who courageously shared their stories in the spirit of helping others gain perspective into the world of mental health counseling. They were my true teachers.

CONTENTS

Acknowledgments

My sincere gratitude is extended to: My valued friend, Pam Pauley, who not only edited each page numerous times but was my relentless cheerleader. She loved each story, and without her months of encouragement, my clients' opportunities to help others would be forever lost in folders deep inside locked file cabinets.

To my daughter Trina, whose suggestions and encouragement continually felt like a supportive, perpetual, warm hug.

To my husband Cal, who consistently conveyed a sense of pride in my goal to reach beyond my office walls, in the form of a book, to promote the noble process of mental health counseling.

To friends, colleagues, and authors, who read my manuscript and contributed quality feedback. I gratefully accepted their expertise and honesty, and I welcomed their counsel and support. All were invaluable mentors as I maneuvered through the vertical learning curve of an unfamiliar industry, book publishing. Each contributed to soothing my wavering belief that my first book, *My Clients…My Teachers*, could be truly possible.

Foreword

It is with great pride that Dr. Goble, Jennifer to me, asked if I would write the foreword for her first published nonfiction book…a true page turner.

First, I must share with you the circumstances of our initial meeting. Jennifer was the innkeeper extraordinaire of a bed and breakfast that had once been an old library. It was funded by Andrew Carnegie and is on the Colorado and National Register of Historic Places. She purchased and supervised the remodeling of the library, and it became a charming three-bedroom bed and breakfast as well as a counseling center. I had the privilege to stay there when I came into town to visit my parents. Her professional offices were on the lower level, and I was taken aback by how she was able to juggle running the inn along with serving her clients.

After several years of friendship, I had the opportunity to read the dissertation she had written, which pertained to growing up with only sisters. Having grown up with only sisters as well, the subject matter interested me; however, I was especially impressed with her writing ability. I then tried to encourage her to go ahead and write the book that she had always wanted to write—one that portrayed her experiences in dealing with some of her many clients, focusing on the various themes and reasons individuals, couples, and families come to therapy.

This project came together like slipping on a glove, and instead of writing in detail about how she helped the fifty-eight clients you'll read about in the following pages, she chose to tell their stories through her eyes. She decided to pen their cases by disclosing what SHE had learned from THEM. What a novel idea, and it worked like a charm.

Like Jennifer, I have learned from these stories and believe you will as well. They are each unique, informative, heartwarming, and offer the opportunity to teach all of us many life lessons. I believe you will want to read this book at least twice, because there is much to take away from each person's story. And if you are thinking of making an appointment to go to counseling or are considering counseling as a career, then this book is a definite must read.

Jennifer is a loving, caring, and talented professional, intricately wrapped with integrity. I believe all of these qualities come through in the following pages.

May her experiences and those of her clients bring you to a deeper understanding of your own life and the lives of those you love.

Pam Pauley

Prologue

My Clients...My Teachers paints a realistic picture of the profession of counseling/psychology. Because this book reveals the reality of individuals I personally counseled, and the reasons they reached out for help, many of the stories are tragic, sad, and dismal—welcome to my world. People do not usually seek therapy because everything in life is rosy. Rather, they come to therapy because something in their life is causing them distress. Also, some of my clients did not make huge strides to recovery—change takes time and a client progresses at his/her own pace. But, all the stories are testimonies of courage. I invite you to read past what each client endured and search for what you can learn from their experiences.

Most of the stories are unfinished, and you might feel like you are left dangling. Again, welcome to my world. A person walks into my office, and we work for as few or as many weeks as the clients determines; they either gain what they came for or eventually run out of time, energy, money, or motivation. When they decide they are finished, they don't come back, and that is the end of their story with me. Even though I care deeply for them, or know more about their hearts and souls than I might know about my own family, I am not ethically permitted to become their friends, to go to lunch with them, or to even call and ask how they are doing. Should we pass each other on the street, I am not permitted to initiate contact with them. It is determined that a friendship outside the office could be harmful to the therapeutic process, and I totally agree. But, because I am human, it was at times difficult for me to sever all contact, especially when I had worked with someone for a long period of time.

Counselors, as all people in most professions, have limitations. I cannot do the work for a person, and I certainly do not have all the answers or all the tools I might need to help everyone. The more I understand my own scope of expertise, my own biases, and my own strengths, the more effective I can be with a client. Above all else, I have to always remember that it is not possible to help every person.

Read each story with an open, neutral mind, just as I tried to do in my office. Try to imagine what you might have done in the same situation, had you been the client...or the therapist.

NOTE: The words counseling, psychotherapy, therapy, and psychology are used interchangeably throughout the book, as are counselor, psychotherapist, and therapist.

Introduction

My career as a mental health counselor began in mid-life, after my three children were grown. After earning an MA and Ph.D. in Counseling Education, I initially believed counseling was all about me—me helping others. Little did I know how strangers walking through my door would broaden my scope of perception and become my unsuspecting teachers.

I invite you, the reader, to also learn from my clients. Not only do I want you to read each of the fifty-eight stories and gain insight into your own challenges and relationships, I wish for you to share in the noble process of psychotherapy. I also hope that the stories you are about to read will answer some of your own questions and ease your apprehensions about seeking therapy.

The media does not always provide a true and realistic view into the psychotherapy process nor offer a perspective that encourages people to seek help. I believe that with real-life examples, and knowing what to expect, one might be more likely to reach out for help. Hopefully, *My Clients...My Teachers* will also serve in a small way to attract men and women into the fascinating career of mental health counseling.

My desire to write this book began as I sat in my first counseling office in 1991 and started a career of listening to incredible stories—each one different and every one valid. It was as if I had chosen a career where a new chapter in a new book began every hour of the day, each with its own characters, dialogue, conflict, and plot.

In 2004, I called the American Counseling Association and asked the legal and ethics divisions if I could write condensed stories about my clients' experiences, explaining that I believed the stories could be helpful to many adults: people who have, and have not, had the luxury of going to mental health counseling; those who enjoy learning from the struggles and achievements of others; those who are battling personal challenges; and individuals considering Counseling or Psychology as a career. The answer I received was, "Yes, you only need to change the clients' names and identities." The book became a possibility on that day.

This is not a technical book about theories and founding fathers. Nor is it a creative piece to conjure up experiences and dynamic struggles. This book simply and purely contains true stories about real people and actual events. Nothing imagined can compete with the realities of life. Each person came with the hope of something—less pain, more solutions, a listening ear, satisfying the courts, or just basic help in getting through something that was going on in their lives.

My Clients...My Teachers was written from memory. I did not review client files. Because of that, along with my deliberate intent to protect clients' privacy, my recounting is subject to error in details, inaccurate recollections, omissions, and embellishments. The stories are real, and any slight inexactitude does not change the true life experiences of my clients or the knowledge I gained from each person.

The clients selected for this collection are from five office locations in two states and span twenty-three years. All names and identities have been changed. Many of the clients have read their stories and given written permission for inclusion in the book. I could not locate every client; a few have been written completely from my recollections, as files and names are shredded seven years after an individual's last session. It is also likely that some former clients are no longer living. I will forever treasure reconnecting with the clients I could locate. They updated their current statuses, read their stories, and gave their blessings and signatures to my project. They too believed their stories could help other people.

The stories are divided into nine common therapeutic categories: Abuse, Addiction, Anxiety, Depression,

Infidelity, Loss, Mental Illness, Parenting, and Relationships. The categories and the stories within each category are alphabetized, showing no preference of significance.

I think life is about learning, and I have learned so much from my clients. They have taught me reality. They have given meaning to psychological terms and fundamental practicality to theories and years of education. More importantly, they have taught me truth about living and the difficulty of change. They have contributed to making my chosen career the supreme experience.

I hope my clients have learned from my knowledge and compassion, but I want this book to headline their stories and the benefits I gained from years of sitting across from some of the most courageous, interesting, humorous, diverse, and challenging examples of the human spirit.

Welcome to my world! I invite you to enjoy and learn.

A Note About the Cover: The graphic on the cover is an example of drawings I used during therapy sessions to help explain a particular concept. The cover picture shows how to deal with a bully:

How to Deal with a BULLY

1) Always look into the eyes of a bully
2) Take up space…feet apart, elbows away from the body
3) Stand very straight…shoulders back
4) Walk slowly and pay attention to all surroundings

Additional illustrations in this book have been used for the same purpose; it is my belief that visuals help clients remember and implement skills after leaving the therapy session.

Abuse

Abuse is a term used to describe an action that is harmful, hurtful, and inappropriate. It usually happens in situations where there is inequality of power. In the counseling profession, abuse is usually seen in physical, verbal, emotional, sexual, religious, and financial scenarios.

People who have experienced abuse often lose their sense of self-worth and their ability to trust their own judgments. They become less connected to themselves and more hyper-attentive to their surroundings. They can also become poor evaluators of others' character or intentions, attracting people who have a tendency to bully, intimidate, or take advantage.

Abuse produces victims, and victims are often mistreated throughout their lives. Relationships and treatment similar to what one experiences in childhood often become the standard for normal, and it is common for one to gravitate to what seems familiar even if it is abusive.

The pattern and repetition of abuse is tough to stop because abuse affects one's self-esteem, perpetuating abuse. Being abused teaches people that they are not worthy of being valued and treated respectfully; they are easy targets to bullying, attacks, and violent treatment. Abused people benefit from consistent counseling because they need the perspective of a trusted person who can offer neutral and frank encouragement to work toward what is healthier and more balanced.

Being abused not only puts one at risk of being regularly abused, but also of becoming an abuser. Abused people often become abusers themselves. One learns how to treat others by how they were treated. One can logically promise and swear never to hit or use cutting words or sexually hurt someone, but when push comes to shove, they do what was done to them. Long-term mental health counseling that includes building a trusting relationship with a trained professional can be very helpful in stopping relational, parental, or workplace abuse.

Consistent counseling can help to break the cycle of abuse, but it is very difficult. The belief that one is not good enough to be treated well is embedded in early experiences that are connected with massive emotions, giving it precedence and power. That explains why bullies have likely been bullied, sexual abusers have likely been sexually abused, and verbal abusers have likely been consistently yelled at and put down. When they hurt someone else, they truly hate themselves, thereby falling back into the victim role and making them again vulnerable for abusive treatment.

It is most essential for a person to understand that it is wrong to hurt or to be hurt. Nobody deserves to be ridiculed, denied privileges, or physically touched inappropriately. Going to regular counseling with a trusted therapist can be extremely instrumental in helping a person rise above abuse. One can unlearn the messages of abuse; it is not easy, but it is possible. Every individual has the right to think, speak, and behave without fear. Counseling can help a person shift their thoughts, build self-esteem, and teach skills to stop abusive treatment or behavior. When a person is ready to change, counseling can be the safe catalyst.

You are respectfully invited into the following eight stories—examples of individuals who were currently being abused or had been abused as children. The varied scenarios offer a glimpse into the complexity and diversity of abuse. They illustrate the devastation and pain of abuse, the needed perseverance to overcome its damage, and the gift of having someone listen, care, and help.

Angel

Angel, a sweet, kind, and gentle woman, originally came to therapy because she was distraught with fear and the feelings of unfairness at the loss of her job. She believed her boss was unduly critical of the contributions and efforts Angel gave to her employer and customers. During the initial and all subsequent sessions, she smiled a lot, spoke softly, and cried quietly. Even as an educated woman with a professional career, she found herself in many cruel, hurtful relationships as an adult.

She came to therapy several weeks before she felt safe enough to disclose what had happened to her as a small child. Her memory of being severely sexually abused by a neighborhood girl who left her naked in a shed with her clothes thrown on the roof caused her to re-experience the trauma with flashbacks and to feel shameful, as if Angel was innately flawed.

In her child mind, Angel learned from her abuse that she was not worthy of being treated with respect. She never developed the skill of looking someone in the eye and letting them know that she had principles and courage. Instead, she learned to lower her head, smile, treat people kindly, and hope that others would copy her example. The hope theory did not serve her well, as she had many bullies in her life: mother, husband, son-in-law, boss, daughter, and colleagues. She seemed to be a beacon for bullies.

She struggled with her weight, her health, her finances, and her personal boundaries. She was sensitive and often felt hurt and violated. We worked on strengthening her self-esteem—assertiveness, communication, consistency, bully management, parenting skills, personality traits, and goal setting.

Even though she found excellent new employment and contributed significantly to family finances, her husband often denied her money for counseling and for buying basic necessities, such as groceries and toiletries. He often dropped her off at my office and picked her up, so she had no independent means of transportation. He did not treat her as an equal, and she chose silence to avoid conflict.

Angel was determined to lose weight, and even though she lost pounds gradually, her husband criticized her brutally for not losing it faster. I was saddened by what she reported he said to her, and she would cry quietly as she repeated his hurtful words.

She often missed therapy sessions because she was called unexpectedly to work, but she always came when she could, and she worked hard when she was in my office. We did intensive Post Traumatic Stress Disorder work using EMDR—Eye Movement Desensitization and Reprocessing. Gradually, she saw a decline in the intensity of disturbance she felt when recalling the childhood abuse. She was a champion at survival. She worked to help leave the past behind; she so wanted to enjoy the present.

Her daily life was difficult because she received random abuse from those she loved. She would proudly report her successes—standing up for herself, saying no when she didn't want to do something, and asking for what she needed. She even began limiting her time with people who didn't treat her with respect; she chose her friends more selectively. As for family, she bravely told her husband how his words hurt and how she needed him to not only speak more kindly, but to offer her support when parenting their children.

I smile when I think of her gentle face and the progress she made while in therapy. I trust that she continues to apply the knowledge she gained in counseling and not define herself by the behavior of one teenage girl.

WHAT I LEARNED FROM ANGEL

Kindness, a valued trait, does not necessarily beget kindness. A person, abused as a child, can benefit tremendously from long-term counseling. Continual patience and compassion from a therapist offers foundational support for building the belief that (s)he is a worthy individual, worthy of being treated respectfully. Each person with courage to tell his/her story, as Angel did, can grow to understand that what happened *then* does not need to sabotage *now*.

Arthur

Married with two children, Arthur was in his early thirties, working in the family business, and serving as youth minister on Sunday morning.

He had a gentle manner, a quick smile, and seemed to be genuine and transparent. During his first session, he presented some marital problems that seemed to be intensified by differences in parenting styles. He reported that his wife was stricter with the children than he deemed necessary and that she had expectations of him that he could not usually achieve.

Arthur reported that she would not let the kids leave the table until they had eaten everything on their plates, would never allow them to have friends visit, would not let them ride the bus to school, and either highly praised them or criticized them harshly. He wanted her to be less extreme, to have more flexibility.

He mentioned that she could be very cruel to him during the day but was always affectionate at night. They had a very fulfilling intimacy that was usually instigated by her. He was confused by her daytime disapproval and her nighttime advances.

He brought her to one session, and I found her to be intelligent, verbally astute, and quite strong in her belief systems. She had fundamental religious guidelines and quoted frequently from the bible. Arthur listened to her and asked her questions for clarity; he wanted to fully understand what she needed. He wanted harmony. She determined she was not the one with the problem and did not join him again for therapy.

Arthur and I worked on communication skills, awareness of when she was most hurtful, and how to gain courage to voice his disapproval and suggestions. He shared his increased concern for his children, became more discouraged, and showed signs of depression.

During one session, Arthur reported being too embarrassed to tell his friends what was happening at home. That is when my light bulb turned on: he was an abused husband. He was afraid of her. She treated him disrespectfully daily and then wanted sex at night. She controlled all decisions in the household and used religion to substantiate all she said and did. She was always the absolute expert, gave him no credence for his opinions, and always had a tone of superiority.

I was disappointed in myself when I realized it had taken me several sessions to recognize that Arthur was a victim of domestic abuse. Had he been a female, I would have identified the symptoms during the first session. I would have certainly seen red flags after meeting the aggressive spouse.

From that moment on, just as I would with an abused woman, we worked on his empowerment and safety. I encouraged him to start stashing cash in case he needed to leave with his children, to get copies of tax records and titles to anything they owned, and to share what was happening with his mom and brothers. He needed support and options. I told him to protect himself and his children, to begin the process of making small changes, and to leave the home if he or his children were in danger.

As I spoke, tears welled up behind his eyes. He nodded and said, "Thank you!" He displayed relief by sitting straighter and breathing deeper. He spoke of gratitude for having a safe place to share his shame and tell his truth.

WHAT I LEARNED FROM ARTHUR

Stereotyping can cause even a counselor with years of training to overlook the obvious. A man can be abused by a woman just as women can be abused by men. It takes courage for anyone to admit that (s)he is being abused by a significant other, and an effective counselor needs to maintain gender neutrality. There is not room in a therapist's office for prejudice or stereotyping.

Audrey

Audrey was a professional woman who suffered with low self-esteem and depression attributed to childhood parental neglect and sibling abuse as well as an abusive marriage.

She was the youngest of four children and had been raised by affluent parents. She was much younger than her next oldest sibling and so was truly raised as an only child. Her childhood memories were incomplete, confusing, fearful, and shameful. When she was quite young, she left her abusive home and married a man who continued the cruelty. When he started acting aggressively toward their children, she divorced him. She took her children and returned to the town where she had been raised. Feeling she had no other options, she gratefully and cautiously accepted her parents' initial help. She used words like shame, fear, and disgust when describing herself through those dark times.

When I met Audrey, her children were grown, her mother had passed away, and her father, who was dependent on her, was not physically well. Her siblings were critical of her decisions concerning their father's care, yet they seldom, if ever, visited him. Their abuse from forty years earlier was reenacted through their verbal disapproval of her caregiving choices. She feared their infrequent visits and carried a dark gray cloud of depression on her shoulders.

I have never worked with a client who was more courageous. Audrey would come to my office with total terror reflecting from her eyes. I knew she did not want to be there, she did not want to uncover her abusive past, and she did not want to leave her safe logical mind. But, she was there and she worked hard to uncover the emotional obstacles that interfered with her present quality of life. She never refused extensive, painful trauma work.

Her father died from a fall in his yard, and she was the one who found him. I thought she was not going to survive the shame she felt and the criticism her siblings placed upon her. They showed no compassion or appreciation for the years and dedication she had given their father.

After her father's death and her chosen estrangement from the family, she developed horrific anxiety. She became fearful of driving and always had to be prepared for the hallucinations that could accompany the paralyzing, dangerous episodes. However, she did not allow her fears to stop her. She wanted the pain from the past and the present to stop. She did not cancel her counseling appointments and was never a *no-show*.

Every week she showed up in my office with the same terrified look in her eyes, not ready, but willing to work on the trauma again. I think she believed in me, in the process, and felt desperate to find relief from her debilitating emotions. She trusted me enough to let her logic wane to expose and examine her guarded vulnerability. It was extremely difficult. I think she kept coming back from blind faith that she would eventually, with tenacity, find the path for healing.

In my mind today, Audrey is a full, dimensional, colored picture of incredible strength. She grew, in front of my eyes, from a hurt little girl to an amazing, accomplished professional woman. She learned to acknowledge that she had no control over her childhood abuse, and she learned to take credit rather than inflict guilt for leaving her abusive marriage. In essence, she learned to live looking forward. She moved fear from a constant companion to a foggy memory; proof that abuse is never gone, but it can be faced, accepted, and the impact diminished.

I thank her for believing in me and never giving up on herself. Because of Audrey, I could lovingly and cautiously help, since, as a therapist, helping is my primary purpose.

WHAT I LEARNED FROM AUDREY

The foundation that moves a client to change and recovery is trust from the therapeutic relationship between the therapist and the client. When trust, as well as undeniable safety, is established and proven dependable, the courage to push beyond what is comfortable becomes easier and more effective for both the client and the therapist. Establishing trust often takes several sessions, yet, for those willing to stick with it, shared trust embodies the positive outcome possible in the therapeutic process; Audrey is an exemplary example.

Corinne

I was in the lunchroom supervising middle school students when Corinne, an adorable thirteen-year-old girl, appeared at my table with news that she was getting married to a thirty-four-year-old man. Hiding my shock, I managed to suggest we visit in my office after lunch.

She came bouncing into my office and continued with her story. Her parents were thrilled about the marriage; they really liked Bob. I asked if he was nice to her and she said, "Yes. He hit me once, but he said he was sorry." She said he approved of her continuing her education. When I asked if they were sexual, she said, "Oh no, I don't believe in that!" I did not believe her.

A week later, Corinne showed up at my office crying hysterically. She and Bob had broken up. Relieved, I told her I was sorry for her sadness, and I listened as she detailed her trauma.

A few days passed and she was at my door again. She was more upset than before. She had received a letter from Bob in which he stated that he had tested HIV positive.

I was thinking, *This is way over my head!*

Instead, I said, "Wow, it is sure a good thing you never had sex with him!"

The sobbing intensified as she said, "I lied!"

With that information, I truly did not know what to do other than to make my mandatory report to Child Protective Services (CPS). I knew I could leave it up to them to involve the police. After she left my office, still visibly upset, I spoke with my principal. He did not know what to do either, beyond reporting this situation to CPS. We decided to ask the parents to come to the school for a conference. After making the necessary phone calls, I brought Corinne back into my office and gave my little speech about her need to be smart and to not have any sexual contact with anyone until she knew she was not HIV positive. I told her that this was very serious. She looked at the floor and nodded her head as if in agreement.

The parent meeting went well but seemed a little strange. Neither parent displayed any emotion; they understood the need for the school's responsibility to report what had occurred to social services and agreed to take her to the hospital for a blood test. They said they would not allow her to see Bob again. They wanted her to continue her schooling.

A week later, Corinne came to my office once more and told me she had a new boyfriend. I reminded her of the responsibility she had to postpone sexual activity. She told me her boyfriend did not care if she was infected; he loved her.

At that point, I was without words. With a culmination of all my thoughts and frustrations and shock, I looked at her and said, "Corinne, as a counselor within a school, it is difficult for me to offer the time it would take to understand what is happening to you and determine exactly how I can be effective. If you and your family are willing to do so, outside counseling could be beneficial to all of you."

Corinne dropped out of school in the spring of her eighth grade year. She came to tell me she was pregnant and that the due date was September 9th. She said her mother was going to raise the baby so she could continue to go to school. She was seemingly happy—laughing and excited. I felt sad, frustrated, and inadequate. I knew I had done everything within the legal and ethical jurisdictions of an educational system, but Corinne's choices and the freedom permitted by her parents left me with limited recourse.

WHAT I LEARNED FROM
THIRTEEN-YEAR-OLD CORINNE

It is very difficult to help a person implement change without an understanding of his/her background and frame of reference. Multicultural education is vital if we truly want to be inclusively helpful. I am referring to the color of one's skin, family systems, income source, and religious beliefs. All are powerful. That power, combined with a school counselor's limitations, often makes the efforts futile. As for Corinne, I'm grateful I was there for her, which allowed her to speak to someone outside her family about what was happening.

Joseph

I saw Joseph off and on for fifteen years. He would be sixty now, but the first time I saw him he was in his early forties. Joseph was single, worked two or three jobs, and enjoyed coaching and volunteering for service organizations.

He initially reported that his father had been and was extremely abusive, not only to him but to his mother, brothers, and sisters. The stories he told of his childhood were horrific. His worse fear was behaving in any manner that resembled his father's.

Joseph's siblings had all moved to other parts of the country, but Joseph had chosen to stay in his hometown where his parents lived. He saw his parents several times a week and worked part-time for them. He also had a full-time job.

When Joseph came to therapy, he usually presented a problem concerning someone who was treating him poorly: his dad, a basketball team member, a girlfriend, someone from work, or someone at church. As he explained the happenings around what was going wrong, he often relayed shame because he had responded with characteristics like his dad's: demanding comments, harsh responses, and defensive excuses.

We worked on identifying the triggers that caused him to behave either like his father or like the little boy who had been physically and emotionally abused. We identified the discrepancy between the feelings he had when he acted like a hurt child or a mean dad. We also worked on how he could be more appropriately assertive and less sensitive to others' opinions.

Joseph was stuck in the middle between childhood and adulthood, with depression and isolation being his primary refuge. If he was healthy and happy, his father often yelled at him and disgraced him in public. If he was sullen and melancholy, his father treated him more kindly but other people seemed to treat him more disrespectfully. He couldn't find a balance, and it caused stress in his life; he felt he was on tight wire, a loser no matter what he did. When his life was out of balance, he became distrustful; he feared people were stalking him, telling lies about him, sabotaging his private business, and criticizing his volunteer work.

His efforts to contribute to the community, the church, and his place of work were commendable. If he was given any praise or appreciation, he would continue to give endlessly. He tried so hard to be accepted that he would give others the benefit of the doubt and either get taken advantage of or spoken to critically. When he tried to not be involved, he felt bad about himself. He didn't know how to create a new normal; he didn't want to imitate how he was raised and he didn't have another reality to model. His solution was usually working harder, staying out of everyone's way, and trying not to get upset with how people treated him.

Joseph was a very kind person. He came into each session with his gentle mannerisms, always asked how I was doing, and usually brought something he had grown in his garden. I truly enjoyed seeing him and trying to help him work through his struggles. I listened to his latest tales and he listened to my suggestions. To his disadvantage, he was not able to commit to regular therapy, which could have been significantly more helpful. Not only did he live a good distance from my office, but he didn't always have spendable income after his regular bills were paid. He knew I understood his internal battle, and I know what he gained in therapy lasted several weeks. On a scale of one to ten, one being awful and ten being fabulous, with a little smile, he would always report, "Almost nine" each time he left my office.

WHAT I LEARNED FROM JOSEPH

Childhood abuse can cause a person to question if they are good or bad, right or wrong, or able to trust their own judgments. It can cause a fight between demons inside one's body, a battle that ebbs and flows but never vanishes. With regular, long-term counseling a person who has been abused, can learn to live a joyful life; learn how to safely let go of the fear, frustration, hurt, and unfairness of what was done to them and around them. They need to relearn and give life another chance.

Mary

Mary had been appallingly abused by her stepfather from the time she was three, the time when her mother became involved with him, until she escaped with her little brother at the age of eighteen. She and her brother were sadistically, sexually, physically, mentally, emotionally, and verbally abused. Other than the Holocaust, I personally had not heard of a more horrific environment for children.

The saddest part of Mary's story is that her mother could have protected them or moved them, but she chose to pretend the treatment was not that bad. She worked outside the home and left her children with her husband, who was, by definition, a pervert and a pedophile.

Mary's saving grace was attending school and playing outside with her brother. The best part of her childhood was stepping onto the school bus and watching the wooded farmstead fade in the distance. When at home, it was the ability to play outside—away from the drinking, smoking, fear, and degradation that awaited her inside the house—which helped her endure. Like many abused children, she excelled in school, and like many other abused children, her brother caused trouble.

Because of her stepfather's threats, she and her brother were too terrified to tell a teacher what was happening at home, and although her mother knew the stepfather was mean and volatile, they did not tell her about the abuse because they thought she knew. Mary and her little brother escaped on a bus when she was eighteen. She lived in fear for years, fear that her stepfather would search until he found them.

Mary came to me when she was in her mid-thirties. She was married to a caring man, and they had three children. She had a professional job that involved helping families. She was kind, sweet, articulate, appreciative, and transparent. More than anything, she was a loving, nurturing parent.

What brought her to therapy were nightmares and fear that her stepfather had hunted her down, was looking in her bathroom window, and lurking in the trees outside her bedroom. Her stepfather's abuse had scarred her emotionally. During months of therapy, she implemented a variety of strategies to help normalize her thoughts and fears. She made her house safer by securing windows with locks and having the door locks changed. She put curtains over windows, so she could not see the black glass at night, and she left lights on. She consciously played outside with the kids more often because that gave her a sense of safety. She wrote detailed memories about the horrendous abuse and burned the writings. She braved her way through extensive, painful trauma work. She had serious conversations with her mother as to why she had not protected the family and why she had not left this brutal man when Mary and her brother were younger. Most importantly, she told me her story. Saying the words helped her dilute the shame and internalize the truth that his actions were not her fault.

During my work with Mary, the police department from her hometown suspected that her stepfather was abusing two small girls in the house where he was presently living. They asked Mary if she had knowledge of any prior abusive behavior and, if so, to describe it in a deposition. The department could use the information as evidence to remove her stepfather from the house, thereby providing protection for the young girls. After all those years, Mary finally had the purpose and support she needed to report her stepfather's abuse and validate the truth of her painful childhood.

Subsequently, Mary learned that her abusive stepfather had died. She had a hard time trusting that he was really gone and could never physically hurt her or her family again. As the weeks past, she became more secure in her safety but still suffered with flashbacks and nightmares, although they were significantly less intense.

Mary found comfort in believing that what she endured as a child helped her to maintain sincere compassion for the many families she encountered during her workday.

WHAT I LEARNED FROM MARY

Mary is proof that angels and heroes truly do walk amongst us. Human beings can have unbelievable strength to rise above horrifying living conditions while maintaining hope that something better is possible. People who have been abused can grow to become loving spouses and parents and succeed in careers that promote programs to recognize, educate, and stop abuse. Working with Mary was an honor; thinking about her gives me hope for healing and recovery.

Melanie

Melanie, a beautiful woman with blond hair, blue eyes, sweet smile, and reserved demeanor, was brought into my office by her husband who claimed she was delusional. He was planning to take the boys away from her, and she was terrified.

When they arrived, I immediately sensed the husband's extreme control. He tried to dominate the initial intake, he was unreasonably strict with the small boys, and he seldom allowed Melanie to speak. He reluctantly left Melanie with me for her therapy session, and it took only minutes to assess that she and her boys were in danger. When the husband came to pick her up, we had a plan. Before the sun went down, she was to draw as much money as she could from their one joint account and, with the help of the local police department, she and her boys were to go into a shelter for abused women.

She was frightened but strong enough to do exactly what we planned. She knew she had to do something to get them all away from her explosive husband.

Because they resided in a state other than where my office was located, she legally had to return the boys to that state. The agency for abused women transferred her and her boys to a shelter in their city of residence, and the father was granted supervised visitation at the shelter.

Melanie found an attorney who had a personal vendetta against abusive men and agreed to represent her with no retainer and small monthly payments. For the next several months, with support from her parents, her sister and brother-in-law, me, and her attorney, she prepared and presented herself well in court hearings, custody evaluations, deposition, and final settlement.

In therapy, we worked primarily on assertiveness skills. I wanted her to be able to look him squarely in the eyes whenever she was in his presence so she might better control her feelings of intimidation and fear. She was a very bright woman who did not have to worry about her recollection or consistency of events but was paralyzed by fear, fear of his retaliation. She knew she had years of future contact with him because of their dual parenting, and she needed skills to equalize and maintain her self-esteem and stability.

We also worked on developing safety strategies after leaving the shelter and renting an apartment. She had new locks put on her doors and windows, she had her car inspected regularly for sabotage (as she knew her husband had done this in the past), and she always had her cell phone charged and programmed with 911.

Her husband monopolized every court hearing and Melanie never had the opportunity to tell her story. She accepted a settlement the night before the trial and was granted a divorce, dual custody of her boys, and enough maintenance for basic survival. She felt like she had won because she was free of his abusive control, his fanatic religion, and his parents who were his mentors as well as his victims. She also felt much more secure in her ability to control her fear when they met to exchange the children. She returned to her previous job and had support from family and friends. Because she lived in a different state, I never saw her again once we waved goodbye after the final court case. I find comfort in believing she is beautiful, inside and out, just as she was during our brief association.

WHAT I LEARNED FROM MELANIE

I learned that even the most broken, with help, can stand up to a bully. I also learned that bullies can intimidate our justice system; few people are immune to an aggressive bully. As a therapist, I had to practice everything I taught Melanie, because he intimidated me too. I found myself being a little more aware of my surroundings and more conscious of locking doors and fastening windows. There is a lot of assistance for women, men, and children who are in abusive relationships. Like Melanie, one needs to be honest about his/her life and ask for help.

Royce

Royce was skinny, short, hyper, and ornery. He was twelve years old. He had short blond hair with a cowlick that looked like a little horn on the back of his head. I never saw him standing still, and he was constantly talking.

Royce liked me, and I liked him. He lived with his elderly grandparents, as his mom was on drugs and he did not know his dad. Every Friday I would go to school early, buy two cinnamon rolls in the kitchen, and Royce would come to my office for breakfast. We were buddies.

He had an upbeat outlook on life, but it bothered him that he did not have any friends. He would dart around the school yard from group to group, but nobody wanted to include Royce in their circle.

When I was on bus duty, I often saw Royce step off the bus pulling a girl's hair or grabbing at her backpack. When he complained to me about not having any friends, I suggested that he try being less pesky. I helped him role-play various behaviors he might try in order to be less annoying. He reported back his few successes and his many failures.

Halfway through the school year, the principal came to me and asked if I would talk to Royce; his grandma had called complaining about his behavior at home.

He came to my office, and when I told him his grandma had called, he burst into tears saying, "I didn't mean to. It was an accident!" Once he calmed down, he explained that he had wet the bed the night before. His grandma was very mad, and she took him into the bathroom and put his head in the toilet; it contained liquid and solid waste. She then forced him to go outside, and she locked him out of the house. He stayed outside all night.

Through his sobs he said he tried not to drink water, and he even tried not to sleep, but nothing helped; he often wet the bed. He said he washed his own sheets so as to not make extra work for his grandma. He said his grandma got very upset, screamed, and made him do double chores or sleep on the floor.

My heart hurt for this little guy. I knew he had no other options for a place to call home, and even though I knew it would not help, I was legally required by law to report the abuse. The person answering the phone, as in another reported abuse, told me if there was no blood or bruises they did not want to hear from me. I knew they had more critical cases and that Royce's grandparents would probably not be contacted. As a reporting counselor, I was never privy to what happened with the information of an alleged abuse. The school principal told me to leave it alone.

I met his grandma and was surprised to see a tiny little woman with white hair tied back in a bun, wearing a blue gingham dress with a tie belt. Proof that what we imagine isn't usually what materializes. I wanted a magic wand, so I could make her behavior match her appearance.

I continued to give Royce positive attention—we enjoyed our Friday cinnamon rolls, and he told me what was going on at home. I didn't always believe him when he said everything was great, but I knew if it was unbearable he had me to tell. When he couldn't find anyone to play with him he would look me up, stand by my side, and chatter non-stop. I think we brought each other a little welcomed joy.

WHAT I LEARNED FROM ROYCE

Against all odds, in spite of adults' incompetence, some kids develop special resilience. Thank goodness! Kids are meant to be loved, and there are many opportunities waiting for each of us inside a school building. Our systems fail us at times and our idealism gets challenged, but we must always continue to advocate for children.

There is always another way to help.

FOCUS on YOURSELF
at least 51% of the time

VALUE YOURSELF

You are the chairman of *your* board of directors,
the president of your company;
keep 51% controlling interest.
Focus on your needs *at least* 51% of the time.
An abused person focuses on everything *but* themselves:
fear, their kids, the abuser, what they can say without
triggering rage, how to hide the abuse,
and how to be perfect.

Addiction

Being addicted to a person, substance, or behavior can be compared to having a monstrous demon running around in one's head and/or body, a demon who wears a "friend" mask over its ugly face. The demon promises, lies, and kills. It does not discriminate by color of skin, gender, age, intelligence, wealth, employment, sexual orientation, or religious preference.

The most effective means of stopping an addiction is to recognize and catch the tendency or pattern early, before a person loses control to the addiction.

Twelve-step programs have proven to be more successful than other approaches, but a person needs to own his/her choices and admit to having no control over the addiction.

People who live with or care about an addict are usually the ones who seek counseling. They live in environments that are laden with fear, anxiety, secrets, false hope, pseudo control, and confusion. What brings them to therapy are their high levels of hurt, frustration, fear, and unfairness.

Addiction poisons relationships, and families need to learn to disengage from the addicted person; their loved one's addiction is not their fault, their choice, nor is it in their control.

Al-Anon is an organization that helps individuals with the difficult skill of disengaging. Anyone who lives with, or worries about someone who is addicted, can find help by attending Al-Anon meetings. They provide support and resources to those lost in someone else's addiction; those who suffer from co-dependency.

The following stories reflect some of the complexities of addiction. I invite you to read them with an open heart and mind.

Jane

Jane was raised by parents who had both died from alcoholism. She came to me because she was drinking too much and did not want to be a drunk like her mom and dad had been.

She was married to the love of her life, though he had recently left her for another woman. She feared he was doing drugs, and she could not wrap her mind around what was happening in her world. She was distraught with grief and realized she had no control over the man her husband had become. She was also very aware that she had little control over herself.

During the first session, she sat across from me and cried like a wounded little child. Jane was in her twenties, had young children, and held a highly skilled job. Her life had gone from near perfect to disaster, and she was afraid it was spiraling further downward.

We briefly reviewed the disease of alcoholism. I told her that she was correct in having concern about her drinking because she innately had strong alcoholic tendencies. I stressed how important it was for her to always have a cap on her consumption of alcohol. We worked mainly on drinking in moderation and making logical decisions. I tried to instill in her the idea that she was not an alcoholic yet and that she had the ability to control how much wine and vodka she drank.

Because her parents centered their life on alcohol, Jane knew a lot about the disease. For the same reason, her faith in recovery systems was skewed. She gave Alcoholics Anonymous no credence. She also knew the shame, despair, and helplessness of the disease, and she was determined to spare her children the pain of an alcoholic family.

I loaned her the book, *How to Quit Drinking without AA* by Jerry Dorsman. She read it cover to cover.

Jane regained some stability, but she could not bear to see her sweetheart with another woman. She, her children, and her good job moved across the country.

A few months later, I received a phone call from Jane. She was drunk. It was 11:00 a.m., and she had not gone to work. I felt sick to my stomach. I talked to her for a long time and told her to go take a shower and call me back. She did as I instructed. Because of her condition, words were of no value, but she said she put the liquor away and was going to lie down and sleep.

I tried several times during the next week to call her, but she never answered her phone.

Years later, I visited with someone who had spoken with Jane, and they said she was remarried and doing well. They didn't mention the drinking. Even if they didn't know or were protecting her, I still felt a huge sense of relief and gratitude.

WHAT I LEARNED FROM JANE

If one clearly does not want alcohol use, abuse, or addiction in his/her life, and they remember they control their choices, they can refuse the drink. Giving up something that has been associated with celebrations, tragedies, and everything in-between for an entire lifetime is a nasty demon to combat. If Jane failed, she did so because her experiences had taught her that nothing was helpful and she would have to try to do it alone. All counselors need training in addictions, however, it is best to refer addicted clients to a certified (CAC) or licensed (LAC) addiction counselor. Like Jane, they might not choose to go, but give them information and offer encouragement. Addiction can be conquered!

Herman

Early in my career, Herman came to my office. He was a sweet, pleasant man in his mid-forties. He wore wire-rimmed eyeglasses, and his hair was short and disheveled. He looked downward most of the time and talked nonstop.

He was married with children but was not happy with his sex life. He read articles and books, and was now asking me for insight concerning his marital sex.

I am not a sex therapist, and I do not claim to be an expert on the subject. I told him so and gave a list of referrals. I knew sex was important to a fulfilling relationship, but technique was really out of my scope of expertise. He determined he wanted to continue with me because he felt comfortable and my office was in a convenient location.

Because of Herman, I am now more enlightened. He would explain, in more detail than I needed, the success and failure between him and his wife. He would suggest some new and exciting foreplay or positions, and he admitted that she was a sport to try. He reported that he was not disappointed in her efforts but in his inability to perform; he was worried.

He spoke about his possible faults or illnesses or disorders that might have caused his decrease in sexual performance. He also wondered if it was his wife's fault. Did she not try hard enough? Did she not love him? Did she have desires for other men or even for women? He informed me at that point that he was not gay.

He would bring articles and books that he thought would help me help him. He was pleasantly persistent, and the information he gathered usually came from viable research, but I certainly did not feel very helpful.

Herman seemed open, transparent, and totally at ease. I felt awkward, uncomfortable, and more than slightly incompetent. I certainly thought I needed some extended studies.

He worried that his problem was connected to his age, but as the weeks passed he became more concerned that he simply was not attracted to his wife. He had sex drive, but he wanted more, he wanted consistent performance with exhilaration.

I discussed changes we go through as we age, how we can feel less excitement after we are with someone for many years, the differences between men and women, and the importance of relaxing and accepting where we are. I told him that I thought he was obsessing and that he needed to balance his thoughts and research connected to sexual activities with possibly a new hobby or a second job.

When he finally accepted that he knew more than I did and decided to discontinue his therapy, he thanked me, stating that our work together had been very helpful. I have not heard from or about him since we said goodbye. On that final day, I watched him walk briskly toward the elevator, chattering cheerfully.

I have to admit I missed his intelligent, creative determination, and his logical approach to an emotional frustration. I hope he is either having improved sexual experiences or he has accepted the reality that sexual fulfillment is a mental challenge.

WHAT I LEARNED FROM HERMAN

Obsessing about sex, as with anything that occupies the majority of our thoughts, can make us unbalanced and cause us to lose perspective. Herman's addiction was not a serious threat to his health or his marriage, but all addictions start small. Learning all he could on the subject was helpful to Herman, as well as his ability to freely communicate his frustrations. As a counselor, I listened to him, challenged some of his thoughts, and supported what I could. That must have been what he needed.

Faces of Addiction

Simply stated, an addiction is a process by which people become dependent on a substance or behavior in order to cope with life. It can become so vital to them that they continue the behavior even when it is harmful to themselves, their families, their employment, and/or their relationships.

I did not consider myself to be an addiction counselor, but the problems surrounding addiction surfaced with clients who came to therapy for relationship, domestic violence, parenting, and work-related issues.

The following are brief stories of clients who suffered the consequences of addictions.

Stacia was in her early twenties and was brought to counseling by her uncle. She had moved from the city because her boyfriend had been shot and killed in a drug deal and she was grieving, scared, and pregnant. She had no money, no home, no job, and an addiction to methamphetamine.

After several months of therapy, no drug use, and a steady job, she met a young man who was using drugs. She moved him into her apartment with the baby and started using meth with him.

I was required to report her choices to the county court where the murder had occurred. She realized what she was doing wrong and she felt intense shame, but she had no power over using and abusing drugs.

Joyce was brought to counseling by a friend. She was forty-something and had promised her friend that she was never going to use meth again. She was done! Her friend gave her a job and paid for her counseling.

Joyce did well for a few weeks, and then I began to notice that she was losing weight. She came to counseling sporadically and finally confessed that she had a lot of work to get done at home. She believed the only way she could stay up and get it done was to use *just a little*. It gave her energy, and she did not have to sleep.

She lost her job, her counseling, her friend, and eventually her health.

Callie was a college student with a five-year-old daughter. She reported being drug free but disclosed that she owed money to a drug dealer who stalked and threatened her.

She came to my office early one morning with cuts and bruises on her face and upper body. She reported that the dealer had gained access to her apartment and attacked her the night before. She said she had reported the incident to the police.

One afternoon she came to my office, sat in a chair hugging her knees to her chest, and shook with tremors. She said she wanted help to stop using. Another employee and I took her to a treatment center of Callie's choice, and we breathed a sigh of relief, hoping she would get the help she needed.

The next day she was back in school. She had checked herself out of rehab.

Nadine was brought to counseling by a man she met at the restaurant where she worked. He paid for her counseling, her rent, her car insurance, and gave her emotional support. He cared about her and was trying to help her break a drug habit.

Instead, she broke him—she used him and enjoyed more drugs with her extra money. He had shown faith in her, and she took advantage of his sincere intentions. He suffered from his own addiction of being victimized and co-dependent. Addicted people can spot a soft-hearted person in a large crowd—someone who has learned the dysfunctional and unsuccessful skills of seeing everyone as more important than themselves. If you see an addict, you don't need to look too far to find a co-dependent.

Joan's husband was addicted to computer pornography. He would stay up late at night looking at sites and then come to bed wanting sex. She told him when he spent hours each day looking at other women she felt hurt and unattractive. She also feared their daughters would gain access to the sites and worried about him being addicted. He said it caused no harm and that he could stop whenever he wanted. But he did not want to stop.

She thought about leaving him, but she did not want her girls to have divorced parents. She decided to stay, thinking about his positive contributions to the family, making excuses to friends and family for why he preferred to stay home rather than attend school events, and ignoring his late night activities with the computer.

I encouraged Joan to become involved with Al-Anon; although it targets alcoholism, it was the most available Twelve Step program in the area.

Blake was a handsome young man in his late twenties. He had been extremely successful in real estate. He was living the highlife. He had plenty of money, owned several exquisitely furnished rentals, and had many friends. He was always on the go trying to close the next deal.

Within a year before he was thirty, he had lost it all to cocaine addiction. He acknowledged he had a problem and admitted himself to a private drug addiction treatment center. When he returned to his fast-paced life, he started using again. He slowly lost his properties, his friends, and his reputation. He said he could not face life without his *fix*.

WHAT I LEARNED FROM STACIA, JOYCE, CALLIE, NADINE, JOAN, AND BLAKE

Addiction is a false friend—it can cause intelligent, talented individuals to self-destruct. Even though they hate what they are doing, nothing is more important, more loved, or more worshiped than their addiction of choice. They lie, manipulate, hook kind souls into helping them, and lose their integrity. Anything one can do to recover from the bondage of addiction or co-dependency is worth his/her time, money, and efforts; it could save their life. For more information: Al-Anon at www.al-anon.org, and Alcoholics Anonymous at www.aa.org.

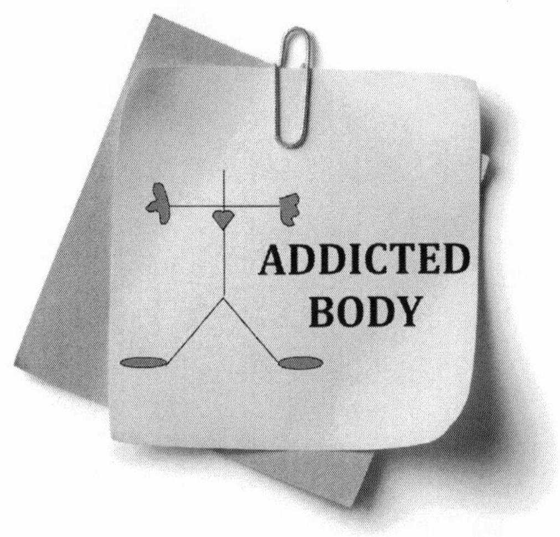

ADDICTED PEOPLE CANNOT THINK

Addicted people lose their heads
to their drug of choice.
They become bodies without heads; bodies without
the ability to think, reason, and choose wisely.
A heart not guided by the head is deficient.

Anxiety

Anxiety involves an intense and persistent fear. In many cases, it can be debilitating, causing deterioration of one's quality of life.

Anxiety brings many people to counseling because the physical feeling and the emotional wearing can be terrifying and exhausting; many people go to the emergency room because they think they are having a heart attack. They experience heart palpitations, tightness in their arms, inability to process clear thoughts, difficulty breathing, intense fear of dying, or fear that it will never go away.

People learn to avoid activities or friendships in an attempt to prevent anxiety. It is healthier to prepare and learn to manage the anxiety than it is to stop participating in life.

It is possible for people to manage their anxiety by learning to control their thoughts. There are also effective medications that can lessen the intensity and lower the frequency of anxiety.

A person who suffers with anxiety needs to go to a medical professional to eliminate all physical factors that could be causing the symptoms. Once they know they are healthy, they can begin learning skills to control the anxiety instead of allowing the anxiety to control them.

People who suffer from anxiety can live productive and fulfilling lives. The first and most important skill is the ability to truly believe that though anxiety is uncomfortable and unwanted, it will not kill them!

As you read the following stories, I encourage you to consider the wide range of expression anxiety can take.

Donna

Donna was a small-framed woman, very thin, forty-something, and suffering with depression and anxiety. She and her husband had two businesses that had failed, and she was engulfed with fear—fear of losing her home, of rejection in the community, and of never recovering.

She reported not sleeping for an entire two weeks and that she was beginning to hallucinate from sleep deprivation. We began by focusing on aids to help one sleep: hot baths; warm milk; a good book; routine; melting into the mattress; saying to herself, "Of course I can sleep, I'm tired;" focusing thoughts on one blue spot or one comforting word; soft peaceful light flowing through her body into her fingers and toes; tightening muscles and relaxing; napping anytime; sleeping in another bed; etc. She had to get some sleep. She could not have successful therapy or manage her low mood and fears unless she got some sleep.

I taught her that she had control of her thoughts and therefore a lot of control over her depression and anxiety. She would get very angry with me. She did not want to believe she had any control; she wanted to be a victim. Donna believed she had nothing to do with the demise of their businesses and therefore she had nothing to do with the extreme change in her emotions. One day, she stomped out of my office because she became so upset at me for suggesting that she was even remotely responsible for the shape she was in; she insisted it was not her fault.

I continually clarified that maybe she had no control of the mistakes or bad luck that contributed to their financial status, but she had 100% control of her thoughts, and her thoughts were strongly contributing to her depression and anxiety.

Donna often looked at me with loathing in her eyes and broke into tears; she did not like what I said. I am not sure what kept her coming back week after week. Neither of us budged on our belief systems. I tried many methods of delivery and gave her many scenarios, proving that what I was saying had some merit, but she was not buying it. I drew pictures, we role-played, we focused on healing from the trauma of loss, and I tried to teach her the symptoms of being a victim and the benefits of rising above that mindset.

Every week, she left with frustration in her stride. I was not feeling sorry for her or supporting her downward spiral, and she did not like it.

As I grew discouraged in my attempts to help her, I loaned her the book, *Gift from the Sea*, by Anne Morrow Lindbergh. It is a beautiful comparison of the author's life to seashells. Donna left with my book but did not return to therapy. I never saw her again.

Several years later, I received a long letter from Donna. She and her husband had moved and were doing well. She reported being happy and thanked me for helping her. She apologized for not returning the book, but explained that she had it on the corner of her dresser in her bedroom, and every time she walked by it, she would touch it lovingly. She was not ready to live without it.

WHAT I LEARNED FROM DONNA

People can listen, learn, and change. They can be cemented in their beliefs and still benefit from change. Change is hard. Change is often resisted even when one's health is at risk. Change requires courageous, determined individuals. As a therapist, when my ideas are rejected, maybe something I try as a last resort can contribute to a person's shift.

I must never give up.

Hillary

I first saw Hillary as she was walking down the street toward my office. I was not sure the person I saw was the woman who had called for an appointment; she looked like a teenager.

She reported having anxiety that was interfering with her quality of life. As the hour progressed, she shared that she was married with two children, lived on a farm, had an unfulfilling marriage complete with interfering in-laws, and she did not want to be like her mother who stayed in an unhappy marriage and suffered from panic attacks.

Hillary was terrified of her anxiety, and over the next several months we examined her past. We discussed when the attacks started, what triggered them, what benefit they gave her, how people treated her when she had them, and what they prevented or rescued her from doing.

We worked on skills that could help control the anxiety. I asked her to memorize and believe the statement, "It is uncomfortable, but it is not going to kill me!" I taught her to make anxiety her friend and rather than fight her anxiety, to focus on it and relax with it. I asked her to practice by focusing on an itch she might have on her nose and not scratch it, helping her to realize that the itch, like anxiety, could float away in less than one minute.

During one period of time, I worked with both her and her husband, Brian. We studied the differences in their innate personalities and practiced communication skills. Her satisfaction with their relationship seemed to improve for a short time.

Ultimately, she wanted out of the marriage and off the farm. Over the course of many years, she moved into a rented house, then back to the farm, and together, she and her husband bought and moved into a house in town. She then moved out of the house into an apartment. All changes helped her for a short period of time, but she continued to want out of her marriage. She was absolutely sure the marriage was the root of her anxiety and her displeasure with life.

Even though she wanted her marriage to end, she could not bring herself to end it. She wanted her husband to go the courthouse and file the papers, but he did not want a divorce. In therapy, we worked on building her courage so she could at least file for separation and begin building the life she wanted or shift her thinking and enjoy the life she had. She could do neither.

She seemed to be paralyzed by the fear that if she left her husband she would be making a huge mistake as well as the fear that if she did not divorce him, her life would be forever miserable.

She was stuck. After not hearing from her for at least two years, she sent an email updating me on her status. Her main message was, "I am having anxiety attacks again and Brian is…and I am…and we are… I just want to be happy!" I had heard the same words for years, and I thought about her for a full day before I replied to her email. My worse thought was that I could be part of the problem—were her counseling sessions enabling her not to change? Had I become her crutch? Since my job is to strengthen and help, I kindly but firmly, and with explanation, responded to her email and told her there was nothing more I could offer. I wished her well and gave her some referral contacts.

I believe it was the long time period between our communication that helped me to hear her words and recognize that therapy with me, although helpful in many ways, was not guiding my client to change. I used every theory in my toolbox to help her change, and she needed me to help her stay safely on the fence.

WHAT I LEARNED FROM HILLARY

I have many limits as a counselor; I can help a client identify the problem, make a plan, clarify their wants and needs, but I cannot place them where they want to be. Try as I may and care as I might, I cannot coerce or entice my clients to use the tools I offer and make desired changes. Being unable to put action behind a decision can frustrate, infuriate, and paralyze a person. The client is always in control of his/her choices. It is the responsibility of the therapist to recognize, long before I did, that progress resembling a gerbil wheel may need to be halted. It may be time to encourage the client to move in a new direction, including a new therapist or modality.

Mrs. Cooper

I had known Mrs. Cooper since I was a little girl. She was the mother of a friend and a teacher I really respected. I actually was a little afraid of her because she stood tall and looked quite stern. Yet, I thought she was beautiful. She wore nicely tailored clothes, and her hair always looked like she had just left the beauty parlor. I remember wishing I could be like her someday. I always behaved when I was around Mrs. Cooper.

When she was in her early eighties, her daughter-in-law called me and said Mrs. Cooper was in a nursing home and wondered if I could visit her. She reported that Mrs. Cooper was not able to function at home. According to her, Mrs. Cooper was nervous, worried, and did not want to leave the house. I told her I would be honored to go and see Mrs. Cooper.

I hung up the phone and regressed. I wondered how I could possibly help *the* Mrs. Cooper. Was I good enough or smart enough to be of any help to such a mountain of a woman?

I arrived in her room, and all I wanted to do was give her a hug. She was sitting on the edge of a small recliner and looked afraid and frail. She was wringing her hands, and her eyes were opened wide. She had some papers organized and spread out on the bed.

She said hi to me and gave me a little smile. I walked over, pulled up a chair beside her, took her hands in mine, and told her how nice it was to see her and how pleased I was that she agreed to see me. She relaxed, and so did I.

She cautiously shared some of her worries. She did not want to go out to eat because of what people might think of her. She was frustrated at not being able to do what she used to do, and she felt too inadequate to get all her work done.

She talked about her family and how she tried to do what they wanted, but admitted they were usually disappointed in her.

We talked about her options and whether or not she wanted to return to her home. We took some walks around the property and she watched the clock, reminding me what time I needed to be back to my office. I could tell she liked the scheduled days of the nursing home: breakfast, hair appointments on Mondays, lunch at noon, and so on.

On the second visit, she told me she did not need to see me again. We hugged and said our goodbyes. Her daughter-in-law called, and I gave her a few suggestions on what the family might consider doing to help and told her that I thought Mrs. Cooper was totally capable of being home if that was what she chose.

I went to my hometown for an event several months after our final session. I was visiting with friends, and I felt this little touch on my shoulder. I looked up and saw Mrs. Cooper walking with her husband. She gave me the sweetest smile and a little wave. She looked beautiful and poised. Her eyes reflected a twinkle, and seeing her made my day.

WHAT I LEARNED
FROM MRS. COOPER

Being a classy individual has nothing to do with age or environment. Aging can be very difficult; watching strengths become less dependable can be fear-inducing, thereby causing anxiety. Sometimes an aging person needs validation for the years when they were strong contributors, along with an understanding of their current struggles and support for any small control they might have over their future.

Like a child, they need advocates.

OUR THOUGHTS CONTROL US

If we do not like what we are doing or feeling, we must change our thinking. We cannot blame another person for what we do or how we feel.

Depression

Depression is a physical disorder, physical because it involves a chemical imbalance in the brain.

Every person at one time or another feels depressed. Life happens, and we fall into a low mood because the life event was painful, traumatic, or sad. We can also feel down if we have physical health problems, are not getting sufficient sleep, or have interpersonal conflicts that are not resolved.

Depression is a thread that runs through many clients' stories, even though they decide to come to therapy for other reasons. Life can be sad, and if we allow our emotions to ebb and flow with what is happening around us, we are going to feel gloomy when the situation warrants that feeling.

It is a mistake to believe that life is only wonderful and joyous and that there is something wrong with us if we get down and a little despondent. We must allow ourselves to be normal—it is normal to feel sad, happy, and everything in-between.

Low mood is only problematic if it interferes with one's quality of life for extended periods of time. Counseling and medication together are the best solutions for taking control and changing the pattern of persistent unhappiness.

It is important to remember that alcohol is also a depressant. It does not work to alleviate depression. Alcohol only makes depression symptoms worse—much worse.

One can choose many activities to smooth the edges of depression: eat colorful food, drink a lot of water, get plenty of sleep, hang out with positive people, turn off the TV, take walks, talk, journal, and always have future plans to anticipate.

As you take in the following stories, remember that there is no reason to ever feel ashamed for the feelings or moods one experiences. When emotions become overwhelming, one can always seek help, whether for a short period or a longer duration.

Candice

Candice suffered from severe depression, but she did not want to take medication. She saw a psychiatrist in the city who prescribed and managed her meds. She would take them for a few days or weeks and then stop.

She was divorced, had two teenagers, a very good job, and one especially good friend. She had a better than usual relationship with her ex-husband and his new wife, and an uncommonly good relationship with her ex-mother-in-law.

Candice was very intelligent, read a lot, and had an extremely sweet personality. She had one major fault: she could *never* cut herself any slack. Candice had been raised on a farm with only sisters and reported feeling inadequate from early childhood. She was very critical of everything she did, had done, or ever wanted to do. She could see the glass half full for everyone and everything but herself. She continued to be angry at herself for not being happy, as she thought she had nothing to complain about.

The minute I saw her I knew whether or not she was taking her antidepressants. If she was, she came in smiling and we could really get to work on issues during the session. If she wasn't, she could barely look at me or answer a question. The difference was always visible and extreme.

She did not want to do any trauma work, as she had no memory of anything other than ordinary family happenings that might be considered traumatic. She did agree to try EMDR (Eye Movement Desensitization and Reprocessing) at my suggestion but was too skeptical to trust the process.

I worked harder than I had worked with anyone to convince her to take her meds. I explained, and she agreed, that she was a great candidate for antidepressants because they actually worked for her. I am not a pill-pushing therapist, but the benefit was obvious, and I pleaded, begged, strategized, and cajoled her. I even gave her a pretty little bling pillbox in my attempts to get her to take two tiny pills once a day.

Because she really wanted to please me, she tried to take her meds, but it never lasted. She would come to her next regular weekly session and sit nearly in tears for the entire hour.

I recommended a book, *Depression Visible*, by Diana Alishouse, that illustrated major depression and bipolar disorder using patchwork quilts. Candice bought the book, read it in its entirety, cried with thankfulness that someone understood what she felt, and still would not take her meds.

She disliked the pills because they reminded her that there was something wrong with her. She believed that, just because pills helped her feel happier, it did not mean she was actually happy. They made her feel like a fake.

Taking antidepressants is difficult for many clients, but they take them because the benefits of feeling less sad outweigh most negative side effects. It is not unusual for a person to stop taking antidepressants periodically because they decide they don't need them. They change their minds once their mood drops to depressive levels. That was not Candice's pattern; she would take them long enough to feel considerably better and then *forget* to take them.

Her inability to allow herself to consistently feel better will forever be a mystery to me.

WHAT I LEARNED FROM CANDICE

Conflict between knowing and doing is a curious battle. When one becomes the barrier to his/her happiness, motives and belief systems need to be challenged. Psychiatrists prescribing medications, collaborating with therapists providing skills, does little good if the client is closed to consistently taking medication. Like a three-legged stool, with three legs it is strong and stable, but with only two it is relatively useless.

Carmen

Carmen was in her late thirties, married, with one adult daughter and one grandchild. Her husband had a good job, but she was unable to work because of her health. She seemed to have every illness other than cancer.

She brought me a list of her medications, and I've never known anyone to take that many pills in one day. She was on so many drugs that I truly did not know how she walked or thought or felt emotions. She reported that doctors continually told her she had two choices: she could take the drugs or die. Because of that, there was no reason to explore the options of less medication.

Carmen and her husband were upside down on a house that was mouse infested and unlikely to sell. They lived in a rented house and therefore had two house payments. Coupled with the astronomical medical bills, they did not have one spare nickel. Her mother paid for her counseling, and because of Carmen's numerous allergies, she also paid for house cleaning once a month. Carmen was not physically able to vacuum, mop, or do the laundry.

Carmen was sweet and seldom complained, even though she had legitimate reasons to be despondent. If she did grumble about something, she would apologize. She was abundant with verbal praises for how helpful her counseling was. I understood her persona when I met her mother. She and her mother were mirror images; both were pleasant, accommodating, and appreciative.

Not only did Carmen have a life centered on health issues with no hope of recovery, but she had little control of her daily activities. She seldom felt clear enough to drive, she had debilitating allergies even in her home, she received monthly infusions, was overcome with doctor appointments, and was in too much pain to hold or care for her grandchild. In addition, her husband controlled all finances. One holiday season, she was not allowed to buy a turkey for Thanksgiving or a one-dollar Christmas present for her daughter or grandchild. He refused to file for bankruptcy, and every month he became more negative as they moved further into debt.

Her daughter was usually unpleasant, and because she dated a guy just released from prison, Carmen worried incessantly about the welfare of her grandchild.

Carmen felt stuck, and I could not disagree with her assessment. In the same story, I would have probably felt worse, because I might not have had her positive attitude. She had dismal and disintegrating health, no means of earning an income, a disrespectful daughter, and a controlling husband. She had five sources of joy: her mother, her grandchild, her positive attitude, flowers in her yard, and me. That was quite daunting. Three of the sources were out of her control, her commendable attitude was difficult to maintain under the circumstances, and her body suffered the consequences if she nurtured her flowers.

Every time she was able to come to therapy, I praised her for her positive outlook on life. I sympathized, listened with a caring heart, and tried to send her on her way with renewed optimism.

I was always pleased when I saw her name on my schedule, as she brought me affirmation to the power of positive thought.

WHAT I LEARNED FROM CARMEN

Sometimes, all a counselor can do is offer sincere compassion with a surge of brightness. Once in a while, that is enough. Sometimes counselors get a client who inspires them with the mystery of how some people rise above despair and others cannot enjoy their blessings. As psychotherapists, we certainly do not have all the answers; we are given many rich opportunities to contemplate the questions.

Melissa

Melissa came to me fifteen days after her second child, a daughter, was born and she was in full-blown postpartum depression. She had a five-year-old son and a husband who was gone twelve hours a day for work.

To her benefit, she lived close to her family, and her mother was a very positive support. Melissa spent most days and evenings at her parents' house because she could not cope with the baby or with being alone. She was afraid she was not capable of taking care of the baby. Life was overwhelming.

She was in such a low mood that her mother brought her to therapy because Melissa did not trust herself to drive. She did not trust herself to take care of the baby. She even seriously considered putting her up for adoption. It was not that she did not love her; she just wanted the pain, fear, and anxiety to go away. Her illogical thoughts told her that if the baby lived somewhere else, Melissa would be fine and return to *normal.*

Melissa resented her husband because he was such an absent parent and did not offer compassion or assistance when he was home. He had the traditional notion that wives did all the housework, and that included serving their husband dinner as he watched TV. She wanted him gone too. She transferred her anger to him because she did not know where else to put it.

She had no trouble taking care of her son. She resented the baby taking so much time and energy away from her son. When she was at her mother's, she would have her family care for the baby as she played and took walks with her son. She transferred her fear and anxiety to the baby because she blamed her presence for her inability to function. Life had been fine before she came.

Melissa was an organized and efficient person who had never struggled with the inability to strategize and make needed changes. Her present life had emotionally paralyzed her. She was frustrated, hurt, afraid, and she felt the whole world was unfair.

Because her symptoms became more severe, I convinced her to go to her medical doctor and get some medication for depression and anxiety. She did so reluctantly.

After several months she stopped therapy, as her insurance benefit ran out and she felt she had the ability to be safe while she rebuilt her life.

Several years had passed when I met her coming out of an office where she was working. She gave me a hug and showed me a picture of the kids. The *baby* was five, and through her laughter, tears welled up behind her eyes when she spoke of those nine dark months of depression and anxiety. She loves her kids, as she always did, and graciously thanked me again for helping her survive her bout with the baby blues.

WHAT I LEARNED FROM MELISSA

Life can unexpectedly take us to our knees, and we need support from family, friends, professionals, and sometimes medication to find our strength and stabilize our lives. Melissa gave new meaning to the word commitment. She never gave up. She was angry—she cried, yelled, and rebelled. She probably regrets some of her actions, but she survived and came through it like a champion. May all therapists be so lucky as to have clients like Melissa; those who work as hard as or harder than they do.

Terri

Terri was a young woman in her late twenties who appeared unkempt—with straggly hair, oversized dowdy jeans, a plaid flannel shirt hanging out, soiled shoes, and slight body odor. She also had poor posture, held her head down, and made no eye contact.

She disclosed that she had developed a seizure disorder in her early twenties and did not know why. She had not had an injury, any family history of seizure disorders, and was not abusing drugs or alcohol. She refused to take medication because she felt meds treated the symptoms and not the cause.

Her life had become chaotic because she did not know when she would have a seizure. She eliminated many activities and limited her contact with people. Often, she would wake up in the emergency room only to learn someone saw her having a seizure and called 911.

She would then have expenses of emergency rooms and ambulances. Terri learned to get to work by bus, but she lived in fear of having seizures on the street, at her desk, or during lunch.

She was a logical thinker and very bright. We spent much of our time playing detective as to what could be the cause of her life-altering disorder. She loved to travel and had no memory of seizures when at lower altitudes, except on the coast of Spain. She monitored her diet and recorded everything she ingested. She made sure she had adequate sleep. Nothing helped and she continued to have random seizures, often when she was most at danger—when crossing the street, riding her bike, getting off the bus, etc.

She loved coming to therapy. When she was in my office she knew she was safe—safe from a 911 call. She knew she could trust me not to panic. Once, she had a seizure in my office, and I witnessed why her life was not safe and how she had lost her confidence and hopefulness. She had no memory of and therefore no details of her bodily activity during the seizure. I explained to her what I saw, hoping to convince her to take the advice of her medical doctor. The information only made her feel embarrassed and angrier.

Her last resort was to go to the Mayo Clinic in Arizona. She borrowed money and used all her savings. She was hopeful that their excellent reputation would uncover the cause for her seizures. She returned very disappointed, as they discovered nothing except a small scar in her brain from a childhood fall. She lost her hope at Mayo Clinic. She gave up but she didn't give in; she still refused medication. She slowly, in a matter of six months following her visit to the Mayo Clinic, lost her job, her medical insurance, her ability to come to my office for therapy, and her hope.

My heart truly ached for her, and I shared her disappointment and hopelessness when she first returned from Arizona. Using logic, her absolute strength, I tried to persuade her to try the anti-seizure medicine. I even tried to convince her to look at it as research, an experiment. She looked at me as if I was a traitor. Similar to Candice, she would not consider medication and I could not do it for her.

I last saw her as she left my office with her head down and her steps slow and sluggish. I visited with her a few times on the phone, but the relationship dwindled and she was never able to come again to my office for continued therapy. I referred her to a therapist close to her home, but I do not know if she chose to call and make an appointment.

WHAT I LEARNED FROM TERRI

Sometimes our logic keeps us from being logical; intelligence can hinder intelligent choices. Every person has the right to refuse or accept medical help. Terri and I had different agendas; I wanted her to try medicine in the hope of her controlling the seizures, and she believed the medicine prevented her from discovering the answers behind her seizures. As always, I was most helpful when I listened with compassion and no judgment.

OVERWHELMED?
ASK FOR
HELP

SOMETIMES WE JUST NEED HELP!

Feeling overwhelmed is when life is too much,
too heavy,
too demanding,
too grief-stricken,
too stressful,
too out of control,
too chaotic.

Infidelity

An affair is denoted if three criteria are present: personal information is shared that would ordinarily be saved for a significant other; there is sexual connotation either physically or in the conversation; and the relationship is secret. Affairs can happen without ever seeing or touching another person. They can happen on the phone or on the computer. A man is usually more upset if their partner has been involved in physical, sexual contact. A woman is obviously upset with the physical too, but she is often more hurt by the emotional betrayal.

Couples facing infidelity are overwhelmed with emotions that are difficult to identify, organize, or diminish. The cheating partner, unless he or she is a sociopath without a conscience, feels the dreadful emotion of guilt. The partner who has not cheated carries emotions of hurt, frustration, fear, jealously, curiosity, inadequacy, and confusion.

Unresolved anger is often at the root of infidelity and can lead to retaliation; what could hurt one's partner more than touching or loving another person?

It is possible to recover from unfaithfulness and rebuild, but it is very time-consuming, humbling, and painful.

To rebuild, both people need to be honest about their commitment to staying together. There is no need, at this point, to pretend. Both need to verbally state that they want the relationship to continue. Appropriate conversations from the heart need to be spoken and heard regularly. Both need to forgive, not just the other person but themselves. Both need to feel empathy for what the other person is feeling.

If the couple has children, severing the relationship is not possible; co-parenting is a given. Therapy is needed even when couples choose divorce, because it can help them move though the hurt and teach them to effectively and appropriately communicate for the benefit of their children. Just because two people do not choose to live together does not mean they have to hate each other. Children need to feel good about both parents, and it is the responsibility of both parents to make that happen.

The cheating partner needs to expect a lot of reprimands, and then he or she needs to be forgiven, with the infidelity placed in the past. I would expect no remorseful people to live the remainder of their lives being reminded of, degraded over, or punished for a mistake they have tried to resolve.

As you read the following stories, once again I invite you to open your minds and hearts to the pain that can occur within relationships when infidelity occurs.

Bob and Becky

Bob and Becky were in their late sixties and came to me because Bob had recently had an affair with a younger woman. Bob was tall, thin, and quiet. He worked on a ranch and removed his big cowboy hat when he came into the office. Becky was short, petite, and soft spoken. She was a clerk in a retail store.

Both appeared to be physically healthy but in considerable distress. They sat on my loveseat with their hands folded in their laps, and both looked at the floor. Silence was heavy, and it was difficult for either of them to speak. When Bob spoke he continued to look at the floor; when Becky spoke she looked at Bob.

The affair had ended several weeks prior to their coming for therapy; the other woman's husband had found out and threatened to divorce her, causing her to end the affair. Bob moved out of the house he and Becky had lived in for forty-plus years. Becky saw the other woman in and around the small town; she was pretty and dressed stylishly, and when Becky saw her it made her feel hurt and inadequate. The couple struggled to determine what they were going to do.

Both claimed they wanted to mend their marriage. He was very remorseful, and she was in the hurt and fearful phases of anger. She cooked dinner for him every night, but he would eat outside on the patio, as he did not think he deserved to go into the house.

They tried to go to events in town, but both were uncomfortable because they felt as if they were the topic of gossip. They tried to go out of town to dinner, and although that was more successful, they were often too tired to drive.

We worked on communication, forgiveness, recollecting happier times, and trying to make some plans for the future. Becky was very willing to forgive, but Bob claimed he did not feel worthy to be taken back. They tried to do sweet things for each other, but they reported that all efforts felt forced and superficial.

They came to weekly sessions for two months. Sometimes they were holding hands and smiling, and at other times they each acted as if the other was contagious. Kindness was shown between them, but speaking about the problems and what had happened prior to the affair was strained and difficult. Becky worried that saying anything would trigger her emotions or push him away, and Bob was too shameful to have an opinion. Many moments of silence were shared in the counseling office.

One week Becky came by herself. She was in tears and said he refused to come. We had a very productive session, as she was comfortable talking and revealing her true perspective without the worry of hurting Bob's feelings.

When it was time for their next appointment, she called and said he had decided he wanted a divorce. He apologized over and over but said that he wanted out; it wasn't going to work. She seemed relieved that he finally admitted to not wanting to live with her, but she was also afraid of life without him. She instinctively knew what the message had been behind his passive behavior and understood that he had not possessed the courage to tell her. She knew she had been living in false hope and that a great deal of his pain was caused by being dumped by the other woman. She knew that he really loved the other woman, who was exciting and interesting.

We spoke briefly when she called, and I encouraged Becky to come back to therapy alone if she felt the need. I reminded her to keep a strong support system and to financially take care of herself in the distribution of property.

They lived quite a distance from my office, and I did not hear from either of them again.

WHAT I LEARNED FROM BOB AND BECKY

Even with love and forgiveness, recovering from infidelity is nearly impossible when loving emotions are directed toward someone else. Infidelity has different dynamics for a couple that is nearly seventy; forty years of marriage, memories, and growing accustomed to one person's continual companionship, even if it is not ideal, is a very heavy loss. Anyone considering an affair should think twice; no matter the age of the couple or how long they have been married, infidelity hurts everyone.

Felicia and Lou

Felicia and Lou, a young couple with two small children, came for marriage counseling. Both worked outside the home, though Lou wanted to quit his job and go to college. Felicia did not want him to do that because they did not have the savings to pay for tuition, books, additional child care, and lost income.

Lou had figured out how they could get student loans and pay for less daycare, as he could watch the kids when Felicia was working. She reported that the previous day he had purchased a big screen TV. It was upsetting to Felicia that he did not have more respect for the budget she planned yet still wanted to quit his job. She reported that he often bought electronics, and she worried about the bills. He said she never wanted to have fun and always nagged him.

Felicia was remorseful for not supporting his desire to go to school to improve their family's future finances, so she agreed to work more hours and gave him her blessing.

Several weeks later, I received a call from Felicia, and she was crying hysterically. She said the police came into her office and served divorce papers, saying she could not go back into her house and could not have her kids.

Felicia and I were astounded; she had no idea that Lou had wanted a divorce, and neither of us could understand how he could legally forbid her access to her house and kids. She learned false accusations, by Lou to the authorities, had warranted the drastic action for the safety of the children. She was beyond distraught and immediately went to Legal Services. Within days, they proved the charges were fabricated and her children were returned to her.

The following week, she learned he was sleeping with her best friend who was going to move into Felicia's house. Her tears came from deep inside her chest and she sobbed in my office. She tried to express how angry she was at her husband as well as her fear about what was next, her frustration in the affair he was having with her best friend, and her hurt over his cruelness. She felt so much unfairness that it was difficult for her to put it all into words.

Felicia rented a low-income apartment, and with the help of her church, she found used and donated furniture and linens. Her mother came to stay with her and cared for the children until she was able to get stabilized financially and emotionally.

I did not see Lou again, but Felicia was able to see me for a few weeks with the help of a nonprofit organization. She was terribly hurt by his actions and afraid that her kids would suffer from the divorce. She raged at the unfairness that he and her best friend showed in having no regard for her or her children.

She was a beautiful young woman, inside and out. She was functioning with the help of her mother, but she went through very hard times. On the seventh, solo appointment, she walked in with a new haircut and an adorable dress she had purchased at the dollar store. I was stunned by the transformation. She smiled and said, "It is his loss, not mine."

Our remaining sessions were spent capitalizing on her shift of attitude, and she slowly started to replace the hurt and unfairness with plans for going to school, opportunities for advancement at her current job, and strategies for how to choose new friends.

Felicia learned from Lou's infidelity to become a stronger woman—to be less trusting and less focused on the needs of others. She knew it was going to be primarily up to her to raise her two small children and to reestablish a working parenting relationship with her ex-husband, his new wife (Felicia's ex-best friend), and their soon-to-be baby.

WHAT I LEARNED FROM FELICIA AND LOU

Deceit is cowardly. From Felicia: Although it may take many tears and years, one can rise above the despicable actions of someone we love. If a young woman with two small children and no formal education can find strength in herself to believe she is going to be okay and move in that direction every day, anyone can. There are nonprofit organizations whose missions are to help women like Felicia—providing counseling, legal services, daycare, food, clothing, housing, job skills, and career planning. One only needs to ask.

Phillip

A handsome man in his early forties called and made an appointment for marriage counseling. When he came into my office he was alone. I initially explained that a couple working together was far more effective and successful. He proceeded to tell me he did not love his wife anymore and that she had no idea he was seeking therapy. He continued to report that he was involved with another woman who was married to a friend of his, and he had always had other women outside his marriage.

As he continued during the first session, I learned that Phillip had children and was financially successful. He admitted that he did not feel good about himself and his indiscretions, he was sincerely worried about his kids, and he knew he was at the end of his luck—the other woman was putting pressure on him and threatening to tell his wife. He was scared.

He said he really did want a divorce, but he did not want his wife to think the reason for his wanting a divorce was that he loved another woman, because he did not. The other woman was needy and showed her insecurities by expecting him to call several times a day and meet her several times a week. Life was getting overwhelming for Phillip.

I suggested that if he sincerely did not want to hurt his wife, he needed to cease contact with the other woman. He left the first session with clear directives to take a break from the other woman and to talk to his wife about his desire for a divorce. I told him it was only right to tell his wife what he was planning.

The second session, he walked in and immediately said his wife had found out about the other woman. He said she was furious. She threatened him by saying, "I am going to take you to the cleaners," implying that she was going to ruin him financially. He was extremely scared.

He began telling stories about his wife and suggesting that he would not have had affairs if she would have been this, that, or the other. He wanted me to believe that his behavior was his wife's fault. I said something like, "Whoa! Maybe she is not as loving as you might want, or puts you second to the kids, or is not much fun, but you are the one who takes off your clothes and crawls into bed with other women. You cannot blame your wife for your behavior. She is responsible for her behavior and you are responsible for your behavior." He looked at me solemnly and slowly shook his head, as if he understood and agreed.

The third session was spent listening to Phillip's worries about how much money he was going to have to give his wife, questioning why she could not be happy with the gorgeous house and a substantial maintenance, and why the law thought she deserved half of everything he owned.

Another reality check—he and his wife had earned all their assets after they were married, she was a contributing partner, and she truly deserved half of what they owned together. Again, he looked at me solemnly and slowly shook his head, as if he understood and agreed.

He had a hard time sitting still, and his eyes shifted back and forth as he spoke. He said he was too tied up with accountants and attorneys to come to therapy. He thought he would be fine. I wished him well and told him to call if he changed his mind. I also reminded him to take good physical care of himself because he had many rough months ahead. I encouraged him to give his best effort in staying connected to the children and trying to rebuild a healthy co-parenting relationship with his wife.

I was sad he didn't come back, as I knew he needed the support and counsel.

WHAT I LEARNED FROM PHILLIP

Clients do not always like to hear the truth, and it takes courage for a counselor to confront inaccurate thought, especially before rapport has been established and trust developed. Ethically, I could not support him in blaming his wife for his unfaithfulness, or his irritation in the position that she deserved half of their property. I was forthright in helping him see his situation with a sense of reality. My responsibility of making the hard calls has precedence over being popular.

Tonya and Rick

It was 10:00 on a dreary winter morning when this handsome couple opened my door for their first appointment.

Tonya and Rick sat close together on the loveseat and held hands. I learned they had been married for twenty years, had grown children and grandchildren, and were both employed. Both moved to the city for job promotions and they loved the restaurants and theater.

They came to counseling because they were struggling with minor differences on how to deal with their oldest son and his current choices. The session went well, and they left with some new ideas on what they might try and what they needed to allow their son to solve.

At the end of the first session, Rick said he would like a session by himself to gain some insight on a few employee issues. Tonya agreed with no hesitation. We set an appointment for the following week.

At his solo session, after he spoke about some employee problems, he reported he was involved in an affair with a woman and that Tonya was totally unaware. With an edge of pride, he reported a history with other women and highly developed skills of discretion. By the end of the session, I fully grasped his message. He liked multiple women, was available, and was hitting on me.

In my naiveté, I was internally shocked and nervous, but he never would have suspected. I slowly and quietly addressed his covert advancements with a direct detour. I calmly looked him straight in the eyes and told him I would be more than glad to meet with him and Tonya and help him disclose his indiscretions to his beautiful wife. I displayed a sense of sympathy in how hard it must be for him. I was being professional, yet sly.

He sat up straight, looked at me with wide eyes, and said, "Oh no…I don't…I don't want you to do that! This has to be between you and me." After a long moment of staring straight at me, he said, "It would break Tonya's heart. She would divorce me."

Nodding, I said, "I am sure it would. As I told you during intake, there are no secrets in this room between couples. What either of you disclose is openly discussed in couples therapy. Healthy relationships are built on trust, and I keep my word."

He stood up to leave, saying he had another appointment. One would have thought he recognized an airborne virus in my office. He could not get to the elevator fast enough.

Tonya called and set up another appointment. Within minutes, she called back and said Rick did not think the counseling was helpful, so they needed to cancel. I visited briefly with her and extended a welcome to call if they ever needed anything. I wished them well.

I would see them occasionally in the city, as we lived in the same condominium complex. They looked stunning, as always, and appeared to be the perfect couple—happy and connected. Beautiful Tonya would acknowledge me with a smile, and Rick would glance my way and tense up. The color would drain from his chiseled face.

WHAT I LEARNED FROM TONYA AND RICK

Just because a person is my client does not mean he/she automatically respects me; I need to remain as savvy as possible and always keep clear professional boundaries. A client can depend on an ethical counselor to do what is right. I have an idea that Rick was helped by our session; he was faced with being busted, and if he didn't do some soul-searching when he left my office, he should have.

We must validate what we need, feel, and want by opening our mouths and saying the words.

Simple as that!

It is not easy to do, but it is a vital skill if you want healthy thoughts, feelings, behaviors, and relationships!

Loss

Loss, at varying levels, is prevalent in every person's life. There is no elitism in the world of loss. It attacks the wealthy, poor, healthy, ill, intelligent, disabled, young, elderly, and everyone else.

Having skills to work through loss is vital. People who had a protected, sheltered upbringing often do not have the tools necessary to deal with the hurt and unfairness of ordinary loss. Parents would be wise to allow their children to experience the pain from loss and then show them how to grieve successfully.

Loss toughens us, and that is good because life is not always kind, fair, or gentle. We learn lessons with loss. If we search for purpose in the letting go, in the inevitable changes, or in the strength demanded, we can reflect on what we are intended to learn, teach, or gain.

If I could eliminate loss from life, I would, but such exclusion would be a mistake. Without occasionally losing what is dear to us, we would be stagnant, shallow, and ungrateful. We would pass little wisdom to the next generation, and we would eventually lose our ability to feel emotions. Our memories would decline, because we remember emotional events. The intensity of our joy has a direct relationship to the depth of our pain. Together they build our range of emotions.

Helping a person recover from major loss is a large percentage of mental health counseling. Loss enters the room when the primary issues are addiction, abuse, parenting, anxiety, mental health, or relationships. Loss cannot be separated from the struggles of living, and knowing the emotional stages following a loss is important to self-management and progress.

Learning to grow through loss could possibly be the secret ingredient to contentment, compassion, and wisdom. I offer the following stories as examples of this inevitable element of life.

Beth

Beth was married to an alcoholic. She and her two grown children had survived years of shame, secrets, and embarrassment. After twenty-plus years of marriage, her husband decided to go to Alcoholics Anonymous. With Beth's dedicated support, he stopped drinking, and in sobriety, he proceeded to divorce her.

She came to see me ten years later, when she was in her late fifties. She and her ex-husband had a healthy parenting relationship, but their son was graduating from college and she realized that she, her ex, and his wife were set to travel on the same flight to and from the celebration. They were booked in the same hotel and had obligations and expectations to associate together and enjoy the activities.

She had been in social situations with them many times and did not understand her apprehension surrounding the graduation. She wanted to be what her son wanted, what her daughter expected, and what her ex had grown to assume.

Beth had a full life, which included a great profession, supportive family, rich faith, and a respected position in the community. I brought to her attention that despite what was going right in her life she had spent 90% of the first session talking about her ex-husband.

She and I both agreed that she had not fully grieved the loss of her marriage, so we spent time talking about her frustrations, hurts, fears, and the unfairness of his divorce choice. We clarified the emotions she had about the new wife and discussed her curiosity about why her kids had such a strong need to be close to their father, who had caused their childhood to be so traumatic. Basically, we refreshed her knowledge of alcoholism.

We still had not targeted the root of her uneasiness concerning the graduation, because she still felt anxious as she packed and prepared for the trip. After much discussion, we finally determined she was intimidated by her ex-husband and always had been. He was a bully and she was a pleaser.

I taught her, and she learned well, to take up space, walk slowly, and to look him square in the eye. She admitted that she wanted to be invisible when he was around, and she never looked directly at him. So, we imagined the various situations she would encounter, and we practiced and role-played. She became a pro, ready to embark on the journey that frightened her.

When she came to her next, and last, session after returning from the graduation, she had a new smile on her face and a new brightness in her eyes. She reported that though she failed a few times, she still gave herself an A-. She could not believe how confident and strong she felt using her new skills and how it enabled her to see him more clearly. She described the details, and I gave her tons of deserved kudos for her strong performance.

Her ex-husband no longer had power over her, and she was able to finally see his weaknesses and celebrate her own strengths. During her final session, Beth seldom mentioned his name. She had a genuine sparkle in her eyes, and it was apparent that she was very pleased with her success. She laughed as she described his surprise when she asserted herself as she told him he could pay for the cab, as she looked him in the eyes when either of them spoke, and how she voiced an opinion about where to go for dinner. She made simple changes but experienced dynamic impact and solid self-esteem.

I was thrilled for her. She came to therapy with fear, and after honest disclosure and a lot of hard work, she left with new skills, renewed confidence, and grew two inches in height.

WHAT I LEARNED FROM BETH

Sometimes the simplest skills can bring the most complex success. It was pure joy to see Beth blossom before my eyes. When a client is both ready and willing, amazing change can happen in a short period of time. Counseling does not always have to be about trauma and long extensive therapy; often it is ordinary people simply smoothing out the bumps and clearing out the rocks.

Bea

Bea came to counseling twelve days after the death of her daughter and only child. Her daughter, Kate, had been on the back of a motorcycle driven by a young man who was speeding. She literally flew to her death. She was eighteen and had just graduated from high school.

Bea stared at the wall as she recalled and relived the details of how she learned of her beautiful daughter's accident and subsequent death—the phone call in the middle of the night that every parent fears. She spoke of her friends and family and how they invisibly carried her and her husband through the night in the emergency room and mortuary, arranging the funeral, church services, and the burial.

She interwove, like satin ribbons in a wicker basket, Kate's friends into every story, memory, worry, and loss. Bea would laugh at the silly teenage escapades she and her husband endured, loved, but ultimately mourned with anguish.

During the next several months, Bea diligently tried to recognize her stages in the loss cycle and those of her husband: denial, bargaining, anger, depression, and release. She learned to understand what I meant when I told her she would swing between those five emotions like the needles on a moving compass.

Bea had some very hard times to work through: the large memorial with a cross and special mementos that friends erected on the edge of the pasture where Kate died; the finality of placing the stone on her grave; dealing with Kate's car and deciding to give it to one of Kate's friends; going into Kate's room and longing for the laughter of teenage girls and imagining the hoodies running out the door again; the realization that there would be no wedding or grandbabies; the unfairness when the boy who *murdered* Kate walked away from his trial with thirty days behind bars, as if there was no crime committed; deciding what to do with memorial money; and trying every day to wake up and put her feet on the floor and breathe.

To her credit, Bea was a little ornery. She would get that look in her eyes, along with a little grin, and defy the pettiness of life. She regained her pragmatic outlook and stood up for what she valued with coworkers, family, and friends. She toughened up. She also softened up and did not allow the insignificant events of work to get her down.

Bea and Clayton bought a house and decorated a *Kate room*. It became their happy place. It was bright and light and held the treasures that defined who Kate had been. They changed jobs and maintained contact with many of Kate's friends.

After many months of therapy, we moved her weekly appointment to twice a month and then to once a month. She decided she was strong enough for *call when needed* and I only saw her occasionally after that. She and her husband were each other's best friend, and together they figured out how to live one day at a time.

I am sure they are still valuable, loveable surrogate parents for many of the young adults that shared their pain and their healing. I can also bet that they are laughing at something. They shared a common sense of humor and appreciated each other's wit and outlook on life.

WHAT I LEARNED FROM BEA

True strength is often forced upon us and cannot be defined, duplicated, or taught. I do not believe, in my experience with those who have lost a child, that there is any deeper pain. I would never pretend to understand their grief and loss. I cannot imagine, after the loss of a child, the mental control it takes to wake up every morning and breathe, walk, eat, talk, and go to work. I truly admire their depth and wisdom.

Dana and Victor

Dana and Victor lost their sixteen-month-old son in their above-ground backyard swimming pool. The toddler was in the kitchen with Dana and their twelve-year-old daughter, Kayla. Victor was farming three miles from home, and their two older boys were visiting family and friends. The baby wandered into the backyard and climbed the swimming pool ladder. Minutes later, when Dana asked Kayla to check on the baby, it was too late. Kayla found him floating on top of the pool and carried him into the house. Victor rushed home after receiving Dana's call, and all three tried frantically to revive little Michael.

I first saw them three weeks after that horrendous day. They were both experiencing obvious despair and fragmentation. The whole family was in crisis. Victor blamed himself for not taking down the ladder. Dana blamed herself for not immediately noticing the absence of the baby's noise, and Kayla was traumatized because she was the one who found him. The three-year-old son, Blain, could not sleep in his room because that was where the baby had slept in his crib, and he was too young to understand why the baby was gone and didn't come home. The oldest son, Chip, who never caused any trouble, continued to be invisible in the chaos.

They all missed the little guy so very much; and each was suffering tremendously with their own thoughts and memories. Kayla, at the most vulnerable age, became defiant, and they sought counseling for her in school and also with the mental health center.

Dana and Victor did many things right that helped them continue. They donated Michael's heart valve to Donor Alliance and became involved with the annual Donor Dash. Before the funeral, they spent much time holding the baby and crying and saying goodbye. They visited his gravesite, often daily. They set up a fund for free swimming lessons to area children. They made a picture quilt of little Michael and the other preschool children at their church and raffled it off at a charity benefit. They set up a memorial in their home with his photo, an angel painting done by a friend, and some of his special belongings. They went to church regularly. They stayed close to family and were involved with their other children's sports and school activities. They teased each other and laughed. They came to therapy for a long time, always together.

They were not financially independent, and they received some free counseling sessions from a local nonprofit agency, but when the assistance stopped, they continued to come to therapy. Throughout their tears and healing, while trying to find a place for their guilt, I never heard them blame each other. They truly felt each other's pain. They found some peace in believing that things happen as they are intended to happen, and that God had a beautiful plan for little Michael.

They also did not neglect their other children. The household obviously had a giant empty space, but they continued with familiar teasing, routine chores, disciplining, and showing affection.

They were the purest example of love I have ever experienced with clients. I marveled at how they looked at each other and softly touched the other's arm when tears surfaced. It was as though they were comforting themselves when they were helping the other—giving and receiving simultaneously.

I always felt a sense of peace when they left my office, and it had nothing to do with what I had said or done; it was the surreal connection they had towards each other.

WHAT I LEARNED FROM DANA AND VICTOR

I learned that a couple can continue a loving relationship, even after the loss of a child, if they support each other and move through recovery together instead of blaming and shaming. Dana and Victor's daily examples model to other grieving parents not to fight the feelings, to go to therapy together for as long as needed, to realize one does not carry the loss alone, and to help each other heal. Also, it is important to filter advice from friends and family—people can say insensitive things when they don't know what to say but want to help.

Marcella

Marcella was a woman in her early fifties who was brought to me by her daughter. Her family was worried about her inability to recover from the death of her baby grandson. His name was TJ, and he died when he was four months old, nearly two years prior to her first session with me.

Marcella cried during therapy every week as she sat and told me story after story of TJ's smile, the way he would look at her with his sweet little eyes, the touch of his skin, and how emotionally bonded they were. She loved her other grandchildren, but TJ had been special.

Every day Marcella would take a lawn chair, go to the cemetery, and sit by TJ's grave. She would read to him, sing to him, and pray for him. She missed him immensely.

I explained the stages in the loss cycle: denial, bargaining, anger, depression, and release. She determined she was stuck between anger and depression. We worked on anger as she spoke about her frustrations, fears, hurts, and her feelings of unfairness. She refused to take meds for her depression. I gave her books to read, asked her to journal, and encouraged her to see friends more often. She made gratitude lists, a fresh bucket list, and wrote about places she had always wanted to visit.

Nothing helped. Everything reminded her of TJ, and the tears would start anew.

As a last effort, I asked if she would be willing to do an unguided visualization exercise. She reluctantly agreed. A counselor never knows the result that might come from visualization, because what the client will envision is totally unknown to the counselor. The exercise can help or it can unleash more unrest. It was worth a try.

With a very soft, slow voice I asked her to close her eyes, sit with her legs uncrossed, and place her hands gently on her legs. I continued with, "Breathe in slowly, exhale slowly. Breathe in, exhale. Breathe in, exhale."

When I determined she was completely relaxed, I said in a slow clear voice, "Imagine you are somewhere so beautiful that it takes your breath away. Notice the colors…the smells…the sounds…anything touching your body…any taste in your mouth. Notice your body…your breathing…any feelings you have."

I continued with a slower and softer voice, "Notice a person, way off in the distance, moving toward you. Watch as they move closer and closer. Open your arms to them. Tell the person what you need them to know. Listen to what they say back to you. Sit quietly in the moment."

When we finished, and after giving Marcella time to open her eyes and become aware of the room, I sat back and listened to what she had seen in the visualization. She looked at me with soft warm eyes and reported that the beautiful place was heaven, and she described it in minute details. The person who came to her was TJ. When she reached out to him, he smiled and playfully floated back and forth above her head. She told him she loved him, and he told her that he loved her too, but that he was happy and did not need her anymore. He said she had already given him everything he needed. As TJ floated away he said, "Please Mam Ma, do not be sad for me."

We met again, but she did not need additional therapy. She was looking at the lists we had created and planning a five-day trip to the Grand Canyon—a place on her bucket list.

WHAT I LEARNED FROM MARCELLA

A person has his/her own answers; a counselor's job is to facilitate the path to self-discovery. Healing from loss is possible. I saw it happen with many, but especially Marcella. It took weeks of building a foundation along with one small hour of providing a technique that allowed answers to questions that only Marcella knew to ask. I was thankful the exercise was successful, but I was prepared to take whatever the outcome and use it to help her move closer to the release stage of her personal grieving process.

Sandy

Sandy came to me months after she had been shot in the face with a shotgun by her boyfriend, who then drove to a deserted field and shot himself. He died, but he left her with the loss of one eye, a disfigured face, nightmares, and a future that was uncertain.

She was an adorable, petite, beautiful junior in high school when the shooting occurred, and she was an adorable, petite, beautiful senior in high school with a white gauze bandage over one-third of her face when she came to see me.

She looked me square in the eyes, spoke clearly and confidently, and appeared to be in no state of despair. She reported that her mother changed her bandages every day and that she had not yet looked to see what damage had been done to her face.

She had a great attitude, was glad to be alive, talked about enjoying school, friends, driving, and having a job. The only problems she mentioned were not being able to sleep without her mother in the house, being upset that her parents were divorcing, and suffering with anxiety.

We worked on her understanding of anxiety, and I gave her the basic skills to manage the attacks. She would leave and I sometimes did not see her again for a month or two. She brought a friend with her once, because she wanted to get some help for her friend who was also having anxiety. If I had to use one word to describe Sandy, it would be authentic.

During her irregular visits for therapy, she never displayed signs of anger. She loved her deceased boyfriend's family and stayed in touch with them after they moved to another state. She never spoke unkindly of her boyfriend and disclosed few details of the day he came pounding on her door, distraught and out of control. I never pushed her to disclose the specifics of the day that changed the course of her life; I trusted her to tell me if she wanted me to know. She was glad to be alive and felt that complaining was a sign of weakness and ungratefulness. I challenged those thoughts and reassured her that I knew she was glad to be alive, but that I would certainly not judge her negatively if she had normal emotions and complained—sometimes we need to speak our truth so what is on the inside moves to the outside.

I asked her if she drank alcohol or used drugs, and she said she would have a beer if she was in a really good mood. She said she never drank if she was sad or mad. She was very wise.

Her plastic surgeon videoed her numerous facial surgeries, and Sandy wanted me to watch the DVD. I did indeed watch as her nose, cheekbone, and eye socket were reconstructed, her nasal passages restored, and her facial muscles repaired. It was very difficult to watch the video, yet I marveled at her endurance, the amazing surgical advancements, and the courage she developed at such a young age. I felt privileged that she wanted me to see what she had been through. I think she allowed me to give her compassion and empathy through the video. She could show me what she had endured without complaining, making her stronger and more grateful.

I hope Sandy has told her story. She needs to share it and not carry it all by herself. If not, I am sure she will when she needs to—she is a mystical, mature, and wise woman.

I can still see her perfect smile and hear her articulate speech as she sat on my black leather sofa wearing flip-flops, short shorts, and a tank top. If I had closed my eyes, I would have never suspected that Sandy had been the victim of a shooting.

I will always hold Sandy in highest esteem.

WHAT I LEARNED FROM SANDY

Maturity and positive attitude have little to do with age or circumstances. One needn't tell the world they are wise, it radiates from eyes and words. Victimization and tragedy do not usually fit in the same scenario with optimism, but people come along and prove that it is possible. As therapists, we must never attempt to inflict our emotions onto clients.

Faces of Suicide

A client suicide is one of a counselor's most tragic realities. Counselors are real people, and we feel the same emotions as any other person. I have been called to emergency rooms when clients have attempted suicide, had clients sign no-suicide contracts, and received phone calls in the middle of the night from suicidal clients. I have lost two clients to suicide, and even though I had not seen either for several months, I experienced a gamut of emotions that float to the surface even today. I know their decision to end their life was not my fault, but I always wonder if I could have done or said something differently that would have given them other options. After a suicide, my compassion is always placed in the hearts of family and friends who are left to recover.

The faces of suicide survivors are tragic, and the effects of suicide ripple like a skipping stone across a peaceful pond. The following recollections offer examples of the tremors of suicide. I include them with the hope that someone contemplating killing him/herself will try to grasp the depth of devastation and search for another solution for easing their pain.

Fran came to me after her husband of forty-five years shot and killed himself at their home while she was taking a bath and preparing to go to bed. He had a chronic illness and she found comfort in believing that he did not want to live as a disabled adult or burden her with the responsibility of caring for him in a wheelchair

Fran brought her son Ron and her grandson Kevin to counseling, because Kevin spoke of wanting to kill himself so he could be with Grandpa in heaven.

Tim, a young man in his early teens, was brought to counseling by his dad after his older brother shot and killed himself. His big brother was his idol, and, years later, Tim continues to struggle. Tim was at a critical developmental age when the tragedy occurred, and he had a difficult time finishing school. The impact from the violent loss of his brother seemed to multiply and intensify as he grew to be a young man.

Martha came to me when she was fifty-four. She had been in counseling her entire adult life. When she was twelve, she found her dad hanging from a rope in the garage. She never recovered. She reported trying unsuccessfully to kill herself several times. Her life was consumed with doctors, drugs, trauma, bad relationships, and despair.

Carman was a client trying to survive the loss of Roger, her significant other, who shot himself while under the influence of alcohol. She logically understood that she was not responsible, but they had argued about something the day he killed himself, and she was distraught with guilt; her life was joyless.

Blake and Valerie were close friends with Carman, and they too were grieving the loss of Roger. Blake was drinking excessively, and their marriage was at risk of failing. They divorced within the year following Roger's suicide.

Jessica was a beautiful woman in her late thirties who came to therapy with extreme anorexia and bulimia problems. During intake, she revealed her father had died from carbon monoxide poisoning in their garage when she was six years old. Food disorders helped her regain control. Twenty years later, married with children, she still controls her life by denying food to her emaciated body.

Elizabeth's brother-in-law shot and killed himself. She spoke of the family trauma that affected her husband, his mother, children, nieces, nephews, grandkids, cousins, high school friends, neighbors, co-workers, etc. The magnitude of grief after he chose death included hundreds of people and will negatively affect future generations.

Carla was referred by her high school counselor because she was distraught and talked about wanting to die. During intake, I realized I had worked with her father years before; his wife, Carla's mother, had taken her own life when Carla was three years old. Carla learned suicide was an option when life became too difficult.

WHAT I LEARNED FROM FRAN, TIM, MARTHA, CARMAN, BLAKE AND VALERIE, JESSICA, ELIZABETH, AND CARLA

The pains of suicide are reflected in a client's eyes, speech, body movements, and total persona. They are instant victims who must discover their inner strengths in order to survive and thrive. If they do not discover their unique strengths, they turn to dysfunctional thoughts and behavior to ease their aching. Being in a state of ultimate despair and hopelessness describes a person who chooses suicide as the solution. Those left to rebuild without their loved one need to allow feelings of fear, frustration, hurt, and unfairness to surface. They must acknowledge their anger. One can love someone and hate what they've done. It's okay. It's normal. It's necessary.

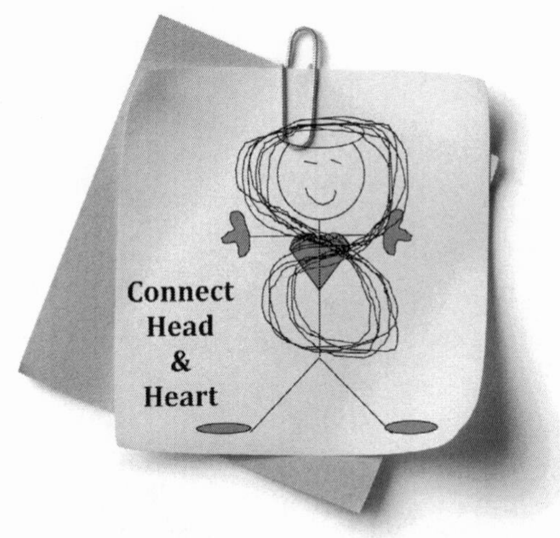

WORK WITH BOTH HEAD AND HEART

Some people operate in their head, above their necks. Other people operate below their heads, in their hearts. The most successful way to operate is to connect the head with the heart. If we operate in both, we have the strength of both, and therefore make better decisions and feel more in balance.

Mental Illness

One could say that mental illness is the opposite of mental wellness. We all have varying situations where our mental state fluctuates between illness and wellness. Nobody is exempt from periods of chemical imbalance.

This is not the place for details on the severity, complexity, or classifications of mental illness. It is my opportunity to plea for acceptance, understanding, and compassion for those innocent individuals who because of genetics, injury, or just bad luck, have minds that do not click like precision clocks.

Some of the finest individuals I have had the pleasure of encountering have a diagnosable mental illness. It is not our responsibility to judge someone who acts, walks, talks, or thinks differently than we might. It is our opportunity to display compassion, offer assistance, and enjoy their company.

Even after counseling a person for several sessions, it can be inaccurate at best to determine the DSM ("Diagnostic and Statistical Manual of Mental Disorders") diagnosis. The need for a mental health provider to subjectively label an individual as a requirement for insurance payment has never been an honorable task.

The individuals in this section of the book hold a special spot in my heart; they taught me more than any university course through their authenticity and tenacity. My hope is that you will be touched by their stories as well.

Debbie

Debbie was my first client to display a serious mental health disorder. Her presence was rough and boisterous, and her current issues were unusual and relayed with "colorful" language. She was friendly yet flippant. Her issues usually were accompanied by tears or embellished drama.

I saw her regularly in the beginning, and then off and on for several years. I moved my practice four times during my tenure as a mental health counselor, and even after we had terminated our therapeutic relationship before each move, she would find my new office and appear out of nowhere.

I had very firm boundaries with Debbie. She could call me at home only if it was an emergency, she had to use appropriate language when she spoke to me, she had to pay me at the end of each session, and if she was late for an appointment, I did not run over into the next client's time allowance.

Her life was always chaotic and full of trauma. As an example, she threatened to kill her husband, and I had to send a written report to the police department so they could inform her husband that his wife had threatened his life. (Duty to Warn or Protect)

She thrived on taking risks: driving at excessive speeds, practicing home nudity with teenagers in the house, drug and alcohol use and abuse, and sexual encounters with both sexes outside her marriage.

She handled actual trauma quite well, but if life was moving smoothly, she would create chaos. Her life was not normal unless there was turmoil. Peacefulness was her feared enemy.

She had been sexually abused as a child, and in the course of therapy she confronted her perpetrator, her father. The majority of our work revolved around Debbie being truthful, not embellishing stories, creating a new comfort level, monitoring risky behavior, learning healthy boundaries, addressing self-destructive habits, and taking medications prescribed by her psychiatrist every day so she could manage her mood swings.

She was a full spectrum of emotions—tears, drama, and many moments of joy.

I terminated my counseling with Debbie and referred her to another therapist because she reported having inappropriate sexual feelings for me. Not only was

I stunned, but the boundary she crossed was unethical and non-therapeutic, as clearly stated in her intake and disclosure forms.

The last time I saw her she called to ask if she could see me. She was working on a Twelve Step program for alcohol and drug abuse and needed to tell me she was sorry. I saw her at my office and she completed Step Nine, making direct amends.

She called a few months later and reported that she had divorced her husband and was living with a guy who drank and was abusive; her life of comedy and tragedy continued.

I could write an entire book about Debbie, but it would never contain the flair and eccentric reality of her life. I learned more from Debbie than she could have possibly learned from me.

WHAT I LEARNED FROM DEBBIE

How we learn to get our needs met is often destructive and resistant to finding healthier ways. Old habits are hard to break, especially if one denies them. People can unconsciously sabotage healthy living and lasting change. One therapist could not handle too many Debbies on his/her caseload simultaneously; boundaries would break down and fatigue would win. On the flip side, however, boredom would never happen and astonishment would thrive.

Denise

Denise drove three hours one way to see me. She had seen an ad in a regional newspaper promoting a group I was forming for survivors of childhood sexual abuse. She wanted nothing to do with the group; she wanted to see me alone.

She was twenty-seven when she came to my office and my only client in twenty-plus years who was the victim of combined satanic ritual, sexual, emotional, mental, and physical abuse.

Denise reported childhood sexual abused by numerous men, including her father and grandfather. She was so emotionally fragmented that she was only able to maintain part-time employment, and when she would get fired, she wouldn't know why.

As a small girl, her father had taken her to her grandfather's house, where she remembered people in black capes standing in a circle holding candles. One person was holding a crying baby. Abruptly, the baby was silent and motionless. Adding to the dichotomy and confusion, as a family they went to church on Sunday and her father taught Sunday school.

She was filled to capacity with shame and fear and terrified of being in close proximity to anyone. Any touching, even shaking hands, was off limits, and she was too fearful to touch or hug the puppets or teddy bears I had in the office.

Denise came to her sessions on time every week and paid cash. There was nothing unusual about her choice of clothing, but she was dangerously thin. She was a sweet, frail, and anxious young woman.

Even though she did not want to be in the group, she did accept my offer to join the group and attend an evening lecture by Marilyn Van Debur, Miss America of 1959, who had been sexually abused by her father until she was eighteen. Denise was in a state of panic the entire trip; she sunk to the floor of the van when she saw the city lights, could not enter the building for the lecture, and chain smoked as she waited outside for the lecture to end.

She was anorexic, and beer was her choice of nutrition. She went beer drinking with a boy one night and ended up pregnant. She had no memory of the sexual encounter, but she was emotionally paralyzed at the thought of having a baby. Two sessions after speaking of the pregnancy, she reported having a miscarriage.

I diagnosed Denise with Dissociative Identity Disorder (DID)—with me she was usually timid, quiet, and respectful. During our sessions she reported being provocative, boisterous, and arrogant with co-workers, with men she was aggressive and sexual, and with her parents she was angry and bossy.

I tried to advocate her acceptance into Menninger's Clinic in Topeka, Kansas, as she needed intensive psychiatric hospitalization, especially for treatment of satanic ritual abuse. However, she had no money, no insurance, and therefore no hope of ever being admitted for treatment. After five or six sessions with me, she did not have the funds to continue with therapy. I gave her a list of referrals in her community, including nonprofits. She said she would never go to therapy in her small town because everyone would know.

I last saw her when she came to my office a year after she had moved to Texas with an older man. She was exhibiting an alter personality—walking with long strides, laughing loudly, wearing a mini-skirt and tank top, smoking cigarettes on the deck, and flicking the butts over the balcony. She was loud and rude and looked twenty years older than her thirty-two years.

WHAT I LEARNED FROM DENISE

I learned that our soul is fragile yet very inventive in the skills of survival. I also learned that my work could be helpful, even though it was not rehabilitating. Denise felt safe with me, and had I initially told her that her condition was beyond my scope of practice, she probably would have never sought counseling again. I was the first therapist she had the courage to call, and I felt a responsibility to offer a little hope. I always treated her as if she was valuable, because she was.

Elizabeth

Elizabeth was a client whom I seldom saw. She was in a group I led for survivors of childhood sexual abuse, and she came for individual therapy only a few times.

She was bright, had a twinkle in her eye, and a smile that let me know she was a little mischievous. She owned her own business and had two small children. She gained her strength and direction from her church and Christian faith; she often referenced both in group sharing.

It was her alcoholic mother who had sexually abused her when she was a baby and small child. She had memories of adults who partied with her parents and also abused her. As a child she learned to dissociate—an experience of having one's attention and emotions detached from the environment. She also developed alter-egos, a second self that is believed to be distinct from a person's normal or original personality.

I learned about her various personalities, not from group or from Elizabeth's behavior, but from her husband who had witnessed them. He came to therapy only once, as he was struggling with her emerging personalities that were opposite from the kind, Christian woman he had married. He understood what she had been through, and he was well aware of the diagnostic criteria for DID, but at the same time, he was very weary and discouraged. I told him he basically had two options: one, he could leave her, or two, he could help her integrate and become well. To his credit, he chose the latter.

Elizabeth was an asset to the group process. She showed compassion for what the other women had experienced, was acutely aware of group members' emotions, and was always willing to offer wise counsel.

One night, during group, something triggered her and she ran into another room and began hysterically screaming, kicking, and hitting. I followed her, put my arms around her from the back, and held her arms tightly to her body. I braced my feet and held her with all my strength until she relaxed and became limp.

I acted instinctually; it was all I knew to do, and I had not learned that in any university class. From that moment, she trusted me. We went back to the group, and she shared what had happened; she wanted her experience to help the other women. Through her flashback, she learned that when she was in my presence, I could keep her safe and not judge her. We developed a trusting, safe relationship that continues to this day.

Elizabeth worked very hard to integrate her personalities. She found a therapist who specialized in trauma recovery and in treating Dissociative Identity Disorder. She learned to recognize her various alter states and her body's warning signals as to when each personality might surface. Through therapy, self-discipline, and her love for God and Jesus, she learned that the disorder did not have to run or ruin her life; she was not going to allow anything to destroy her or her family.

As with many clients, I would occasionally see her in the community. She always spoke or waved, and she brightened my day with her visible enthusiasm, calm demeanor, and quick smile.

WHAT I LEARNED FROM ELIZABETH

Mental disorders are real and debilitating, but people can survive, recover, and thrive. It is possible! Anyone who is feeling defeated or beyond the circle of recovery needs to remember Elizabeth and her success. She is an exemplary example of working until she won the battle. Even therapists need to remember Elizabeth; clients can and do recover. Treatment is valuable and our work is significant in helping people heal. Additionally, it is helpful for therapists to remember that not everything we use when working with patients will come from our formal education. Sometimes, our inner guidance will point the way.

Karl

Karl was a small child when his mother first brought him to my office. He had Down syndrome and was showing aggressive behavior toward kids at school. We worked on teaching him "no hitting, no kicking, no biting, and no shoving." He got it.

He was a very cute kid. He always wore a big cowboy hat. Karl had a treasurable innocence, and I could almost see his brain churning as he tried to understand what was being said. He always looked me square in the eyes and nodded his head as I spoke.

His mother brought him to see me only when the family could not get him to understand what was happening in his world. When each session was over, and the two stood to leave, he always gave me a big, strong hug and said, "I love you!"

Karl had two older brothers, and both were involved with the family farm and very connected with Karl's welfare. But, it was his mother who was his anchor. When I saw one, I saw the other; their love for each other was apparent and unquestionable.

His mother brought him to see me again when he was sixteen so together we could have "the talk," because he had told her that he was in love with a girl at school. His expression was one of disbelief when I explained the differences between a girl and a boy and the fact that girls did not have what he had. He could not imagine how a girl could pee. He then turned and looked at his mom with the look of, "Tell me it's not true!" He looked back at me and his eyes opened wider as he looked back to his mom. We knew he had made the connection that Mom was a girl too. He then asked about every girl he knew:

"Carol?"

"Yes."

"Angie?"

"Yes."

"Bonnie?"

"Yes."

He did not understand, but he believed us.

Years later, when he was in his late twenties, his dad brought him to see me. His mother was very ill and near death. Karl's dad wanted me to help Karl understand that his mom was leaving and not coming back. That session ranks right up there with one of the toughest sessions in my career.

We worked on reassuring him that he was going to be okay. He had other people who would care for him and whom he could care for in return. His dad assured him that he would still live in the same house with the same bed and that his brothers would still come to see him.

As they left, I received my much needed hug and an "I love you!"

That was the last time I saw Karl. I occasionally had the opportunity to ask his sister-in-law how he was doing, and she would smile and tell me another cute story of something he had done. He was a gem.

WHAT I LEARNED FROM KARL

Absolute, true love has nothing to do with IQ. Our lessons come to us, often without being invited, as do our gifts. Karl, his mother, his dad, and his extended family gifted me with an enduring image of love and family. Their genuine authenticity, that was apparent in their words, behavior, and compassion toward each other, will always be my example of a family to emulate.

BALANCE. . .

Balance is the single most important
element in a mentally stable existence.
Balance thoughts, feelings, activities,
time, work, love, rest, parenting, etc.
Also balance strengths—if not, they become weaknesses.
Example: Being a good listener equals strength.
Only listening and never having a voice
or opinion of one's own equals weakness.

Parenting

Parenting is the responsibility of two people—the one giving the sperm and the one contributing the egg. Initially, both individuals know little to nothing about caring for a baby. The baby needs immense amounts of love and nurturing; therefore, parenting must be a joint, cooperative effort as both strive to love and raise a child.

I just described the ideal, yet our world does not always provide the ideal. Parenting can involve one parent, male or female, two males, two females, grandma and/or grandpa, relatives, foster, natural, adopted, divorced, rich, poor, educated, disabled, willing, abusive, etc. The ones providing the sperm and egg are not always the available, competent, or involved parents, even though in a perfect world they would be.

We all have the opportunity throughout our lives to set the standard for kids. Parenting is the hardest, most important, and often, the most challenging job we will ever have in our lifetime. It pays no salary, awards little kudos, and costs more money than our budgets intended.

I believe *balance* to be a major word in the attempt to define the traits found in good parents. For example: neglect is shameful, as is absolute control; filthiness can be harmful, as is sterility if it prevents exploration; rudeness is irritating, as is having no freedom to speak; no interest in education is despicable, but so is over-involvement and rigidity with no time for play; inappropriate sexual touch is unforgivable, but so is giving no hugs or affection.

I have the greatest admiration and respect for any person who helps in the endeavor to grow honorable, responsible, dependable people. The following stories highlight some of the challenges faced in the role of parenting.

Christine

Christine first came to see me because she was feeling disrespected by her supervisor at work. Before her sixth session, she was fired, had major surgery, and the man she was dating touched her fourteen-year-old daughter inappropriately. I was required by law to report the incident.

For the next two years, she saw me through funding from the Department of Social Services. She continued to have serious health and unemployment issues. Her daughter was placed in foster care and eventually in residential treatment.

Christine's life was a mess. Her mother financially and emotionally supported her, as she had for many years. Christine's ex-husband was an abusive alcoholic who provided no child support. She had no place to go but up, and her life defied the odds; still, it kept getting grimmer. She chose unproductive men who used her for their own needs, and even though she needed to step up her parenting skills, she was too broken to find the strength or the determination.

Years of counseling were provided for her and her daughter individually and for the two of them together. They provided school monitoring, foster care, residential treatment, mileage reimbursement or transportation to and from counseling for her daughter, tuition for job training, and continual emotional support. We all did everything in our imagination and ability to give her the tools she needed to help herself and her family.

She tried; she really did. She came every week to therapy and never missed the joint sessions with her daughter. She always did her therapy homework and tried to keep her attitude positive. She had a great sense of humor and a quick contagious belly laugh.

It seemed her background and her present situation had her trapped. She continued to lose her level of physical health, and she continued to need services provided for her and her daughter.

Because I had made a decision to move to another state, she was referred to another female counselor. The last time I asked about her, social services had closed the case because the daughter became of legal age.

Christine had a lot of potential—an upbeat personality and a true desire to be employed and maintain a happy home. She utilized the services offered to her, but as she tried to keep up with all the appointments and paperwork, I think she lost the connection with her strengths.

WHAT I LEARNED FROM CHRISTINE

Too much assistance can cause a person to become dependent on the wrong system. Systems can be found guilty, even though they provide continual quality services. Christine was overwhelmed by two systems—her family and the Department of Social Services. Both demanded more of her—more time and commitment as well as proof of her continual improvement as a parent. As therapists we must help strengthen our client so (s)he might best utilize the needed assistance.

Hannah

Eighty-nine-year-old Hannah was brought to me by her son. There was dissention in the family, and he thought she could benefit from therapy.

Hannah was a widow and had many adult children. She had a very strong Christian faith and lived alone with a disabled son who was in his forties. The two of them were good buddies. They would go to bingo together, she would help him deliver papers on his paper route, and he would mow her lawn.

As the story unfolded, the family was split on the issue of the disabled son moving to another state to live with an older sister who was also her brother's guardian. Some of the siblings believed the older sister could offer more to the disabled son. The siblings who felt the son was fine living with their mother were the ones who visited regularly and helped whenever help was needed.

In my opinion, Hannah was very capable of taking care of her son. She helped with church dinners and walked to church several times a week. She baked a lot and continued to prepare large meals for whoever showed up for dinner. She was also cognitively very stable.

I worked with the family members who were supportive of their mother. I held mediation for the whole family, but the ones trying to move the son away from the mother did not attend.

With little financial means, Hannah hired an attorney, and I accompanied her to court so she could tell her side of the story to the judge, but the daughter and her husband monopolized the judge for eight hours and Hannah did not get her chance to speak.

I reported the situation to Adult Protective Services because Hannah's health was in jeopardy. Her children and their families were her entire life, and six of her children kept her in constant stress and chaos. The daughter who wanted the disabled son to live with her in another state would sometimes secretly take him for days and not say if or when she would bring him back. Hannah deeply loved her special son. She had always been his primary caretaker, and she was distraught with fear and frustration knowing that some of her kids would intentionally hurt her by trying to remove her son from his lifelong home, friends, and community of forty-seven years.

Hannah would ruminate about the repeated on-goings, and I determined I was not being helpful to the family, as nothing had changed. I referred them to marriage-family therapy in the hopes that someone else could be more productive in solving the family dynamics.

The last time we visited, they were still in court battles, still trying to get Hannah's son back, and individuals remained unwilling to compromise for the benefit of the family.

I am an advocate for the elderly, and both Hannah and I felt helpless. I still feel sadness for her.

WHAT I LEARNED FROM HANNAH

Elder abuse is not just about neglect and money. Adult children can be brutally cruel in ways never imagined. Large families have unique dynamics. The differences in age between the oldest and youngest can be a full generation. Even though they all grow to be functioning adults, the role of each person in the family is imbedded in memories and emotions because of natural hierarchy, jealousy, and conflict. A unified voice for the benefit of the whole can be a lofty, unrealistic goal. I learned the need for elder protection.

Jackie

Post-secondary school counseling has its challenges. One is the fact that a counselor might see a student once and never see them again. There is very little time for rapport building, because students have only a few minutes between classes or sports practice. They usually drop by during that time for a very specific reason. Such was the case with Jackie.

Jackie was an attractive, well-dressed honor student who walked into my office, closed the door, and burst into tears. She sat down, covered her face with her hands, and sobbed uncontrollably.

She told me she was pregnant, her parents would not speak to her, and they had kicked her out of the house. She was staying with a friend, and the father of the baby was out of the picture.

She was nineteen, two months pregnant, and she had come to me because she didn't know what to do about the baby. I was frank and told her she basically had three options: keep the baby, let the baby be adopted, or have an abortion. I spoke about the basics of each choice. She sat staring at the wall and wringing her hands. Looking at the floor, she said she still did not know what she wanted to do. I asked if she was willing to do an exercise that might help her make the difficult decision. She said she was willing to do anything that could help her decide.

I placed three chairs in the middle of the room and brought a baby puppet out of the counseling props box. I wrapped it snuggly in a baby blanket, asked Jackie to sit in the first chair, and handed her the *baby*.

I explained that sitting in this chair meant she had decided to keep the baby. I asked her to imagine what life was like in this chair. As she held the *baby* in her arms, she talked about her struggles with money, worry about being a good mom, fear of not having any friends, concern about school, and hopes that her parents would forgive her and love the baby. When she could think of nothing more to say, I asked her to sit in the next chair.

I told Jackie the second chair was the adoption chair. I asked her to take the *baby* and place it on my desk where she could not see it. As she sat in the chair without the *baby* she said, "That was hard." As she spoke about what it was like in the second chair, she said she wondered how the baby was doing, if the adoptive parents loved her/

him, and if the baby would hate her. She said she felt sadness, and she started to cry. Her sobs were soft and quiet.

I asked her to sit in the third chair and told her this chair was about abortion. I gave her the *baby* and asked her to take the *baby* and place it back in the prop box. She did as I asked and returned to the third chair. After she sat down, she looked at me. She stood, walked to the box, and retrieved the *baby*. She brought the *baby* back to the third chair. She said, "I cannot do that."

Jackie left my office with visible strength and a smile. She had decided to again try to approach her parents. She still did not know if she wanted to keep her baby or go the adoption route, but she knew she wanted to give birth to her baby. She had seven months to decide.

Jackie dropped out of school and did not return to my office. Whatever she decided, I knew that the exercise had helped her make the tough choice, a choice that only she could make.

WHAT I LEARNED FROM JACKIE

When focusing on the needs of the client, counseling can be helpful even with the disadvantage of only one visit. Working with young adults is rewarding. They still believe they have options, they are full of energy, and they are excited about being grownup. Even with Jackie's pregnancy and her parent's rejection, she knew there was hope beyond the present situation, and it motivated her to have a plan for action. Rapport building was still important, but it happened instantly, out of necessity, instead of through the process of information gathering over time.

Julia

From my counseling office window, I watched a man get out of a car, open the trunk, and lift out a wheelchair. He methodically proceeded to unfold the chair, rolled it to the passenger side of the car, lifted a woman from the car into the chair, and began pushing the chair down the ramp toward my office door.

That was the first moment I was grateful my office was handicap accessible. I opened and held the door for them. The lovely young woman used her left hand to help extend her right hand up to me, and as I accepted her small hand, she said, "Hi, I am Julia and this is my dad."

He rolled her into my office and told her he would be back in one hour. That was the beginning of the ritual that happened every three to four weeks for several months.

During the first hour, I learned she had muscular dystrophy. She also had a sweet twelve-year-old daughter and lived with her parents. Julia was divorced but had a good relationship with her ex-husband, because they were both devoted to their daughter and wanted to provide quality parenting. She had a gift for music and writing but was not able to be employed outside the home.

She had feelings of inadequacy that intensified as her daughter grew older. She was painfully aware that other young girls had mothers who could take them shopping and practice volleyball with them, and who were not an embarrassment. She talked briefly about her illness, but mainly about her concerns for her daughter and how appreciative she was for her parents and her ex-husband. She had a strong Christian faith, and her daughter, who shared her love of music, was involved in a youth group at church.

After a few sessions, she came for her appointment and began quietly sobbing the moment her dad shut the door. Her ex-husband was dating someone and getting married. She realized she was losing her best friend, and she said her heart was broken.

From that day, her life rapidly went downhill. The new wife did not like the daughter. The daughter was suddenly not the center of her dad's life, so she was hurt and frustrated. The ex-husband stopped co-parenting with Julia and turned all communication over to the new wife for scheduling activities. Julia's adorable affectionate daughter turned into a rebellious teenager.

Her daughter hated the new wife, and the feeling was mutual. Julia's ex continued his passivity, and her life literally felt like it was falling apart. He refused to talk to her. The new wife was very unpleasant, and Julia became the target—the identified problem. Her sweet, beautiful daughter told her she hated her too and was going to live with her dad and stepmom-zilla. Her daughter started staying out late with undesirable friends, and Julia's illness became more of a blatant disability. She carried perpetual tears behind her soft grey eyes; worry and stress replaced the warm glow I had grown to expect.

Julia cancelled her last appointment because she found a therapist who accepted her ex-husband's insurance. She wanted therapy for her daughter and didn't have funds to pay out of pocket. I totally understood her decision, but I really missed helping her adjust to life's altering situations that were mostly out of her control. She was a client who truly touched my heart. It was not because I felt sorry for her—I was seldom aware of her illness when she was in my office—but because she loved so deeply and tried so hard.

WHAT I LEARNED FROM JULIA

Life is especially unfair, and parenting teenage children is particularly difficult for sweet souls trapped in ill bodies. A young life of wheelchairs, medicine, home healthcare, and near total dependence on others would not be ideal to most. To have a disorder that is no fault of one's own, and to still maintain a positive outlook, develop talents, maintain friends, and grow in faith is to be commended. I have the utmost respect for Julia.

Tom

Tom was a handsome man in his forties who was referred by a friend. He was going through a nasty divorce and had four children for whom he had sole legal and physical custody. He was successful, bright, and a very logical thinker.

He was experiencing parenting problems. His daughters were having a difficult time with his divorce, and he admitted that his kids were all spoiled. He saw himself as the stable parent and also the financial provider. He was feeling unappreciated and was also fearful that he was losing his positive relationship with his children.

He always stated that the strategies and visuals we developed were very helpful, and he applied them on a regular basis. I would draw pictures, lines, and scribbles, and he followed along. Sometimes, I would put an empty chair in the room and have him imagine one of his kids in the chair, asking him to say what he needed to say to the person in the chair. My solutions made sense to him, and he was excellent at implementing change when he left my office.

We also worked on relationship issues. He became involved and eventually married a woman who was very wealthy and had two small children of her own. She was not as dependent on him as he was accustomed, and he had to make major paradigm shifts.

Together, we were diligent at digging through all the personalities and dynamics of each situation. We would roll up our sleeves, so to speak, and search until we knew we had captured the true problem. I would present logical solutions, and his eyes would tell me that we had discovered the true essence of the big picture. It made sense to him. His mood would visually heighten as we concluded each session, and I knew I had truly helped him to help himself. He would leave with renewed energy and a clear direction.

He only came to therapy when his life seemed upside-down. He continues to call when he needs to work through something. Our therapeutic relationship has lasted over twenty years.

He was the epitome of my perfect client; he worked as hard as or harder than I did. He was mentally healthy and only needed my help to get him over the hurdles of life. He really wanted change, and he listened to what I had to offer. He was strong enough to make the needed changes, and he asked for help when life presented him with another challenge.

Tom has created a life for himself far different from the one he had been living when I first met him. He and his wife are doing well, and he reports being happy. He is involved in many community events that keep him motivated and informed, and he continues to be a responsible, supportive parent for his now adult children. I feel a little smug when I think I contributed in some small way to his success.

WHAT I LEARNED FROM TOM

Therapeutic success is a combination of the client's determination and the therapist's knowledge and contributions. When a client is ready, change happens. When a client and therapist have similar ways of processing information and both communicate clearly and honestly, being the client or the therapist is an enjoyable, stimulating exchange. When respect is established along with rapport, the therapeutic process is effective and effortless.

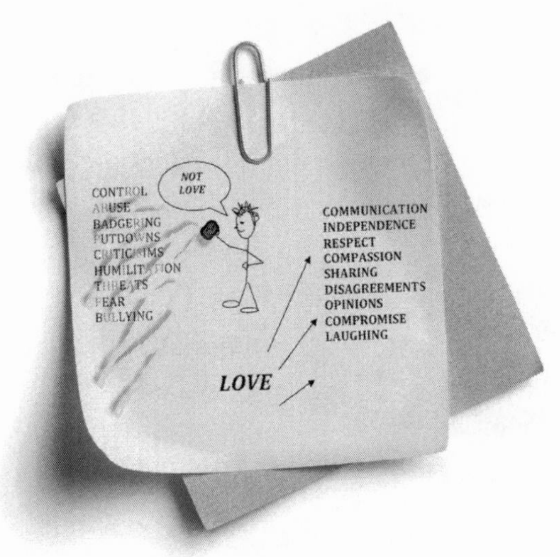

CHANGE YOUR THOUGHTS ABOUT LOVE

What we have learned about love
is often not correct.
Like a chalkboard,
we might need to erase what we learned
and rewrite healthier guidelines.

Relationships

The value of dependable, respectful, sincere relationships is priceless. People can survive almost anything and rise to excellence if they are valued, supported, and encouraged by one or more individuals.

Relationship issues are present in nearly all counseling sessions. Whether a client's identified problem is addiction, abuse, parenting, anxiety, mental health, or loss, relationships are involved.

There is a fine balance needed between healthy relationships and safe boundaries. We must maintain our individualism if we want to build strong, trusting relationships. Quality relationships are not possible if we value what others believe and practice but do not give equal worth to our personal experiences and opinions.

We must love and build a respectful relationship with ourselves if we hope to join a loving, trusting relationship with someone else. "I love you!" means little if the words *I* or *you* in the statement are absent or fake. To have the quality of relationships most people desire, one must take an authentic person into the union.

Relationships are challenging because each person is unique and has preferences and expectations. Relationships are as varied as the individuals we meet. They are always worth the time and energy necessary to make them healthy and fulfilling.

This final group of stories is presented to show you the variety, as well as the depth and breadth of relationships. I offer them as an invitation to understand and deepen your own relationships, most especially the one you have with yourself.

Bonnie

I have worked with Bonnie since 1999 in two different office locations. Her story is in the category of relationships because connections with friends, family, and co-workers were the primary focus of nearly every session. She is a current client.

In her twenties when I first met her, Bonnie was a striking young woman; tall and thin with black silky hair and a sophisticated demeanor. Together we worked through issues of a psychotic dad, a passive mother, dating, a toxic work environment, marriage, a house purchase and remodel, sisters-in-law wrath, husband's infidelity, divorce involving attorneys and court hearings, serious health issues, earning a master's degree, breaking a lease because a neighbor's marijuana smoke was coming through vents into her apartment, more dating, employment with bullies, as well as noncompliant disability accommodations at work.

I could say I have been "through hell and back" with Bonnie. Truthfully, Bonnie is a trooper. She has searched, discovered, survived, contributed, developed, and flourished. I have hung onto her belt loops and admired her journey.

Bonnie is an extroverted, intuitive feeler who likes to get things done. She is idealistic and is driven to be understood. She therefore is verbally astute. She can recall details and emotions evoked from a situation as well as any novelist. In her personal and professional life, she continually strives to condense her stories so others will listen long enough to hear what she wants them to know.

Because of her transparency, she is often the recipient of other's frustrations and nastiness. She has encountered a number of significant bullies in her life and has done a fabulous job of toughening up over the years, but not without a lot of stress. She describes emotions in detail as she dissects an experience, recalls conversations, and identifies problems so she can understand the big picture and attempt to put the pieces back together.

She repeatedly reports what we did in therapy that was most helpful: her Myers Briggs personality assessment helping her understand why she responds as she does to various issues, saying the words and asking for what she needs, stating her opinion even if it is not popular, being her own advocate for the vision accommodations needed for school and work, and trusting her instincts.

I attribute her forward progress to her positive, appreciative attitude. Bonnie never tells a story without giving the good before the bad. She always takes responsibility for how she contributes to any situation, she listens to what I say, and she is excellent at implementing change. Mainly, she cares about her wellness and strives to improve her outlook on life, her relationships, and herself. She calls when she has a hurdle to overcome and only needs me to listen and offer some historical reference or logical understanding.

Bonnie continues to be her most proactive advocate. She continues to strive, improve, and stand up for herself. I marvel at her positive attitude and her management of time, energy, and schedules. She graduated with her master's degree and earned a certificate in a complementary program. Bonnie is employed in a professional job, has a healthy love relationship, and a strong support system of family and friends. I am continually pleased with her tenacity, her critical thinking skills, and her desire to improve.

WHAT I LEARNED FROM BONNIE

If a person gets the chance to tell the whole story and have someone really listen, often solutions are discovered without a lot of effort. Sometimes, people need to speak their story and have someone reflect what was heard. People have answers to their own hurdles if only they can organize all the pieces, as in a puzzle, and let the solution emerge as the various components are connected. A counselor can be very instrumental in the process of identifying key issues and recognizing viable solutions.

Hank

When I think of Hank, I envision a big soft teddy bear. A stocky man with soft eyes, an easy laugh, and a lot to say, he spoke of the various issues and personalities at work, everything imaginable about his children and siblings, and all the favorable and undesirable traits of his wife.

He was trying some medications for depression but found himself not dealing with life as well as he had in the past. He thought counseling might help. I praised him for taking care of his needs and being aware when he wasn't on top of his game. We did a personality assessment so he could know and accept how he innately operated. He liked learning that he was an extroverted, sensing, thinking, and judging person. Since it was fun and helpful, he wanted his wife to come with him to the next session and do the same assessment.

She joined him the following week. She sat on the opposite corner of the loveseat, and five minutes into the session she abruptly turned her head, looked him straight in the eyes, and said, "I rented a house and moved out this morning. I want a divorce!"

I was stunned and Hank had a look on his face as if thinking, "Who am I? Where am I? What did this woman just say?" None of us spoke for what seemed like several minutes. Needless to say, we did not have a fun personality insight session.

From that day forward, Hank dealt with clearly-defined depression and questions such as: "What did I do wrong?" "How did I not know she was so unhappy?" and "What will I do now?"

Future sessions revolved around her new boyfriend, separation of property, divorce settlement, reaction of grown kids, and Hank's despair. He was broken. What started as a man who came to talk about life in general turned into heavy therapeutic counseling. I worried about his emotional stability and told him he could call me whenever he needed. He never called, as he had a supportive family, a regular routine, and he stayed in his home with familiar surroundings.

Hank and I worked together for many months. He continued meeting his buddies at a local restaurant for breakfast and started going to a few dances and school activities with his kids. He stopped obsessing about his ex-wife and what she was doing, although he felt hurt when he saw her or her guy friend by chance around town or heard about her new hairdo or change of vehicles.

When he was stabilized and could imagine moving forward without counseling, we gradually terminated therapy. At his last session, we reviewed his strengths, his support systems, how to stay in his logical mind, and a reminder that he did have control of his thoughts and therefore his feelings.

Several months later, I saw him with a woman at a restaurant. He motioned me over, so I stopped to say hello. He introduced me to his fiancée and told me that they were very involved with her church and he had found peace in God. He had a little glow showing through his gentle eyes and had regained his generous smile; I knew he was going to be okay.

WHAT I LEARNED FROM HANK

Good can come from painful events if we give ourselves time, reach out for help, and keep our options open. Lessons in life often come, just as Hank's did, with total surprise, absolute finality, and out of one's control. How one regains composure and direction after a traumatic event reveals much about a person's stamina, resourcefulness, and integrity. I gave Hank an A+.

Leanne

Leanne, a business owner, called and said she needed some help with low office morale. She had a competent employee (IP—Identified Patient) who was rude, cross, demanding, critical, and disrespectful to her and the other employees. Leanne did not terminate the employee because finding a comparable replacement would have been difficult. The IP was pleasant and appropriate to customers and performed at a level of excellence.

I suggested mediation, which would allow opportunities for all employees to have a voice, identify the problem, and determine solutions. Everyone from the office, including the IP, arrived for their appointment, and we sat in chairs placed in a circle. The mediation process is simple: (1) We go around the circle and everyone has a determined number of minutes to tell the story as they see it; (2) After everyone is finished, together they identify and agree upon one statement that defines the problem; (3) Everyone determines what they can personally do to help solve the problem; and (4) Everyone signs a contract confirming what they agreed to do.

Of all the mediations I have conducted, this one started with more tension and ended with significantly more disappointment. The owner volunteered to speak first. She said everyone in the group was her family and she wanted them all to feel loved. She did not mention the attitude of the IP, which was why she had brought her employees to my office. She was more intimidated by the woman than either of us had realized previously. The IP cried when it was her turn to speak. Everyone knew the reason for the mediation, but nobody could challenge the bully in the workplace, especially one who appeared weak.

I was personally baffled. In past mediations, improvement happened beyond my expectations. In this group, the dynamics of each person choosing to overlook the truth was interesting. The group defined the problem as gossip and not getting along. Their solutions included actions such as: "I will not be so sensitive." "I will express my feelings more and be more confrontational." "I will listen and put things in perspective." The mediation process I trusted as near foolproof disillusioned me with this group.

I sensed that each person was as disappointed as I was. I felt frustrated that the employees did not address the issue. Something went awry, and I concluded that the boss and I should have had a finite plan instead of depending mainly on the mediation process. A counselor facilitates versus guiding the process, but I could have given the boss a few directives before the mediation on how to directly verbalize why she had asked employees to participate.

The group left with little visible optimism for improved work morale, and they decided not to return for follow-up mediation. I did not blame them—it had not been overtly helpful.

I visited with Leanne at a later date, and she reported that the mediation truly did meet her expectations of improved office morale. She said the change was gradual and that the IP still "has her days," but Leanne thought the mediation helped the IP to shift her thoughts and consider how her behavior negatively affected the employees, the morale of the office, and ultimately the customer. She said they all still laugh when they remember the time they went to "marriage counseling."

WHAT I LEARNED FROM LEANNE'S MEDIATION

We should not judge the success or failure of our efforts immediately after a session. It often takes time for a person or group to process and implement what they heard and what they found to be valid. It takes time to integrate change. One needs first to recognize what isn't working and understand where the behavior originated before change can begin. Non-confrontational mediation does not work as well with an intimidating individual, a bully; people are reluctant to confront him/her, and the IP is not likely to politely give up his/her power.

Lucy

Lucy was a pillar of her community, and either you did not like Lucy or you loved her. She was a no-nonsense straight shooter. She lived through gossip, heartache, feast, and famine. She was solid, good-hearted, and funny.

Fun was had by all who stopped by Lucy's for coffee or a good visit. If you were lucky enough to have Lucy as a friend, you were truly lucky; she was trustworthy, loyal, would tell you honestly what she thought, and help you out of any mess without asking questions. She would also defend you if someone decided to make you the topic of gossip. On many occasions, I heard her firmly put a stop to nasty rumors.

She came to counseling twice, but I had casual associations with her for three or four decades. The two sessions were approximately fifteen years apart. The first one had something to do with one of her exes. The second had to do with a current relationship, a younger man who enjoyed her affections but would not invite her to gatherings of friends and family. She basically disliked herself for putting up with him and his shenanigans. Her exclusion from his social life was hurtful, and she knew that she deserved more than being someone's convenience. Because she understood him and had loving emotions for him, she conceded to his needs but knew in her heart that she was being used.

The last session with Lucy was most entertaining. She was hilarious, like a stand-up comic, as she talked herself in and out of her present situation. She told funny stories, criticized her decisions, and looked at me with an expression of, "Can you believe that?" Her eyes searched my face for any sign of acceptance, and she shook her head and disclaimed any sense of intelligence. We laughed hard.

I can still see the ornery twinkle in her eyes as she schemed and connived to balance the playing field. She had no secrets and no shame. She told it like it was—stupid, embarrassing, and worth it.

I do not recall one minute of therapeutic consult during that last session, but I think she left my office with renewed determination to treat herself better. She was an independent, adult woman with the means to do whatever she chose, and that is exactly what she was doing and always had done. She also knew that she could change her mind any time she wanted—with or without approval from others.

If Lucy's life was a movie, I would download it so I could watch it over and over. She was full of wisdom, anchored cynicism, and my kind of humor. A little like Willy Nelson: talented, passionate, with a stride in her step that said, "Don't mess with me!" She was the person we might all like to be, if we had the courage.

I felt flattered that Lucy believed I could help her figure things out. In reality, she was the twinkle in my day.

WHAT I LEARNED FROM LUCY

A healthy person takes responsibility for their choices and enjoys the lessons along the way. Mistakes, friends, changes, and amends are made, and the sun comes up. History is possible because of survivors, scrappers, and creators like Lucy. Good attitudes, laughter, and an acceptance of self are key ingredients to balanced living and resiliency.

Misty

Misty, with her two-year-old son, left her husband a few months prior to her first session with me. She was granted a restraining order against him by local authorities, and she and her son were living with her parents. She knew she was going to need emotional support, because he had filed for sole physical and legal custody of their son.

She had met her husband at college. She reported that she knew he was controlling when she dated him but succumbed to his pleading and his promises that their life would be great once they were married. After four years of marriage, she realized she was afraid of him. He was a large man and very verbally demanding and critical. He forced her to do things she did not want to do, and he wanted her to have very little contact with her family. She thought he was too physically rough and tough with their son and did not approve of how he would shame the child when he cried. He said he didn't want to raise a *sissy*.

Leaving him was the easiest part of the struggle that awaited her. For more than two years, Misty cooperated with CFI (Child and Family Investigator) family visits and reports, a MMPI (Psychological Assessment), the child's hysterical crying when they exchanged him for visitation, and the father's continual harassment. They had several court appearances, two CFI investigations (the father felt the first one was biased), numerous attempts at mediation, medical exams for their son's autistic symptoms, and the father's cruel, religiose intimidations.

She fought until she had no finances left to pay for legal fees. Her attorney believed the judge would rule for joint/shared custody, which is what they could agree on without going into court, and strongly urged her to not spend money she did not have and to settle out of court. Because Misty had no means of borrowing more money and she was emotionally exhausted, she agreed to her ex-husband's demands for joint custody.

Once the courts awarded shared custody, Misty had to straighten her shoulders, hold her head high, and shift her thoughts to believe their son would be healthy, well, and safe with his father. She had exhausted her resources, and she knew she had to continue to be the positive force in her son's life.

The child was four years old by the time the heart-wrenching ordeal was over. Nobody won; the husband lost his wife and the sole custody battle, Misty lost her fight for sole physical custody, and the son lost his intact family system and his mother's protection fifty percent of the time. Her worst fears had come true. We both felt the system had failed her and her child.

She only had one place to go, and that was up. She used the skills she had learned in therapy to move forward and to continue providing a calm and loving home for her son. Basically, she shifted gears. She felt defeated, for sure, but she didn't let that stop her from finding a new home and building a new life with her son. She did not enjoy the routine of driving eighty miles every Friday and Sunday for exchanges, sharing holidays, and splitting summers, but she let go of the fear; she replaced it with faith that they were all going to be okay.

WHAT I LEARNED FROM MISTY

Emotional tenacity is the magic it takes to fight with all your heart, so you can wake up with yourself in the morning knowing you did your best. It is not always the decision that is good or bad; it is often the action after the decision is made that determines its destiny. Shifting thoughts to accept what is, and stopping the fight, can contribute amazingly to the success of achieving what one wants, even though it often comes wrapped in a different package.

Sarah and Ken

Ken first came to me because his wife had left him for another man. As I listened to his story, I realized the man his wife was involved with was the husband of one of my female clients, Sarah. Before a month was over, to my surprise, Sarah and Ken walked into the office together. They had met by chance, realized their common connection, and began dating.

I knew it was out of the ordinary to counsel them as a couple, but together we determined that working through their emotions together could be helpful and not detrimental to either. I told them their relationship was likely a pleasant detour from the pain in their chests, but that it would not prevent them from experiencing the denial, bargaining, anger, and depression of the grief cycle. They understood that, and they also understood when I explained that involvement with someone, anyone, and so soon after a breakup, was probably not the best decision.

Sarah and Ken were witty and resourceful, and they were both caregivers. They shared common interests and communicated freely. Each was respectful of the other and had empathy that strengthened them individually. Most importantly, they laughed a lot.

Their relationship was built around the hub of the two cheating spouses. Sarah and Ken provided each other with support plus accurate information as both retraced their spouses' behaviors during the past several months. They helped each other put the pieces together. They diverted their pain to a future time, and together they targeted their anger toward the spouses, where it belonged.

Ken had a good job and provided well for his wife. Their adult children were not living in the home, and they had two little dogs they both loved. Ken had no financial problems, only frustration and the feeling of unfairness; he had done everything for his wife and treated her like a princess.

Sarah, on the other hand, was married to an alcoholic. She was employed and owned a small house. She had little means of paying her bills and was overwhelmed with fear and hurt. She had stuck it out with him through his alcoholic embarrassments and abuses, and then he'd had the nerve to leave her for another woman.

Sarah and Ken tried to make the center of their love relationship something other than their spouses, but they were unsuccessful. Both needed to retract and work on their own recovery, as neither had processed through their individual loss.

Both were very raw and vulnerable, and it was helpful that they found each other and regained a little self-esteem. They stopped dating but maintained a friendship that was rich and sincere. They truly cared about each other.

The divorces happened, and Sarah found a stable job. The last time I saw her, she was smiling and on the verge of a big hearty laugh. I have no doubt that she is enjoying life and spending quality time with her grandkids. She had all the tools for a happy life, but she had been wasting them on an alcoholic.

Ken finally had the courage to stand up to his ex-wife and required her to get her belongings out of his house. He received custody of the dogs and his routine did not change significantly. I encouraged Ken and Sarah to not choose love relationships that were a project; feeling sorry for a person is a seed for co-dependency.

He experienced some psychosomatic symptoms that brought him occasionally to my office, but the last time I saw him, he too seemed healthy, well, and enjoying life.

WHAT I LEARNED FROM KEN AND SARAH

Sometimes our best gifts come from the most unlikely people, places, and things. Caregivers search for someone to care for; a characteristic they need to address. Their spouses were users. Users can spot a caregiver through a concrete wall, and vice versa. If likeness instead of opposites attracted, there might be less conflict and more longevity in relationships.

Sheila and Frank

Frank called to schedule an appointment for himself and his girlfriend, Sheila. When they came, they were in jovial moods. Frank was dressed in jeans and a T-shirt. Sheila was in cutoff short-shorts and a tank-top. Both were in their early forties, had met at a party, and worked in restaurants.

They had dated for a year, had a fight, and broken up. Frank thought it was just a little spat, but Sheila felt the relationship was over and had since become involved with another man. When Frank called her and said he really missed her and wanted to try again, she broke it off with her boyfriend because she really loved Frank. All she had ever wanted was for Frank to love her in return.

They had been together three to four weeks and reported everything was going great. When Frank wasn't working, he spent a lot of time with Sheila's boys and made a real effort to attend school events. What made Sheila really happy was that Frank proved he really loved her by not hanging out after work with the guys and drinking beer.

She showed her renewed love by being sexual every night, which made him very happy. Because he was feeling loved, he agreed to grant her wish and called me to set up an appointment. They really wanted a good relationship.

The second week, all was not so great. He stayed after work one night because some friends came to his restaurant for a late dinner and wanted to visit when he finished his shift. The sex stopped, and the tears started. He tried to explain what a tough spot it put him in when he had to hurry home to the *little woman* instead of occasionally relaxing with friends. He did not understand why it was such a big deal.

She expressed to him that when he chose his friends over coming home, it made her feel unimportant and unloved. When he would say something in his defense, she would cry and make comments about how their relationship was just not going to work.

Every week they came in smiling and left upset. It was possible that therapy was working well; however, the process seemed quite difficult for Sheila and Frank.

I pointed out the patterns I observed: if he did what she wanted, they were loving and sexual, and they were both happy; if, however, he did not do what she wanted, they were not sexual and both were unhappy. I brought up general information—a relationship works both ways, giving and receiving in some sort of balance is important; interdependence is the goal, where both people have an identity plus a connection; compromise is important and communication is essential; and it is healthy for both to have friends other than each other.

Whenever I had those conversations, Sheila would turn to him and say something like, "You never care about how I feel. I just want to feel important and loved!" And, the tears would start.

I do not know if they chose to continue dating, but their efforts to reach their stated goal of building a healthy relationship was less than successful for several reasons—Sheila's goal was to change Frank. What she needed from him in order to feel loved was rigid and unrealistic. Frank and I were the only ones working hard, and there was an established imbalance of power. Because they were at a stalemate as a couple, I ultimately provided them with a list of therapists who might be able to move them through their impasse.

WHAT I LEARNED FROM FRANK AND SHEILA

Men and women need to know that another person cannot *make* him/her happy. Nobody has that kind of power. Frank was in a no-win situation, and even if it was possible for him to succumb to Sheila's expectations, losing oneself so another might feel loved is ridiculous and never a viable option. Frank, like many people, tried to become what somebody wanted instead of finding someone who loved him just as he was.

Trish and Shawn

A woman in her early thirties rang my home doorbell on a Saturday morning as I was leaving to go for a run. She was crying hysterically and pleaded to see me, "Right now!"

Dressed in my shorts and baseball cap, we walked into my office. Her name was Trish, and she was very upset. She had just learned she was pregnant. She reported that she and her husband Shawn did not have a good marriage and another child was not what they needed. It was a second marriage for both, and between them, they had three other children. She cried, sobbed, and talked incessantly, stopping only long enough to blow her nose and breathe. She was frantic.

During the course of that first session, to her credit, she determined that she and her husband needed marriage counseling. When I met Shawn, I was not surprised, as he was exactly as Trish had described him—kind, calm, and quiet. After a few weekly sessions, they were doing much better as a couple and both reported feeling more confident in their innate strengths. Our work together transitioned from every week to every two weeks and then to only when needed.

Their problems, varied as they were, were always rooted in one dysfunctional pattern: after a disagreement he would stop talking and so would she. The problem with that cycle was that he was extremely introverted, quiet by nature, and during stress needed to withdraw more than usual. She was extroverted, very verbal by nature, and during stressful times she needed to talk. When her frustrations and hurt got the best of her, she would become like him and not speak. That did not work for either of them. By the time the sessions were over, and she had a chance to voice her bottled-up thoughts and feelings, they would leave with a smile and a strong reminder that she needed to talk even if he never said a word, which was common.

Over the years, they worked relentlessly on a broad variety of challenges: struggles with combining his, her, and their children; painful experiences with ex-spouses and their opposing parenting practices; kids who would flip between households; kids involved with drugs and teen-pregnancy; parents who were going through divorce and reverting to childish behavior; a serious illness; and friends who would hit on one or the other. Life was never boring for Trish and Shawn.

When life was good it was very good, and when it was bad it was because communication had stopped. The basis of their success, no matter the issue, was so simple yet so difficult to remember and practice.

I had the privilege of working with them intermittently for several years. Trish would call right before she was ready to explode and together she and Shawn would soon be sitting on my loveseat looking at me, knowing I was going to say what they had heard many times before. I would facilitate conversation between them and it was always helpful.

From the first moment I looked into Trish's overwhelmed eyes on that beautiful autumn morning, we connected. She bubbled over with life's blisses and glitches. If she thought it or felt it, she said it. I never had to guess or read between the lines. Whether it was listening, thinking, or talking, she did it with determination and passion. Shawn, living through exactly the same scenarios, handled life by observation and private thought.

My consistent hope for Trish is that she is clearly, always saying the words. My hope for Shawn is that Trish is clearly, always saying the words. Isn't it interesting how that works?

WHAT I LEARNED
FROM TRISH & SHAWN

We can have healthy relationships if we capitalize on our basic strengths and never give up, no matter the hurdles. It might feel silly or like a waste of time and money to go to therapy to gain help for repeating a simple exercise, but if a good relationship grows and sustains from the pattern, it would be counterproductive to stop. One counseling session usually lasts fifty minutes and costs about the same as going out for dinner; consider the benefit-cost ratio.

HEALTHY RELATIONSHIPS HAVE EQUALITY

When one person is superior, more powerful, more important, and/or more significant,
the relationship is unbalanced.
One should not have to be small in order
for another to be big.
Both should be big.

Epilogue

When my husband and I were ready to work less and play more, I was unable to continue my private counseling practice. A therapist, as well as mental health agencies, must be available in emergency situations or have a referral system in place. The decision to sell our businesses and embark on a life of travel was not conducive to adequately providing for clients in a consistent, ongoing manner.

I have enjoyed our new life, but I must admit that I have missed my work and my clients beyond what I would have imagined. I learned long ago that if I leave something I love for something I want, there is still loss. Giving up my private counseling practice most definitely left me with a sense of loss that I have had to move through.

Whether I am on the back of our Harley Davidson, riding shotgun in a vehicle, or writing, the many people I have worked with in my counseling practice continue to be in my thoughts. I carry their triumphs and struggles, their smiles, and their commendable courage with me wherever I travel.

For those readers who are practicing therapists or pursuing a mental health counseling career, my hope is that *My Clients…My Teachers* reinforces for you the noble process of psychotherapy. Be proud of your work; it is valuable. Along with continuing education, it takes a lot of courage to be an effective counselor. Talking and listening, both very essential, can be more effective when used with a variety of visuals, techniques, and strategies.

Most importantly, I want my clients' stories to instill a respect for each person who reaches out to you for help. Whether their presenting issues are extreme or casual, laced with sympathy or disapproval, all are there to get the best you can provide. So, take care of yourself, have clear boundaries, and balance the client's struggles with your own mental wellness.

My Clients…My Teachers is my way of continuing to offer help to people, without the confines of four walls or a weekly schedule. It does not, however, take the place of sitting across the room from an apprehensive face or building a new therapeutic relationship; but it comforts me to think it can be the catalyst for individuals and couples to ask questions, find answers, or even call a licensed therapist for an appointment.

We all connect through, and everyone deserves, a good story. May the sharing of some of my clients' stories help you, the reader, understand at a deeper level one of the foundational premises of human life. While you might not have control over many things that happen to you, you do have complete control over how they affect you—because you always have control over your reactions.

Like my clients, you too can create your desired life story. The good news is that it's up to you, and counseling can help.

About the Author

Jennifer Goble, a rural Colorado native, feels fortunate to have been born and raised with four sisters in Akron, a small town on the northeastern plains.

A farm wife for thirty years, she has three children, and seven grandchildren. She has taught, counseled, and developed educational programs for students from preschool through university graduates, earning a Ph.D. in Counseling Education from Colorado State University. Jennifer has owned and operated her private counseling practice for twenty-three years in Colorado and Arizona.

Semi-retired, Jennifer and her husband enjoy traveling. They currently call Estes Park, CO and Bisbee, AZ home.

Her weekly newspaper column, "Mental Matters," can be viewed at www.southplattesentinel.com/health.

To contact Jennifer with comments, questions, or to schedule a speaking engagement please visit her website and blog at www.jennifergoble.com

QUESTIONS TO CONTEMPLATE AND DISCUSS

1. As you read the stories, what did you discover about the process of psychotherapy?
2. How did the stories help you think about your own life situations differently?
3. What kind of courage do you think it takes to be a client? A therapist?
4. How could a client who only goes to one or two sessions find counseling to be helpful?
5. If you had been to therapy, would you sign a permission form to have your story told in a book? If not, why not? If you would, why would you?
6. The therapist shared what she learned from her clients. What did you learn from the stories? How do your insights differ from what the therapist learned?
7. What story evoked your strongest emotions? Why?
8. Consider if and how the visuals helped you understand the concepts presented to the clients. What one was most impactful for you?
9. What part of the book was most encouraging? Discouraging? In what ways?
10. Consider the statement, "People connect with each other through their pain." What does this statement mean to you? Have you seen this play out in your own life? If so, how?

Made in the USA
San Bernardino, CA
27 July 2014

The Bible and the

The Liturgical Context of Patristic Exegesis

Contributors

~: Khaled Anatolios :~

Khaled Anatolios is Professor of Historical and Systematic Theology at Boston College School of Theology and Ministry. Among his publications are: *Retrieving Nicaea: The Development and Meaning of Trinitarian Doctrine* (Baker Academic, 2011); *Athanasius. The Coherence of his Thought* (Routledge: 1998 & 2004); and the *Athanasius* volume of the Routledge Early Church Fathers series (2004).

~: Mark Armitage :~

Mark Armitage lives in England, where he studied Theology at the Universities of Oxford and Durham. He is the author of *A Twofold Solidarity: Leo the Great's Theology of Redemption*, and has written on Leo, Thomas Aquinas, and G. K. Chesterton for *Marianum, New Blackfriars, Nova et Vetera, The Thomist, Pro Ecclesia,* and *The Chesterton Review.*

~: Michael Patrick Barber :~

Michael Patrick Barber is the Chair of the Graduate Program in Biblical Theology at John Paul the Great University in San Diego, California. He completed his Ph.D. in Theology at Fuller in Pasadena, CA, writing a dissertation entitled, "The Historical Jesus and Cultic Restoration Eschatology: The New Temple, the New Priesthood, and the New Cult" (2010). Barber also earned an M.A. in Theology from Franciscan University and a B.A. in Theology and Philosophy from Azusa Pacific University. He has published a number of popular books on Scripture. With two other Senior Fellows of the St. Paul Center, John Bergsma and Brant Pitre, Dr. Barber writes for the weblog, www.TheSacredPage.com, a site affiliated with the Society of Biblical Literature. He lives in San Diego, CA, with his wife Kimberly and their three children.

~: Scott W. Hahn :~

Scott W. Hahn, founder and president of the St. Paul Center for Biblical Theology is professor of Scripture and Theology at Franciscan University of Steubenville, Ohio. He has held the Pio Cardinal Laghi Chair at the Pontifical College Josephinum in Columbus, Ohio, the Pope Benedict XVI Chair of Biblical Theology and Liturgical Proclamation at St. Vincent Seminary in Latrobe, Pennsylvania (2005-2011), and has served as visiting professor at the Pontifical University of the Holy Cross and the Pontifical University, Regina Apostolorum, both in Rome. Hahn is the general editor of the *Ignatius Catholic Study Bible* and *Catholic Bible Dictionary*, and is author or editor of more than thirty books, including *The Kingdom of God as Liturgical Empire: A Theological Commentary on 1-2 Chronicles* (2012), *Kinship By Covenant: A Canonical Approach to the Fulfillment of God's Saving Promises* (The Anchor Yale Bible Reference Library, 2009), *Covenant and Communion: The Biblical Theology of Pope Benedict XVI* (2009), *Letter and Spirit: From Written Text to Living Word in the Liturgy* (2005), *Understanding the Scriptures* (2005), and *The Lamb's Supper: The Mass as Heaven on Earth* (1999).

⁓: Stephen Hildebrand :⁓

Stephen Hildebrand is an Associate Professor of Theology and Director of the Master's Program in Theology at Franciscan University of Steubenville. He received his Ph.D. in Historical Theology from Fordham University in 2002. He published *The Trinitarian Theology of Basil of Caesarea* (CUA press) in 2007 and a translation of St. Basil's *On the Holy Spirit* (St. Vladimir's Seminary Press) in 2011. Most recently, he has translated Robert Grosseteste's *On the Cessation of the Law* in CUA's Fathers of the Church, Mediaeval Continuation series.

⁓: Fr. William Kurz, S.J. :⁓

Fr. William Kurz, S.J., is Professor of New Testament at Marquette University. He specializes in Luke-Acts, John, narrative criticism, intertextuality, and theological interpretation. His 2004-2005 sabbatical found patristic models for interpreting Scripture as God's Word, resulting in his seventh book, *Reading the Bible as God's Own Story: A Catholic Approach for Bringing Scripture to Life* (2007). His theological commentary on Acts (Catholic Commentary on Sacred Scripture) is being edited for 2013 publication by Baker Academic. He has published over forty scholarly articles in professional journals and books. The most recent of his six previous books include *Reading Luke-Acts: Dynamics of Biblical Narrative* (1993); *The Future of Catholic Biblical Scholarship: A Constructive Conversation* (co-author Luke Timothy Johnson, Eerdmans, 2002); and *What Does the Bible Say about the End Times? A Catholic View* (2004, first place in Scripture by Catholic Press Association 2005, Polish translation 2007).

⁓: Matthew Levering :⁓

Matthew Levering is Professor of Theology at the University of Dayton. With Reinhard Hütter, he is co-editor of the theological quarterly *Nova et Vetera*. He is Chair of the Board of the Academy of Catholic Theology and serves as the Director of the University of Dayton's Center for Scriptural Exegesis, Philosophy, and Doctrine. He is the author or editor of numerous books, including most recently *Jesus and the Demise of Death: Resurrection, the Afterlife, and the Fate of Christians* (2012); *Predestination: Biblical and Theological Paths* (2011); *Reading Paul with St. Thomas Aquinas* (2012); *The Betrayal of Charity: The Sins that Sabotage Divine Love* (2011); and *The Oxford Handbook of the Trinity* (2011). He is the translator of Gilles Emery's *The Trinity: An Introduction to Catholic Doctrine on the Triune God* (2011).

~: Owen M. Phelan :~

Owen M. Phelan is Associate Professor of Church History at Mount Saint Mary's University and Seminary. Dr. Phelan holds an M.A. and Ph.D. from the University of Notre Dame, where his concentration was medieval history. His Ph.D. dissertation was entitled "The Formation of Christian Europe: Baptism under the Carolingians." He specializes in late antique and early medieval history. His articles have appeared in journals such as the *Journal of Ecclesiastical History* and the *Harvard Theological Review*. Currently, he is working on a book examining the role of baptism and sacramental thinking in Carolingian Europe.

~: Fr. Stephen Ryan, O.P. :~

Fr. Stephen Ryan, a member of the Order of Preachers, is an Associate Professor of Sacred Scripture in the Pontifical Faculty of the Immaculate Conception at the Dominican House of Studies in Washington, D.C. He received his licentiate in Theology (S.T.L.) from the Pontifical Faculty of the Immaculate Conception (1994), and his Ph.D. in Hebrew Bible from the Department of Near Eastern Languages and Civilizations at Harvard University (2001). He has published an edition of *God and His Image: An Outline of Biblical Theology* (San Francisco: Ignatius Press, 2007) by the late Dominique Barthélemy, O.P., and his most recent publications include an article on the ancient versions of the Book of Judith and book reviews in *The Thomist* and the *Catholic Biblical Quarterly*.

~: Fr. Jared Wicks, S.J. :~

Fr. Jared Wicks, S.J., gained his Th.D. in the Faculty of Catholic Theology of the University of Münster, where he heard lectures given by Prof. Joseph Ratzinger. He taught at the Jesuit School of Theology in Chicago from 1967–79 and at the Gregorian University from 1979–2004. His research and publications have treated the theology of Martin Luther, Vatican II, and especially *Dei Verbum*. He served on the world-level Catholic–Lutheran dialogues on church and justification and on the church's apostolicity. After moving to John Carroll University, he joined the US Catholic-Lutheran dialogue that produced the consensus document, *The Hope of Eternal Life* in 2011. In late 2011, Fr. Wicks became scholar-in-residence at the Pontifical College Josephinum in Columbus, Ohio.

~: William Wright :~

William Wright is an associate professor of theology at Duquesne University in Pittsburgh, PA. A specialist in New Testament studies, his work focuses on the Gospel according to John, the history of biblical interpretation, and the relationship between biblical studies and Catholic theology. He is the author of *Rhetoric and Theology: Figural Reading of John 9* (Walter de Gruyter, 2009) and is the co-author (with Fr. Francis Martin) of *The Gospel of John*, forthcoming in the Catholic Commentary on Sacred Scripture Series (Baker Academic).

~: Christine E. Wood :~

Christine E. Wood received her Ph.D. in Systematic Theology from Marquette University, Milwaukee, in 2011. Her dissertation was entitled, "The Metaphysics and Intellective Psychology in the Natural Desire for Seeing God: Henri de Lubac and Neo-Scholasticism." In light of a clear distinction between Suarezian and Thomistic theologies in the early twentieth century, her research investigated de Lubac's concerns over the "extrinsicist neo-scholastic" theology of the nature-grace relationship. Dr. Wood currently teaches Scripture, Systematics, and Moral Theology at John Paul the Great Catholic University in San Diego.

Letter & Spirit 7 (2011): 7-12

Introduction

This volume of *Letter & Spirit* responds to the call of Pope Benedict XVI in his Apostolic Exhortation *Verbum Domini* for a thoughtful return to the Fathers of the Church and how they approached Sacred Scripture. First and foremost, for the Fathers, the reading and interpretation of Scripture was something that took place within an *ecclesial setting*. Pope Benedict maintains that authentic biblical interpretation "can only be had within the faith of the church."[1] The Pope cites St. Bonaventure on the necessity of faith, which acts as a "key" to "throw open the sacred text": "...it is impossible for anyone to attain to knowledge of that truth unless he first has infused faith in Christ, which is the lamp, the gate, and the foundation of all Scripture."[2]

To appropriate this ecclesial outlook, this faith-oriented approach, we need to return to the Church Fathers and understand their *tradition of interpretation*. This is not in any way to jettison historical-critical methods and the valuable insights that modern biblical scholarship has brought to light. It is simply to acknowledge what Pope Benedict calls for—again, in *Verbum Domini*—a measured return to the interpretive methods employed by the Fathers. Pope Benedict urges that the Church Fathers be given renewed attention—attention to the interpretive methodology they brought to the Sacred Text as well as the theology that flowed from their exegetical labors. Pope Benedict states that "The Church Fathers present a theology that still has great value today because at its heart is the study of sacred Scripture as a whole. Indeed, the Fathers are primarily and essentially *commentators on sacred Scripture*." The Pope holds up the Church Fathers as examples that can "teach modern exegetes a truly religious approach to sacred Scripture, and likewise an interpretation that is constantly attuned to the criterion of communion with the experience of the Church."[3]

Once we recognize the importance and relevance of the ecclesial setting for reading scripture, and recognize also the importance of the patristic interpretive tradition that enriches it, then we can see what the Fathers saw—that *the liturgy* was then, even as it is now, *the privileged setting for the Word*. It is a matter of historical fact that the Bible was compiled from the context of the liturgy, to be read in the liturgy, and was to be actualized by the liturgy. Pope Benedict expresses himself in precisely these categories, speaking of the liturgy as "the privileged setting in which God speaks to us in the midst of our lives; he speaks today to his people, who hear and respond.[4] He goes on to say how "Every liturgical action is

1 *Verbum Domini*, 29.

2 *Verbum Domini*, 29.

3 *Verbum Domini*, 37.

4 *Verbum Domini*, 52.

by its very nature steeped in sacred Scripture. In the words of the Constitution *Sacrosanctum Concilium*, 'sacred Scripture is of the greatest importance in the celebration of the liturgy. From it are taken the readings, which are explained in the homily and the psalms that are sung. From Scripture the petitions, prayers, and liturgical hymns receive their inspiration and substance. From Scripture the liturgical actions and signs draw their meaning.' Even more, it must be said that Christ himself 'is present in his word, since it is he who speaks when Scripture is read in Church.'"[5]

Having formed this understanding—with respect to the ecclesial setting, the patristic traditions, and the privileged liturgical setting for the Word—we begin to discover the *sacramentality* of Scripture and experience its *performative power* precisely as it is proclaimed in the liturgy and then fulfilled in the celebration of the Eucharist. Christ himself is present when God's life-giving word is proclaimed at the Eucharistic celebration. He who is the Way and the Truth and the Life speaks life to us, and, when we listen, we are transformed and renewed by that life-giving Word so that we can walk in His Way and live the Truth. Saint Jerome speaks of this wonderful mystery, almost *equating* the Eucharist *with* the Proclamation of the Word of God: "We are reading the sacred Scriptures. For me, the Gospel is the Body of Christ; for me, the holy Scriptures are his teaching. And when he says: *whoever does not eat my flesh and drink my blood* (*Jn* 6:53), even though these words can also be understood of the [Eucharistic] Mystery, Christ's body and blood are really the word of Scripture, God's teaching. When we approach the [Eucharistic] Mystery, if a crumb falls to the ground we are troubled. Yet when we are listening to the word of God, and God's Word and Christ's flesh and blood are being poured into our ears, yet we pay no heed, what great peril should we not feel?"[6]

Saint Jerome had no intention of suggesting there be an eighth sacrament. His rhetoric was employed to emphasize and draw attention to the notion that as the Word is proclaimed and expounded in the Liturgical assembly of the Church, it has *performative power*—it functions *sacramentally* in renewing and elevating the life of the Christian.

None of the fathers set these ideas out in terms of an exacting theoretical framework, but all of them contributed significant insights that would lead to the sort of synthesis that Pope Benedict sets forth in *Verbum Domini*, especially recognizing the sacramentality of the word and its performative character. This volume of Letter & Spirit will explore the insights of the Fathers of the Church in the hope of bringing renewed interest in the contribution they bring to the study of the bible.

In his article, "Cures of the Soul and Correction of Heart: Pope Leo the Great on the Healing Power of Holy Week," **Mark Armitage** explores how sermons by Pope Leo the Great on Christ's agony in Gethsemane and cry of dereliction on

5 *Verbum Domini*, 52.

6 *Verbum Domini*, 56.

Calvary are designed to foster both contemplation of these events and participation in them. Pope Leo teaches that in the Sacraments, and particularly in the Eucharist, we participate in the paschal mystery, enabling us to experience something of the cross, to relive the passion with Christ, to share in the healing remedy of Christ's death and resurrection, and so to "pass over" with him from death to life. In other words, as mysteries and remedies the events of Christ's passion—effected in and through the Sacraments—bring healing and transformation. These remedies are thus ordered towards our participation with Christ in the brightness and glory of the kingdom of God. This participation confers inner healing and freedom from the fear of suffering and death. Anticipating the motto of John Paul the Great, the message "be not afraid" is also the gospel of his great predecessor Leo.

Fr. William Kurz, S.J., in his study, "Patristic Interpretation of Scripture within God's Story of Creation and Redemption," considers how two great Fathers of the church, Saints Irenaeus and Athanasius, teach us how to read Scripture in a way that will deepen us theologically as well as guide us practically. Fr. Kurz shows how Irenaeus and Athanasius read individual biblical passages as within and as part of God's overarching biblical story of creation and redemption. This approach provides the key to understanding the meaning of the entire canonical Bible, from Genesis to Revelation, as well as any individual passage. They were aided in deriving this overarching biblical narrative by a traditional and ecclesial reading and use of Scripture. Like most patristic biblical scholars, Irenaeus and Athanasius were both teachers and pastors in the Church, not academic biblical specialists, as is common today. Their context of interpretation was ecclesial, liturgical, and pastoral. Fr. Kurz demonstrates how patristic interpretative methods, far from being irrelevant for today, actually enable modern readers to attain greater theological and spiritual insight into any biblical passage.

Christine E. Wood's article, "Anamnesis and Allegory in Ambrose's *De sacramentis* and *De mysteriis*," shows how St. Ambrose of Milan used typology to explain the notion of ritual memorial or *anamnesis*, something central to the early Church's understanding of making a past event present to those participating in the liturgical action. Ambrose understood the Sacraments, and the Eucharistic liturgy in particular, within the context of the Jewish liturgical tradition which was formed upon *anamnesis* or ritual memorial. Thus the event and effects of Jesus' paschal mystery are actualized for each generation of Christians through the mode of liturgical memorial. Without the liturgy, we would be incapable of being present at the cross or the empty tomb. For Ambrose, as with many other fathers of the church, divine providence has provided a means by which we are not mere spectators in these pivotal events of human history, but are rather *actually present* as contemporaries with Mary and the others at the foot of the cross. For Ambrose, the Liturgy becomes our teacher and a primary source for our theology.

Michael Barber's "'The Yoke of Servitude': Christian Non-Observance of the Law's Cultic Precepts in Patristic Sources," considers an important early Patristic interpretive tradition which understood Israel's sin of worshipping the golden calf as triggering dramatic changes in Israel's laws and its relationship with God, particularly with respect to the imposition of sacrificial and cultic laws that are no longer observed by Christians. Dr. Barber shows how this Patristic tradition, sadly neglected today, helps to explain the New Testament's continuity with the Old, in that certain precepts, instituted after the sin of the golden calf, were not originally part of God's covenant relationship with his people. Thus, patristic sources argue that Christian non-observance of certain Old Testament precepts results not from a "selective reading" of the Scriptures but from a holistic understanding of God's plan for humanity.

Matthew Levering's "Scriptural and Sacramental Signs: Augustine's *Answer to Faustus,*" provides a much-needed overview of portions of Saint Augustine's *Answer to Faustus.* Dr. Levering shows how Augustine, in taking on the Manichean heretic Faustus, employs extensive use of typology, shows how the Old Testament foreshadows the New, and how the advent of Christ does not negate the Old Testament. For Augustine (unlike Faustus), the Old Testament remains absolutely necessary for attesting to the truth of New Testament realities. Having rejected the Old Testament, Faustus and the Manicheans are unable to understand accurately the New Testament. Dr. Levering demonstrates that, taken as a whole, Augustine's *Answer to Faustus* constitutes an extraordinary Christian theology of the Old Testament and its relation to the New.

In his article, "Scripture, Worship, and Liturgy in the Thought of St. Basil the Great," **Stephen Hildebrand** examines St. Basil's understanding of Scripture's relationship to dogma, tradition, and liturgy. We learn that for St. Basil, the Scriptures could not be rightly understood apart from apostolic and patristic tradition, a tradition that was liturgical. As with the Fathers and Apostles that came before him, Basil taught that the Scriptures do not interpret themselves, but rather that authentic tradition—consistent with and enshrined in apostolic liturgy and worship—holds a special and indispensable place in the question of Church authority and the formation of dogma.

Owen Phelan's "Patristic Exegesis and the Liturgy: Medieval *Ressourcement* and the Development of Baptism," traces how St. Jerome's late fourth-century commentary on the Gospel of Matthew influenced important early medieval theologians—Bede, Alcuin, Hrabanus Maurus, Paschasius Radbertus, and others—in their baptismal catechesis. Dr. Phelan shows how Jerome's comments on the Great Commission (Matt. 28:16–20) were transformed by Bede and then synthesized and made popular by Alcuin. These theologians practiced what we understand as *ressourcement*—a return to the (often ancient) sources of Christian tradition and Scriptural interpretation—in responding to their own contemporary pastoral concerns. Dr. Phelan shows how Jerome's exegesis of Matthew 28:16–20 exemplifies the impact that patristic interpretation of the Bible had on later Christian liturgy and suggests the importance of engaging this same tradition and *ressourcement* methodology as we move forward in our own day on important questions of catechesis and conversion.

In 1988 then Cardinal Joseph Ratzinger called for the development of a new exegetical method that would take advantage of the strengths of both the patristic-medieval exegetical approach and the modern historical-critical approach. In his article "Psalm 22 in Syriac Tradition," **Fr. Stephen Ryan, O.P.**, examines how early patristic Syriac commentary on Psalm 22 can contribute to Cardinal Ratzinger's appeal. After a brief survey of the reception of Psalm 22 in the Syrian Orient, Fr. Ryan suggests several areas in which this tradition might contribute to moving biblical scholarship forward. Though generally overshadowed by the ancient Greek, Latin, and even Coptic interpretive traditions, the Syriac tradition has distinctive and important features that should not escape the attention of scholars seeking to develop a more theologically relevant exegesis for today.

In his article "Interiority and Extroversion in Biblical Trinitarian Faith in Augustine's *De Trinitate*," **Khaled Anatolios** looks at St. Augustine's classic work, *De Trinitate*, from the perspective of the dialectic of interiority and exteriority in the appropriation of Trinitarian faith—and thus, of Christian faith in general. He shows that Augustine offers enduring resources for mediating and transcending this polarity. Three principles arise in Dr. Anatolios' treatment of this dialectic on the basis of a reading of *De Trinitate*: first, that the originating moment and enduring content of Christian faith is the inter-section of divine and human *extroversion* which is distinctly configured by the Christocentric-Trinitarian economy of revelation and salvation; second, that a crucial negative moment in the assent of faith is the repudiation of an interiorist foundationalism that allows the subject to judge the contents of faith by reference to the standards of his own interiority; and, thirdly, that Nicene Trinitarian faith views the human person as radically and irreducibly extroverted and defines the life of faith as a Christological reformation of this extroversion.

William Wright's "Patristic Biblical Hermeneutics in Joseph Ratzinger's *Jesus of Nazareth*," reflects on Ratzinger's retrieval of patristic biblical hermeneutics by focusing in detail on his interpretation of a specific biblical text: the Good Shepherd discourse in John 10:1–18. Dr. Wright shows how *Jesus of Nazareth* offers a model for post-conciliar theological interpretation of the Gospels, which combines both "the new and the old" (Matt. 13:52), in service of the readers' spiritual transformation by Christ. Ratzinger's retrieval of patristic biblical hermeneutics allows God's Word to sound forth in the Church and in the world today, a task most appropriate to the man who serves as Chief shepherd of Christ's sheep.

Fr. Jared Wicks, S.J., offers a new translation of Joseph Ratzinger's (Pope Benedict XVI) entry, "Stellvertretung" (Vicarious Representation), originally published in *Handbuch theologischer Grundbegriffe* [Manual of Basic Theological Concepts] in 1962–63. Joseph Ratzinger wrote this entry during the years 1959–63, when he was professor of Fundamental Theology in the Catholic Theology Faculty of the University of Bonn. Pope Benedict's article is an outstanding example of a *Christology* worked out from biblical sources, as well as being an exemplary presentation of central convictions about Christ and the Church which he has held throughout his theological career. The article also shows the foundational role played by the Pope's Christology in the two volumes of Jesus of Nazareth, in which the Pope speaks often of Jesus' representative role, and repeatedly takes the Servant of Deutero-Isaiah as the key to Jesus' understanding of his mission.

In his article, "Liturgy: The Context of Patristic Exegesis," **Patrick McGoldrick** examines the relationship between the liturgy and the interpretation of Scripture in patristic exegesis. Dr. McGoldrick will shed light on how for both the Church Fathers and for us, the liturgy will not allow the Scriptures to be treated simply as written texts. Because, in the final analysis, it is Christ who is present and who addresses the hearers of the Word, the reading of Scripture must be proclaimed by a minister so as to be heard. The setting of the proclamation must be such as to heighten expectation and engage the hearers actively. So too, from the early church and down through the centuries the liturgy has had the tradition of preaching and continues to insist on it. The word contained in the Scriptures and proclaimed in the Christian assembly is made alive and given its cutting edge in the celebration of the liturgy. In the celebration of the Sacraments the mysteries contained in Scripture are actualized for us and we are carried into reaches that lie beyond space and time. This is the understanding that liturgy has of itself, an understanding that the Fathers shared, and an understanding that influenced their exegesis.

Letter & Spirit 7 (2011): 13-34

Cures of the Soul and Correction of Heart
Pope Leo the Great on the Healing Power of Holy Week

~: **J. Mark Armitage** :~

The idea of "sacrament" or "mystery" (*sacramentum; mysterium*) and "example" (*exemplum*) is fundamental to the patristic understanding of the redeeming power of Scripture and liturgy. Explaining the way in which the Fathers of the Church employ these terms, Pope Benedict XVI writes:

> By sacramentum they mean, not any particular sacrament, but rather the entire mystery of Christ—his life and death—in which he draws close to us, enters us through his Spirit, and transforms us. But precisely because this sacramentum truly "cleanses" us, renewing us from within, it also unleashes a dynamic of new life. The command to do as Jesus did is no mere moral appendix to the mystery, let alone an antithesis to it. It follows from the inner dynamic of gift with which the Lord renews us and draws us into what is his.[1]

Characteristically Augustinian,[2] this dynamic of *sacramentum* and *exemplum* lies, as Philip Barclift has shown, at the heart of Pope Leo the Great's soteriology.[3] For Leo, the terms *sacramentum* and *mysterium* are interchangeable. Both refer to "mysteries" understood liturgically, and to "mysteries" understood soteriologically as the saving life, death, and resurrection of Jesus. For Leo, liturgy is a "mystery" in which past events are not just remembered but rendered sacramentally and efficaciously present.[4] Operating at the level of *mysterium* and *exemplum*, the mysteries of the nativity, passion, and exaltation of Christ are recapitulated in the liturgy and in the Church in such a way that the members of the Mystical Body partake in the mysteries undergone by the Head.[5] *Sacramentum* and *mysterium* are also interchangeable with *remedium*, which is again coupled with *exemplum*: "unless

1 Pope Benedict XVI, *Jesus of Nazareth: Holy Week: From the Entrance into Jerusalem to the Resurrection* (San Francisco: Ignatius Press, 2011), 62.

2 Basil Studer, "Sacramentum et Exemplum chez saint Augustin," *Recherches Augustiniennes* 10 (1975): 87–141.

3 Philip L. Barclift, *Pope Leo's Soteriology: Sacramental Recapitulation* (Unpublished dissertation, Marquette University, 1992).

4 Jean Gaillard, "Noël, memoria ou mystère," *Maison-Dieu* 59 (1959): 37–59; Marie-Bernard de Soos, "Présence du mystère du salut dans la liturgie d'après saint Léon," *Ephemerides Liturgicae* 73 (1959): 116–135.

5 Philip L. Barclift, *Pope Leo's Soteriology*, 243.

Christ were true God, he would not bring us a remedy; unless he were true man, he would not offer us an example."[6] The interchangeability of *sacramentum, mysterium* and *remedium* suggests that the paschal mystery is to be understood as operating therapeutically—a theme which I intend to develop during the course of this study. As mysteries and remedies, the events of Christ's life effect a healing transformation in the human nature assumed by the Word. As examples, they model the recapitulation (Barclift's term) by the faithful of the various phases of that transformation. This recapitulation is in turn empowered by the liturgical *memoria* and *mysterium* of Christ's saving *sacramenta*, and by the *mysteria* of baptism and the Eucharist, in such wise that faith and liturgy are translated into human living.[7]

In his preaching Leo generally begins with the "narration of the gospel" (*evangelica narratio*),[8] the "narration of the gospel reading,"[9] the "narration from the scriptures,"[10] in virtue of which the minds of the faithful are inspired to wonder and their hearts are raised on high (a reference to the *sursum corda* of the Eucharistic Prayer).[11] The "narration of the gospel" is followed by a combination of scriptural exegesis, doctrinal exposition, and, finally, exhortation to an amendment of life which will give expression to the mystery being celebrated, and which may take the form of prayer, fasting, almsgiving, moral renewal, fighting against demons, upholding doctrinal orthodoxy, and ascetic endeavor.[12] The threefold schema—scripture, doctrine, ascesis—is sketched out in the introduction to *Tr* 71 (on the resurrection). It is, explains Leo, by "our participation in the cross of Christ" that "the very life of believers contains in itself the mystery of Easter (*paschale sacramentum*)." Moreover, "what is honored at the feast is celebrated by our practice," and "we should feel something of the cross (*aliquid sentiremus crucis*) in the time of the Lord's passion." In this way "we must strive to be found partak-

6 *Tr* 21.2. For Leo's sermons, abbreviated as *Tr* (*Tractatus*), I have used the critical edition of Antoine Chavasse, *Corpus Christianorum, Series Latina*, vols. 128 and 128A (Turnhout: Brepols, 1973). For the letters, abbreviated as *Ep* (*Epistolae*) I have used the Ballerini edition in *Patrologiae Cursus Completus: Series Latina*, ed. J. P. Migne, 221 vols. (Paris: Garnier and J. P. Migne, 1844–1864), vol. 54. Translations are my own. I have consulted the translations by Charles Lett Feltoe in *A Select Library of Nicene and Post-Nicene Fathers*, Second Series, vol. 12, ed. Philip Schaff (Edinburgh: T&T Clark, 1895, reprint 1989), and by Sr. Jane Patricia Freeland and Sr. Agnes Josephine Conway in the *Fathers of the Church* series, vol. 93 (Washington: Catholic University of America Press, 1986).

7 See D. Antonio Piloni, La "fides Christiana" nelle opere di S. Leone Magno dalla "celebratio fidei" alla "vita credentium" (per una teologia della celebrazione) (Pontificio Ateneo S. Anselmo, 1985).

8 *Tr* 38.1.

9 *Tr* 36.1.

10 *Tr* 35.2.

11 *Tr* 67.1.

12 Leo explores these themes in more detail in his sermons for the Lenten and other fast seasons. See J. Mark Armitage, *A Twofold Solidarity: Leo the Great's Theology of Redemption*, Early Christian Studies 9 (Strathfield, Australia: St Pauls Publications, 2005), 153–168.

ers (*consortes*) also of Christ's resurrection, and, while we are in this body, to pass over from death to life."[13] In the present study I wish to examine one particular aspect of "our participation in the cross of Christ"—namely, our participation in the interconnected mysteries of the agony in the garden of Gethsemane and of the cry of dereliction on Calvary—and to sketch out some of the ways in which Leo's exegesis of the relevant passages of liturgically occurring scripture enables us to "feel something of the cross," to recapitulate the *paschale sacramentum*, to share in the healing *remedium* of Christ's death and resurrection, and to "pass over" with him from death to life.

Freedom from Fear

In his sermon on the transfiguration,[14] Leo tells how, on the road to Caesarea Philippi, Jesus asks the apostles who they think he is, and Peter answers "you are the Christ, the Son of the living God."[15] Anxious lest the apostles "should believe that human nature was glorified in him in such a way that he could neither suffer punishment nor be dissolved in death," Jesus proceeds to tell them of his forthcoming passion, death, and resurrection.[16] Peter rejects the idea that Jesus might suffer and die, but is "corrected by a kindly reproach from Jesus," and "animated with the desire of participating in his passion."[17] Jesus instills into the apostles "that they who wished to follow him should deny themselves, and, in the hope of eternal things, consider the loss of temporal things unimportant, because only those who do not fear to lose their soul for Christ can achieve its salvation."[18] Desiring "that the apostles might embrace with their whole heart this happy and constant courage without trembling at the harshness of taking up the cross," Jesus leads Peter, James, and John up a mountain and reveals to them the "kingly brilliance" (*regia claritas*) of "the Son of Man coming in his Kingdom."[19] According to Leo, Christ's primary object in the transfiguration was "to remove the scandal of the cross from the hearts of the disciples, so that the faith of those to whom the excellence of his hidden dignity had been revealed might not be upset by the lowliness of his voluntary passion."[20] His second object was to establish "the foundation ... of the holy

---

13 *Tr* 71.1.

14 This sermon was delivered in Lent, 445. See Bernard Green, *The Soteriology of Leo the Great* (Oxford: Oxford University, 2008), 182–186; Elena Cavalcanti, "The Sermon of Leo the First on the Transfiguration (*Serm LI* Chavasse)," *Studia Patristica* 38 (2001): 371–376.

15 Matt. 16:16.

16 *Tr* 51.2.

17 *Tr* 51.2.

18 *Tr* 51.2.

19 *Tr* 51.2. The reference is to Matthew 16:28. Leo's thought echoes that of Hilary of Poitiers in *De Trinitate* (On the Trinity) 11, 37 (*Corpus Christianorum, Series Latina*, vol. 62A, 565; *Nicene and Post-Nicene Fathers*, Second Series, vol. 9, 213–214). See Green, *Soteriology*, 183.

20 *Tr* 51.3.

Church's hope" in such a way that "the whole Body of Christ might acknowledge exactly what sort of change was to be bestowed upon it, and that the members might promise themselves a fellowship in that honor which had already shone forth in their Head."[21] Leo adduces a catena of biblical quotations in favor of this idea that the members of Christ's Mystical Body can take hope and courage from the glory of the Head manifested in the transfiguration: "Then the righteous will shine like the sun in the kingdom of their Father;"[22] "I consider that the sufferings of this present time are not worth comparing with the glory that is to be revealed to us;"[23] "for you have died, and your life is hid with Christ in God. When Christ who is our life appears, then you also will appear with him in glory."[24]

Leo emphasizes that we have no choice but to follow the way of the cross if we wish to share in Christ's glory:

> Although we ought not to entertain any doubt about the promises of happiness, nevertheless we should understand that among the trials of this life we must ask for the power of endurance rather than for glory, because the joyousness of reigning cannot precede the times of suffering.[25]

The inevitability of suffering, however, should not be a cause of dismay. Out of the cloud the Father addresses the fear of the disciples in the face of Christ's impending death, asking them "Why do you tremble at being redeemed? Why do you … fear to be set free?" He exhorts them to "let that happen which Christ wills and I will,"[26] to "cast away all fleshly fear," and admonishes that "it is unworthy that you should fear in the passion of the Savior what by his gift you will not have to fear even at your own end."[27] In this passage at the climax of *Tr* 51.7 Leo uses no fewer than five words to denote "fear": *trepidatis, pavetis, formidinem, timeatis,* and *metuetis*. The message that Christ has conquered fear is directed to all believers: "in these three Apostles the whole Church has learned all that their sight beheld and their hearing received."[28] The corollary of Christ's victory is clear: "let not anyone be afraid to suffer for righteousness' sake, or lack trust in the fulfillment of the

21 *Tr* 51.3.

22 Matt. 13:43.

23 Rom. 8:18.

24 Col. 3:3–4; *Tr* 51.3.

25 *Tr* 51.5.

26 Lars Thunberg's remarks about Maximus the Confessor (580–662) apply equally to Leo: "The act of salvation … is … a cooperative act, an act of reciprocity." See Lars Thunberg, *Man and the Cosmos: the Vision of St Maximus the Confessor* (New York: St. Vladimir's Seminary, 1985), 65–66.

27 *Tr* 51.7.

28 *Tr* 51.8.

promises," for "through toil comes our passing over (*transitur*) to rest, and through death our passing over to life." Accordingly, "since he assumed all the infirmity of our lowly state, if we abide in our confession and love of him, we conquer as he conquered, and receive what he promised."[29] Suffering and death are not to be feared, for it is by sharing in the cross of Christ that we share in his resurrection, passing over with him from death to life, and entering into the "royal brilliance" of his kingdom.

Correcting the Heart

Christ's victory over fear—fear of suffering, fear of persecution, fear of death—presupposes an orthodox understanding of the incarnation. In *Tr* 54 Leo begins by affirming that the properties of Christ's divine and human natures remained in such a way that "we may not think of him as God without that which is man, nor as man without that which is God."[30] This in turn means that "the one is passible, the other inviolable; and yet the indignity (*contumelia*) belongs to the same person, as does the glory." This same person, therefore, "is present at once in weakness and in power; at once capable of death and the conqueror of death."[31] Leo speaks of "two forms," each of which "does that which is proper to it (*agit utraque forma ... quod proprium est*) ... in communion with the other (*cum alterius communione*)."[32] That is to say, the Word performs that which belongs to the Word and the flesh performs that which belongs to the flesh.[33] It follows from this that "even his very endurance of sufferings does not so expose him to the mental condition (*affectio*) of our lowliness as to disjoin him from the power of the Godhead."[34] Indeed, his sufferings are an exercise of the incarnate Word's power, and of the human will of Christ acting freely in communion with the divine: "all the persecution and

---

29 *Tr* 51.8.

30 *Tr* 54.1. Basil Studer understands the two natures in terms of a "double consubstantiality," which denotes a twofold solidarity according to which the incarnate Son is simultaneously *consubstantialis Patri* and *consubstantialis Matri*. See Basil Studer, "'Consubstantialis Patri', 'Consubstantialis Matri'. Une antithèse christologique chez Léon le Grand," *Revue des Études Augustiniennes* 18 (1972): 87–115.

31 *Tr* 54.1.

32 The sentence should be translated not "he acts in each form" but "each form acts." On this see George L. Prestige, "The Greek Translation of the 'Tome' of St Leo," *Journal of Theological Studies* 31 (1929–30): 183–184. On the patristic context of Leo's use of the *utraque forma* formula, see Herman Michel Diepen, "L'*Assumptus Homo* patristique," *Revue thomiste* 64 (1964): 32–52, 364–386.

33 *Tr* 54.2. Leo does not envisage Jesus as doing certain things in his divine capacity and others in his human capacity. Rather, he discerns the reality—and hence the distinctness—of the two sets of *proprietates* in the one subject.

34 On the idea that the two *proprietates* are *passibilitas* and *impassibilitas*, see Geoffrey D. Dunn, "Divine Impassibility and Christology in the Christmas Homilies of Leo the Great," *Theological Studies* 62 (2001): 71–85; "Suffering Humanity and Divine Impassibility: The Christology of the Lenten Homilies of Leo the Great," *Augustinianum* 41 (2001): 257–271.

punishment which the fury of the wicked inflicted on the Lord was not endured of necessity but undertaken of free will."[35]

Leo underscores the divine initiative by quoting St. Paul to the effect that "in Christ God was reconciling the world to himself,"[36] adding "and the Creator himself was wearing the creature which was to be reformed to the image of its Creator."[37] Christ prepares for this image-restoration through his ministry of teaching and miracle-working,[38] but it begins in earnest in the garden of Gethsemane. Leo quotes Matt. 26:38–39—"my soul is very sorrowful even to death" and "Father, if it be possible, let this cup pass from me"—and suggests that "professing a certain fear with these words, he was curing (*curabat*) the mental state (*affectus*) of our weakness by sharing it, and checking our fear of punishment by undergoing it."[39] "In that which is ours," explains Leo, "the Lord trembled with our fear that he might be clothed with our weakness and vest our inconstancy with the firmness of his own strength."[40] Initially dismayed by Christ's humiliation, Peter is soon "restored to vigor, taking up the remedy (*remedium*) from the example (*exemplum*), so that the suddenly-shaken member returns to the firmness of the Head."[41]

In a lapidary expression at the close of *Tr* 54.4, Leo affirms that Christ "preferred to entertain our fears, rather than exercise his own power," thus bringing together the key themes of the co-existence in Christ of weakness and power and of his voluntary embracing of human fear. As in *Tr* 51, the members of the mystical body can triumph over fear by finding a *remedium* in the victory of the Head. Christ first feared in order that Peter might conquer fear—Peter "could not have vanquished the trembling of human frailty had not the vanquisher of death first feared."[42] Drawing on Luke 22:61, Leo paints a vivid portrait of Jesus looking back at Peter, and offers a theologically charged interpretation of the scene, according to which Christ "met his perturbed disciple with eyes which had foreseen his perturbation," and "the gaze of the truth entered into him who was in need of correction of heart (*cordis ... correctio*)." It is, says Leo, as if Christ were saying,

35 *Tr* 54.2. In order for Christ to save us, it was first necessary that his human will should freely accept and embrace suffering. This insight is taken further by Maximus the Confessor. On this, see François-Marie Léthel, *Théologie de l'agonie du Christ: La liberté humaine du Fils de Dieu et son importance sotériologique mises en lumière par saint Maxime Confesseur* (Paris: Editions Beauchesne, 1979), 18.

36 2 Cor. 5:19.

37 *Tr* 54.4.

38 *Tr* 54.4.

39 *Tr* 54.4.

40 *Tr* 54.4.

41 *Tr* 54.5.

42 *Tr* 54.5.

> Turn to me, put your trust in me, follow me. This is the time of my passion. The hour of your suffering is not yet come. Why do you fear what you, too, shall overcome? The weakness which I accepted will not confound you. I was fearful (*trepidus*) for you; you should be secure in me.[43]

The victory over fear of the Head of the Mystical Body, accordingly, brings correction of heart—*cordis correctio*—to the members (among whom Peter and the apostles are foremost). Immersed in the narration of the gospel, the faithful "feel something of the cross"—of Christ's fear of suffering and death. Christ, however, has healed and overcome this fear, and, empowered by his *mysterium* (sacraments) and inspired by his *exemplum*, the members of his Mystical Body can face future suffering by looking to the resurrection in which, through the liturgy and the sacraments, they already possess a share.

To Heal and to Vanquish

Leo returns to the drama of Gethsemane in *Tr* 58. He begins by discussing the scene in John 13:27 in which Jesus says to Judas "what you are going to do, do quickly." "This," Leo contends, "is the voice ... not of fear but of readiness," and Jesus "carries out the Father's will for the redemption of the world in such a way as neither to promote nor to fear the crime which his persecutors were preparing."[44] Whereas in *Tr* 54.4 Leo says that "the Lord trembled with our fear," in *Tr* 58.4 the emphasis is a little different: "the Lord, unperturbed by any fear, but anxious only for the salvation of those who needed redeeming," devoted the time before his passion to "holy teaching" (*sacrata doctrina*). This holy teaching culminates in the Gethsemane prayer of Matthew 26:39—"Father, if it be possible, let this cup pass from me."[45] Leo juxtaposes this text with that from John 18:11 in which Jesus asks "shall I not drink the cup which the Father has given me?"—also an example of *sacrata doctrina*—noting that "it is not to be thought that the Lord Jesus wished to escape the passion and the death whose mysteries (*sacramenta*) he had already handed over to his disciples' keeping."[46] Although in *Tr* 58.4 he seems to think less in terms of Christ sharing our fears and more in terms of his teaching us to overcome them, Leo makes it very clear that Christ embraces genuine physical and psychological suffering: "in assuming true and entire manhood he took the true sensations (*sensus*) of the body and the true feelings (*affectus*) of the mind."[47] The fact that "everything in him was full of sacraments, full of miracles" does not in

---

43 *Tr* 54.5.

44 *Tr* 58.4.

45 *Tr* 58.4.

46 *Tr* 58.4. As for Maximus, so also for Leo the work of redemption depends on the freely willed acceptance of suffering by the incarnate Son operating in concert with the Father.

47 *Tr* 58.4.

any way mean that "he either shed false tears or took food from pretended hunger or simulated sleep."[48] On the contrary, "in our humility he was despised, with our grief he was saddened, with our pain he was crucified."[49]

The two forms—the form of a servant and the form of God, the form of lowliness and the form of glory—co-operate to effect a twofold salvation: "his mercy underwent the sufferings of our mortality in order to heal them (*ut sanaret*), and his power encountered them in order to vanquish them (*ut vinceret*)."[50] For Leo, the therapeutic dimension of salvation (*ut sanaret*) is admirably expressed in Isaiah 53:4–5—"he carries our sins and is pained for us. ... He was wounded for our sins, and was stricken for our offences, and with his bruises we are healed."[51] Leo then offers an analysis of Jesus' words "Father, if it be possible, let this cup pass from me; nevertheless, not as I will, but as thou wilt," and "My Father, if this cannot pass unless I drink it, thy will be done."[52] Regarding "let this cup pass from me," Leo suggests that Christ "uses the voice of our nature, and pleads the cause of human frailty and trembling so that, in those things which we have to bear, he might strengthen our patience and drive away our fears."[53] Once again, the purpose of Jesus' words—of his *sacrata doctrina*—is that he might heal and vanquish (*ut sanaret* and *ut vinceret*), after which "he passes into another mental state (*affectus*)" which finds expression in "not as I will, but as thou wilt" and "if this chalice may not pass away, but if I must drink it, may thy will be done."[54]

Leo refers to Christ's *sacrata doctrina* not as "words" (as in the Feltoe translation),[55] but as his "voice" (*vox*), indicating that what the faithful encounter in the gospel narrative and in the liturgy of the passion is far more than just a teaching or an example. Rather, it is Christ's own voice crying out in the apostles, in the suffering Church, in the liturgical community.[56] Leo writes:

> This voice of the Head is the saving-health (*salus*) of the whole Body. This voice has instructed all the faithful, kindled the zeal

48 *Tr* 58.4.

49 *Tr* 58.4.

50 *Tr* 58.4.

51 *Tr* 58.4. Leo quotes from a version which literally translates the Septuagint but which differs markedly from the Vulgate (Feltoe, *Nicene and Post-Nicene Fathers*, 170). On the idea of Christ as a physician, see B.W.M. Speekenbrink, "Christ the 'medicus humilis' in St. Augustine," *Augustinus Magister: Congrès international augustinien* (Paris, Sep. 21–24, 1954, vol. 2), 623–639.

52 Matt. 26:39, 42; *Tr* 58.5.

53 *Tr* 58.5.

54 *Tr* 58.5.

55 Feltoe, *Nicene and Post-Nicene Fathers*, 170.

56 On the theme of "Christ present in the Church" (*Christus praesens in ecclesia*), see Hans Feichtinger, *Die Gegenwart Christi in der Kirche bei Leo dem Grossen*, Patrologia: Beiträge zum Studium der Kirchenväter; Bd. 18 (Frankfurt am Main: P. Lang, 2007).

> of all the confessors, crowned all the martyrs. For who could overcome the world's hatred, the whirlwinds of trials, the terrors of persecutors, had not Christ, in the name of all and for all, said, to the Father, 'Thy will be done'?[57]

The voice of Christ in Gethsemane and on Calvary becomes the prayer of the faithful in such a way that the prayer through which he heals and vanquishes fear (*ut sanaret* and *ut vinceret*) becomes that by which they, too, are empowered to overcome. Leo exhorts, "let everyone learn this voice, ... and when the adversity of some violent trial overshadows them, let them use the protection of this powerful prayer, that, overcoming their trembling fear, they may accept their burden of suffering."[58] In *Tr* 66.3 he continues with this same thought, "There is no one to whom the prayer of Christ does not bring help,"[59] and, in the paschal liturgy, Christ's prayer—Christ's voice—becomes the voice of the Church and her members. Leo reaffirms the view of Augustine that Christ prays in us and for us.[60] In the liturgy his prayer is uttered in and through and on behalf of the faithful in such a way that the liturgy itself heals and vanquishes fear, bringing "correction of heart" and effecting in the life of believers that "passing over" from death to life in which the mystery of Easter consists.

The Glory of the Cross

In *Tr* 59 Leo's narration of the gospel begins in the moments after Jesus' agony in the garden and subsequent arrest. Leo discerns in Jesus' agony a dramatic demonstration of the two natures according to which the human nature is afraid to suffer while the divine nature enables the human to overcome fear and engage in combat with the devil:

> By the words of his sacred prayer the Lord declared that the divine and the human nature was most truly and fully present in him, showing that from the human nature came his unwillingness to suffer and from the divine his determination to suffer. Then, when the trembling of weakness had been expelled and the loftiness of power confirmed, he returned to the purpose of his eternal plan, and in the form of a sinless slave encountered the devil who was raging at him.[61]

---

57 *Tr* 58.5.

58 *Tr* 58.5.

59 *Tr* 66.3.

60 St. Augustine, *Commentary on Psalm 85.1 in Corpus Christianorum, Series Latina*, vol. 39, 1176–1177; *Nicene and Post-Nicene Fathers*, First Series, vol. 8, 409–410).

61 *Tr* 59.1. For Leo, the idea of victory over the devil and victory over (and freedom from) death are closely related. See Jean Rivière, "La rédemption chez s. Léon le Grand," *Revue des sciences*

Christ's triumph over fear in Gethsemane and over the devil on Calvary means that we need to see the cross as an instrument of victory and glory. Indeed, whereas in his sermon on the transfiguration Leo depicts the cross as preceding the glory to which it leads (and which is prefigured on Mount Tabor), here the time of suffering and the time of glorification converge. Switching from the Matthean account to the Johannine, Leo presents Christ's prayer for glorification in John 12:23–32 as a kind of parallel to the Gethsemane narrative, inviting himself and his flock to

> let our understanding, illumined by the Spirit of Truth, take up with a pure and free heart the glory of the cross (*gloria crucis*) which irradiates heaven and earth, and perceive interiorly what the Lord meant when he said of his impending passion: "The hour is come that the Son of man may be glorified."[62]

The true significance of the Father's glorification of the Son finds expression in Leo's paradoxical exclamation "O wondrous power of the cross! O ineffable glory of the passion, in which is contained ... the power of the Crucified." Here the formulae "power of the cross," "glory of the passion," and "power of the Crucified" echo the earlier reference to the *gloria crucis*.[63] The glorious cross becomes "the fount of all blessings, the source of all graces," conferring on believers "strength for weakness, glory for shame, life for death," so that it is through the *gloria crucis*—through the cross which is already radiant with the resurrection glory to which it gives access—that Jesus brings the beginnings of healing and victory to those oppressed by the fear of suffering and death.

In virtue of the incarnation, Christ's voluntary sacrifice—understood in *Tr* 59 primarily in terms of glory and victory—accomplishes the destruction of death. Leo writes that "though the nature of the Godhead could not sustain the sting of death, nevertheless he took from us in being born that which he might offer on our behalf."[64] He assumed our weakness and mortality precisely in order to offer his own death as a sacrifice, and also in order to heal our weakness and vanquish our fear. Leo places the Vulgate translation of the words of Hosea 13:14—"O death, I will be thy death; O hell, I will be thy bite"—on the lips of the incarnate Son of whom he writes that "he threatened our death with the power of his death," and that "by dying he underwent the laws of hell, but by rising he dissolved them, and so broke off the perpetuity of death as to render it temporal instead of eternal."[65] It is in this destruction of the perpetuity of death that Christ puts an end to death's

religieuses 9 (1929): 17–42; 153–187; Filippo Carcione, "I 'diritti del diavolo' nella soteriologia di S. Leone Magno," *Rivista Cistercense* 2 (1985): 113–126.

62 *Tr* 59.6; John 12:23.

63 *Tr* 59.7.

64 *Tr* 59.8.

65 *Tr* 59.8.

power to instill terror. The cross becomes a cross of glory and of victory from which the *claritas* of the kingdom already shines. In carrying the cross Simon of Cyrene "pre-signifies the Gentiles' faith, to whom the cross of Christ would be not shame but glory" and shares Christ's sufferings, embodying the Pauline teaching that "if we suffer with him, we shall also reign with him."[66] By his own free and willing acceptance of death—made present in the Holy Week liturgy as mystery and example—Christ is glorified on the cross with the glory which will be fully revealed in the resurrection. This convergence of cross and resurrection—of suffering and glory—serves to heal and vanquish in us the fear of death, so that, even in the midst of our sufferings and anxieties, we may follow the path of the Cyrenian and begin to be united with Christ in his resurrection, his glorification, and his kingly reign.

The Cry of Dereliction

In *Tr* 67, in which he brings before his congregation the gospel reading of the cry of dereliction on Calvary, Leo continues this investigation into the way in which we participate in the mystery of Christ's therapeutic suffering. Expounding the connection between Scripture, liturgy, and the mystery of being "in Christ," he affirms that the principal reason for our eucharistic lifting up of our hearts[67]

> is that those things which the gospel truth has narrated have been sung by the voices of the prophets not as events which are destined to happen but as events already accomplished, and that the Holy Spirit was proclaiming as already fulfilled things that human ears had not yet learnt were to take place.[68]

More specifically, Christ is the seed of David, the author of the Psalms (and, in this case, Psalm 22). David "endured none of those punishments which he relates as inflicted upon himself." However, "because by his mouth one spoke who was to assume passible flesh from his stock, the history of the cross is rightly anticipated in the person of him who bore in himself the bodily origin of the Savior." The corollary of this is that "David truly suffered in Christ, because Jesus was truly crucified in the flesh in David."[69] Having thus prepared the ground for the climax of the sermon, in which he discusses Jesus' quoting of David in the cry of dereliction, Leo reprises the idea that his suffering is therapeutic for humanity. Although the birth and ministry of Jesus are full of wonders and "signs of Godhead,"[70] nevertheless "he

66 *Tr* 59.5, with reference to 2 Tim. 2:12 and Rom. 8:17.

67 *Erigendi sursum nostri cordis*. As in 74.5, this is a liturgical allusion to the *sursum corda* of the Eucharistic Prayer.

68 *Tr* 67.1.

69 *Tr* 67.1.

70 *Tr* 67.5.

had assumed the reality of our weaknesses, and without share in sin had excluded himself from no human frailty, that he might impart what was his to us and heal (*curaret*) what was ours in himself."[71]

Continuing the medical metaphor, Leo writes:

> A double remedy (*remedium*) was prepared for us in our misery by the almighty physician (*medicus*), one part consisting of mystery and the other of example (*in sacramento; in exemplo*), so that by the one divine things might be bestowed, by the other human things driven out.[72]

Leo adds that, in order to enable us to appropriate for ourselves "this ineffable restoration of our health (*salutis ... reparationem*)," Christ invites us to follow in his footsteps.[73] Christ is rightly called our "way" (Leo is referring to John 14:6) "because except through Christ there is no coming to Christ," and "the one who walks the path of Christ's endurance and humiliation advances through him and towards him." All these things, however, "the Lord of hosts and King of glory passed through in the form of our weakness and in the likeness of sinful flesh,[74] so that amidst the danger of this present life we might find it preferable not to escape them by refusing them but to conquer them by enduring them."[75] As in *Tr* 58, Leo juxtaposes the twin themes of healing and vanquishing (*ut sanaret* and *ut vinceret*), depicting salvation in terms both of *salus* and *gloria*. Moreover, just as "David truly suffered in Christ, because Jesus was truly crucified in the flesh in David," we are all, in mysterious fashion, included in Christ's cry of dereliction on the cross:

> The Lord Jesus Christ, our Head, transforming (*transformans*) all the members of his body in himself, cried out amidst the torture of the cross in the voice of those redeemed by him that cry which he had once uttered in the psalm, "O God, my God, look upon me: why hast thou forsaken me?"[76]

Leo proceeds to explain that "that cry (*vox*) ... is a lesson (*doctrina*), not a complaint." He argues that because "in him there is one person of God and man, and he could not have been forsaken by him from whom he could not be separated, Christ asks

71 *Tr* 67.5.

72 Feltoe (*Nicene and Post-Nicene Fathers*, 179) suggests that the alternative reading *erigantur* ("elevated") might make more sense than "driven out" (*exigantur*).

73 *Tr* 67.6.

74 Rom. 8:3.

75 *Tr* 67.6.

76 *Tr* 67.7, quoting Ps. 21:1.

on behalf of us trembling and weak ones why the flesh that is afraid to suffer has not been heard."[77]

Once again Leo quotes from Matthew 26:39, 42 Christ's words in Gethsemane uttered "to cure (*ad sanandum*) and correct (*ad corrigendum*) the fear born of our weakness."[78] This leads him to pose an important question about the cry of dereliction on Calvary:

> Once he had vanquished the trembling of the flesh and passed over (*transierat*) to the Father's will and trampled all dread of death under foot and was completing his ordained work, why does he seek, at the very moment of his triumphant exaltation in so great a victory, the cause and reason of his being forsaken, that is, not heard?[79]

In Gethsemane, Christ the incarnate Word of God embraces suffering and death in his human nature—by his own free and deliberate choice—as an act of salvation-as-healing (*salus*), thereby both healing and vanquishing the fear of suffering and of death. On Calvary, however, in his cry of dereliction, we see Christ "transforming all the members of his body in himself"—the members of his Mystical Body, who, in his own voice, are crying out (just as in the original cry of dereliction in Psalm 22 David is crying out as a member of Christ).[80] In *Tr* 58 Leo presents Christ in Gethsemane as praying in and on behalf of the members of his Mystical Body, but in *Tr* 67 he depicts the Mystical Body as praying in and through Christ on Calvary. If Christ's prayer in Gethsemane is the therapeutic and salvific action of his human will operating in perfect union with his divine will, his cry on the cross is the action of his Mystical Body appealing in Christ's own voice for that healing and vanquishing of its fears and for that "correction of heart" which the incarnate Word alone can bring. The Holy Week liturgy makes Christ's Calvary prayer present as *mysterium* and *exemplum*. It gives concrete expression to that prayer precisely in so far as it is the prayer not just of the Head but also of the entire Mystical Body—of the whole Christ—which is thereby enabled to participate in Christ's passion and resurrection and thus appropriate and recapitulate his healing and victory. It is when the prayer of Christ on Calvary truly becomes the prayer of the Mystical Body that the faithful "feel something of the cross at the time of the Lord's Passion,"

---

77 *Tr* 67.7. This strong affirmation of the unity of person in Christ reflects the fundamental continuity between Cyril of Alexandria and Leo.

78 *Tr* 67.7.

79 *Tr* 67.7.

80 *Tr* 67.1. Augustine portrays the faithful as being included in the Gethsemane prayer—which he sees as a prayer of the "whole Christ" uttered "in the name of his body"—in his Commentary on Psalm 140, 2–3 (*Corpus Christianorum, Series Latina*, vol. 40, 2028–2029; *Nicene and Post-Nicene Fathers*, First Series, vol. 8, 644–645).

sharing in the healing *remedium* of Christ's death and resurrection, and "passing over" with him from death to life.

Interior Remedies

In *Tr* 68 Leo continues his exegesis of Psalm 22:1 and Matthew 27:46—"My God, my God, why hast thou forsaken me?"—focusing once again on the salvific role of Christ's human will. He begins by emphasizing that we should not take these words in the sense that "when Jesus was fixed upon the wood of the cross, the omnipotence of the Father's deity departed from him."[81] On the contrary, "the nature of God and the nature of man came together in a unity so great that it could neither be destroyed by punishment nor disjoined by death."[82] This solid and inseparable *unitas* guaranteed that, "while each substance remained in what belonged to itself, God did not forsake the suffering of his body, and flesh did not make God passible, because the divinity which was in the sufferer was not in the suffering." Rather, "divine power joined itself to human weakness in order that, while making his own what belonged to us, God might make ours what belonged to him." Leo makes a direct comparison between the christological unity of the human and divine natures in the incarnate Son and the Trinitarian unity of the Father and the Son: "Although the dispensation of becoming incarnate belonged properly to the only-begotten Son of God, the Father was not disjoined from the Son any more than the flesh was divided from the Word."[83] Consequently, the cry "why have you forsaken me?" reflects not "the deprivation of assistance" but "the determination to die."[84] Leo marvels at the way in which Christ's life could be laid down and taken up again by his own power, and adds:

> That the Lord was handed over to his passion was as much of the Father's will as of his own, so that not only did the Father "forsake" him, but in a certain sense he also abandoned himself, not in frightened withdrawal, but in voluntary surrendering.[85]

In virtue of this voluntary self-surrendering "the might of the Crucified ... refused to make use of his manifest power,"[86] willing instead that, in the weakness of his

81 *Tr* 68.1.

82 *Tr* 68.1. The two natures come together in a unity because the person of the Son—the ground of that unity—brings human nature into unity with his own divine nature. The unity of the person (in the language of Maximus the Confessor, of the *theandric person*) is paramount. See Basil Studer, "Una persona in Christo. Ein augustinisches Thema bei Leo dem Grossen," *Augustinianum* 25 (1985): 453–487.

83 *Tr* 68.1.

84 *Tr* 68.2.

85 *Tr* 68.2.

86 *Tr* 68.2.

human nature, he should experience fear and abandonment to the point of crying out "My God, my God, why hast thou forsaken me?"

This freely willed refusal on the part of the incarnate Son to avail himself of his proper power constitutes a sacrifice which has salvation-historical implications. Christ effects "a transition from the Law to the Gospel, from the synagogue to the Church, from many sacrifices to the one victim."[87] In *Tr* 95—an extended exegesis of Matthew 5:1–12 (on the beatitudes)—Leo depicts this transition from Law to Gospel in terms of Jesus bringing interior remedies (*remedia interiora*) and cures of the soul (*curationes animarum*) in virtue of which the Spirit of adoption dispels the "terror of bondage."[88] These cures of the soul culminate in peace (*pax*), adoptive sonship, and harmony of wills between God and man.[89] In *Tr* 68 the transition from Law to Gospel, from the "terrors of bondage" to adoption, is decisively effected by the incarnate Word's own harmony of wills—by his voluntary surrendering, his self-abandonment, and his refusal to deploy his own power in order to evade physical and psychological suffering. Christ's saving sacrifice consists precisely in his abandonment of himself to fear and forsakenness—that is, to a synergy of the divine and human wills in accordance with which, always in perfect unity with the will of the Father, his divine will determines in perfect unity with his own human will that in his human nature he should be (in effect) abandoned to fear and suffering. In virtue of that self-abandonment to physical and psychological suffering in which the synergy of divine and human wills in Christ finds perfect expression, the incarnate Son effects a transition from Law to Gospel with its attendant "interior remedies" and "cures of the soul." In order to liberate them from the "terror of bondage" and the fear of suffering and death, the risen Christ extends these remedies to the members of his Mystical Body who, inasmuch as they "feel something of the cross at the time of the Lord's passion," participate in the healing *remedium* of Christ's death and resurrection, and so "pass over" with him from death to life.

The Flesh of the Crucified

The statement in *Tr* 67.7 that the cry of dereliction is uttered by "the Lord Jesus Christ, our Head, transforming all the members of his body in himself," picks up on a theme which Leo develops in greater depth in *Tr* 63. He begins by explaining:

> Human nature has been received by the Son of God into such a union that not only in that man who is the first-begotten of all creation,[90] but also in all his saints there is one and the self-same

87 *Tr* 68.3.

88 *Tr* 95.1.

89 *Tr* 95.9; *Tr* 26.3. See Armitage, *A Twofold Solidarity*, 139–145.

90 Col. 1:18.

> Christ (*unus idemque sit Christus*), and, as the Head cannot be separated from the members, so the members cannot be separated from the Head.[91]

Leo is keen to underline the scriptural foundations of this doctrine of the "whole Christ," Head and members.[92] Firstly, in direct reference to 1 Corinthians 15:28, he affirms that "although it is not in this life, but in eternity that God is to be 'all in all,' even now he is the undivided indweller of his temple, which is the Church." Secondly, he cites in support of his argument Matthew 28:20: "Lo, I am with you always, to the close of the age,"[93] which he understands in terms of Christ—the incarnate Son—effectively prolonging his incarnation in the Church and in individual believers.[94] Finally, he provides a brief exegesis of Colossians 1:18–20—"he is the head of the body, the Church ... for in him all the fullness of God was pleased to dwell, and through him to reconcile to himself all things."[95]

Leo proceeds to ask "what is suggested to our hearts by these and many other testimonies but that in all things we shall be renewed in his image who, remaining in the form of God, deigned to take the form of a slave?"[96] Leo's answer is that Christ provided us with a *sacramentum* and an *exemplum* (or, as we have seen above, a *remedium* and a *doctrina*):

> He took on himself all our weaknesses, the consequence of sin, without sharing in sin, so that he might not lack the feelings (*affectiones*) of hunger and thirst, sleep and fatigue, grief and weeping, but might undergo the fiercest sufferings unto the extremity of death, because no one could be released from the snares of death, unless he in whom alone the nature of all was innocent allowed himself to be slain.[97]

Leo adds that "all that the Son of God did and taught (*et fecit, et docuit*) for the world's reconciliation we not only know as a matter of past history, but feel

91 *Tr* 63.3.

92 The scriptural and patristic foundations of this idea are explored in Émile Mersch, *The Whole Christ: The Historical Development of the Doctrine of the Mystical Body in Scripture and Tradition*, trans. John R. Kelly (Milwaukee: Bruce Publishing Company, 1938).

93 At the heart of Leo's teaching on incarnation and salvation is a "theology of the Emmanuel"—a theology of God-with-us in the incarnate Son and in the Church. See Herman Michel Diepen, "L'Assumptus Homo à Chalcédoine," *Revue thomiste* 51 (1951): 573–608; 53 (1953): 254–286.

94 See Manuel Garrido Bonaño, "Prolongación de Cristo en su cuerpo místico, según San León Magno," *Studium. Revista de filosofía y teologia* 15 (1975): 491–505.

95 *Tr* 63.3.

96 *Tr* 63.4; Phil. 2:6.

97 *Tr* 63.4.

in the power of its present effect (*in praesentium operum virtute*)."[98] Here "did and taught"—a clear reference to Acts 1:1—correspond to *sacramentum* and *exemplum*, to *remedium* and *doctrina*, while "in its present effect" corresponds to the sacramental and liturgical activity of the Church which provides the context for Leo's exposition.

The "present effect" of Christ's saving mysteries is first experienced in baptism, which is nothing other than a "passing over" into the Mystical Body of the incarnate Son who dwells in his Church and renews his members in his own image. Christ's sufferings, accordingly, "are shared not only by the martyrs' glorious courage, but also in the very act of regeneration by the faith of all the new-born." Leo states:

> To renounce the devil and believe in God, to pass over (*transitur*) from our old condition into newness of life, to cast off the earthly image and to put on the heavenly form—all this is a kind of death and a similitude of resurrection, so that he that is received by Christ and receives Christ is not the same after the baptismal washing as he was before, for the body of the regenerate becomes the flesh of the Crucified.[99]

In virtue of the incarnation, the Word assumes human nature. In his cry of dereliction, his *vox* is the voice of the members of his Mystical Body. We "pass over" into his Mystical Body—becoming, indeed, the "flesh of the Crucified"—through the mystery of baptism, in consequence of which we are identified with the fearful, suffering, abandoned Christ of Gethsemane and Calvary, and are able to share in his "interior remedies" and "cures of the soul"—in his healing and vanquishing of the fear of suffering and death (*ut sanaret; ut vinceret*), and in his "correction of heart" (*correctio cordis*). Moreover, because in sharing in Christ's suffering we share in his healing and victory, it follows that we also share—even in the present—in his glory: "the same brightness (*splendor*) appears everywhere through the many rays of the one Light, and there can be no merit on the part of any Christian that is not part of the glory of Christ."[100]

Passing Over into Christ

This participation in the divine light is effected by the Eucharist, which effects a further "passing over" (*transitus*) into Christ: "Partaking of the Body and Blood of Christ effects nothing other than that we pass over (*transeamus*) into that which we then take up, and both in spirit and in flesh carry him everywhere, in and with

98 *Tr* 63.6.

99 *Tr* 63.6.

100 *Tr* 63.7.

whom we died, were buried, and rose again."[101] A similar expression is found in one of Leo's letters: "in that mystic distribution of spiritual nourishment, that which is imparted and taken is of such a kind that, receiving the virtue of the celestial food, we pass over (*transeamus*) into the flesh of him who became our flesh."[102] As we saw at the beginning of this study, Leo believes that "we must strive to be found partakers (*consortes*) also of Christ's resurrection, and, while we are in this body, to pass over from death to life."[103] It is, above all, our eucharistic "passing over" into Christ which accomplishes this participation. It is the Eucharist that establishes Christians as fully "in Christ" while at the same time establishing Christ as fully "in the Church" and "in the individual Christian" to the extent that the mysteries of Gethsemane and Calvary—mysteries through which the incarnate Son heals and vanquishes the fear of suffering and death—give expression to the identity between his own *vox* and the cry of his Mystical Body.

In *Tr* 63 Leo uses different forms of the verb *transeo* to denote the way in which we pass over (*transitur*) from oldness to newness in baptism and in which we pass over (*transeamus*) into the Body and Blood of Christ which we receive in the Eucharist. In *Tr* 72 (on the resurrection) he explores this idea of "passing over" in even greater depth. He begins by reminding his congregation that Christ's self-emptying (*exinanitio*) "was the dispensation of compassion, not the privation of power,"[104] in virtue of which he made "the impassible passible" in order "not that power might fail in weakness, but that weakness might pass over (*transire*) into incorruptible power."[105] Elaborating on this theme, Leo observes that Pascha/Passover becomes *transitus* in Latin,[106] and that the Pascha/Passover of Jesus is nothing other than his passing out of the world to his Father (*ut transeat ex hoc mundo ad Patrem*).[107] Commenting on John 13:1 ("when Jesus knew that his hour had come to depart out of this world to the Father") he asks "in what nature would it be that he thus passed out (*erat transitus iste*) unless it was ours, since the Father was in the Son and the Son in the Father inseparably?" On the eve of his passion, Christ prepares "a blessed passing over (*beatum transitum*) for his faithful ones" so that they might share in the "ineffable gift" of his exaltation into divine glory.

Leo concludes by quoting John 17:20–21—"I do not pray for these only, but also for those who believe in me through their word, that they may all be one; even as thou, Father, art in me, and I in thee, that they also may be in us"—understanding this not as a prayer for ecclesial unity but as a request for glorification "not

101 *Tr* 63.7.

102 *Ep* 59.2.

103 *Tr* 71.1.

104 *Tr* 72.5. Similar expressions are found in *Ep* 28.3 and *Tr* 23.2.

105 *Tr* 72.5.

106 *Tr* 72.6.

107 *Tr* 72.6.

only for his Apostles and disciples but also for the entire Church."[108] Whereas in *Tr* 63 the *transitus* language is used to denote the passing over of the believer into Christ's body in virtue of the sacraments of baptism and the Eucharist, in *Tr* 72 it gives expression to the entire scope of Christ's saving work, inasmuch as the incarnation, passion, resurrection, and ascension constitute a single movement in which Christ's assumed humanity—with all its weakness and lowliness and passibility, with all its susceptibility to suffering and fear and death—passes over, firstly, into union with the divinity and, secondly, into risen glory (from the *forma servi* to the *forma gloriae*).[109] Finally, the *transitus* of Christ's human nature from the *forma servi* to the *forma gloriae* is itself intrinsically bound up with the *transitus* of the incarnate Son to the Father. *Transitus*, accordingly, has a threefold significance for Leo, denoting as it does the sacramental *transitus* of the believer into the body of Christ, the christological and soteriological *transitus* of Christ's assumed human nature from lowliness to glory, and the Trinitarian *transitus* of the Son who passes over from the world to his Father.

Possessors of Paradise

The *transitus* of Christ's human nature from lowliness to glory is one of the principal themes of Leo's sermons for the liturgical celebrations of the Resurrection and Ascension, and it is this *transitus* which completes the process by which Christ heals and vanquishes our fear of suffering and death. Taken on its own, the passion had not so much healed the disciples' fear of death as intensified it: "Christ's death had greatly perturbed (*turbaverat*) the disciples' hearts, and, after his torture on the cross, ... a kind of torpor of distrust had crept over the minds weighed down with grief."[110] Their initial doubt concerning the reports of the empty tomb were the result of human weakness—weakness which "the Spirit of Truth would in no way have permitted to exist in his preachers' breasts had not their trembling anxiety and careful hesitation laid the foundations of our faith."[111] The fear, doubt, and weakness experienced and exhibited by the disciples were for the sake of the rest of the Mystical Body: "It was *our* perplexities and our dangers that were counseled in the Apostles. ... Others doubted, that *we* might not doubt."[112] During the period between the resurrection and ascension "great sacraments (*sacramenta*) ... were confirmed ... great mysteries (*mysteria*) revealed" in which "the fear of awful death

108 *Tr* 72.6.

109 This soteriology is similar in structure to that outlined by Hilary. See Paul Galtier, "La *forma Dei* et la *forma servi* selon saint Hilaire de Poitiers," *Recherches de science religieuse* 48 (1960): 101–118.

110 *Tr* 73.1. On Leo's theology of the ascension, see Armitage, *A Twofold Solidarity*, 199–134; Henri Denis, *La théologie de l'ascension d'après saint Léon le Grand* (unpublished dissertation, University of Lyons, 1959).

111 *Tr* 73.1.

112 *Tr* 73.1.

(*metus dirae mortis*) was removed, and the immortality not only of the soul but also of the flesh was declared."[113] On the Emmaus Road, Christ challenges our own doubt by upbraiding the two disciples for their "terror and bewilderment."[114] Even in the midst of the resurrection appearances the disciples were "storm-tossed by fearful thoughts" (*trepidis cogitationibus aestuarent*) until Christ says "peace be unto you,"[115] and so reassures them that "what was swirling around in their hearts might not be their fixed opinion."

The purpose of these appearances is to demonstrate to the disciples—and, through them, to the entire Church—that the agonized, crucified, abandoned Jesus of the passion narratives is truly glorified. Christ, accordingly, "presents before the doubters' eyes the signs of the cross ... that the wounds of unbelieving hearts (*infidelium cordium vulnera*) might be healed by the marks of nails and lance."[116] As a result of the resurrection appearances, the Apostles, "who had been both trembling (*trepidi*) at his death on the cross and doubtful about believing his resurrection, were so strengthened by the clearness of the truth" that sadness gave way to joy.[117] More specifically, they rejoiced that, in the ascended Christ, human nature was "associated on the throne with his glory, to whose nature it was united in the Son."[118] Because it is our human nature which is exalted in Christ, and because the whole Christ—the Mystical Body together with the Head—is taken into heaven, "Christ's ascension is our uplifting (*provectio*), and the hope of the Body is called whither the glory of the Head has preceded."[119] In consequence, heaven already belongs to us: "not only are we confirmed as possessors of paradise today, but in Christ we have penetrated the heights of heaven."[120]

All of this presupposes the threefold *transitus*, according to which human beings pass over into Christ's body through baptism and the Eucharist, Christ's human nature passes over from passibility and lowliness to impassibility and glory, and the incarnate person of the Son passes over to his heavenly Father. Just as the Holy Week liturgy presents before Leo's flock the picture of Christ fearing and suffering on our behalf (as a *remedium* and *doctrina*; a *sacramentum* and *exemplum*) in order to heal and conquer (*ut sanaret; ut vinceret*) our fear of suffering and death, so the Resurrection and Ascension liturgy sets before the faithful "the signs of

113 *Tr* 73.2.

114 *Tr* 73.2.

115 *Tr* 73.3; Luke 24:36; John 20:19.

116 *Tr* 73.3.

117 *Tr* 73.4.

118 *Tr* 73.4.

119 *Tr* 73.4.

120 *Tr* 73.4.

the cross"—the wounds of the risen Christ—for the healing (*ad sananda*) of the wounds of our unfaithful hearts. It recapitulates—today, within the eucharistic celebration, and through the means of the "narration of the gospel"—the passing over (*transitus*) into heaven, into glory, into union with Christ's divinity and with the person of the Father, of the human nature which the Son assumed. It makes present, in the *paschale sacramentum*, that human nature whose weakness and fear he healed and conquered in Gethsemane and on Calvary, and whose lowliness he exalted and glorified in the resurrection and ascension. Containing in itself "interior remedies" and "cures of the soul," it ensures that, in their "passing over" with Christ and in Christ from death to life, the faithful possess within themselves the mystery of Easter.

Conclusion

Leo's exegesis of those gospel passages—the agony in Gethsemane, the cry of dereliction on Calvary—which depict the prayer of the suffering Christ is designed to foster both contemplation and participation. In *Behold the Pierced One* Pope Benedict echoes Leo's understanding of the *mysterium* and *exemplum* of the prayer of Jesus:

> We see who Jesus is if we see him at prayer. The Christian confession of faith comes from participating in the prayer of Jesus, from being drawn into his prayer and being privileged to behold it; it interprets the experience of Jesus' prayer, and its interpretation of Jesus is correct because it springs from a sharing in what is most personal and intimate to him.[121]

Leo likewise believes that we both behold Jesus' prayer and are drawn into it. We who "feel something of the cross at the time of the Lord's passion" cause the prayer of the Head to resound throughout the Mystical Body. Participating in his cross, we come to share in his resurrection and glorification, appropriating his "interior remedies" and "cures of the soul," his healing of—and victory over—our fear of suffering and death.

Daniel A. Keating notes that, while he never uses the term, Leo "is one of the clearest exponents of the content of the doctrine of divinization in the Western tradition."[122] Drawing on the Greek Fathers and later Byzantine authors,

---

121 Joseph Cardinal Ratzinger, *Behold The Pierced One*, trans. Graham Harrison (San Francisco: Ignatius, 1986), 19.

122 Daniel A. Keating, *Deification and Grace* (Naples, Fl.: Sapientia, 2007), 9. Keating discusses Leo's understanding of deification at greater length in *The Appropriation of Divine Life in Cyril of Alexandria* (Oxford: Oxford University Press, 2004), 251–288. A similar point is made by John

Metropolitan Hierotheos Vlachos portrays deification as a process which begins with healing of the *nous* and culminates in the possession of the divine light.[123] Leo, too, understands the *sacramenta* of Christ—the saving *mysteria* and the liturgical *mysteria*—as *remedia* which effect "correction of heart" (*correctio cordis*), bring healing of the will, and apply "interior remedies" and "cures of the soul." These remedies are in turn ordered towards the brightness—the *claritas*—of the kingdom of God, and towards our sharing in Christ's passing-over—his *transitus*—from the *forma servi* to the *forma gloriae*. Christ's prayer to the Father in Gethsemane and on Calvary is a "remedy" that brings *salus*—that salvation which confers inner healing and freedom from the fear of suffering and death, and in virtue of which "the life of believers contains in itself the mystery of Easter." Forever associated with Pope John Paul II, the message "be not afraid" is also the gospel of his great predecessor Leo.

Meyendorff in his work *Christ in Eastern Christian Thought* (Crestwood, NY: St. Vladimir's Seminary Press, 1987), 25.

123 Metropolitan Hierotheos Vlachos, *Orthodox Psychotherapy*, trans. Esther Williams (Levadia, Greece: Birth of Theotokos Monastery, 2005).

Letter & Spirit 7 (2011): 35-50

Patristic Interpretation of Scripture within God's Story of Creation and Redemption[1]

~: William S. Kurz, S.J. :~

Introduction

Many exegetes have grown increasingly dissatisfied both by the limitations and secularistic presuppositions of historical criticism, and also by the seemingly endless proliferation of undisciplined or ideological post-modern reading strategies, few of which seem to respect or even relate to the Bible as God's revelation. How instead can exegetes more effectively treat and interpret Scripture as God's Word to his people? Contemporary Christian and Jewish biblical scholars continue to develop approaches to theological interpretation of Scripture that are both contemporary as well as traditional and biblically grounded.

They are again looking to the Fathers of the Church for inspiration and guidance on how to interpret for today the Bible as God's Word. However, some of the interpretive approaches for which the Fathers are well known seem quite alien to contemporary scholarly sensitivities and preferences, particularly because of their apparent lack of methodological controls to prevent eisegesis into the text of one's own biases, or fanciful applications that bear little apparent relation to the obvious meaning of the biblical passage. Such concerns prompt the following questions:

> (1) Do patristic authors have anything to teach today's Catholic interpreters of Scripture (especially teachers and preachers) about reading Scripture?
>
> (2) If so, what?

Probably least attractive to contemporary biblicists are allegorical meanings that seem to be arbitrarily imported into the sense of the passage. Also foreign to contemporary exegetical approaches are the "four senses of Scripture," for which medieval exegesis is also especially known. Although the four senses do not appear as arbitrary as patristic and medieval allegorizing, their complexity and their grounding in medieval philosophy seem to presuppose a philosophical competence that many contemporary exegetes do not have.

---

1 I am very grateful to The Word Among Us Press and to Editorial Director Patricia Mitchell for granting me copyright permission to borrow heavily in this article from Chapter Two, "Developing a Theological Approach to Scripture," in my *Reading the Bible as God's Own Story: A Catholic Approach for Bringing Scripture to Life* (The Word Among Us Press, 2007). There the reader will find a fuller context, development, and exemplification of this article's arguments and conclusions.

Some early patristic figures, however, exemplified a much simpler and more direct theological approach to interpreting Scripture. For example, St. Irenaeus generally avoided allegory because he was combatting the heretical allegories by which the Gnostics managed to deform the basic meanings and narratives of Scripture either into their polar opposites or into completely unrelated myths and theologies. Also, against Arians, St. Athanasius was defending the pivotal doctrine of the Incarnation of the Son of God, who was both true God and true man (and ultimately the dogma that God is One and Triune). The Arians did not depend on allegory, but they used literalistic interpretation of particular words and expressions of Scripture (the Greek Old and New Testament) as proof texts for their doctrine, without sufficient account of their fuller biblical context. They especially failed to consider the context of a given text within the overall sweep of Salvation History.

The principal defense of Fathers like Irenaeus and Athanasius against heretical interpretations, whether of undisciplined allegorizers like Gnostics, or of proof-texting readers like Arians, was to interpret individual scriptural passages within the overarching biblical narrative from God's creation to redemption and ultimately to eschatological judgment and new creation. This approach is proving quite attractive to contemporary scholars who respect and use historical criticism to determine the human meaning of passages, but also want to read those passages as part of God's overall biblical narrative and revelation.

Patristic Biblical Interpretation

Catholics do not have to create theological biblical readings *ex nihilo*, from nothing. They have centuries' worth of examples of theological readings of Scripture—beginning in the Bible itself with the later Old Testament and the New Testament, in which subsequent biblical texts reinterpreted and reapplied earlier passages. Theological interpretation of Scripture flourished through the patristic and medieval periods, up until the widespread rejection of those "pre-critical" interpretative approaches in the modernist age. A significant, if partial, reason for that rejection was Enlightenment rationalism and its rejection of dogma.[2]

Catholic Church authorities for some time resisted this modernist rejection and the use of the new critical methods, but the "Dogmatic Constitution of Divine Revelation" in Vatican II finally gave full official ecclesial approval to

2 See Luke Timothy Johnson, "Rejoining a Long Conversation," in Luke Timothy Johnson and William S. Kurz, *The Future of Catholic Biblical Scholarship: A Constructive Conversation* (Grand Rapids, MI: Eerdmans, 2002), 35–63. Johnson discusses and recommends consulting Church Fathers and pre-critical interpreters of Scripture. Because the Enlightenment period in the eighteenth century followed the bloodshed and devastation from the religious wars in Europe, it sought to replace by critical reason such irrational and destructive behaviors and beliefs that were generated by conflicting religious beliefs and denominations.

reasonable use of historical-critical biblical exegesis.[3] Within a surprisingly short time after Vatican II, however, the hard-earned authorization from Catholic teaching authorities to use historical-critical exegesis of Scripture has been followed by intensifying dissatisfaction by some Catholic biblical scholars with the increasingly apparent pastoral limitations of exclusively historical-critical readings. This has led to some tension not only among Catholic biblical researchers, but also between Catholic biblicists and patristic and medieval historians who specialize in "pre-critical" biblical interpretation by ancient and medieval Church Fathers. Systematic theologians also can find themselves torn between grounding their use and citation of Scripture predominantly on historical-critical biblical interpretations (as they typically seem to have done since Vatican II), or seeking scriptural interpretations more attuned to theological explanations and views of reality.

The recent reclamation of the Fathers of the Church for lessons and models of theological interpretation of Scripture has not been without its strains. Therefore, it will be helpful to revisit some tensions, misconceptions, and prejudices regarding patristic and pre-critical biblical interpretation in recent Catholic scholarship. Although the allegorical tendency for which patristic and medieval writers are most widely known will not be the primary approach followed in this essay, it does seem important to explain briefly what is usually meant by allegorical interpretation of Scripture. Related and sometimes overlapping terms are used when discussing allegory, such as typology and figural reading, which we need not fully distinguish nor individually explain here.

The *Catechism of the Catholic Church* provides a readily available summary of the chief distinctions among kinds of interpretation or senses of Scripture. Its two principal and most important categories are the literal sense and the spiritual senses (nos. 115–119); the spiritual senses are usually subdivided into the "allegorical, moral, and anagogical senses" (no. 115). The *Catechism* explains that because of the unity of God's saving plan (no. 112), the realities and events about which Scripture speaks can be signs of other realities (no. 117). The three spiritual senses are, therefore, the *allegorical* (in which one referent can stand for another, for example, crossing the Red Sea as a sign of Christ's victory and Christian baptism); the *moral* sense (which relates Scripture to acting justly, as "written for our instruction," 1 Cor. 10:11); and the *anagogical* sense (which relates Scripture to its eternal significance and our future hope, e.g., seeing the church on earth as a sign of the heavenly Jerusalem, no. 117).[4]

3 Second Vatican Council, *Dei Verbum* [the Word of God], Dogmatic Constitution of Divine Revelation, (November 18, 1965) 12–13, in *The Scripture Documents: An Anthology of Official Catholic Teachings*, ed. Dean P. Béchard, S.J. (Collegeville, MN: Liturgical Press, 2002), 19–31, at 24–25.

4 *Catechism of the Catholic Church*, 2d. ed. (Vatican City: Libreria Editrice Vaticana, 1997), nos. 112, 115–119.

To allegorize a biblical (or any) text usually involves isolating individual words, phrases, or details in the passage from their natural meaning in their original contexts, and then correlating those words with some other word or reality that was not part of the passage's original meaning or context. For example, it was common for Christians in ancient and medieval times to allegorize the two human lovers in the ancient biblical Hebrew love song, the Song of Solomon (or Canticle of Canticles), as referring to the love of Christ for the Church, his bride. This allegory from the Song of Solomon illustrates the perduring value that some biblical allegory retains. The symbolism of Christ and his bride the Church, which has been especially immortalized in the comparison of husband and wife to Christ and his bridal Church in Ephesians 5:21–33, remains of crucial importance in Catholic biblical interpretation and doctrine.

Augustine

At the heart of the disputes over approaches like allegory is the extent to which allegory does or does not express or presume the apparently intended meaning of the original human biblical writer. Roland Teske exemplifies the issues at stake in an illuminating case study comparing Augustine's literal and christological (spiritual) interpretations of the Good Samaritan. Augustine generally interprets this parable christologically (allegorically correlating the Good Samaritan who helps the fallen man with the incarnate Son helping fallen humankind). Augustine also, however, can interpret the parable literally (in ways acceptable to historical critics), and has produced several examples of its literal interpretation. Nevertheless, there is an added theological richness in Augustine's christological interpretation, which can exemplify the entire economy of God's salvation of fallen humans through the Incarnation of the Son. Augustine himself admits the difference between the meaning intended by the human author and a meaning which the text can call to the reader's mind even if it was not part of the author's original point. If the latter spiritual meaning is congruent with the overall message of Scripture as interpreted in the Church, Augustine would consider it as a legitimate understanding of the text's message from God to the reader.

Contrary to historical criticism, however, Augustine held that the christological interpretation of the Good Samaritan can even be considered the teaching of Jesus himself. Teske suggests three lines of argumentation that Augustine might use to argue his point with modern exegetes. First, in *Confessions* Book 12, Augustine made the following argument against those who would claim that although his interpretation of Genesis has merit, it was not intended by the author of Genesis: there is no harm if one does not arrive at the author's intended point if we reach a truth that God shows us to be true. Similarly, Augustine might argue that without determining what Luke's intended meaning for the parable itself was,

Luke would have surely intended readers to be able to find in the parable other biblical truths even if he himself did not have them in mind.

Second, although Augustine clearly prefers the meaning of the author himself, this is not always ascertainable. If it is not, we should choose an interpretation that is supported by the context of Scripture and is prescribed by sound faith. His christological interpretation does agree with both the biblical message and sound faith. Additionally, sometimes a biblical passage has several true interpretations. Further, even if the human author was not aware of the christological meaning, the Holy Spirit who inspired him certainly foresaw and providentially arranged that such a meaning would occur to believing readers. Therefore, that sense is true even if unintended by Luke.

Third, for Augustine the goal of all biblical exegesis is practical—the love of God and neighbor. Through the instrumentality of the biblical text God directly works on the individual reader. Thus, for Augustine, no matter how learned an interpretation may be, if it does not build love in the reader, it has failed to understand Scripture as Scripture. Whereas an interpretation that does build love, even if it does not convey the precise meaning intended by the biblical author, does no harm and is guilty of no untruth. Augustine would, therefore, consider his christological interpretation of the Good Samaritan to be more theologically useful than a merely literal interpretation of the parable, and, therefore, to fulfill the ultimate purpose of exegesis of building love in the reader.[5]

Another important consideration about allegory is that already some New Testament passages had allegorized Old Testament details. An example is 1 Corinthians 10:1–4, especially verse 4, "and all [the Israelites in the desert] drank from the same supernatural [or *spiritual*] drink. For they drank from the supernatural [*spiritual*] Rock which followed them, *and the Rock was Christ*."[6] Other examples of patristic or medieval allegorizing, especially the further removed their allegorical details are from the central point of the biblical passage, are less attractive today. There may not be much current interest in allegorizing Martha and Mary, respectively, as active and contemplative spiritualties (for example, of "active" Jesuits and "contemplative" Trappists or Poor Clare sisters).

Irenaeus and Athanasius and Other Fathers

As mentioned above, other approaches of the Church Fathers that seem more inviting today for interpreting Scripture theologically (as God's biblical message) are exemplified by Saints Irenaeus (ca. A.D. 125–203) and Athanasius

5 See Roland Teske, "The Good Samaritan (Lk. 10:29–37) in Augustine's Exegesis," in *Augustine: Biblical Exegete*, eds. Frederick Van Fleteren and Joseph C. Schaubelt, O.S.A. (New York: Peter Lang, 2001), 347–367, at 353–357.

6 *The Holy Bible containing the Old and New Testaments*, Revised Standard Version Catholic Edition (San Francisco: Ignatius Press, 1965, 1966), emphasis added. Unless otherwise noted, all English quotations in this essay are from this version.

(A.D. 298–373). Both of these Church Fathers had to deal with alien or harmful interpretations and applications of Scripture, which supported non-Christian religious mythology or heretical forms of Christianity that denied vital Christian dogmas. To counter these misleading approaches to Scripture, both Irenaeus and Athanasius explicitly read and interpreted Scripture in the context of the entire biblical message of creation and salvation and of traditional Church summaries of biblical revelation in various versions of the "rule of faith." They interpreted this way because they were Church teachers and pastors, instructing believers in ecclesial, liturgical, and pastoral settings, not in school settings like contemporary universities. Misinterpretations of Scripture threatened the faith of Christians entrusted to their care. This helps account for the vehemence with which Fathers like Irenaeus and Athanasius rejected heretical interpretations of the Bible.

For example, when ancient Gnostics took biblical words and passages out of context to elaborate their peculiar polytheistic myths of creation and salvation, which were quite foreign to biblical revelation and Christian salvation, Irenaeus insisted on reading biblical words and passages in both their immediate biblical context and in the context of the Church's understanding of the central biblical message. Later, at the time of the Council of Nicea (325), when Arian Christians were using the literal meanings of biblical words, phrases, and passages to argue that the Word or Son of God was not divine but only a creature made by God (even if they admitted that he was the first to be created), Athanasius responded with an extremely close and careful reading of the same passages used by the Arians. Nevertheless, he was guided in his close reading by the overall biblical message of salvation as interpreted by the Church, in which the divine Son of God was begotten by the Father as equally divine without being a second God.

The problematical forms of interpretation in both Gnosticism and Arianism tended not only to take words, phrases, or passages out of their natural biblical context. They tended also to read those words or passages with an exaggerated literalist interpretation that failed to respect the overall biblical revelation about the relationship of God to the world and about the history of God's salvation of fallible humans.

At the heart of the approaches of both Irenaeus and Athanasius was a relatively simple and straightforward principle and procedure. Both Fathers read each biblical passage quite closely and with concentrated attention to details in the text, as biblical scholars do today. However, unlike most contemporary academic biblicists, Irenaeus and Athanasius also purposefully read each individual passage in the light of Scripture's overall message of God's creation and salvation.

Early Christian Fathers regularly read and steeped themselves in Scripture and participated in liturgies that featured biblical readings over the course of the Church's liturgical year (readings which together commemorate most of God's story of salvation). They expressed their personal and communal prayers in the words of the Old Testament psalms, and they consciously lived within the biblical worldview. They understood themselves as created by God, as sinners with Adam and his descendants, as reconciled to God by the death and resurrection of Jesus, God's Son. Through the Church's liturgical year, they placed themselves within the biblical events as participants in them. An especially striking Jewish example of such personal insertion into God's biblical story is the explanation to the youngest participant at a Jewish Seder celebration that God has freed "*us*" from slavery. In these ways both Jews and Christians derived from the Bible an overarching narrative.[7] From the Bible's myriad details, plot lines, books, theologies, and cultural contexts, patristic writers discerned an underlying unified story line, a foundational biblical story. Commencing from the very beginning—the creation of the world and of humans by God—this story recounted the human fall from God's friendship and God's response through divine promises, covenants, saving acts, and use of human instruments to implement divine providence.

This biblical story finds its climax in the Incarnation of the Son of God and in the life, death, and resurrection of Jesus. It continues with the life of the Church up until the final judgment. Using this fundamental story as implied context and background for all the individual accounts and perspectives in both Old and New Testaments enabled the patristic authors to pay extremely close attention to individual details of particular biblical passages without losing a sense of God's overall biblical message.

As a further shorthand guide to keep the reader from getting lost in the maze of diverging and sometimes apparently even misleading strands among the many Old and New Testament books and authors, the Fathers used a "rule of

7 Christopher Seitz demonstrates that this kind of overall biblical narrative approach developed by the patristic authors is grounded in the New Testament itself. Using Lukan examples in particular, he illustrates how the expression "according to the Scriptures" situates the identity and mission of Jesus in the context of God's saving plan and actions recounted in the Old Testament. The Gospels and Fathers from the second and third centuries described Jesus by situating him in God's saving plan as revealed in their Scripture (= Old Testament) combined with the apostolic witness to Jesus (before the completed "canonized" New Testament). See Christopher R. Seitz, *Figured Out: Typology and Providence in Christian Scripture* (Louisville, KY: Westminster John Knox, 2001), 104. Seitz also relates the patristic use of the *rule of faith* to this use of the Old Testament narrative of God's saving plan. Because for Christians the Son and Father are one, both Old and New Testaments provide a unified witness to them via the Holy Spirit (Seitz, *Figured Out*, 6). See Lk. 16:31: "He said to him, 'If they do not hear Moses and the prophets, neither will they be convinced if someone should rise from the dead.'" Compare also Lk. 24:27: "And beginning with Moses and all the prophets, he interpreted to them in all the scriptures the things concerning himself." See also Lk. 24:44–49: "Then he said to them, 'These are my words which I spoke to you, while I was still with you, that everything written about me in the law of Moses and the prophets and the psalms must be fulfilled.' Then he opened their minds to understand the scriptures, and said to them, 'Thus it is written, that the Christ should suffer and on the third day rise from the dead, and that repentance and forgiveness of sins should be preached in his name to all nations, beginning from Jerusalem. You are witnesses of these things. And behold, I send the promise of my Father upon you; but stay in the city, until you are clothed with power from on high.'"

faith," or a basic hypothesis or story line of Scripture. They judged that the Bible's foundational narrative had been authentically summarized by the Church in theological and philosophical terminology as the Church's rule of faith:

> It [the rule of faith] began with the confession of God as creator, briefly narrated the coming of Christ, told of his suffering, death and resurrection, the sending of the Holy Spirit, and ended by pointing to the return of Christ in glory. By presenting the story of the Bible in capsule form, the rule of faith or "pattern of truth" defined the subject matter of the Bible, thereby offering a commentary on the whole.[8]

This rule of faith was based on scriptural narratives, teachings, and evidence. It helped to keep readers' bearings focused on the essentials of the overall biblical story and message and not to get lost in voluminous biblical details, stories, and theologies.

The education of most ancient and patristic writers was grounded in Greco-Roman rhetoric. In their book, *Sanctified Vision: An Introduction to Early Christian Interpretation of the Bible*, John J. O'Keefe and R. R. Reno describe how Irenaeus borrows from classical rhetoric three key terms: *hypothesis, economy,* and *recapitulation*. Rhetorical teaching and theory called "the gist of a literary work" its *hypothesis*.[9] The hypothesis of an *argument* is the argument's basic outline, whereas the hypothesis of a *narrative* is the basic story line of that narrative.

According to Irenaeus, the main problem with heretical interpretation of Scripture is that it ignores the primary hypothesis of the Bible. While focusing on details and symbols, it fails to show how "the beginning, middle, and end hang together."[10] For Irenaeus, the hypothesis of Scripture is that Jesus fulfills all things. Jesus came according to God's economy, and recapitulated everything in himself.[11]

For Irenaeus the *economy* is the "outline or table of contents of scripture."[12] Later generations tended to prefer the expression "salvation history" to the patristic word "economy." An ancient rhetorical *recapitulation* is a work's final summing up, repetition, drawing to a conclusion. In oratory it refers especially to the summary at the end of a speech that drives home the point of its strongest arguments. For

8 Robert Louis Wilken, "*In Dominico Eloquio*: Learning the Lord's Style of Language," *Communio* 24 (1997): 846–866, at 863.

9 See John J. O'Keefe and R. R. Reno, *Sanctified Vision: An Introduction to Early Christian Interpretation of the Bible* (Baltimore: Johns Hopkins University, 2005), 34.

10 O'Keefe and Reno, *Sanctified Vision*, 35.

11 O'Keefe and Reno, *Sanctified Vision*, 37.

12 O'Keefe and Reno, *Sanctified Vision*, 38.

Irenaeus, Jesus is the Father's summary statement, his Logos or Word, the purpose for the biblical economy as incarnating the purpose of God's economy.[13]

Patristic Reading of Scripture with the Rule of Faith

There were actually multiple early examples and variations of this rule of faith, even within a single author such as St. Irenaeus. The rule of faith was like a Creed, but the rule of faith was particularly meant for theologians and biblical interpreters, whereas the original setting for Creeds was the sacrament of Baptism.[14] Later interpreters and readers of Scripture also came to use official Creeds as they would a rule of faith. The most significant Creed for biblical interpretation came to be the Nicene Creed, which Athanasius helped to formulate at the Council of Nicaea in A.D. 325.

The Nicene Creed was defined to counteract the heretical denial of Jesus' divinity by the Arians. Even though Arians accepted the biblical claim that the Son existed with God before the creation of the material world, they based their denial of his divinity on their interpretation of several biblical passages that seemed to imply that the Son of God was a creature. Compare John 1:1–3 ("In the beginning was the Word, and the Word was with God, and the Word was God ...) with the claim by Wisdom in Proverbs 8:22–23: "The LORD *created me at the beginning of his work*, the first of his acts of old. Ages ago I was set up, at the first, before the beginning of the earth."[15] The principal rejoinders that Athanasius makes against Arian biblical interpretation were for the most part his alternative exegetical arguments and interpretations of the same passages that were being used by Arians to deny Jesus' divinity.

St. Irenaeus emphasized the church's "rule of faith" as an indispensable key to reading Scripture, especially to counteract dramatically alien gnostic interpretations of Scripture. *Gnostics* (from the Greek for *knowing*) were heretical thinkers who were quite influential at the time of Irenaeus. They claimed to have extra-biblical oral revelation and inside knowledge that ordinary (and implicitly inferior) Catholic Christians did not have. At the heart of their religion was an alien mythology that claimed that human souls were sparks of the divine that somehow got trapped in evil matter. Salvation came primarily through souls *knowing* their true identity as sparks of the divine and, consequently, being freed from the shackles of their material bodies. Though the ancient gnostic religion is in the past, gnostic tendencies occasionally reappear, as in some aspects of recent "New Age" religiosity.

---

13 O'Keefe and Reno, *Sanctified Vision*, 39.

14 See Joseph T. Lienhard, *The Bible, the Church, and Authority: The Canon of the Christian Bible in History and Theology* (Collegeville, MN: The Liturgical Press [A Michael Glazier Book], 1995), 49–52, at 51.

15 RSV, Catholic Edition, emphasis added.

Irenaeus emphasized how Gnostics took biblical details completely out of their biblical context and significance, from which they then fashioned their eccentric unbiblical doctrines by using biblical vocabulary in unbiblical ways. Irenaeus likened their interpretations to taking apart a beautiful mosaic image of a king into its constituent pieces, and then rearranging those pieces into a new mosaic image of a dog.[16] To counter such chaotic and arbitrary "proof-texting" of biblical words and passages in ways that were completely foreign to their biblical contexts and meanings, Church leaders emphasized that the Scriptures needed to be read in light of their basic message, which had been summed up in the church's "rule of faith."

The Church Fathers frequently recall how when humans rejected God and his commands in their desire to be as God themselves, no mere human could make up for that offense against God's infinite dignity. Therefore, they often emphasized that the turning point in God's biblical story of salvation was the occasion on which the Second Person of the Trinity (the Son or Word) became man (in the Incarnation) to reconcile humans to God and to "re-open the gates of heaven" as the unique mediator between God and man.[17] To be able to function as mediator, God's incarnate Son, Jesus, could not be merely a creature. It is because the Son of God is both truly God and truly man that he can mediate between and reconcile God and the alienated human race. Because the Son is of the same being as the Father, the Son also is God. Thus, the incarnate Jesus is both God and man.[18]

16 See *Irenaeus Against Heresies* (Bk. 1, Chap. 8, in *Ante-Nicene Fathers* [*ANF*], vol. 1, ed. Alexander Roberts and James Donaldson, rev. A. Cleveland Coxe [American reprint of Edinburgh ed.; Grand Rapids, Mich.: Eerdmans, reprinted 1969], 326): "How the Valentinians pervert the scriptures to support their own impious opinions: Their manner of acting is just as if one, when a beautiful image of a king has been constructed by some skillful artist out of precious jewels, should then take this likeness of the man all to pieces, should rearrange the gems, and so fit them together as to make them into the form of a dog or of a fox, and even that but poorly executed; and should then maintain and declare that this was the beautiful image of the king which the skillful artist constructed, pointing to the jewels which had been admirably fitted together by the first artist to form the image of the king, but have been with bad effect transferred by the latter one to the shape of a dog, and by thus exhibiting the jewels, should deceive the ignorant who had no conception what a king's form was like, and persuade them that that miserable likeness of the fox was, in fact, the beautiful image of the king. In like manner do these persons patch together old wives' fables, and then endeavour, by violently drawing away from their proper connection, words, expressions, and parables whenever found, to adapt the oracles of God to their baseless fictions."

17 Wilken ("*In Dominico Eloquio*," 862) quotes Henri de Lubac: "Jesus Christ brings about the unity of the Scripture, because he is the endpoint and fullness of Scripture. Everything in it is related to him. In the end he is its sole object. Consequently, he is, so to speak, its whole exegesis" (citing *Exégèse Médiévale* 1:322 [ET 1:235]).

18 Especially helpful as a guide to patristic biblical interpretation are Frances Young, *Virtuoso Theology: The Bible and Interpretation* (Eugene, OR: Wipf and Stock, 1993), ch. 3, "Tradition and Interpretation," 45–65, and ch. 4, "Jewish Texts and Christian Meanings," 66–87. (*Virtuoso Theology* was originally published in London in 1990 by Darton, Longman and Todd, Ltd., as *The Art of Performance: Towards a Theology of Holy Scripture*.)

Because of the predominant role played by the Incarnation in the biblical account of salvation, the key to Scripture was generally recognized to be the doctrine that the Son was of the same being, nature, or essence as the Father, even though the wording of that teaching is more philosophical than biblical. To expound this doctrine, Athanasius and other Church Fathers used the philosophical term, *homoousios* (of the same being or essence), which they admitted was not even found in the Bible. They neither found this term or doctrinal teaching explicitly expressed in Scripture, nor did they extract this term from the Bible. Nevertheless, they judged that this word most fully and accurately expressed the fundamental biblical teaching about the Son, that he was not only "with God" in the beginning, before the creation of the world, as the Arians also held, but that he "was God," as John 1:1 put it.[19]

The Scope of Scripture according to St. Athanasius

Athanasius accuses the Arians of misinterpreting Scripture because they do not read individual passages from within the "scope of Scripture." The scope of Scripture refers to the reality about which the Bible is speaking. As he explains:

> Now the scope and character of Holy Scripture ... is this,—it contains a double account of the Saviour [*sic*]; that he was ever God, and is the Son, being the Father's Word and Radiance and Wisdom; and that afterwards for us he took flesh of a Virgin, Mary, Bearer of God [*Theotokos*], and was made man. And this scope is to be found throughout inspired Scripture, as the Lord Himself has said, "Search the Scriptures, for they are they which testify of Me."[20]

---

19 See Thomas Forsyth Torrance, *Theology in Reconstruction* (Grand Rapids, MI: W.B. Eerdmans, 1966), 33: "Theological statements are made by hard exegesis in light of the truth to which Scripture points. For Athanasius, the supreme example of exegetical and theological activity is the *homoousion* of Nicea. As a compressed statement, it becomes normative for all theological statement that is to be faithful to its proper object and consistent with other faithful statements." See also p. 36: "The epistemological significance of the Nicaean *homoousion* doctrine of consubstantiality of the Incarnate Word and Son of God lies in the rejection of the Valentinian and Arian dichotomy that made the *Logos* in the last resort a creature of God ... and lies in the insistence that in Jesus Christ we have a *Logos* that is not of man's devising but One who goes back into the eternal Being of God for he proceeded from the eternal Being of God. The Incarnation means that God has really given himself and communicated himself in his eternal Word to man." See also for corroboration Thomas F. Torrance, *Divine Meaning: Studies in Patristic Hermeneutics* (Edinburgh: T&T Clark, 1995), 253.

20 St. Athanasius, *Four Discourses Against the Arians*, Bk. 3, Chap. 29, in *A Select Library of the Nicene and Post-Nicene Fathers of the Christian Church*, Second Series, vol. 4, ed. Philip Schaff (Grand Rapids: Eerdmans, 1957), 409. Two key Scriptures Athanasius cites to express this "scope" are Jn. 1:1–3, 14 and Phil. 2:6–8.

When the Old Testament is read in light of the New, the primary reality being revealed is that the Word or Son of God, who pre-existed creation with the Father and through whom the world was created, was not only "with God"[21] but also "was God."[22] This divine "Word became flesh and dwelt among us, full of grace and truth; we have beheld his glory, glory as of the only Son from the Father."[23]

Athanasius then refers to the Word's pattern of emptying or *kenosis* expressed by Paul in Philippians 2:6–8. Though "he was in the form of God" (to be contrasted later with "form of a servant") he "did not count equality with God a thing to be grasped."[24] Rather, "he emptied himself, taking the form of a servant, being born in the likeness of men."[25] Further, "in human form he humbled himself and became obedient unto death, even death on a cross."[26] Not clinging to his being "in the form of God," he took on "the form of a servant" which is identified with the human outward appearance or form.[27]

Implicit is the contrast between the Word, who was in the form of God, not grasping at equality with God that he already had, and Adam, who was in the image of God, coveting: "you will be like God."[28] In contrast to Adam who therefore disobeyed God, the Word in human form humbly obeyed God unto death, even that of the cross.

Athanasius goes on to argue: "Any one, beginning with these passages and going through the whole of the Scripture upon the interpretation which they suggest, will perceive how in the beginning the Father said to Him, 'Let there be light,' and 'Let there be a firmament,' and 'Let us make man'"[29]; "but in fulness [*sic*] of the ages, He sent Him into the world, not that He might judge the world, but that the world by Him might be saved ..." And the Son conceived by the Virgin shall be called "Emmanuel, which, being interpreted, is God with us."[30] Thus reading all the Scripture in light especially of John 1 and Philippians 2, Athanasius perceives the scope of Scripture as extending from the pre-existent Word through his Incarnation, death and exaltation, to his status as Judge at the end of time. Thus, all interpretation must account for the objective reality revealed in Scripture. That object or scope of Scripture is Jesus himself, who is both God and man. Biblical

21 John 1:1.

22 John 1:1.

23 John 1:14.

24 Phil. 2:6.

25 Phil. 2:7.

26 Phil. 2:8.

27 Phil. 2:7.

28 Gen. 3:5.

29 Gen. 1:3, 6, 26.

30 See Matt. 1:23.

statements must therefore be interpreted according to both his divine and human natures.[31]

Athanasius' Understanding of "Tradition" in "Scripture and Tradition"

Athanasius expounds Church "Tradition" by the command of Christ at the end of Matthew's Gospel: "Go therefore and make disciples of all nations, baptizing them in the name of the Father and of the Son and of the Holy Spirit, teaching them to observe all that I have commanded you; and lo, I am with you always, to the close of the age."[32] Having "all authority in heaven and on earth,"[33] Christ commands his disciples (the Church), to convert all nations and to baptize them "in the name of the Father and of the Son and of the Holy Spirit,"[34] that is, in the single name of the one God as Trinity.

Disciples are to teach all nations "to observe all that I have commanded you." Their teaching is grounded firmly on the deeds and sayings of Jesus and neither adds to all those sayings or deeds nor subtracts from them. For Athanasius, therefore, the content of Church Tradition matches what is revealed in Scripture. Providing protection against human additions to and subtractions from Tradition (as in Arianism), the risen Jesus remains present with the Church. Tradition is not sustained in separation from Jesus' continued presence in the Church and guidance of all that the Church teaches: "lo, I am with you always, to the close of the age."[35]

Catholic teaching and Tradition comes from Jesus, through the apostles, to Church leaders and members, up to the present time, and until the end of time. Thus, for Athanasius, Tradition is equivalent to apostolic tradition, which in turn is equivalent to the content of Scripture. Since he considers the scope or core revelation and content of Scripture to be Jesus, God and man, who remains with the Church as Immanuel, Tradition is not separated from the continued presence of the risen Jesus, God with us. Grounded in the person of the risen Jesus, the God-man, Tradition is passed on not by mere human reasoning and speculation alone. It is passed on and received by both faith and by reverent (and obedient) reasoning from within the teachings and practices of the Catholic Church, not by profane meanings or mere human opinions.[36]

---

31 Compare Torrance, *Divine Meaning*, 238–239.

32 Matt. 28:19–20.

33 Matt. 28:18.

34 Matt. 28:19.

35 Matt. 28:20.

36 Compare Torrance, *Divine Meaning*, 240–244, and St. Athanasius, *Contra Arianos* [Against the Arians], Bk. 3, Chaps. 29–30, in *A Select Library of the Nicene and Post-Nicene Fathers of the Christian Church*, Second Series, vol. 4, ed. Philip Schaff (Grand Rapids: Eerdmans, 1957), 409–410.

Monotheism and the Trinity in Reading the Old Testament

Despite the Church Fathers' belief in the Trinity, which differentiated them from their contemporary Jewish readers of Scripture, they never lost sight of the foundational truth, which the Old Testament and Judaism repeatedly emphasize, that there is only one God. The Fathers consistently confirm the Catholic understanding that the God who acts in the Old Testament is the same God who is Father of Jesus in the New Testament.

Gnostics at the time of Irenaeus had used St. Paul's phrase in 2 Corinthians 4:4, "the god of this world," to argue that there is a second god who created and rules this material world, different from God the Father of Jesus. Their second god (the creator) was jealous, vengeful, and inferior to the New Testament God of love and Father of Jesus Christ. Such gnostic arguments presumed also that they rejected the Old Testament as Christian revelation. By thus contending, Gnostics implicitly rejected also the unity of Scripture, which clearly emphasizes there is only one God.[37]

Further disproof of the gnostic understanding of "the god of this world" comes from contemporary historical critical interpretation. Scholars today generally understand that "the god of this world" in 2 Corinthians 4:4 refers to a fairly common belief in later Old Testament writings and in the New Testament that Satan had usurped much of Adam's original dominion over earth, which had been debilitated when Adam rebelled against God. As a Jewish monotheist, Paul certainly was not referring to a second god in the strict sense.

Contrary to misinterpretations of such ancient heretics as the Gnostics, Irenaeus and other Church Fathers have demonstrated that the God who creates, saves his people from Egypt, gives them the Law, promises them a Messiah and Savior from David's line, and sends prophets to them is actually the Trinity. That is, not only is he the one and only God to whom Judaism has given constant witness; but he also is now recognized by Christians to be Trinitarian—Father, Son, and Holy Spirit. In hindsight, Christians know how God's Old Testament story of salvation is concluded—that is, in the reconciliation of alienated humans to God through the Incarnation, death, and resurrection of God's Son. Therefore, it is no longer instinctive or typical for Christians to continue to read the Old Testament as if they were the original Hebrews who were ignorant that their one God is actually Trinity.

Nevertheless, there remains a value in sometimes trying to re-read the Old Testament through the eyes of the original readers. Even though Christians may know "the rest of the story," they can come to a deeper appreciation of the richness of God's providential plan by attending to its intricate windings from its early stages with "fresh eyes." Still, this seems a matter of "both-and" rather than "either-or": ordinary Christians or students should not be forced to choose between

37 Wilken, "*In Dominico Eloquio*," 862.

reading and understanding the Jewish books "*either* as the Hebrew Scriptures *or* as the Old Testament." They might profit, however, from reading them "*both* as Hebrew Scriptures *and* as the Old Testament."

Saints Irenaeus, Athanasius, other Church Fathers, and medieval saints have modeled for contemporary Christians how to read biblical passages both very closely in themselves as well as with theological insight into their deeper meaning. They give today's Christians a methodology for reading any particular passage in either the Old or New Testament just as closely and carefully as is currently expected in academic exegesis, but also within the theological context of God's overarching biblical story of salvation. Employed judiciously, patristic interpretative methods enable modern readers to attain greater theological and spiritual insight into any biblical passage.[38]

Conclusion

Do the patristic authors have anything to teach today's Catholic interpreters of Scripture (especially teachers and preachers) about reading Scripture? If so, what? They can teach us how to read Scripture theologically as God's revelation and message addressed explicitly to us. The contemporary search for more explicitly theological interpretations of Scripture finds simple and appropriate models and examples in the Fathers of the Church. Patristic and medieval authors read the Bible as God's Word addressed to them and to the Christians over which they were pastors and teachers.

They were able to do this because they read Scripture not merely as scholars who closely studied every word and expression in the passages they read, but as pastors, teachers, and believers who read individual passages from within the overarching biblical account of creation and salvation as God's revelation addressed to them and to the Church which they pastored. They not only read and taught and preached Scripture. They also prayed Scripture in the context of sacraments and liturgical rites, and they expressed their prayers in the words of biblical psalms and canticles. They also lived within the biblical worldview as creatures of the one true Creator God, as sinners who needed and received reconciliation with God through the Incarnation, death, and resurrection of God's Son, and as filled with the Holy

---

38 Especially helpful aids to theological interpretation have been the essays by Henri de Lubac ("Spiritual Understanding"), David C. Steinmetz ("The Superiority of Pre-Critical Exegesis"), and especially David S. Yeago ("The New Testament and the Nicene Dogma: A Contribution to the Recovery of Theological Exegesis") in *The Theological Interpretation of Scripture: Classic and Contemporary Readings*, Stephen E. Fowl, ed. (Malden, MA: Blackwell, 1997), 3–25 (de Lubac), 26–38 (Steinmetz), and 87–100 (Yeago). Catholic underpinnings for concerns discussed in Johnson and Kurz, *The Future of Catholic Biblical Scholarship*, can be found in Peter S. Williamson, *Catholic Principles for Interpreting Scripture: A Study of the Pontifical Biblical Commission's* The Interpretation of the Bible in the Church (Subsidia Biblica; Rome: Editrice Pontificio Istituto Biblico, 2001), and David M. Williams, *Receiving the Bible in Faith: Historical and Theological Exegesis* (Washington, D.C.: Catholic University of America Press, 2004).

Spirit and therefore members of the Son's Body, the Church, and children of the Father and brothers and sisters of Christ. This is what our patristic authors have to teach contemporary Catholic biblical interpreters.

Letter & Spirit 7 (2011): 51-66

Anamnesis and Allegory in Ambrose's *De sacramentis* and *De mysteriis*

~: Christine E. Wood :~

The importance of the liturgy for theology cannot be overstated. The phrase *legem credendi lex statuat supplicandi*, ascribed to Prosper of Aquitaine,[1] means that the Church's "law of belief" is seen in her "law of prayer" (*lex orandi, lex credendi*).[2] We see in the catechetical instructions of the Church Fathers, including Ambrose of Milan,[3] that this relationship of the liturgy to belief was well understood by the early Church. Since the liturgy is a primary source for theology, the maxim *lex orandi, lex credendi* takes a prominent position in the method of liturgical theology.

This article will investigate two of the key elements of Ambrose of Milan's catechetical instructions: (1) *anamnesis* or ritual memorial, and (2) how Ambrose used allegory (or typology) as a pedagogical tool to convey the meaning of the sacraments to his neophyte audience.[4] The study will be restricted to the *De sacramentis* and *De mysteriis* commonly called mystagogies because their subject matter was the "mysteries" or sacraments.

Before entering into a discussion of the mystagogy of Ambrose, it is germane to the question to first state that any authentic theology must show how it directs man to a proper and full response to and worship of God, who reveals Himself as a "Thou," and who invites all men into a relationship with Himself. It is primarily through the liturgy that man encounters the living God and is empowered to make an adequate and full response to Him. It is in this light that the expression, *lex orandi, lex credendi*, receives its full meaning. In his everyday life, the supernatural

---

1 It was St. Prosper of Aquitaine who first articulated the expression *legem credenda lex statuat supplicandi* (that is, "the law of prayer may establish the law of belief"), later to be formulated as "the law of belief is the law of prayer." Prosper was born in France, *c.* A.D. 390; d. probably in Rome, after 455. He dialogued with St. Augustine of Hippo on the theology of grace, predestination, and the semi-Pelagian heresy. See F. X. Murphy, "St. Prosper of Aquitaine," *New Catholic Encyclopedia*, Vol. 11, 2nd ed. (Detroit: Gale, 2003), 771–772.

2 Kevin Irwin, "Liturgical Theology," in *The New Dictionary of Sacramental Worship*, ed. Peter E. Fink (Collegeville, MN: Liturgical Press, 1990), 722.

3 St. Ambrose (b. Trèves [Trier, Germany], *c.* A.D. 339; d. Milan, 397): Bishop of Milan, Father and Doctor of the Church. Ambrose was influenced in his theology by St. Athanasius, Didymus the Blind, St. Cyril of Jerusalem, St. Basil, and Hippolytus. His exegesis of Scripture was profoundly influenced by the allegorical method of Philo and Origen. St. Ambrose was instrumental in the conversion of St. Augustine of Hippo to Christianity. See M. R. P. McGuire, "St. Ambrose," *New Catholic Encyclopedia*, Vol. 1., 2nd ed. (Detroit: Gale, 2003), 337–340.

4 The term *neophyte* (Gr. νεόφυτος; L. *neophytus*—new plant) refers to the newly initiated Christian, that is, a person who has recently converted and received the sacraments of baptism, confirmation, and Eucharist. In the Catholic Church today, a new convert is called a *neophyte* for a year after baptism.

faith of man is expressed most fully in the liturgical act. With that said, let us now take a step back into the fourth century.

Although doubted for a long time, scholars are now quite certain that Ambrose was the author of *De sacramentis* (*On the sacraments*), a set of six sermons that were probably preached in the week after Easter, about 391. *De mysteriis* (*On the mysteries*) appears to be an abridged version of *De sacramentis*, which was prepared for publication. Probably due to the *disciplina arcani*, *De mysteriis* is a much shorter text, which omits certain parts found in *De sacramentis*.

The purpose of mystagogy[5] in the fourth century was to introduce the newly baptized Christian to the knowledge of the "mystery."[6] Consequently, mystagogy can refer to the initiation, via the liturgy, of the neophyte into the mystery of salvation that has taken place in history. For us to understand this, it is worth investigating how the Church Fathers saw the liturgical rites as embodying the mystery of salvation and enabling the Christian to participate in it.

There were four writers in the Patristic period whose mystagogical instructions are available to us today: John Chrysostom, Cyril of Jerusalem, Theodore of Mopsuestia, and Ambrose of Milan. Due to the depth and mystery of the subject matter, each Father tends to emphasize different aspects. John Chrysostom concentrates on the moral implications for participating in the sacramental life and the attainment of the eschatological realities that the sacraments promise,[7] "Cyril stress[es] how the liturgical present image[s] the scriptural past; Theodore stress[es] how the liturgical present foreshadow[s] the eschatological future; and Ambrose stress[es] how visible rites point to invisible realities."[8] There is a great mystery in each of these.

For Ambrose, it is a question of how a ritual action makes present the mystery of salvation accomplished in Jesus Christ centuries earlier. Ambrose believes that it has been actuated throughout salvation history, even prior to the coming of Christ, by way of figure and truth, shadow and reality. The typological interpreta-

---

5 Mystagogical catechesis, or liturgical catechesis, is the specific form of catechesis given to neophytes in order to explain the significance of rituals, signs, and symbols that they experienced at their initiation at the Easter Vigil. Mystagogy contrasts with the pre-baptismal catechesis of the catechumen (that is, the unbaptized person) which is didactic in nature and focuses on the foundational Christian beliefs formulated in the Creeds. See "Mystagogy," *New Catholic Encyclopedia*, vol. 10, 2nd ed. (Detroit: Gale, 2003), 77. Catechesis, in general, refers to the instruction given to those whom, having been evangelized, have come to initial faith. Catechesis "has the twofold objective of maturing the initial faith and of educating the true disciple of Christ by means of a deeper and more systematic knowledge of the person and the message of our Lord Jesus Christ" (Pope John Paul II, *Catechesi tradendae: Apostolic Exhortation on Catechesis in Our Time* [Rome: 1979], 19).

6 Enrico Mazza, *Mystagogy: A Theology of Liturgy in the Patristic Age* (New York: Pueblo, 1989), 25.

7 Mazza, *Mystagogy*, 166.

8 William Harmless, *Augustine and the Catechumenate* (Collegeville MN: The Liturgical Press, 1995), 364.

tion of salvation history by Ambrose is a useful pedagogical tool to provide great insight into the eternal mysteries which every human person is called to enter.[9] It is through typology that Ambrose explains the notion of ritual memorial or *anamnesis*,[10] which was central to the early Church's understanding of making a past event present to those participating in the liturgical action.

Ritual Memorial

Although Ambrose does not use the terms *anamnesis* or ritual memorial, he does show the meaning of the Christian sacraments by referring to the key concepts of *anamnesis* and actualization. The liturgies of ancient Israel constituted memorials of an ancient event not by way of mere reminiscence, but by making the actual event present or by making each person (liturgically) a contemporary of the past event. In the *Mishnah* (a collection of Jewish law from the early third century), Rabbi Gamaliel puts it this way:

> In every generation a man must so regard himself as if he came forth himself out of Egypt, for it is written, "And you shall tell your son on that day saying, 'It is because of that which the Lord did for me when I came forth out of Egypt.'"[11]

The Christian Eucharist instituted by Christ at the Last Supper conforms with, and continues, this ancient Jewish concept of liturgical memorial. As we shall see, Ambrose follows this tradition in his catecheses, *De sacramentis* and *De mysteriis*, using allegory as his pedagogical method of explanation.

Jewish cultic practice was based upon an historic-prophetic memorial due to the fact that God has manifested Himself in history. There are two types of memory: simple memory which is static, and a living act of commemoration which

---

9 The use of the phrase "eternal mysteries" here must be clearly understood. Just as the saving events of Christ's life were historical, so also are each succeeding liturgy we celebrate throughout our lives. They are events in our historical lives which have eternal effects in us. At the liturgy, through our memorial of what Christ accomplished once and for all, the cross is realized anew in the historical events of our lives precisely insofar as his offering is realized in our self-offerings. Thus, through the sacraments we are able to participate in the mysterious, eternal self-offering of Christ to the Father—expressed historically on the cross—and the Father's loving acceptance of this offering by historically raising Jesus from the dead.

10 The Greek word *anamnesis* has been translated variously as "memorial," "remembrance," "commemoration," and "memory" (Hahn, *Letter and Spirit*, 91). Max Thurian (*The Eucharistic Memorial*, trans. J. G. Davies [Richmond, VA: John Knox Press, 1962], 18) prefers to translate *anamnesis* as "memorial" and to abandon "remembrance" and "memory" since the modern conception of these terms implies a mere mental act, a limitation which is lacking in the ancient meaning of the term.

11 Robert Louis Wilken, *The Spirit of Early Christian Thought* (New Haven: Yale University, 2003), 34. Wilken comments, "Those who celebrate Pesach [Passover] are not spectators, they are participants." See also Nahum Glatzer, *The Passover Haggadah, with English Translation, Introduction, and Commentary* (New York: Schocken Books, 1969), 5.

makes the event alive in the present and enables the participants to look to the future.[12] Both the Jewish and Christian cultic practices include this second memorial in which the communal memory enables a people to regenerate itself. The paradigm for *anamnesis* in ancient Israel's liturgical tradition was the Passover *seder*.[13] Although no texts are available to us for the Jewish Passover dating from the time of Jesus, the civil and religious rules which are contained in a body of works called the *Mishnah*[14]—particularly the *Pesahim, Tosefta,* and *Sifrei*—do relate an outline of the Passover meal.[15] To use an expression of John McKenna, this *c.* A.D. 200 text shows a "communal memory that regenerates those remembering."[16]

Key to understanding the liturgy and scriptures of ancient Israel is the notion of covenant. Scripture is clear that Yahweh formed the people of Israel and saw it as His first-born son (see Exod. 4:22; Hos. 11:1). The covenant relationship between Yahweh and Israel is therefore best understood as a family or kinship bond.[17] A solemn ritual oath was always a common element in the establishment of an ancient covenant. Such oaths were not mere words, but "speech acts" or "performative language" because they accomplished what they signified, hence really making a kinship bond between God and Israel.[18] These covenants were frequently sealed by ritual actions (signs) such as sacrifices and meals, which became synonymous with the covenant itself.[19] Further, "The meal was a familial communion between God and man."[20] Covenant signs such as these meals were performed by future generations within a liturgical context in order to renew and remember the historical sealing of the covenant.[21] Following the Exodus event, covenant remembrance was essential for the identity of Israel because it was through the work of Yahweh liberating the people from Egyptian slavery and giving them the Promised Land, in accordance with His promises to their father Abraham, that Israel was formed as a nation. Without this heritage, Israel would not have come into existence.

12 Louis-Marie Chauvet, *Symbol and Sacrament* (Collegeville: The Liturgical Press, 1995), 235.

13 From the Hebrew meaning "order" or "sequence," *seder* is the word used to denote the ritualized dinner observed during Passover.

14 The *Mishnah* (A.D. c. 200) is the first major edition of the Jewish oral traditions. In this document, Rabbi Judah the Patriarch compiled the oral traditions of the Pharisaic period, that is, the end of the Exile until the destruction of the Temple in A.D. 70.

15 Sofia Cavalletti, "Memorial and Typology in Jewish and Christian Liturgy," *Letter and Spirit* 1 (2005): 75.

16 John McKenna, "Eucharist and Memorial," *Worship* 79 (2005): 505.

17 Scott Hahn, *Letter and Spirit: From Written Text to Living Word in the Liturgy,* (London: Darton, Longmann, and Todd, 2006), 55. For a thorough treatment of biblical covenants see Scott Hahn, *Kinship by Covenant: A Canonical Approach to the Fulfillment of God's Saving Promises* (New Haven: Yale University Press, 2009).

18 Hahn, *Letter and Spirit,* 56.

19 Hahn, *Letter and Spirit,* 56.

20 Hahn, *Letter and Spirit,* 57.

21 Hahn, *Letter and Spirit,* 58.

It is for this reason that Chauvet says that the memory of the people both forms and regenerates their identity.[22] In realizing, or better still, *actualizing* their liberation from Egyptian slavery through the liturgical celebration of Passover, future generations of Israelites are formed as God's People and continue the hope of future redemption. It is not a mere looking back at history, but a making present or actualization of the event with its effects, as well as a hope for the future: "In its Passover memorial, Israel receives its past as present, and this gift guarantees a promise of a future."[23] Let us now take a look at the Passover ritual to better appreciate the notion of *anamnesis*.

An integral part of the Passover meal consists of the Haggadah[24] in which the Exodus story is narrated. Here, the youngest *child* asks his father, the celebrant or master of the *seder*, "Why does this night differ from all other nights?"[25] In reply, the father places the *seder* meal in the context of their family story "beginning with the humiliation [namely, Egyptian slavery and idolatry (Deut. 26:5–9)] and ending with the glory [that is, entrance into the Promised Land and the building of the Temple]."[26] This ritual of question and reply had to be performed even if everyone present knew the story, or if there was just one person celebrating Passover because it was the ritual enactment of the *seder* that actualized the ancient event, making it present for the participants. Cavalletti explains, "this history is never really past, since it is reenacted in the person of every Jew who participates in the Passover rite. According to the Mishnah, every Jew must 'consider himself as having come forth from Egypt'."[27] This practice follows that of Moses, who taught the second generation of the Israelites who escaped the clutches of Egypt: "The Lord our God made a covenant with us in Horeb. Not with our fathers did the Lord make this covenant, but with us, who are all of us here alive this day" (Deut. 5:2–3). It is the very act of remembering that inserts one into the event which the celebration commemorates.[28]

---

22 Chauvet, *Symbol and Sacrament*, 233.

23 Chauvet, *Symbol and Sacrament*, 234.

24 *Haggadah* refers to the text that guides the ritual action and prayer of the Jewish *Seder* celebrating Passover. This text provides a commentary of the Exodus story including a religious philosophy of Jewish history, and responses to the children's questions during the ritual. More broadly, the *Haggadah* refers to the non-legal part of Rabbinic literature.

25 Glatzer, *Passover Haggadah*, 21.

26 *Pesahim* 10.4; Glatzer, *Passover Haggadah*, 7.

27 Cavalletti, "Memorial and Typology," 77. See also *Pesahim* 10.5; Glatzer, *Passover Haggadah*, 5.

28 J.J. Von Almen, *Essai sur le repas du Seigneur (Essay on the Lord's Supper)* (Neuchâtel: Delachaux-Niestlé, 1996), 24, cited in Chauvet, *Symbol and Sacrament*, 232.

According to the Mishnah Pesahim, the midrash[29]on Deut. 26:5–8 forms the crux of the Passover Haggadah.[30] The ritual prayers in this section include the narration of past events in the past and present tenses:

> A wandering Aramean was my father; and he went down into Egypt and sojourned there. ... Then we cried to the Lord the God of our fathers, and the Lord heard our voice, and saw our affliction ... and the Lord brought us out of Egypt ... into this place and gave us this land. ... And behold, now I bring the first of the fruit of the ground, which thou, O Lord, has given me.' (Deut. 26:5–10).[31]

The narration switches from the first person singular to the first person plural to enable the narrator to be identified with those of the historical event thus "snatch[ing] it out of its pure anecdotal 'pastness' to reveal its power as a *founding present* ... today, Yahweh gives the promised land to Israel."[32] Chauvet comments that such a narration has the intention of inserting those who are remembering into the very event which the celebration commemorates.[33]

For centuries Christians have seen the link between the Jewish liturgical function and the Christian sacraments. Max Thurian explains that while the Passover was being celebrated:

> ... the Jews could re-live mystically, *sacramentally*, the events of the deliverance and Exodus from Egypt. They became contemporaries of their forefathers and were saved with them. There was in the mystery of the paschal meal a kind of telescoping of two periods of history, the present and the Exodus. The past event became present or rather each person became a contemporary of the past event. ... It is the mystery of this redemptive act accomplished once for all [that is, Christ's act of redemption] and yet ever renewed, present, and applied, that the Church came to designate by the word ... *sacramentum*.[34]

29 Midrash is a type of Rabbinical exegesis of the Hebrew Scriptures compiled between A.D. 400–1200. It is comprised of two forms: the *Haggadah*, which explains non-legal texts (e.g. stories, parables, legends, history, etc.), and the *Halakah*, which explains legal texts.

30 Glatzer, *Passover Haggadah*, 30.

31 The translation is the RSV.

32 Chauvet, *Symbol and Sacrament*, 236.

33 Chauvet, *Symbol and Sacrament*, 232.

34 Thurian, *The Eucharistic Memorial*, 19.

As we can see here, Thurian believes that the Christian sacraments follow the Jewish tradition of memorial or *anamnesis*. Thurian is not alone in this belief.[35] We shall see below that Ambrose shared this notion of *anamnesis*, as evidenced in his mystagogical catechesis on the meaning of the sacraments to his neophyte audience.

Ambrose's Notion of *Anamnesis*

Although he does not use the terms *anamnesis* or memorial, Ambrose refers to a ritual memorial act when he catechizes the newly baptized about their having died with Christ when they descended into the baptismal waters, and having risen with Christ as they came out:

> You were asked: "Do you believe in God the Father almighty?" You said: "I do believe," and you dipped, that is: you were buried. Again you were asked: "Do you believe in our Lord Jesus Christ and in His cross?" You said: "I do believe," and you dipped. So you were also buried together with Christ. For who is buried with Christ rises again with Christ. A third time you were asked: Do you believe also in the Holy Spirit?" You said: "I do believe," you dipped a third time, so that the threefold confession absolved the multiple lapse of a former life.[36]

This passage demonstrates the belief that performative language or "speech-acts" constitute this liturgical rite, enabling the catechumens to truly die with Christ, to enter into His tomb and to rise again with Him to newness of life.[37] Through the liturgical ritual the catechumen is *actually* conformed to Christ in His death and resurrection. Ambrose is far from innovative here. Rather, he is within a constant tradition stemming from the testimony of St. Paul:

> Do you not know that all of us who have been baptized into Christ Jesus were baptized into this death? We were buried therefore with him by baptism into death, so that as Christ was raised from the dead by the glory of the Father, we too might walk in newness of life. For if we have been united with him

35 Other authors have noted such a relation: Chauvet, *Symbol and Sacrament*, 231–233; Wilken, *Spirit of Early Christian Thought*, 34–35; Cavaletti, "Memorial and Typology," 75–82; Hahn, *Letter and Spirit*, 88–102.

36 *De sacramentis* ["On the Sacraments"], bk. II, c. 7, n. 20, in *Patrologiae Cursus Completus, Series Latina*, ed. J.P. Migne (Paris: Garnier and J.P. Migne, 1844–1864), 16:429. Hereafter abbreviated *PL*.

37 Hahn, *Letter and Spirit*, 89.

> in a death like his, we shall certainly be united with him in a resurrection like his (Rom. 6:3–5).[38]

The abstruse nature of the sacramental realities for the neophytes does not escape the purview of Ambrose. He is keenly aware of the need for his audience to appreciate the power of the sacraments to put the faithful in contact with the saving events of Christ's life. In order to provide credibility to his argument, Ambrose enumerates example after example of Old Testament events, all demonstrating God's power to save. The virtue of this method of mystogogical teaching highlights what Louis Bouyer sees as the memorial content of the Eucharist: first, the cross of Christ; second, all the events and persons leading up to Christ throughout history; and, finally, the effects resulting from the passion of Christ including His resurrection, ascension, and second coming.[39] Bouyer points out that through the Liturgy of the Word, God's actions throughout human history are remembered by the faithful. The Liturgy of the Word consequently functions to lead into the Liturgy of the Eucharist where the climax of God's actions through the total giving of Himself in the Word made flesh is commemorated. We therefore can see an integral relationship between the two successive parts, which together form "one liturgy of the Word."[40] Mystagogical catechesis, like that of Ambrose, opens up to the faithful a deep understanding of the mysteries that are commemorated through the Eucharistic memorial of Christ acting through, with, and in the community.

By relating the story of Christ opening the deaf mute's ears to hear the Gospel (Mark 1:31–37), Ambrose hopes to show that the sacramental rites have opened the hearts of the neophytes that they may perceive the mysteries of salvation hidden in the Old Testament and made manifest in the Christian sacraments.[41] Beginning with St. Paul's words, "His [God's] eternal power also and divinity are estimated by His works" (Rom. 1:20),[42] the catechetical instruction boldly moves to the Old Testament to consider the figures of the great Christian mysteries.

Baptism

In the baptismal liturgy, Ambrose likens the *power* of the sacrament to that which occurred in the Old Testament when the Hebrews passed through the Red Sea through the power of Moses as he placed his staff into the waters,[43] or when the prophet Elisha spoke the word and raised the head of the axe to the surface of the

---

38 RSV.

39 Louis Bouyer, *Liturgical Piety* (Notre Dame, IN: University of Notre Dame Press, 1955), 78–79.

40 Bouyer, *Liturgical Piety*, 79.

41 *De mysteriis*, ["On the Mysteries"], c. III, nn. 3–4 (*PL* 16:389–390).

42 *De mysteriis*, c. III, n. 8 (*PL* 16:391).

43 *De mysteriis*, c. III, n. 12 (*PL* 16:392–393).

water,[44] or when Naaman went to Elisha seeking a cure for his leprosy and was told to bathe in the waters of the Jordan seven times.[45] Each of these events prefigured the Christian sacrament of baptism in different ways.

First, the Hebrews were fleeing the slavery of the Egyptians but were faced with certain death when hemmed in by the Red Sea with their enemy at their heels.[46] It was only through the promise that God would deliver them that Moses was able to perform the miracle of parting the Red Sea to enable the people to be liberated with the subsequent destruction of their enemy when the waters returned. Second, Ambrose understands the episode of Elisha raising the submerged axe head (2 Kings 6:5) as a symbol of the unbaptized who, submerged by sin, will surely die without the powerful word of God which raises them to new life.[47] Third, Ambrose interprets Naaman's miraculous cure as symbolizing liberation from sin, a disease of the soul.[48] Ambrose is emphatic that these Old Testament mysteries were inferior to the Christian sacraments for they did not bring eternal life, but only temporal blessings.

These three Old Testament events help interpret the institution of Christian baptism by Jesus at His own baptism by John in the Jordan (Matt. 3:13–17). We read that John's objection is that Jesus should be baptizing him, as this would seem more fitting considering He is the Son of God. However, Jesus explains that in order to fulfill all righteousness, it must be John who does the baptizing. It is not Jesus who is cleansed when He descends into the waters; rather it is the water that is sanctified by the Word of God with the descent of the Holy Spirit and the blessing of the Father. The waters of the Jordan were made holy for the sake of our sanctification. It is clear to Ambrose that the baptismal act must be seen in this context.[49] All who descend into the baptismal waters descend with Christ and are sanctified by the Holy Spirit. Just as the Father in speaking of Jesus declared: "This is my beloved Son in whom I am well pleased," so too those who are baptized into Christ are transformed into the likeness of Christ to be the Father's beloved children. They are made righteous and are filled with the justice of Christ by the work of the Trinity.

Ambrose provides other types or figures of baptism found in the Old Testament. First, at creation the Spirit hovered over the waters and brought about the first creation.[50] Later, Noah entered the ark while the waters flooded the earth

---

44 *De mysteriis*, c. IX, n. 51 (*PL* 16:405–406).

45 *De mysteriis*, c. III, nn. 16–17; c. IV, n. 21 (*PL* 16:393–395).

46 *De mysteriis*, c. IX, n. 51 (*PL* 16:405–406); *De sacramentis*, bk. I, c. 6, nn. 20–22 (*PL* 16:423–424).

47 *De mysteriis*, c. IX, n. 51 (*PL* 16:405–406); *De sacramentis*, bk. II, c. 4, n. 11 (*PL* 16:426–427).

48 *De sacramentis*, bk. I, c. 5, n.13–15 (*PL* 16:421–422).

49 *De sacramentis*, bk. I, c. 5, n.15–19 (*PL* 16:422–423).

50 *De mysteriis*, c. III, n. 9 (*PL* 16:392).

and purified it from sin.[51] Noah sends out a raven which does not return—symbolic of sin—then sends out a dove which returns with an olive branch—symbolic of peace of soul and the dwelling of the Holy Spirit who brings about a new creation.[52] The episode of Moses sweetening the bitter waters of Marah by casting a piece of wood into the fountain is a figure of the wood of the Christ's cross which bestows the sweetness of grace to the waters of baptism.[53]

Ambrose uses these and other Old Testament stories to demonstrate that since God has worked wonders for His people in former times, there is nothing to prevent Him from working even greater wonders now that His Son has come to dwell among us.[54] The graces and blessings that the neophytes have experienced in the Easter liturgy are of surpassing worth compared to the works of God in the Old Testament. For example, Ambrose compares the "manna [which] rained upon the Jews from heaven" and the true bread from heaven, which is the body of Christ.[55] Ambrose states, "He who ate the manna died; he who has eaten this body will effect for himself remission of sins and 'shall not die forever'."[56] Using this method of allegory and figure, Ambrose demonstrates again and again the surpassing greatness of the New Testament sacraments.

The Eucharist

In so far as the Eucharistic liturgy is concerned, there is evidence that Ambrose recognizes the aspect of memorial here too. In his teaching about the Eucharistic prayer to the neophytes, he relates how the narrative begins in the past tense, but switches to the present tense when Christ speaks the words of institution: "Take and drink of this, all of you; for this is my blood." For Ambrose, it is not the priest who speaks these words at the Mass, but Christ Himself.[57] As with every performative action which accomplishes the reality that it describes, so too Christ's words have a performative effect. The wine in the cup "becomes blood by heavenly consecration"[58] that the "price of redemption may be effected."[59] This aspect of memorial enables the participants in the liturgical rite to be present at the offering of Christ in His Paschal Mystery.

---

51 *De mysteriis*, c. III, n. 10 (*PL* 16:392).

52 *De mysteriis*, c. III, n. 11 (*PL* 16:392).

53 *De mysteriis*, c. III, n. 14 (*PL* 16:393).

54 Pamela Jackson, *The Holy Spirit in the Catechesis and Mystagogy of Cyril of Jerusalem, Ambrose, and John Chrysostom* (Ann Arbor, MI: University Microfilms International, 1987), 219.

55 *De sacramentis*, bk. IV, c. 5, n. 24 (*PL* 16:444).

56 *De sacramentis*, bk. IV, c. 5, n. 24 (*PL* 16:444).

57 *De sacramentis*, bk. IV, c. 5, n. 22 (*PL* 16:444).

58 *De sacramentis*, bk. IV, c. 4, n. 19 (*PL* 16:442).

59 *De sacramentis*, bk. IV, c. 4, n. 20 (*PL* 16:443).

Again, Ambrose does not deviate from tradition, for the Eucharistic prayer that he describes in detail was widely used. Aimé Martimort has analyzed the various parts of the prayer used by Ambrose and concludes: "The formulas so far mentioned within the Eucharistic prayer of the Roman rite—the Preface, narrative of the Last Supper, the anamnesis and the offering—are witnessed to in the *Apostolic Tradition* of Hippolytus and have been practically fixed in the Roman usage since the time of St. Ambrose."[60]

Ambrose further explains that as often as we receive the body and blood of Christ, we proclaim His death and the remission of our sins.[61] In support of this, Ambrose provides us with part of the Eucharistic prayer that was heard at the Easter celebration:

> Therefore, mindful of His most glorious passion and resurrection from the dead and ascension into heaven, we offer you this immaculate victim, a reasonable sacrifice, an unbloody victim, this holy bread, and chalice of eternal life. And we ask and pray that you accept this offering upon your sublime altar through the hands of your angels, just as you deigned to accept the gifts of your just son Abel and the sacrifice of our patriarch Abraham and what the highest priest Melchisedech offered you.[62]

This being "mindful" or this "remembrance" of Christ's most glorious passion and resurrection from the dead and ascension into heaven, as Ambrose explains, is the "remedy" for our sins.[63] In faith we believe that Christ's redemptive act frees us from our sins, but how is this freedom appropriated in each individual person? Ambrose would answer: *liturgically*—through the power of the sacraments to make the redemptive work of Christ actualized here and now for us. It must be remembered that as with the Passover *seder*, where the participants are actually considered to be liberated from Egypt with their predecessors, so too the Christian faithful, as members of Christ's mystical body, are not mere spectators, but real participants in the actualization of Christ's death and resurrection and thereby receive remission for their sins.

How are we to understand Ambrose's connection of the ritual action with Jesus' saving works? An early twentieth century debate about the "*Mysteriengegenwart*," the "mystery presence," may shed some light on the issue. Odo Casel, a German Benedictine liturgical scholar, initiated the debate when he claimed that Christ and His saving works are the basic mystery. In John McKenna's brief summary of the debate, he notes that Casel believed: "To be saved by Christ's actions, we must

60 Aimé Martimort, *The Signs of the New Covenant* (Collegeville, MN: Liturgical Press, 1963), 168.

61 *De sacramentis*, bk. IV, c. 6, n. 28 (*PL* 16:446).

62 *De sacramentis*, bk. IV, c. 6, n. 27 (*PL* 16:445–446).

63 *De sacramentis*, bk. IV, c. 6, n. 28 (*PL* 16:446).

somehow come into contact with them. Christ [...] makes himself present in the liturgy together with those saving deeds."[64] In a partial affirmation of Casel's theology, Edward Kilmartin writes: "The Eucharist renders present the reality of the mystery of the cross in the form of a sacramental memorial meal of the Church. .... The goal of the Eucharist is the self-offering of the Church with Christ ... in order that believers be changed into the true body of Christ, and become themselves a holy sacrifice."[65] This sheds valuable light upon Ambrose's emphasis on being "mindful" in order that "we proclaim the death of the Lord."[66] In so doing, we are put in direct contact with the saving work of Christ.

Allegorical Method

The most striking thing about Ambrose's *De sacramentis* and *De mysteriis* is his dramatic allegorical method for interpreting the Scriptures.[67] This method, developed within the Alexandrian school, was probably adopted by Ambrose due to his familiarity with the writings of Origen. The method employed three senses of Scripture: the literal, moral, and mystical.[68] The Alexandrian school tended to "see everything as symbolic of the eschatological blessings revealed in Christ,"[69] and as a result they were able to arrive at a profound grasp of what Scripture meant as a whole.

The presupposition behind the Alexandrian method is that since all truth comes from the Holy Spirit, "the words of scripture can be used to illuminate any truth to which they can be made to apply."[70] In addition, the precedent for the allegorical or typological method is found in the New Testament itself. For example, in 1 Corinthians 10:1–11 St. Paul sees the cloud and the passage through the Red Sea as prefigurements of Christian baptism. He sees in the manna and water from the rock a prefigurement of the Eucharist, the rock being a type of Christ.[71] St. Paul explains that under the literal historical sense of the Old Testament texts, there is a spiritual sense from which we can draw instruction, for which reason these ancient events were committed to writing. Since Ambrose saw Scripture as

64 McKenna, "Eucharist and Memorial," 513; see also Odo Casel, "Mysteriengegenwart," *Jahrbuch fur Liturgiewissenschaft* 8 (1928): 145.

65 Edward Kilmartin, *The Eucharist in the West: History and Theology*, ed. Robert J. Daly (Collegeville, MN: Liturgical Press, 1998), 199–200, 202.

66 *De sacramentis*, bk. IV, c. 6, nn. 27–28 (*PL* 16:445–446).

67 Edward Yarnold, *The Awe Inspiring Rites of Initiation: The Origins of the R.C.I.A.*, 2nd ed. (Collegeville, MN: The Liturgical Press, 1994), 98.

68 Jackson, *Holy Spirit*, 91.

69 Henri Crouzel, "Biblical Exegesis: III Spiritual Exegesis," in *Sacramentum Mundi: An Encyclopedia of Theology, Absolute and Contingent to Constantinian Era*, eds. Karl Rahner *et al* (New York: Herder and Herder, 1969), I: 205.

70 Yarnold, *Awe Inspiring*, 99.

71 Crouzel, *Biblical Exegesis*, 202. See also St. Paul's use of allegory in Gal. 4:21–31.

the authoritative source in answering all questions, he draws narrative material, moral instruction, imagery, and typology from Scripture for the content of his catechetical instruction.[72] As with his contemporaries, Ambrose understands that the "eschatological good things of the Old Testament are the figure, the hope, the foretaste, but that the New Testament gives us their true form here below, a real though imperfect possession of them 'in a mirror, dimly.'"[73]

Ambrose begins *De mysteriis* by explaining how he used Scripture in his pre-baptismal catechesis. He reminds the catechumens that they drew from the scriptures a Christian rule of life: "to walk in the paths of our elders and to read in their steps, and to obey the divine oracles."[74] This exhortation referred to the lives of the patriarchs or the precepts of the Proverbs which were read to them during their prebaptismal catechesis. Ambrose is attempting to show that the catechumens are like the Old Testament people who journeyed through the desert in preparation for entering the Promised Land. Since the catechumens are on their way to meet Christ in and through the sacraments, they must be morally and spiritually purified for this encounter. As Chauvet notes, there is an "authentic evangelical tension" between life and cult, ethics and ritual practice.[75] The liturgy must be lived out in one's ethical life for the very living of it is a self-reflective act since the liturgy is thus accomplished.[76] The truth of one's gratitude to God as expressed in the liturgy must be verified in the recognition of the poor. God did not require mere lip-service or ritual sacrifice, but steadfast love and a humble and contrite heart (see Ps. 51:18–19; Isa. 1:10–17; Hos. 6:6; Matt. 9:13, 12:7). This connection between liturgy and ethical life is the basis for Ambrose's moral catechetical instruction of the catechumens. We can see here that it is by reading the Scriptures that the people are formed.

Ambrose's use of Scripture in his post-baptismal catecheses, *De sacramentis* and *De mysteriis*, was aimed at giving a "reasoned account of the sacraments."[77] Although Ambrose does not speak again of his Scriptural method in these works, we are able to garner deeper insights into it through the rhetorical techniques he used to explain how the realities recorded in the Gospels are personally applied to the neophytes in the sacraments.[78]

Using the Old Testament events, persons, and symbols as types of the sacraments of the Christian dispensation, Ambrose explains the details of the single Christian story that has been gradually disclosed over the course of salvation

72 Jackson, *Holy Spirit*, 90.

73 Crouzel, *Biblical Exegesis*, 202.

74 *De mysteriis*, c. 1, n. 1 (*PL* 16:389).

75 Chauvet, *Symbol and Sacrament*, 228.

76 Chauvet, *Symbol and Sacrament*, 238.

77 *De mysteriis*, c. 1, n. 2 (*PL* 16:389); *De sacramentis*, bk. I, c. 1, n. 1 (*PL* 16:417).

78 Jackson, *Holy Spirit*, 91.

history. This follows the principle that God has entered human history to reveal Himself as a "Thou," inviting people into covenantal relationship with Himself. Jean Danielou explains:

> The sacraments are conceived in relation to the acts of God in the Old Testament and the New. God acts in the world; His actions are the *mirabilia*,[79] the deeds that are His alone. God creates, judges, makes a covenant, is present, makes holy, delivers. These same acts are carried out in different phases of the history of salvation. There is, then, a fundamental analogy between these actions. The sacraments are simply the continuation in the era of the Church of God's acts in the Old Testament and the New. This is the proper significance of the relationship between the Bible and the liturgy. The Bible is a sacred history; the liturgy is a sacred history.[80]

Ambrose perceives the fundamental analogy between the works of God in the Old Testament and in the New Testament. It is for this reason that he reminds his audience of the *mirabilia* of God in the Old Testament; and in doing so he explains the formative and regenerative power of the sacramental liturgy to make the Christian people. Without the memory of where they have come from, the Christian people lose their identity.

Proceeding in this fashion, Ambrose shows in *De mysteriis* that baptism and the mystery of the cross of Christ were present in the great flood and Noah's ark.[81] As stated above, the flood was a symbol of the cleansing of the flesh from all carnal sin, while the raven was the figure of sin that went out and did not return. Likewise, Ambrose sees images of the power of baptism in the cloud that the Hebrew people were under as they traveled through the wilderness, as well as by their passing through the sea. The cloud cools the carnal passions and the waters destroy the slavery of sin as symbolized in the Egyptians.[82]

The correspondence between the Old Testament and New Testament persons, events, and things is referred to as "figure" or "truth" by Ambrose: "the figure itself was of benefit to us, since it is an indication of the truth."[83] Following this principle, Ambrose provides the example of the angel who descended upon the pool of Bethesda (John 5:4), giving it the power to heal whoever was first to enter the waters. In the angel, Ambrose sees a figure of Christ who has come to heal the

79 *Mirabilia* is the Latin word for wonders, miracles, or marvelous works.

80 Danielou, "The Sacraments in the History of Salvation," in *The Liturgy and the Word of God* (Collegeville, MN: Liturgical Press, 1959), 28.

81 *De mysteriis*, c. 3, nn. 10–11 (*PL* 16:392).

82 *De mysteriis*, c. 3, nn. 12–13 (*PL* 16:392–393).

83 *De sacramentis*, bk. II, c. 1, n. 2 (*PL* 16:425); see also, Jackson, *Holy Spirit*, 93.

infirmities of all men through His death and resurrection, the effects of which are applied to us through the sacrament of Baptism.[84] In *De mysteriis,* Ambrose refers to the angel as the "shadow" of Christ who would heal all men together.[85] For Ambrose, the truth or reality not only surpasses the figure or shadow, but is also the exemplar and archetype of it. In contrasting Christ with Melchisedech, Ambrose states:

> As for Melchisedech, it is said that he has neither beginning of days nor end. If Melchisedech does not have beginning of days, could Christ have had it? Yet it is not more a figure than truth. You see, then, that He himself is both the first and the last: first, because He is the author of all; last, not because he finds the end, but because He includes all things.[86]

Ambrose utilizes images to manifest to the neophytes the great dignity they receive in becoming children of God through baptism. He identifies them with the bride of the Canticles who goes out to meet her Bridegroom, who is Christ the Lord. According to Ambrose, upon seeing the newly baptized, the angels exclaimed: "Who is this that cometh up from the desert whitewashed?"[87] It is impossible not to see this as a reference to the great love song of the Old Testament: "Who is that coming up from the wilderness, leaning upon her beloved?" (Song 8:5). Traditionally the Jews saw this canticle as the dialogue of love between God, the bridegroom, and Israel, His beloved. The Fathers of the Church, however, saw it as an allegory of the mystical union between Christ and His Church (see Eph. 5:21–33).

By means of typology, Ambrose is able to demonstrate the unity of God's saving plan for humanity when the Old and New Testaments are superimposed. He does this by showing Christ, the protagonist, being present by way of prefigurements in the Old Testament and by imitations in the sacramental life. "Typology unites past, present, and future."[88] The prefigurements are so real for Ambrose that it seems that they are identical with what they prefigure in the New Testament. For example, he likens the rod of Aaron to the newly baptized. The "baptized are no longer 'dry sticks,' but have begun to bear fruit"[89] in the baptistery or tent of the high priest. Again, the washing of Naaman from leprosy (2 Kings 5:14) is identified with the cleansing of baptism that washes away the leprosy of sin.[90]

84 *De sacramentis,* bk. II, c. 2, nn. 3–7 (*PL* 16:425–426).

85 *De mysteriis,* c. 4, nn. 22, 24 (*PL* 16:395–396).

86 *De sacramentis,* bk. V, c. 1, n. 1 (*PL* 16:445–446).

87 *De sacramentis,* bk. IV, c. 2, n. 5 (*PL* 16:437).

88 Mazza, *Mystagogy,* 34.

89 Mazza, *Mystagogy,* 35.

90 Mazza, *Mystagogy,* 36.

Conclusions

The Eucharistic liturgy was given by Christ to His apostles within the context of the Jewish liturgical tradition which was formed upon *anamnesis* or ritual memorial. Given this context it is clear that the event and effects of Jesus' paschal mystery are actualized for each generation of Christians through the mode of liturgical memorial. Without the liturgy, we would be incapable of being present at the Cross or the empty tomb. But divine providence has provided a means by which we are not mere spectators in these pivotal events of human history, but are rather actually present as contemporaries with Mary and the others at the foot of the cross.

The maxim *lex orandi, lex credendi* also bears new or deeper meaning when we consider that our prayer, which includes the memorial of various mysteries, rules our faith. For it is through our prayer that we are present at the mysteries of our faith. All of this shows to us that liturgy is our teacher and a primary source for our theology. Liturgy teaches us that the best way to show the importance of a past event is to recount it in the way that liturgy memorializes such an event in the present. We do not tell the liturgy, rather we liturgically tell the story that we memorialize.[91]

Much more could be said on the manner in which memorial actually operates and how the various aspects of the mysteries hidden for all ages are made manifest to us through the liturgy. But suffice to say, Ambrose and his contemporaries have contributed much to our insight into these mysteries.

91 Chauvet, *Symbol and Sacrament*, 194.

Letter & Spirit 7 (2011): 67-90

"The Yoke of Servitude"
Christian Non-Observance of the Law's Cultic Precepts in Patristic Sources

~: **Michael Patrick Barber, Ph.D.** :~

John Paul the Great Catholic University
San Diego, CA

Introduction

The early Church Fathers' emphasis on the unity of the Old and New Testaments[1] has deservedly received a great deal of attention. St. Augustine's famous dictum is frequently and appropriately cited as representative of early Christian hermeneutics: "The New Testament is concealed in the Old; the Old Testament is revealed in the New." The belief that the scriptures were to be read as "a single book" provided the basis for the Fathers' typological and spiritual analysis of the biblical texts. [2] The rise of heretical movements such as Gnosticism and Marcionism in the second century—groups that disputed the validity of the scriptures of Israel—necessitated an even more pronounced emphasis on the continuity of God's plan in the Bible. What is often neglected, however, is the way the Fathers also recognized *discontinuity* in salvation history. In a way, this recognition also crystallized out of theological controversy.

Long before Marcion insisted on jettisoning Israel's scriptures, the Church's leadership had to deal with radical claims made by heretics who stood at the opposite end of the spectrum. Famous in the apostolic period were the Judaizers,

---

1 Using the terminology of "Old Testament" and "New Testament" in a paper on patristic interpretation poses difficulties. Clearly ancient Jews would not have used these terms. Indeed, in ancient Judaism there was no universal recognition of a closed set of authoritative sacred books. In the Talmud the book of Sirach is (apparently) quoted as Scripture (see *Baba Batra* 92b; *agigah* 13a)—a book that was later excluded by the rabbis. Moreover, in the Dead Sea Scrolls there appears to be no distinction between "biblical" books and other sectarian documents. Moreover, the Christian canon only received its final authoritative shape after the councils at Rome (A.D. 382), Hippo (A.D. 393) and Carthage (A.D. 397). For a thorough discussion of issues relating to the development of the canon see Lee Martin McDonald and James A. Sanders, eds., *The Canon Debate* (Peabody: Hendrickson, 2002). Rather than constantly offering qualifications for the terminology, and for the sake of convenience, the phrase "Old Testament" will be used in this article to describe Israel's sacred texts that the Church came to recognize as authoritative Scripture.

2 See the discussion of the patristic approach to the Bible in Robert Louis Wilken, *The Spirit of Early Christianity* (New Haven: Yale University Press, 2003), 61–69, especially 62. See also Jean Danielou, *From Shadows to Reality: Studies in the Biblical Typology of the Fathers* (London: Burns & Oates, 1960).

who insisted that faith in Christ required acceptance of *all* the precepts of the Torah, including circumcision. This controversy was addressed at the council of Jerusalem and recorded in Acts 15. A decision was rendered that would forever impact Christian understanding: Christians need not be circumcised or abide by all of the dietary regulations of the Mosaic Law.[3] Christ has "fulfilled" the Law, releasing Christians from many of the requirements of the Old Testament. In explaining why Gentiles should not be forced to submit to certain precepts of the Law, Peter put it this way: "Now therefore why do you make trial of God by putting *a yoke upon the neck of the disciples which neither our fathers nor we have been able to bear*? But we believe that we shall be saved through the grace of the Lord Jesus, just as they will" (Acts 15:10–11, emphasis mine). Christ's "fulfillment" of the Law paradoxically involved some level of "discontinuity" with portions of the Old Testament.

The decision of the council, however, is somewhat perplexing. On the one hand, the narrative in Acts makes it clear that it was Peter's appeal that finally moved the council to its resolution. Before Peter's speech there had been "much debate," but after the speech we are told that "the assembly fell silent" (see Acts 15:7, 12). On the other hand, the interpretive principles behind Peter's resolution are not expressly spelled out. What enabled Peter to identify a subset of laws—a "yoke ... which neither our fathers nor we have been able to bear"—from which believers could be dispensed?[4] The task of unpacking the interpretive and theological principles intuited by the apostolic decree was left to the fathers.

Other early Jewish criticisms of Christianity occasioned the need for precise, exegetical answers to the type of questions found in Acts 15. Christian non-observance of Old Testament ordinances scandalized the Jews. Justin's interlocutor in his *Dialogue with Trypho* appears to voice the concerns many Jews had about Christianity:[5]

---

3 While it was decided that Christians should abstain from certain foods (for example, food offered to idols and meat containing blood), there is no indication that this applied only to the "clean" foods of the Old Testament (compare Acts 15:28–29).

4 It is well known that emergent Judaism referred to the Law in terms of a "yoke." See, for example, James D. G. Dunn, *The Epistle to the Galatians* (London: A. & C. Black), 263; E. P. Sanders, *Paul and Palestinian Judaism* (London: SCM Press, 1977), 93–94. See also a quote from the Mishnah: "He that takes upon himself the yoke of the Law, from him shall be taken away the yoke of the [oppressing foreign] kingdom and the yoke of worldly care; but he that throws off the yoke of the Law, upon him shall be laid the yoke of the kingdom and the yoke of worldly care" (*m. Abot.* 3:5; cited from Herbert Danby, *The Mishnah* [Oxford: Oxford University Press, 1933; reprinted 1985]).

5 Some scholars have questioned whether or not Justin's *Dialogue* was directed towards a Jewish audience. See, for example, C. H. Cosgrove, "Justin Martyr and the Emerging Christian Canon," *VC* (1982): 211. For an excellent defense of the traditional view see Allert, *Revelation*, 37–61. For a recent and comprehensive overview of scholarship on Justin Martyr see Michael Slusser, "Justin Scholarship: Trends and Trajectories," in *Justin Martyr and His Worlds*, eds. S. Parvis and P. Foster (Minneapolis: Fortress Press, 2007), 13–21.

> But this is what we are most puzzled about, that you who claim to be pious ... do not keep the feasts or Sabbaths, nor do you practice the rite of circumcision. You place your hope in a crucified man, and still expect to receive favors from God when you disregard his commandments. ... [You] spurn the commandments ... and then you try to convince us that you know God, when you fail to do those things that every God-fearing person would do. If, then, you can give a satisfactory reply to these charges and can show us on what you place your hopes, even though you refuse to observe the Law, we will listen to you most willingly, and then we can go on and examine in the same manner our other differences (*Dialogue* 10.3).[6]

From this Jewish challenge we can see how a second century Christian apologist might feel obligated to explain not only the *unity* of the divine plan (vs. the Gnostics) but also how that unity made *discontinuity* possible (vs. Jewish antagonists).

This article will focus on how Patristic writers took up this challenge by looking at how they addressed the question of Christian non-observance of ordinances in the Old Covenant Law. What emerges is a substantive and coherent set of interpretive principles which the Fathers derive from a close reading of biblical texts. As we will endeavor to show, these principles can be summarized as follows:

1. Within Israel's scriptures one can distinguish between different categories of law, including those with universal and abiding application (usually identified with the Ten Commandments) and a set of precepts specifically necessitated by the historical circumstances of God's people.

2. Certain laws were not part of God's original arrangement with Israel but were only given later as a means of dealing with their sin. In particular, patristic sources argue that the sacrificial and purity laws were imposed as a response to the sin of the golden calf.

3. Christian non-observance of Israel's ritual code was, paradoxically, anticipated in the Patriarchal period. In some ways, Christianity can be seen as a *return* to this period.

6 *St. Justin Martyr: Dialogue with Trypho*, ed. Michael Slusser, trans. T.B. Falls (Washington, D.C.: Catholic University of America Press, 2003), 18–19. The standard critical edition is *Iustini Martyris: Dialogus cum Tryphone*, ed. Miroslav Marcovich (Berlin: Walter de Gruyter, 1997).

In order to explain Christian non-observance of Israel's cultic laws, Patristic writers make the case that certain laws constituted a "secondary legislation"; "secondary" both in terms of chronological appearance and of importance. As we shall see, advocates of this approach include some of the most influential early Christian writers and sources. Indeed, by the third century this approach becomes so firmly and widely established in Christian understanding that it is treated as part of apostolic tradition itself.

New Testament Origins of the "Secondary Legislation" View

The Fathers' strategy for explaining Christian non-observance of the Old Testament's ritual requirements does not appear *ex nihilo*. Basic components of the "secondary legislation" approach can be traced back to the New Testament itself. Aside from the decree of the Jerusalem council mentioned above, other texts can be highlighted.

Of particular significance is the Gospels' presentation of Jesus' prohibition of divorce and remarriage, something expressly permitted by Moses in Deuteronomy. When challenged to explain this controversial teaching, Jesus explains: "For your hardness of heart [*sklērokardian*] Moses allowed you to divorce your wives, but from the beginning it was not so" (Matthew 19:8; Mark 10:5). Jesus' answer involves three important ideas. First, he makes it clear that he has not introduced discontinuity into God's design for marriage. Israel's scriptures are *themselves* in tension with one another since Deuteronomy's accommodation for divorce is discontinuous with the vision for marriage found in Genesis. Second, Jesus implies that he has come to restore the standards that applied prior to Moses' allowance for divorce and remarriage; he has come to uphold the standards that were "from the beginning." Third, Jesus identifies the reason for Moses' concession: Israel's hardness of heart (*sklērokardian*). Jesus' teaching establishes precedent for a recognition that certain laws—in this case, the procedure for divorce and remarriage in Israel—were given not because such precepts were inherently good and necessary. Rather, they were given as a result of Israel's sinfulness.

While Jesus never explicitly applies these principles to the cultic and ritual regulations of the Old Testament, Christian non-observance of such ordinances does find a basis in the writings of the evangelists. Jesus displays the miraculous power to make "clean" that which the Law stipulated as "unclean" (see Mark 2:40–45). Further, in a sweeping statement that renders distinctions between "clean" and "unclean" as no longer relevant, Jesus states: "There is nothing outside a man which by going into him can defile him; but the things which come out of a man are what defile him" (Mark 7:15). Mark then clearly affirms: "Thus he declared all foods clean" (Mark 7:19). Here Jesus effectively does away with the need for the dietary laws of the Mosaic Code.

In other places Jesus also appears to relativize Sabbath regulations and the importance of the temple. His healings on the Sabbath suggest that he himself transcends its significance (see Mark 3:1–6; Luke 13:10–17; 14:1–6; John 5 and 9). Moreover, he describes himself as "something greater than the temple" (cf. Matt 12:6). Jesus even suggests that he will ultimately replace the physical building standing in Jerusalem with a new temple, his body (John 2:13–22; Mark 14:58).[7] Stephen also appears to relativize the significance of the temple in Acts 7, highlighting prophetic criticism of the cult.[8] Likewise, the author of Hebrews comes to the epoch-changing conclusion that Christ's sacrifice has rendered all the sacrifices required by the Old Testament Law as utterly obsolete (see Hebrews 10:9).

Moreover, the apostle Paul, as clearly seen from his discussion of circumcision in his letter to the Romans, did not believe that Christians were bound by all of the Old Testament laws. Paul appeals to Abraham as precedent for the idea that justification can be found apart from circumcision, pointing out that Abraham was "justified" *prior* to his circumcision (see Romans 4:9–10). For Paul, Christian freedom from the requirement of circumcision is anticipated in the Patriarchal period (prior to Genesis 17).

Further, as with Jesus, Paul advocates that certain aspects of divine legislation were added because of sin. In Galatians 3 he writes:

> Why then the Law? *It was added because of transgressions,* till the offspring should come to whom the promise had been made; and it was ordained by angels through an intermediary. Now an intermediary implies more than one; but God is one (Gal. 3:19–20).

The question of what Paul specifically had in mind when he speaks of the "Law" is difficult. One possibility is the Mosaic Law in its entirety. A closer look at Paul's language, however, suggests that he had in mind certain laws given to Israel after the sin of the golden calf. The Law given to Israel at Sinai was not "added" to a pre-existing set of laws; at Sinai God revealed his Law to Israel *for the first time.* Also, Paul's description of the Law as being given through intermediaries conflicts with the biblical description of the Sinai experience. In Deuteronomy 5:22 Moses explains that the Lord himself spoke *directly* to Israel at Sinai, not through intermediaries. Given these difficulties, Paul's language is best understood as describing precepts imposed *after* the golden calf debacle. There is solid warrant for this

7 For a fuller discussion of Jesus as the new temple, see Nicholas Perrin, *Jesus the Temple* (Grand Rapids: Baker Academic, 2010). See also Michael Barber, "The Historical Jesus and Cultic Restoration Eschatology: The New Temple, the New Priesthood and the New Cult" (Ann Arbor: UMI Dissertation Services, 2010).

8 For a fuller treatment of Stephen's speech see John Kilgallen, *The Stephen Speech* (Rome: Biblical Institute Press, 1976); Martin Scharlemann, *Stephen: A Singular Saint* (Rome: Biblical Institute, 1968).

interpretive approach: Paul himself links the giving of the Law to the aftermath of the golden calf (see 2 Corinthians 3:7–18).[9]

To conclude and summarize: the secondary legislation approach of many patristic writers follows a trajectory of thought that comes straight from the New Testament itself. Turning now to the Patristic sources, we shall see that the interpretive principles employed by the Fathers represent a coherent elaboration of the basic principles found in the teachings of Jesus and in New Testament writers such as St. Paul.

St. Justin Martyr (c. A.D. 100–167)

The first clear articulation of the "secondary legislation" view is found in Justin Martyr's *Dialogue with Trypho* (A.D. 155–167).[10] Justin argues that Christian non-observance of the rite of circumcision finds its precedent in the freedom the Patriarchs enjoyed from such commands:

> For if, as you claim, circumcision had been necessary for salvation, God would not have created Adam uncircumcised; nor would he have looked with favor upon the sacrifice of the uncircumcised Abel, nor would he have been pleased with the uncircumcised Enoch, *who was seen no more, because God took him*. The Lord and his angels let Lot out of Sodom; thus was he saved without circumcision. Noah, the uncircumcised father of our race, was safe with his children in the ark. Melchizedek, the priest of the Most High, was not circumcised, yet Abraham, the first to accept circumcision of the flesh, paid tithes to him and was blessed by him; indeed, God, through David, announced that he would make him a priest forever according to the order of Melchizedek (*Dial.* 19:3–4).[11]

The critical point for Justin is this: if the ceremonial laws were not necessary for holiness in earlier periods, why should we conclude that they have enduring value? He writes, "For if circumcision was not required before the time of Abraham, and

---

9 For more on Paul's treatment of the Law in Galatians 3 see Scott W. Hahn, *Kinship by Covenant: A Canonical Approach to the Fulfillment of God's Saving Promise*; Anchor Yale Bible Reference Library (New Haven: Yale University Press, 2009), 264–267; Terrance Callan, "Pauline Midrash: The Exegetical Background of Gal 3:19b," *Journal of Biblical Literature* 99 (1980): 549–67; John Bligh, *Galatians* (London: St. Paul, 1970), 292–312.

10 See Craig D. Allert, *Revelation, Truth, Canon, and Interpretation: Studies in Justin Martyr's Dialogue with Trypho* (Leiden: Brill, 2002), 33–34; Oskar Skarsaune, *The Proof from Prophecy, A Study in Justin Martyr's Proof-Text Tradition: Text-Type, Provenance, Theological Profile* (Leiden: Brill, 1987), 9; Eric Francis Osborne, *Justin Martyr* (Tübingen: Mohr-Siebeck, 1973), 8.

11 Cited from Slusser, *St. Justin*, 31–32.

if there was no need of Sabbaths, festivals, and sacrifices before Moses, *they are not needed now* [that Christ has come]" (*Dial.* 23:3).[12]

Moreover, Justin identifies the reason why God imposed certain cultic regulations on Israel: idolatry in general and, more pointedly, as a response to the sin of the golden calf:

> We, too, would observe your circumcision of the flesh, your Sabbath days, and, in a word, all your festivals, if we were not aware of the reason why they were imposed upon you, namely, *because of your sins and your hardness of heart* [*sklērokardia*] (*Dial.* 18:2).[13]

> [Israel] showed itself wicked and ungrateful to God *by molding a golden calf* as an idol in the desert. Therefore, God, adapting [*harmosámenos*] his laws to that weak people, *ordered you to offer sacrifices to his name, in order to save you from idolatry* ... (*Dial.* 19:5–6).[14]

> Thus, your sacrifices are not acceptable to God, nor were you first commanded to offer them because of God's need of them, but because of your sins. The same can be said of the temple, which you refer to as the Temple in Jerusalem. God called it his house or court, not as if he needed a house or a court, but because, *by uniting yourselves to him in that place, you might abstain from the worship of idols* (*Dial.* 22:11).[15]

For Justin, God gave Israel certain regulations "in order that, by observing these many precepts, *you might have him constantly before your eyes and refrain from every unjust and impious act*" (*Dial.* 46:5).[16]

Justin's argument is not based merely on allegorical readings of Old Testament texts (though certainly he does employ spiritual exegesis at various points). Rather, his argument is primarily rooted in a salvation-historical approach that makes recourse to what he sees as the literal sense of biblical passages.

This is especially clear in chapter 22 of the *Dialogue with Trypho*. Here Justin identifies four passages which make it clear that the ceremonial laws were not part of God's original arrangement with Israel but were added because of sin. Justin observes that the prophet Ezekiel described how the Lord gave Israel laws that "were

12 Cited from Slusser, *St. Justin*, 37 (my emphasis).

13 Cited from Slusser, *St. Justin*, 30.

14 Cited from Slusser, *St. Justin*, 32.

15 Cited from Slusser, *St. Justin*, 36 (my emphasis).

16 Cited from Slusser, *St. Justin*, 36 (my emphasis).

not good" (Ezekiel 20:25) after the people turned away from him in the wilderness (*Dial.* 21:3). Next, Justin turns to Amos 5:18–6:7, a passage in which the Lord condemns the sacrifices offered by Israel, promising to reject their offerings (*Dial.* 22:2–5). Third, Justin turns to Jeremiah 7:22, a text which he believes supports his view that such precepts were not part of God's original arrangement with Israel: "*For I commanded not your fathers, in the day that I brought them by the hand out of the land of Egypt, concerning the matter of burnt offerings and sacrifices*" (*Dial.* 22:6).[17] Fourth, he cites texts from Psalm 50 where the psalmist explains that the Lord has no need for sacrifices. Finally, he cites from Isaiah 66:1 where the temple's significance is relativized: "*What is this house that you built for me? says the Lord. Heaven is my throne and the earth is my footstool.*"[18]

Justin does not treat these passages allegorically in his argument. Instead, he relies on what he thinks is the text's literal-historical meaning. Justin's strategy is not surprising; Jewish interlocutors would hardly have found Christian allegorical readings persuasive.

Justin's repeated use of the terminology of "hardness of heart" (*sklērokardia*) in describing the rationale for the imposition of the sacrificial laws also seems to evoke another biblical text. The same terminology occurs in Jesus' prohibition of divorce and remarriage in the Gospels of Matthew and Mark. Though Moses allowed for the practice, Jesus explains: "For your hardness of heart (*sklērokardian*) Moses allowed you to divorce your wives, but from the beginning it was not so" (Matthew 19:8; Mark 10:5). The parallel is striking. As Jesus explained that the allowance for divorce and remarriage was temporary and only given because of Israel's "hardness of heart," Justin makes a similar argument regarding the sacrificial precepts of the Law no longer observed by Christians.

St. Irenaeus (c. A.D. 140–200)

By the end of the second century we encounter another significant voice advancing this same interpretive approach, Irenaeus. Irenaeus is often spoken of as "the most important Christian theologian of the second century."[19] In Book 4 of his famous work, *Against Heresies* (*A.H.*),[20] which can be safely dated to the last quarter of the

17 Cited from Slusser, *St. Justin*, 35.

18 Cited from Slusser, *St. Justin*, 36.

19 See Ronald E. Heine, *Reading the Old Testament with the Ancient Church: Exploring the Formation of Early Christian Thought* (Grand Rapids: Baker Academic, 2007), 62. For more on Irenaeus' biography, see Dennis Minns, *Irenaeus: An Introduction* (London: T & T Clark, 2010), 1–3; Eric F. Obsorne, *Irenaeus of Lyons* (Cambridge: Cambridge University Press, 2001), 2–5.

20 For a fuller discussion of the authenticity, dating and textual traditions of *Against Heresies* see Dominic J. Unger, "Introduction," in *St. Irenaeus of Lyons: Against Heresies*, J. J. Dillon, trans.; Ancient Christian Writers, vol. 55 (Mahwah: Newman Press, 1992), 1–18; Matthew Craig Steenberg, *Irenaeus on Creation: The Cosmic Christ and the Saga of Redemption* (Leiden: Brill, 2008), 217–19. Unless otherwise noted, the translation used in this article of Book 1 of *Against Heresies* is taken from *St. Irenaeus of Lyons: Against Heresies*, trans. J. Dillon. Translations from

first century,[21] Irenaeus echoes many of the arguments used by Justin, though with more sophisticated nuance.

Unlike Justin's argument in his *Dialogue with Trypho*, which primarily addressed Jewish criticisms of Christianity, *Against Heresies* is principally concerned with refuting heretics such as the Gnostics who rejected the validity of the Jewish scriptures.[22] Irenaeus is primarily concerned with demonstrating the *unity* of the divine plan throughout salvation history, which he describes in terms of a "whole *economy*" (*oikonomia*).[23] Irenaeus places great emphasis on his notion of "recapitulation" (*anakephalaiôsis*), that is, the way Christ "sums up" salvation history:

> It was necessary, therefore, that the Lord, coming to the lost sheep, and making *recapitulation* of *so comprehensive a dispensation*, and seeking after His own handiwork, should save that very man who had been created after His image and likeness, that is, Adam, filling up the times of His condemnation, which had been incurred through disobedience,—[times] "which the Father had placed in His own power." [This was necessary,] too, inasmuch as *the whole economy of salvation regarding man* came to pass according to the good pleasure of the Father ... (*A.H.* 3.33.1).[24]

Despite insisting on the unity of God's plan, Irenaeus does not overlook the diversity of God's dealings with his people. He speaks not only of a "whole economy" but also of various "economies" (*oikonomiai*) within salvation history. While affirming

---

the rest of the work will be taken from, *The Ante-Nicene Fathers* [henceforth: *ANF*], eds. A. Roberts and J. Donaldson, (10 vols.; repr., Peabody, Mass.: Hendrickson, 1994). Most of the original of the Greek has been lost, though some Greek fragments remain. The critical edition is found in *Irénée de Lyon: Contre les heresies* (Sources Chrétiennes [Christian Sources] 100, 151, 152, 210, 211, 263, 264, 293 and 294; Paris: Cerf, 1990–2001).

21 For a fuller treatment see Unger, "Introduction," 3–4.

22 See Unger, "Introduction," 1. For a fuller examination of the particular heretical notions addressed in *Against Heresies*, see Sebastián Moll, *The Arch-Heretic Marcion*; (Wissenschaftliche Untersuchungen zum Neuen Testament [Scientific Investigations to the New Testament] 250 (Tübingen: Mohr-Siebeck, 2010), 17–20.

23 A helpful overview of the notion of *oikonomia* in Irenaeus' thought can be found in Tyler J. Vandergaag, "The Role of Justin Martyr's *Dialogue with Trypho* in the Early Christian Understanding of God's Plan (*Oikonomia*)" (M.A. Thesis, Trinity Western University, 2010), 46–55. See also Jean Daniélou, *The Gospel Message and Hellenistic Culture;* A History of Early Christian Doctrine Before the Council of Nicaea. Volume 2; ed. and trans. J. A. Baker (Philadelphia: Westminster Press, 1973), 157–161: "The history of salvation is thus regarded by Justin as a great design, spanning the whole of history, expressive of the Father's purpose, and carried out by the Son. The incarnation represents only the high point of a permanent *oikonomia*. ... To the Word then are ascribed all the acts by which God intervenes in history; and this is an outstanding characteristic of Justin's theology." See also Allert, *Revelation*, 108–109; 239–240.

24 Cited from *ANF* 1:455 (my emphasis).

"God's *dealings* [singular: *pragmateian*] and *Economy* [singular: *oikonomian*]" (*A.H.* 1.10.3), Irenaeus affirms that the orthodox faith believes in "one God the Father Almighty ... and in one Christ Jesus, the Son of God, and in the Holy Spirit who through the prophets preached the *Economies* [*tas oikonomias*]" (*A.H.* 1.10.1).[25] Osborne summarizes Irenaeus' presentation of the *oikonomia* as follows: "The economy [*oikonomia*] is the whole plan of God ... The *universal economy* is made up of *smaller diverse economies* of events which form the different saving dispositions which God has granted."[26]

In speaking of a universal *oikonomia*, Irenaeus appears to be drawing on terminology also used by Paul (see Ephesians 1:10, 3:9). Intriguingly, Justin Martyr also used the term *oikonomia*. Irenaeus, however, seems to have worked out more fully the significance of applying the terminology to salvation history as whole. While Justin uses the word to speak of God's *many* plans (plural: *oikonomiai*),[27] each of which find their fulfillment in Christ, Irenaeus uses the term to describe one *unified* plan for all of salvation history.[28]

Moreover, Irenaeus' usage of *oikonomia* points to something more than just a simple "plan," though it certainly has that meaning. Other ancient writers used the word to describe the "management" of a household,[29] a meaning also associated with *oikonomia* in the Septuagint[30] and the New Testament.[31] For Irenaeus, God's *oikonomia* is not simply about realizing a design for history; it also has familial implications—God is raising up sons and daughters. That Irenaeus has this meaning in mind is clear from his explanation in Book 4 of *Against Heresies*, when in reference to Jesus he states:

> For the Lord is the good man of the house [*Paterfamilias*], who rules the entire house of His Father; and who delivers a law

25 Cited from Dillon, *St. Irenaeus of Lyons*, 49.

26 Obsorne, *Irenaeus*, 77–78 (my emphasis).

27 See, for example, *Dialogue* 134.2.

28 For further studies see A. D'Alès, "Le mot *oikonomia* dans la langue théologique de Saint Irénée [The word *oikonomia* in the theological language of St. Irenaeus]," *Revue des études grecques* [Journal of Hellenistic Studies] 32 (1919): 1–9; M. Widemann, "Der Begriff *oikonomia* im Werk des Irenäus und seine Vorgeschichte [The Term *Oikonomia* in the Work of Irenaeus and His Historical Background]" (Ph.D. diss., Tübingen University, 1956). It seems Irenaeus' unified approach to the term is often read into Justin's work. See, for example, Daniélou, *Gospel Message*, 159, who fails to translate the word, which clearly in the Greek is plural, as singular. The author of this paper owes this insight to Vandergaag, "The Role of Justin," 7.

29 The word is used with this meaning by both Greco-Roman writers (see Xenophon, *Oeconomicus*, 2.12; 3.15; 8:3) and Jewish writers (see Philo, *On the Life of Joseph*, 38.4–7; *Special Laws*, 3.170–1; Josephus, *Against Apion*, 2.57; 2.89). For further references see William F. Arndt, Frederick W. Danker, and Walter Bauer, *A Greek-English Lexicon of the New Testament and Other Early Christian Literature* (3rd ed.; Chicago: University of Chicago Press, 2000), 697.

30 See the description of the responsibilities of the chief steward in Isa. 22:19, 21.

31 See Luke 16:1–4.

> suited both for slaves and those who are as yet undisciplined [*indisciplinatis*]; and gives fitting [*congruentia*] precepts to those that are free, and have been justified by faith, as well as throws His own inheritance open to those that are sons (*A.H.* 4.9.1).[32]

God's plan for salvation history is presented in terms of fatherly pedagogy. God is raising up sons in his Son, Christ Jesus. This pedagogy forms the rationale behind the different laws imposed by God in history. God imposes "fitting precepts" designed to properly discipline his children in their specific circumstances. Iain M. MacKenzie explains how Irenaeus describes God's dealings with his people in the Old Testament as a dispensation "which takes into consideration particular historical estates and conditions, and adapts itself to them, making itself appropriate to the lot of the people therein."[33]

How does Irenaeus find an overarching *oikonomia* in the various episodes of salvation history? The answer seems to be found in his notion of the covenant. As a growing number of scholars are beginning to recognize, at the heart of Irenaeus' approach is a sophisticated "covenantal theology."[34] Irenaeus observes that if one looks closely at salvation history one finds *many* different covenants. He insists that true understanding involves recognizing "why several covenants were made with the human race; by teaching what the real nature [*charachtēr*] of each of the covenants was" (*A.H.* 1.10.3).[35] For Irenaeus, God established various covenants tailored to the specific needs of his people at different times in history. He writes:

> They (the Jews) had therefore a law, a course of discipline, and a prophecy of future things [*lex, et disciplina erat illis, et prophetia futurorum*]. For God at the first, indeed, warning them by means of natural precepts, which from the beginning He had implanted in mankind, that is, by means of the Decalogue (which, if any

32 Cited from *ANF* 1:472.

33 Iain M. MacKenzie, *Irenaeus's Demonstration of the Apostolic Preaching: A Theological Commentary and Translation* (Aldershot: Ashgate, 2002), 149.

34 Only recently has the significance of covenant been fully appreciated in Irenaeus scholarship. Susan L. Graham ("Irenaeus and the Covenants: 'Immortal Diamond,'" in *Studia Patristica* [The Study of the Patristics] *Vol. XL* [Leuven: Peeters, 2006], 393–398) points out that Irenaeus "employs the term 'covenant' more often than 'recapitulation,'" something which seems striking given that most are far more familiar with Irenaeus' use of the latter term. For more on the study of Irenaeus' covenantal approach, in addition to Graham's article, see Everett Ferguson, "The Covenant Idea in the Second Century," in *Texts and Testaments: Critical Essays on the Bible and the Early Fathers*, ed. W. Eugene March (San Antonio: Trinity University Press 1980), 144–8; J. Ligon Duncan, "The Covenant Idea in Ante-Nicene Theology," (Ph.D. diss., University of Edinburgh, 1995), 132–156; *idem.*, "The Covenant Idea in Irenaeus of Lyons: An Introduction and Survey," in *Confessing our Hope: Essays in Honor of Morton Howison Smith on His Eightieth Birthday*, eds. J. A. Pipa, Jr. and C. N. Willborn (Taylors: Southern Presbyterian Press, 2004), 31–55.

35 Cited from Dillon, *St. Irenaeus of Lyons*, 50.

> one does not observe, he has no salvation), did then demand nothing more of them. As Moses says in Deuteronomy, "These are all the words which the Lord spoke to the whole assembly of the sons of Israel on the mount, and He added no more; and He wrote them on two tables of stone, and gave them to me." (*A.H.* 4.15.1).[36]

Irenaeus here presents God's law in terms of familial pedagogy or "discipline." Moreover, Irenaeus explains that when God led Israel out of Egypt he simply commanded the people to keep the decalogue, identified with the "natural precepts" that are "implanted in mankind." To make his case for this he highlights Deuteronomy 5:22, which seems to indicate that these were the *only* laws imposed upon Israel when God first brought Israel to Mt. Sinai: *"He added no more."*[37]

Irenaeus further explains that a time came when God required more of Israel than simply the decalogue. Irenaeus identifies the specific sin that triggered the imposition of new precepts, namely, the worship of the golden calf:

> But *when they turned themselves to make a calf,* and had gone back in their minds to Egypt, desiring to be slaves instead of freemen, *they were placed for the future in a state of servitude suited to their wish,*—[a slavery] which did not indeed cut them off from God, but subjected them to the yoke of bondage; as Ezekiel the prophet, when *stating the reasons for the giving of such a law, declares: "And their eyes were after the desire of their heart; and I gave them statutes that were not good, and judgments in which they shall not live"* (*A.H.* 4.15.1; my emphasis).[38]

Irenaeus thus explains that God gave Israel the ritual precepts to counter the people's proclivity to idolatry. As in Justin's argument in his *Dialogue,* Irenaeus highlights Ezekiel's statement about God giving Israel "laws that were not good." In addition, also like Justin, Irenaeus later highlights Jeremiah 7:22 to make the case that the sacrificial laws were not required from Israel from the beginning (*A.H.* 4.17.3).

---

36 Cited from *ANF* 1:479.

37 Here it seems that Irenaeus is attempting to refute the claims made by Jewish writers who insisted that all of the laws given to Israel, including the ceremonial laws and the oral tradition of the rabbis, were revealed to Moses at Sinai. On this, see Marcel Simon, "The Ancient Church and Rabbinical Tradition," in *Holy Book and Holy Tradition: International Colloquium Held in the Faculty of Theology, University of Manchester,* eds. F. F. Bruce and E. G. Rupp (Grand Rapids: Eerdmans, 1968), 102–103.

38 Cited from *ANF* 1:479.

In order to demonstrate that the cultic code was only instituted because of Israel's sin and not because such laws were inherently redeeming, Irenaeus points out that such laws were not imposed during the Patriarchal age:

> And that man was not justified by these things, but that they were given as a sign to the people, this fact shows,—that Abraham himself, without circumcision and without observance of Sabbaths, "believed God, and it was imputed unto him for righteousness; and he was called the friend of God" (*A.H.* 4.16.2).[39]

Irenaeus goes on to highlight the righteousness of Lot, Noah, and Enoch, who were all righteous without circumcision (*A.H.* 4.16.2). The freedom enjoyed by Christians from such laws is thus understood as anticipated in the Patriarchal age.

In arguing that God had to accommodate himself to his people's sinfulness, Irenaeus appeals not only to the Old Testament but also to the teachings of Jesus (referencing Jesus' teaching on divorce and remarriage). He writes, "the Lord also showed that certain precepts were enacted for them by Moses, on account of their hardness [of heart], and because of their unwillingness to be obedient" (*A.H.* 4.15.2).[40]

According to Irenaeus, the ceremonial laws are now no longer in force—not because Jesus has revealed a different God but because there is now no need for them. He explains, "These things, therefore, which were given for bondage, and for a sign to them, He cancelled by the new covenant of liberty" (*A.H.* 4.16.5).[41] For Irenaeus, there is one plan—a plan to set humanity free in Christ. This one plan, however, takes shape in different ways as God is deals with the specific needs of his children at various times in history.

Tertullian (c. A.D. 160–220)

Despite the fact that he eventually became a schismatic, it is widely recognized that the writings of Tertullian played a major role in the developing theology of the Catholic Church.[42] Tertullian advances the secondary legislation interpretation in his works *Against the Jews* (*A.J.*)(*c.* A.D. 200), and *Against Marcion* (*A.M.*)(*c.* A.D. 207–8).[43]

39 Cited from *ANF* 1:481.

40 Cited from *ANF* 1:480.

41 Cited from *ANF* 1:482.

42 Joel Stevens Allen writes, "Even with his rejection of Catholicism, Tertullian's influence in the Church is surpassed by few others" (*The Despoliation of Egypt in Pre-rabbinic, Rabbinic and Patristic Traditions* [Leiden: Brill, 2008], 195). For a discussion of Tertullian's life and work see T. D. Barnes, *Tertullian: A Historical and Literary Study* (Oxford: Oxford University Press, 1971).

43 Many scholars only accept the authenticity of chapters 1–8 of *Against the Jews* and so our study

First, Tertullian speaks of a "natural law" (*lex naturalis*) that was "anterior even to Moses" *(A.J.* 2). He writes:

> In short, before the Law of Moses, written in stone-tables, I contend that there was a law unwritten, which was habitually understood naturally, and by the fathers was habitually kept. For whence was Noah "found righteous" [Gen 6:9; 7:1] if in his case the righteousness of a natural law had not preceded?[44]

This law, first given to Adam and Eve, is principally identified with the commands to love God, to love one's neighbor, and with the Ten Commandments:

> For in this law given to Adam we recognise in embryo all the precepts which afterwards sprouted forth when given through Moses; that is, Thou shalt love the Lord thy God from thy whole heart and out of thy whole soul; Thou shalt love thy neighbour as thyself; Thou shalt not kill; Thou shall not commit adultery; Thou shalt not steal; False witness thou shall not utter; Honour thy father and mother; and, That which is another's, shall thou not covet. For the primordial law [*lex primordialis*] was given to Adam and Eve in paradise, as the womb of all the precepts of God. *(A.J.* 2).[45]

Here we find something similar to what we saw in Irenaeus.[46]

Second, and also like Irenaeus, Tertullian emphasizes the unity of God's plan by speaking of how God adapts his laws to the needs of his people at various times in history. He teaches that although a natural law was given at the dawn of time, it was necessary for God to apply it in different ways to the specific circumstances of his people. Thus Tertullian speaks of the power of God, which

---

here will focus on these chapters. On this, see David Efroymson, "Tertullian's Anti-Judaism and Its Role in His Theology" (Ph.D. diss., Temple University, 1976), 116 n. 6. The most recent critical Latin text is found in Hermann Tränkle, ed., *Q.S.F. Tertulliani Adversus Iudaeos [Tertullian's Against the Jews]: Mit Einleitung und kritischen Kommentar [With Introduction and Critical Commentary]* (Wiesbaden: Steiner, 1964). The authoritative Latin text of *Against Marcion* is found in René Braun, ed. and trans., *Adversus Marcionem: Contre Marcion [Against Marcion]*; Sources Chrétiennes [Christian Sources] 4 vols. (Paris: Cerf, 1990–2001). English translations used here are taken from *ANF* 3:151–73; 269–475.

44 Cited from *ANF* 3:152.

45 Cited from *ANF* 3:152.

46 Others have recognized the similarities between Tertullian and Irenaeus here. See, for example, F mi Adey mi, *The New Covenant Torah in Jeremiah and the Law of Christ in Paul*; Studies in Biblical Literature, 94 (New York: Peter Lang, 2006), 25: "... Tertullian concurs with Irenaeus that the natural law was the primordial law, the 'womb' of all God's precepts."

"reforms [*reformantem*] the law's precepts in a way suitable [in the Divine mind] to the circumstances of the times, with a view to man's salvation" (*A.J.* 2).[47]

In particular, Tertullian identifies the way God adapted his law to Israel after they had abandoned him by falling into the sin of idolatry. In *Against Marcion*, he writes:

> As for the burdensome sacrifices also, and the troublesome scrupulousness of their ceremonies and oblations, no one should blame them, as if God specially required them for Himself: for He plainly asks, "To what purpose is the multitude of your sacrifices unto me?" and, "Who hath required them at your hand?"[48] But he should see herein a careful provision on God's part, which showed His wish to bind to His own religion a people who were prone to idolatry and transgression by the kind of services wherein consisted the superstition of that period; that He might call them away therefrom, while requesting it to be performed to Himself..." (*A.M.* 2.18).[49]

Here we see that, for Tertullian, the giving of the sacrificial laws to Israel represented an expression of God's wise jurisprudence.

Third, Tertullian argues that since certain precepts came later, it should be obvious that these laws only had *temporary* value. He explains that God "has premonished that it should come to pass that, just as 'the law was given through Moses'[50] at a definite time, so it should be believed to have been temporarily observed and kept" (*A.J.* 2).[51] He points out that while God did enjoin Israel to worship on the Sabbath, God nonetheless made exemptions concerning its observance. For example, Joshua commanded the priests to carry the ark in procession around Jericho on the Sabbath (see Joshua 6:1–20). Similarly, he explains that the Maccabees were justified in violating this precept in order to defend the city (*A.J.* 4 citing 1 Maccabees 2:41). From such situations he concludes, "... it is manifest that the force of such precepts was temporary, and respected the necessity of present circumstances; and that it was not with a view to its observance in perpetuity that God formerly gave them such a law" (*A.J.* 4).[52] Tertullian also references Jeremiah 31, focusing on God's announcement that the new covenant will not be "according to the covenant that I made with their fathers in the day when I arrested their dispensation in order to bring them out of the land of Egypt" (Jer. 31:32). He explains:

47 Cited from *ANF* 3:153.

48 Isa. 1:11–12.

49 Cited from *ANF* 3:311–12.

50 See John 1:17.

51 Cited from *ANF* 3:153.

52 Cited from *ANF* 3:156.

"He thus shows that the ancient covenant *is temporary only*, when He indicates its change. ... Forasmuch then as He said, that from the Creator there would come other laws, and other words, and new dispensations of covenants" (*A.M.* 4.1).[53]

Finally, like Justin and Irenaeus, Tertullian argues that the New Covenant involves a return to a more pristine era, that of the Patriarchs:

> Therefore, since God originated Adam uncircumcised, and inobservant of the Sabbath, consequently his offspring also, Abel, offering Him sacrifices, uncircumcised and inobservant of the Sabbath, was by Him commended; while He accepted what he was offering in simplicity of heart, and reprobated the sacrifice of his brother Cain, who was not rightly dividing what he was offering.[54] Noah also, uncircumcised—yes, and inobservant of the Sabbath—God freed from the deluge.[55] For Enoch, too, most righteous man, uncircumcised and in-observant of the Sabbath, He translated from this world;[56] who did not first taste death, in order that, being a candidate for eternal life, he might by this time show us that we also may, without the burden of the law of Moses, please God (*A.J.* 2).[57]

The New Covenant thus replaces the Old, though certain aspects of it, such as the decalogue, abide:

> But still we make this concession, that there is a separation, by reformation, by amplification, by progress; just as the fruit is separated from the seed, although the fruit comes from the seed. So likewise the gospel is separated from the law, whilst it advances from the law—a different thing from it, but not an alien one; diverse, but not contrary. (*A.M.* 4.11)[58]

In summary, Tertullian echoes many of the same themes found in Justin and Irenaeus. The God of the Old Testament is the God of the New, but this God wisely *adapts* his Law to the needs of his people at certain points in salvation history. Moreover, while portions of the Law endure, the ritual precepts that were simply added to deal with Israel's sins are no longer binding in the New Covenant age.

---

53 Cited from *ANF* 3:346 (my emphasis).

54 Gen. 9:1–7, especially in the LXX. Compare Heb. 11:4.

55 Gen. 6:18; 7:23; 2 Pet. 2:5.

56 See Gen. 5:22, 24; Heb. 11:5.

57 Cited from *ANF* 3:153.

58 Cited from *ANF* 3:361.

The Didascalia Apostolorum (c. A.D. 220–240)

By the middle of the third century, the "secondary legislation" interpretive approach advocated by Justin, Irenaeus, and Tertullian had become so well established and widespread that it was embraced as part of the apostolic tradition itself. This is clearly evident from its presence in the *Didascalia Apostolorum* (*The Teaching of the Apostles*), a work that purports to be the proceedings of the apostolic council recorded in Acts 15. The text comes to us through a fourth-century Syriac manuscript,[59] which in turn is believed to be a translation of a third-century Greek manuscript.[60] The original work, whenever it was actually written (or compiled) appears to have undergone several recensions and likely includes much earlier material.[61] Much of the original Greek apparently is preserved in the *Apostolic Constitutions*.[62] The appearance of the *Didascalia Apostolorum* in so many languages (Greek, Latin, Syriac, and Coptic), its widespread geographical distribution, as well as the reappearance of its material in the *Apostolic Constitutions* indicate how widely received and well-established its ideas were in the early Church.

The special emphasis given to the secondary legislation approach in the *Didascalia Apostolorum* is remarkable. Marcel Simon calls the *Didascalia* the "classic example" of this interpretive tradition.[63] In its second chapter we are told that not everything in the Law should be considered as perpetually normative:

> Let this be before your eyes, that you know what in the law is the law and what the bonds of the secondary legislation which, subsequent to the law, was imposed bringing severe burdens for those who under the law, and under the repeated legislation,

59 The standard critical edition of the Syriac text is Arthur Vööbus, *The Didascalia Apostolorum in Syriac, Corpus Scriptorum Christianorum Orientalium*, vols. 401, 402, 407, 408 (Louvain: Secrétariat du CorpusSCO, 1979). The English translation used here from Alistair Stewart-Sykes, *The Didascalia Apostolorum: An English Translation with Introduction and Annotation* (Turnhout: Brepols, 2009). The author is grateful for the help he received from Andrew Younan in working with the Syriac texts of the *Didascalia* and Aphrahat's *Demonstrations*. Younan is the rector of Mar Abba the Great Seminary in San Diego and professor of philosophy at John Paul the Great Catholic University.

60 On this see Lawrence J. Johson, *Worship in the Early Church, Volume 1: An Anthology of Historical Sources* (Collegeville: Liturgical Press, 2009), 224.

61 Stewart-Sykes, *Didascalia Apostolorum*, 11–55.

62 See Vööbus, *The Didascalia Apostolorum in Syriac*, 408:32: "the amount of the original Greek preserved in the *Apostolic Constitutions* must be reckoned as considerable." For a critical edition of the *Apostolic Constitutions* see Marcel Metzger, *Les Constitutions Apostoliques*, 2 vols; *Sources Chrétiennes*, 320, 329 (Paris: Éditions du Cerf, 1985–1986). See also Alistair Stewart-Sykes, *On the Apostolic Tradition* (Crestwood: St. Vladimir's Seminary Press, 2001), 1–50; Paul F. Bradshaw, Maxwell E. Johnson, L. Edward Phillips, and Harold W. Attridge, *The Apostolic Tradition* (Hermeneia 85; Fortress Press, 2002).

63 Marcel Simon, *Verus Israel: A Study of the Relations between Christians and Jews in the Roman Empire* A.D. *135–425*; trans. H. McKeating (London: The Littman Library of Jewish Civilization, 1996), 88.

> sinned so severely in the wilderness. For the law is that which the Lord God spoke before the people made the calf and turned to idolatry, that is, the decalogue and the judgments. However, after their idolatry he commanded, and justly laid bonds upon them, but do not therefore lay such chains upon yourself, for our Saviour came for no other reason than to fulfill the law and weaken the chains of the secondary legislation. Therefore he calls out to those from the people who believed in him, releasing them from these very chains, as he says: 'Come to me, all who labour and are heavily burdened [and I will give you rest]'[64]. You, therefore, who are unburdened, read the simple law, that which is in accordance with the Gospel ... (*D.A.* 1.6.7–11)[65]

The *Didascalia* here states that: (1) it is possible to distinguish between two types of laws in the Torah, namely, those given prior to Israel's act of worshipping the golden calf and those given afterwards as well as (2) Christians are not bound by the "secondary legislation."

It is, however, in the final chapter of the *Didascalia* that we find the fullest expression of the secondary legislation approach. Here the concern is with keeping those who have converted to Christianity "from *the people*"—that is, from *the Jewish people*—from "continuing to keep your former conduct, keeping pointless obligations, and purifications, and separations, and baptismal lustrations and distinction between foods" (6.15.1).[66] Here we discover that the "Law" of Jesus is to be specifically identified with the Ten Commandments:

> Therefore, as you know Jesus Christ the Lord and his dispensation *for all* which was made *in the beginning*, be aware that he gave a simple law, pure and holy, in which the Saviour set his name. *For the decalogue which he gave indicates Jesus.* For ten represents iota, yet iota is the beginning of the name Jesus. (*D.A.* 6.15.2)[67]

Christ, we read, has come to show that he "does not undo the law but teaches what is the law and what is the secondary legislation" (*D.A.* 6.15.3).[68] When Christ explained that he has "not come to destroy the law, nor the prophets, but to fulfill them" (Matthew 5:17), the *Didascalia* explains that Christ was referring to the decalogue and not to the secondary legislation:

64 Matt. 11:28. The words in the brackets only appear in the Syriac. See Stewart-Sykes, *Didascalia Apostolorum*, 108 n. 30.

65 Cited from Stewart-Sykes, *Didascalia Apostolorum*, 108–109; my emphasis.

66 Cited from Stewart-Sykes, *Didascalia Apostolorum*, 238.

67 Cited from Stewart-Sykes, *Didascalia Apostolorum*, 238; my emphasis.

68 Cited from Stewart-Sykes, *Didascalia Apostolorum*, 238.

> Thus the law is indissoluble, whereas *the secondary legislation is transitory. For the law is the decalogue*, and the judgments to which Jesus bore witness when he said: 'Not one iota letter shall pass away from the law.'[69] Now it is the iota which does not pass away from the law, *for the iota is known, through the decalogue, to signify the name of Jesus*. (*D.A.* 6.15.3–4)[70]

The document therefore distinguishes between the "transitory" nature of the secondary legislation and the enduring value of the dispensation of Christ which is made "for all" and which is associated with "the beginning."

The *Didascalia* grounds the distinction between "law" and "secondary legislation" in a close reading of the biblical text. It points out that prior to the sin of the golden calf God gave Israel a simple list of commandments. In this, the first law code given to Israel at Sinai (Exodus 20–23), none of the specific commands for regular animal sacrifices or purity regulations seen in later books such as Leviticus are found:

> Thus the law consists of the decalogue and the judgments which the Lord spoke before the people made the calf and worshipped idols ... For this law is simple and is light, is not burdensome with regard to the separation of foods, or incensations, or sacrifices or burnt offerings. In this law he speaks only of the church and of the foreskin. (*D.A.* 6.16.1, 2).[71]

The document then points out that all of this changed after the sin of the golden calf:

> When they denied him and said: "We have no God to go before us" and made themselves a molten calf and worshipped it, and sacrificed to the statue, then was the Lord angry, and in the heat of his anger, yet in his merciful goodness, he bound them to the secondary legislation as to a heavy load and the hardness of a yoke. Thus no longer did he say: "If you should make [an altar]" as previously, but said: "Make an altar, and sacrifice continuously", as though he had need of such. Thus he imposed on them as a necessity that they should make frequent burnt offerings and he made them abstain from foods by means of the distinction of foods. From then on [after the sin of the golden calf] were clean animals and unclean foods defined, from then

69 Matt. 5:18.

70 Cited from Stewart-Sykes, *Didascalia Apostolorum*, 239; my emphasis.

71 Cited from Stewart-Sykes, *Didascalia Apostolorum*, 240.

> on there were separations and purifications and baptisms and sprinklings. From then on were there sacrifices and offerings and tables. From then on were there burnt offerings, and offerings and shewbread, and the offering of sacrifices, and firstlings, and ransoms, and scapegoats, and vows, and much else that is astounding. On account of the great number of their transgressions were customs laid on them which cannot be described. (*D.A.* 6.16.6–9)[72]

The secondary legislation is therefore understood as God's response to Israel's idolatry.

In addition, the *Didascalia* cites biblical passages to support the claim that the ritual requirements of the laws were added because of sin. Many of the same passages employed by Justin, Tertullian, and Irenaeus reappear in the *Didascalia*. For example, it uses Jeremiah 7:22 to support the claim that the sacrificial precepts were not part of the original covenant legislation (*D.A.* 6.17.2). Likewise, it appeals to Ezekiel 20:25, explaining, "the secondary legislation is that which he calls judgments which are unprofitable, and they are incapable of saving" (*D.A.* 6.18.6).[73]

Moreover, the *Didascalia* evokes the language of Peter's speech at the Jerusalem council in Acts 15, associating the secondary legislation with "yoke" imagery:

> Therefore those who take upon themselves what was imposed on account of the worship of idols shall be inheritors of the woes: "Woe to them who prolong their sins like a long rope, and like the strap on a heifer's yoke." Now the yoke of the bonds is a heifer's yoke, and the bonds of the law were put on the people like a long rope. ... Everyone who seeks to be under the secondary legislation therefore is "guilty of the calf-worship, for the secondary legislation was not imposed except on account of the worship of idols, and so any who observe them are prisoners and idol-worshipers." (*D.A.* 6.18.9–10)[74]

Thus, after coordinating the same essential arguments of Justin, Irenaeus, and Tertullian, the *Didascalia* concludes that since the secondary legislation was a yoke of servitude added because of idolatry, to return to it constitutes nothing less than a return to the bondage of idolatry.

72 Cited from Stewart-Sykes, *Didascalia Apostolorum*, 241–242.

73 Cited from Stewart-Sykes, *Didascalia Apostolorum*, 246.

74 Cited from Stewart-Sykes, *Didascalia Apostolorum*, 246.

The Secondary Legislation View in Other Early Christian Sources

Given the appearance of the secondary legislation view in such influential writers as Justin, Tertullian, and Irenaeus, as well as its occurrence in the *Didascalia Apostolorum*, a widely circulated work, it is no surprise to find later writers of considerable stature also taking it up. For example, St. Augustine writes:

> Thus the sacraments of the Old Testament, which were celebrated in obedience to the law, were types of Christ who was to come; and when Christ fulfilled them by His advent they were done away, and were done away because they were fulfilled. For Christ came not to destroy, but to fulfill. And now that the righteousness of faith is revealed, and the children of God are called into liberty, and the yoke of bondage which was required for a carnal and stiff-necked people is taken away, other sacraments are instituted, greater in efficacy, more beneficial in their use, easier in performance, and fewer in number.[75]

Here Augustine specifically identifies the "yoke of bondage" in terms of the Old Testament rituals (="sacraments") that were added because of Israel's sin. He contrasts the "yoke" of the Old Testament "sacraments" with the ease of those in the New. Whereas Israel's sacraments were numerous, lacking in efficacy, and difficult to perform, those of the New are few, powerful, and simple.

Many of the most influential fathers and doctors of the Church also advocated the secondary legislation view. Here three examples will suffice:

> Now it appears to me ... that not at first[76] were the commandment and the law concerning sacrifices given, neither did the mind of God, Who gave the law, regard whole burnt-offerings, but those things which were pointed out and prefigured by them. ... Therefore, the whole law did not treat of sacrifices, though there was in the law a commandment concerning sacrifices, that by means of them it might begin to instruct men and might withdraw them from idols, and bring them near to God, teaching them for that present time. Therefore neither at the beginning, when God brought the people out of Egypt, did He command them concerning sacrifices or whole burnt-offerings, nor even when they came to mount Sinai. For God is not as man,

75 St. Augustine, *Contra Faustus* [*Against Faustus*], 19.13. English translation taken from *A Select Library of Nicene and Post-Nicene Fathers of the Christian Church*, 2nd series [*NPNF1*], 14 vols., ed. Philip Schaff (Peabody, MA: Hendrickson, 1994 [reprint]), 4:244. Text in *PL* 42:355.

76 Evidently (see further on in the quote), the time-frame that Athanasius has in mind here is at the departure of Israel from Egypt at the Exodus.

> that He should be careful about these things beforehand; but His commandment was given, that they might know Him Who is truly God, and His Word, and might despise those which are falsely called gods. ... For when He saith, "I have not spoken concerning sacrifices, neither given commandment concerning whole burnt-offerings," [Jer. 7:22] He immediately adds, "But this is the thing which I commanded them, saying, Obey My voice, and I will be to you a God, and ye shall be to Me a people, and ye shall walk in all the ways that I command you" [Jer. 7:23]. Thus then, being before instructed and taught, they learned not to do service to anyone but the Lord.—St. Athanasius (*c.* A.D. 397)[77]

> The Jews will ask: "How is that [God] ... did permit the Jews to sacrifice?" He was giving into their weakness. ... The physician grants his patient the lesser evil because he wishes to prevent the greater and to lead the sick man away from a violent death. This is what God did. He saw the Jews choking with their mad yearning for sacrifices. He saw that they were ready to go over to idols if they were deprived of sacrifices. I should say, he saw that they were not only ready to go over, but that they had already done so. So he let them have their sacrifices. The time when the permission was granted should make it clear that this is the reason. After they kept the festival of the evil demons, God yielded and permitted sacrifices. What he all but said was this: "You are all eager and avid for sacrifices. If sacrifice you must, then sacrifice to me." But even if he permitted sacrifices, this permission was not to last forever; in the wisdom of his ways, he took the sacrifices away from them again.—St. John Chrysostom (*c.* A.D. 387)[78]

> ... another reasonable cause may be assigned to the ceremonies of the sacrifices, from the fact that thereby men were withdrawn from offering sacrifices to idols. Hence too it is that the precepts

---

77 St. Athanasius, *Epistula festalis* [*Festal Letter*] 19.3,4. English translation taken from *A Select Library of Nicene and Post-Nicene Fathers of the Christian Church*, 2nd series [*NPNF2*], 14 vols., ed. Philip Schaff (Peabody, MA: Hendrickson, 1994 [reprint]), 4:546. Text in *Patrologiae Cursus Completus, Series Graeca* [*PG*], ed. J.P. Migne, 161 vols. (Paris: Garnier and J.P. Migne, 1857–1891), 26:1425–1426.

78 St. John Chrysostom, *Adversus Iudeaos* [*Against the Jews*], 4.6.4–5; English translation taken from St. John Chyrsostom, *Discourses Against Judaizing Christians*, trans. P. W. Harkins, The Fathers of the Church, vol. 68 (Washington, D.C.: Catholic University of America Press, 1979), 153. Text in *PG* 48:879–880.

> about the sacrifices were not given to the Jewish people until after they had fallen into idolatry, by worshipping the molten calf: as though those sacrifices were instituted, that the people, being ready to offer sacrifices, might offer those sacrifices to God rather than to idols. Thus it is written (Jer. 7:22): "I spake not to your fathers and I commanded them not, in the day that I brought them out of the land of Egypt, concerning the matter of burnt-offerings and sacrifices."—St. Thomas Aquinas (*c.* A.D. 1271–1272)[79]

Conclusions

Broadly speaking, the patristic sources examined in this article find striking agreement on the following points:

1. A distinction is made in the Old Testament between a universal / natural law, understood primarily as moral laws (especially identified with the decalogue), and other laws made necessary by the circumstances of God's people.

2. Israel's sin of worshipping the golden calf triggers dramatic changes in Israel's relationship with God, particularly with respect to the imposition of sacrificial and cultic laws no longer observed by Christians.

3. The Patriarchal age is highlighted as a precedent for Christian non-observance of the ceremonial laws.

Moreover, in support of these claims early patristic sources appeal to many of the same texts. For example, they frequently turn to Jeremiah 7:22 to demonstrate that the ceremonial laws were not part of God's original design for his people. Likewise, Ezekiel's account of God's imposition of "laws that were not good" is often cited as part of the secondary legislation argument.

Yet, despite its ancient pedigree and near universal appearance in early Christian literature, this interpretive tradition is widely overlooked today.[80] Even works devoted to the recovery of patristic exegesis appear to ignore it. The reasons for this neglect are not entirely clear. This neglect might be partially due to one of

---

79 St. Thomas Aquinas, *Summa theologiae* IIa IIae, q. 102, art. 3; cited from St. Thomas Aquinas, *Summa Theologica*, trans. Fathers of the English Dominican Province, 5 vols. (New York Benzinger Bros., 1948), 2:1058.

80 There are however some exceptions. See Simon, "The Ancient Church and Rabbinical Tradition," 94–112.; *idem.*, *Verus Israel*; Richard Patrick Crosland Hanson, *Allegory and Event: A Study of the Sources and Significance of Origen's Interpretation of Scripture* (London: SCM Press, 1959), 289–310.

the most fascinating features of the secondary legislation interpretive tradition: it is rooted not in a spiritual or allegorical reading, but in a *literal* approach to the canonical form of the text.[81] As we have seen, this tradition seeks to explain the New Testament's continuity with the Old by arguing that, according to the biblical narrative itself, certain precepts were not originally part of God's covenant relationship with his people. Thus, patristic sources that employ this view make the case that non-observance of certain Old Testament precepts results not from a "selective reading" but from a holistic understanding of God's plan for humanity and a recognition that divine jurisprudence wisely accommodates itself to the particular needs of specific periods in salvation history. For the Fathers, it is precisely the *unity* of the divine plan that explains the discontinuity within it.

81 This perhaps makes this approach unappealing to writers interested in recovering patristic exegesis—writers who are oftentimes more interested in the fathers' spiritual exegesis—while at the same time somewhat unpalatable to historical-critics preoccupied with diachronic explanations of the text.

Letter & Spirit 7 (2011): 91-118

Scriptural and Sacramental Signs
Augustine's *Answer to Faustus*

~: **Matthew Levering** :~
University of Dayton

Introduction

In exile during the mid-380s, the Manichean Bishop Faustus wrote a work titled *The Chapters*, in which he defends Manichean doctrine against Catholic criticisms. Almost half of these chapters defend some aspect of Manichean rejection of the Old Testament, while most of the other chapters take up the Manichean denial that Jesus was born. Augustine's *Answer to Faustus, a Manichean*, composed in 397–398 on the heels of *On Christian Doctrine*, takes up each of Faustus's thirty-three chapters in turn.[1] I will focus my attention on those chapters that have particularly to do with the Old Testament: thus, in Augustine's work, Books 4, 6, 9, 10, 12–19, 22, and 30–32. Although these Books inevitably contain some repetition, nonetheless when taken as a whole they constitute an extraordinary Christian theology of the Old Testament and its relation to the New. Having developed his theology of scriptural signs in *On Christian Doctrine*, he here develops it further. As Paula Fredriksen observes, "Typology served Augustine as his weapon of choice against Faustus."[2]

Few theologians today, however, are aware of the contribution that *Answer to Faustus, a Manichean* makes to later theology of Scripture and theology of the sacraments. Despite his frequent quotations from Augustine, Peter Lombard does not directly cite *Answer to Faustus* even once in Book 4 of his *Sentences*, where he treats the sacraments.[3] In their eleventh-century controversy with Berengarius, too, Lanfranc of Canterbury and Guitmund of Bec repeatedly cite Augustine but never his *Answer to Faustus*.[4] By contrast, Thomas Aquinas quotes *Answer to Faustus*

---

1 See Augustine, *Answer to Faustus, a Manichean*, trans. Roland Teske, S.J. (Hyde Park, NY: New City Press, 2007). All subsequent quotations are taken from this translation and page numbers in subsequent footnotes refer to this edition.

2 Paula Fredriksen, *Augustine and the Jews: A Christian Defense of Jews and Judaism* (New York: Doubleday, 2008), 240 (see pages 213–223 and 232–234 for discussions of Faustus's critique of the Old Testament in the context of the anti-Judaism of earlier Catholic authors).

3 He does cite *Answer to Faustus* once by mistake (he attributes the quotation to Augustine's *On Genesis*). See Peter Lombard, *The Sentences*, Book 4: *On the Doctrine of Signs*, trans. Giulio Silano (Toronto: Pontifical Institute of Mediavel Studies, 2010), 192.

4 See Lanfranc of Canterbury, *On the Body and Blood of the Lord* and Guitmund of Aversa, *On the Truth of the Body and Blood of Christ in the Eucharist*, trans. Mark G. Vaillancourt (Washington, D.C.: Catholic University of America, 2009).

frequently in his treatises in the *Summa theologiae* on the Old Law and on the sacraments, and later scholastic theologians follow his lead.[5] Yet modern scholars other than Paula Fredriksen have severely neglected *Answer to Faustus*. Eugene TeSelle's 350-page *Augustine the Theologian* ignores *Answer to Faustus* entirely, as does Peter Brown's *Augustine of Hippo* and Henry Chadwick's *Augustine: A Very Short Introduction*.[6] Even the *Catechism of the Catholic Church* contains abundant citations of Augustine but only one from *Answer to Faustus*, and then not with any relation to Scripture or to the sacraments.[7]

In a lecture delivered at the inaugural Wilken Colloquium at Baylor University, Peter Leithart highlights the influence of *Answer to Faustus* in the sixteenth-century controversies between Catholics and Protestants. As Leithart remarks, due to the lack of secondary literature on *Answer to Faustus*, "We need a brief overview of the treatise, and it would not hurt to have a monograph on it."[8] In what follows, I cannot offer a monograph but I do hope to provide a "brief overview" of the portions of *Answer to Faustus* relevant to Scripture and the sacraments. For each Book I first review Faustus's critique of the Catholic position, and then examine in detail Augustine's reply. My goal is to assist in reinserting *Answer to Faustus* into contemporary theological discussion of Scripture (especially regarding typological interpretation) and the sacraments.

Book 4: The OT Promises

In Book 4, Faustus responds to the question, "Do you accept the Old Testament?" His reply is that he could only accept it if it contained his inheritance. He argues that the Old Testament speaks only of the inheritance of the Jews, namely the land of Canaan. Only those who obey the laws of Israel—circumcision, the food laws, and so forth—will receive this land. Since Faustus does not obey these laws, and is not among those who will inherit the land of Canaan, he finds that the Old Testament has nothing to offer him.

Augustine answers Faustus by conceding that the laws and promises of the Old Testament refer literally to the people of Israel alone, but he argues that these laws and promises prefigure something greater. Since the Manicheans accept St.

5 See, for example, Thomas Aquinas, *Summa theologiae* [Summary of Theology], I–II, q. 100, a. 12; I–II, q. 103, a. 4; I–II, q. 106, a. 4, ad 2; I–II, q. 107, a. 1, obj. 2; I–II, q. 107, a. 3, ad 2; III, q. 61, a. 1, *sed contra*; III, q. 61, a. 3, obj. 2; III, q. 61, a. 4, *sed contra*; III, q. 65, a. 1, obj. 4; trans. Fathers of the English Dominican Province (Westminster, MD: Christian Classics, 1981).

6 See Eugene TeSelle, *Augustine the Theologian* (New York: Herder and Herder, 1970); Peter Brown, *Augustine of Hippo: A Biography*, 2nd ed. (Berkeley, CA: University of California, 2000); Henry Chadwick, *Augustine: A Very Short Introduction* (Oxford: Oxford University, 1986).

7 See *Catechism of the Catholic Church*, 2nd ed. (Vatican City: Libreria Editrice Vaticana, 1997), no. 1849.

8 Peter J. Leithart, "More than a Dainty Sip: Old and New in Augustine's *Contra Faustum*," unpublished essay, p. 3, n. 7. See also Leithart's "Conjugating the Rites: Old and New in Augustine's Theory of Signs," *Calvin Theological Journal* 34 (1999): 136–147.

Paul as an authority, Augustine seeks to ground his theology of the Old Testament in the teachings of Paul. Paul makes clear that the Old Testament has a strongly figural meaning: "All these were symbols of us. … All these things happened to them as symbols, but they were written down on account of us, upon whom the end of the ages has come" (1 Cor. 10:6, 11). The Greek word is *tupikos*, from which the English word typology derives. The "symbols" that Paul has in view have to do with the exodus of the people of Israel from Egypt, especially God's guiding the people in a "pillar of cloud" (Exod. 13:21), leading the people across the sea on dry land (Exod. 14:22), feeding the people with "bread from heaven" (Exod. 16:4), and giving the people water from a rock (Exod. 17:6). Paul holds that these events from Israel's history prefigure Christ and the Church: "I want you to know, brethren, that our fathers were all under the cloud, and all passed through the sea, and all were baptized into Moses in the cloud and in the sea, and all ate the same supernatural food and all drank the same supernatural drink. For they drank from the supernatural Rock which followed them, and the Rock was Christ" (1 Cor. 10:1–4). For Paul, this typological interpretation of Israel's exodus serves as a warning to Christians, since God punished the murmuring of the Israelites and their desire to return to Egypt, by allowing them to die in the wilderness rather than to reach the promised land.

Augustine argues that Paul here instructs the Church on how to understand the covenantal promises and laws that God gave the people of Israel. These covenantal promises and laws prefigure their fulfillment in Christ. The Israelites who received these promises and laws in expectation of their fulfillment were already united by faith with Christ. On this view, the Church of Christ was already present in Israel, although Israel knew Christ only through figures rather than in the way that we now know him. Augustine quotes the risen Jesus: "It was necessary that all the things be fulfilled that were written about me in the law of Moses and in the prophets and the psalms" (Luke 24:44). It thus cannot be that the Old Testament, as Faustus supposes, teaches only about the promise of the land of Canaan to the Jews who follow circumcision, the food laws, and so forth. It must be that the Old Testament teaches about the saving power of Jesus, including his crucifixion and resurrection. The fact that Jesus is not raised to a renewed earthly life, but rather is glorified, shows that the promises of God to Israel are about more than long life for the Jews in the land of Canaan. The promises of God pertain ultimately to the glory that has been revealed in the risen Lord.

On this basis, Augustine holds that the authors of the Old Testament were guided by God, both in their words and in their deeds, to signify prophetically through material images the glorious fulfillment that was to come. The whole history of the people of Israel was prophetic. God used even the sins of the people to show his intention to fulfill his covenants with Israel in a manner that would go well beyond the literal sense of dwelling peacefully in the land of Canaan.

Books 6, 9, and 10: The Law

Whereas Book 4 focuses on the promises, Book 6 takes up the law. Recall that Faustus thinks that he must reject the Old Testament not only because he does not want (nor is he included in) the reward of dwelling forever in Canaan, but also because he does not observe circumcision, the food laws, and so forth. Faustus argues that Catholics too reject the law as useless, and he criticizes Catholics as dissemblers for their attempt to praise the Old Testament while rejecting its core practices.

Augustine replies that God in fact gave Israel two kinds of laws: laws that are intended to regulate behavior, and laws that are intended to symbolize something regarding the relationship of Israel to God. Circumcision and the food laws are the latter kind. They are symbolic indicators of the people's relationship to God. Because they cannot achieve the intimacy that they symbolize, they foreshadow their own fulfillment. They do not serve any other necessary purpose, by contrast to laws that regulate behavior in a necessary way, such as we find in the Decalogue. Now that the fulfillment has come, Christians do not observe the laws that have a symbolic function in the Old Testament, since Christians observe the realities that these laws symbolized. An example is circumcision: Christians observe the circumcision of the heart prefigured by the circumcision of the flesh (see Deut. 30:6, Rom. 4:11). Faustus holds that holiness could not be signified by the circumcision of the male sexual organ, but Augustine points out that sexual generation is not despised by God. To become children of God, we must first become children through sexual generation. If God wishes, God can symbolize spiritual begetting by means of the circumcision of an organ involved in physical begetting.[9]

The strict Sabbath rest of the Old Testament provides Augustine with an example of why Christians should continue to care about the Old Testament's symbolic laws, even though we no longer practice them. The law regarding the Sabbath rest symbolizes the eternal rest to which Jesus, at the right hand of the Father, is leading his people. By reading about this reality as prefigured by the deeds and words of the people of Israel, we are helpfully taught to make this reality the center of our lives. Similarly, reading about the various animal sacrifices guides the Christian to reflect upon the sacrifice of Christ, symbolized by all the animal sacrifices. Since the laws about animal sacrifices symbolize Israel's intimacy with God in worship, without being able in themselves to accomplish this reality, the meaning of the animal sacrifices is fulfilled, not evacuated, by Jesus' death on the Cross and our participation in this sacrifice in Eucharistic worship. In the same

9 As Fredriksen shows, Augustine's positive interpretation of circumcision contrasts sharply with earlier pagan and Catholic critiques of circumcision. See Fredriksen, *Augustine and the Jews*, 250–254; 316–319. Fredriksen's thesis is that by affirming that the Jews had been right to observe God's commandments literally and that these commandments were good (even though now fulfilled), Augustine "stood centuries of traditional anti-Jewish polemic, both orthodox and heterodox, on its head" (*Augustine and the Jews*, 244).

vein, the food laws forbid eating certain things on symbolic grounds. Thus an animal that does not ruminate is "unclean" because it symbolizes humans who do not recall and meditate upon the words of wisdom that they have heard (see Prov. 21:20). By abstaining from eating this kind of animal, people are guided in avoiding this defect. Again, the laws regarding the feast of tabernacles or regarding wearing a garment woven of wool and linen (Deut. 22:11) have symbolic rather than regulative value. Now that Jesus has shown us the path of life, the symbolism of these laws is no longer necessary and his followers no longer need to observe the laws.

Even so, we can still benefit from the prophetic authority of these laws. As Augustine says, "The scripture that then required symbolic actions is therefore now a witness to the realities that were symbolized, and those practices that were then observed for the purpose of foretelling events are now read out for the purpose of confirming them."[10] He finds confirmation of this in 1 Corinthians 9:9–10, "For it is written in the law of Moses, 'You shall not muzzle an ox when it is treading out the grain.' Is it for oxen that God is concerned? Does he not speak entirely for our sake? It was written for our sake." Throughout Book 6, Augustine pauses frequently to show that the practices and beliefs of the Manicheans are rooted in profound contradiction and absurdity, by contrast to the meaningfulness of the Jewish and Catholic practices and beliefs.

In Book 9, Faustus notes that the apostles who were born Jews were permitted to abandon the laws of the Old Testament. He argues therefore that as a gentile he is justified in ignoring the Old Testament completely. He compares the Old Testament to a bitter tree and the New Testament to a sweet tree. Augustine points out in reply that Paul thinks of the gentiles as grafted onto the root of Israel (see Rom. 11). To be a Christian means to be joined to that root, rather than to do as Faustus has done and reject the root.

Book 10 records a similar argument on Faustus's part. He urges that the Old Testament and its promises regarding long life in Canaan are the property of the Jews, and in obedience to the Decalogue (as recorded also in Jesus' teaching) he must not covet the Jews' property. Augustine repeats the distinction between regulative and prophetic laws. Christians do not need to obey the prophetic laws, but neither can these laws be ignored. Rather, these laws now bear testimony to their fulfillment by Christ. The arrival of the reality does not displace the figure, because the figure continues to instruct us about the reality. Augustine again appeals to 1 Corinthians 10:11 to make clear that the Old Testament was written for Christians as well as for the Jewish people, even though the Jews were specially chosen by God to receive and obey the laws in a literal way prior to Christ's coming.

10 Augustine, *Answer to Faustus*, Bk. 6, Chap. 9, p. 104.

Books 12 and 13: The Prophets

In Book 12 Faustus argues that there is no need for prophetic testimony to Christ, because God testifies to Christ at his baptism by John (Matt. 3:17), and because Jesus also testifies that he has come forth from the Father (John 8:18; 16:28). Augustine replies that the Jewish prophets foretold Christ and that their prophecies remain important for Christian faith. Since, as has already been noted, Faustus accepts the authority of Paul, Augustine uses Paul's authority to make the case regarding the testimony of the prophets to Christ and the value of their testimony for Christians. Romans 1:2, for instance, teaches that the gospel of Jesus Christ was promised through the prophets; Galatians 3:16 speaks of the promises made to Abraham and to his offspring (Christ) in whom all nations will be blessed. Elsewhere Paul praises the advantages that God has given to the Jewish people. By listening to the prophets' testimony, we avoid inventing a false understanding of Christ like the one into which the Manicheans have fallen. Augustine goes through the Old Testament and finds numerous prophecies, including the creation of man in the image of God (perfected in Christ as the new Adam), the creation of Eve from the rib of Adam (fulfilled by the Church being formed through the blood that flowed from Christ's wounded side), the marriage of man and woman being an image of Christ and the Church (Eph. 5:32), the death of Abel as a figure of the death of Christ, the mark of Cain as foreshadowing the mark (and bodily protection) of the Jewish people after the crucifixion of Christ and the destruction of the Temple,[11] Noah's ark as a figure of the Church, Joseph's suffering at the hands of his brothers and being honored by the Egyptians (gentiles) as a figure of Christ, the symbolism of the Passover lamb, the royal and priestly power of David, Isaiah's prophecy of the suffering servant, Daniel's prophecy of the son of man, and many others. Faustus claims that no Jewish witnesses are needed, but Paul himself quotes Isaiah in Romans 10 precisely to show that the testimony of the Jewish prophets is needed in the proclamation of the gospel, to whose truth the prophets attest.[12] It is not for nothing that Abraham is "the father of all believers" (Rom. 4:11).

Book 13 continues the same debate: Faustus argues that even if the Jewish prophets foretold Christ, it should not matter to gentile Christians. Gentile Christians owe nothing to the Jewish prophets, but rather owe all to Christ himself. For Jews, the indirect testimony of the prophets may be of value, but not to non-Jews to whom the prophets never preached. Christ's direct word and example convert the gentiles, and so they do not need the prophets.

Augustine replies by taking another angle, this time focused on the term "Christ." Where, he asks, did Faustus learn the name "Christ"? It has its meaning from the Old Testament. The people of Israel were expecting a "Christ," an

11 For discussion see Fredriksen, *Augustine and the Jews*, 263–277, 319.

12 See Fredriksen, *Augustine and the Jews*, 320–324.

anointed one, to come and fulfill the role of priest and king in Israel. Paul and the Gospels introduce Jesus Christ in terms of the expectations of the prophets of Israel. Here Augustine has recourse again to Paul's affirmation that God had promised the gospel of Jesus Christ "through his prophets in the holy scriptures" (Rom. 1:2), and Augustine also appeals to Matthew's use of Isaiah 7:14 in announcing the birth of Jesus Christ. Against Faustus's claim that no witnesses other than Christ are needed, Augustine points to the role that Mani plays for Faustus, since Mani styled himself in his letters "an apostle of Jesus Christ." Mani's errors show Augustine how important it is to understand what "Christ" means through the Jewish people whom God had instructed on this matter. Whether Jesus is the "Christ" becomes apparent in light of the Jewish testimonies to the coming of the Christ. Not only Paul and Matthew, but also Jesus in the Gospel of John makes precisely this point: "Search the scriptures in which you think that you have eternal life; they bear witness concerning me. ... If you believed Moses, you would also believe me, for he wrote about me" (Jn. 5:39, 46). Believing truly about Christ requires learning from trustworthy witnesses, and the very witnesses that Christ himself commends (the Old Testament prophets) are rejected by Faustus in favor of Mani.

In addition, Augustine argues that the prophets bear witness to events that have occurred since the coming of Christ and thus have to do with the gentiles rather than strictly with the Jews. Regarding the Roman persecution of the Church of Christ, and of the Church's universal extension, he quotes Psalm 2:2, "The kings and princes of the earth have risen and gathered together against the Lord and against his Christ," and Psalm 2:8, "I will give you the nations as your inheritance and the ends of the earth as your possession." He also quotes various passages from Isaiah and Jeremiah, and from Paul quoting Isaiah, that prophesy the destruction of the idols and the rise of faith among the gentile nations. The Old Testament also assists in understanding why some members of the Church of Christ fall away from holiness and produce divisions. As Paul says, "whatever was written before was written to teach us so that through patience and the consolation of the scriptures we may have hope in God" (Rom. 15:4).

Book 14: Did Moses Curse Christ?

According to Faustus, Moses is anathema because he cursed Christ in Deuteronomy 21:23: "His body shall not remain all night upon the tree, but you shall bury him the same day, for a hanged man is accursed by God." This is the topic of Book 14. Augustine first points out that the Manicheans deny that Christ had a mortal body, so that the curse would not, therefore, apply to their Christ. He goes on to connect Moses' curse in Deuteronomy with the curse that God applied to eating of the tree of the knowledge of good and evil. When the first humans ate of that tree, human nature was disordered and they suffered the curse of death. When the innocent

Christ hung on the tree, he bore the curse for us. In this regard Augustine quotes Paul extensively: "He became a curse for us" (Gal. 3:13); "God sent his son in the likeness of sinful flesh so that from sin he might condemn sin in the flesh" (Rom. 8:3); "Him who did not know sin he made sin on our behalf so that we might be the righteousness of God in him" (2 Cor. 10:21). On the wood of the cross, Christ bore the curse of sin and death for us and redeemed us from this curse. Augustine expresses his gratitude for being rescued both from the curse and from the false teaching of the Manicheans, whose doctrine had captivated him for many years. The death that we must avoid is the death of the soul. Christ's death, which bears the curse, frees us from the condemnation of our souls.

Book 15: Accepting Both Testaments a Monstrosity?

Book 15 contains yet another argument from Faustus for rejecting the Old Testament. He proposes that one can be fully nourished by the Old Testament (as the Jews were and are today), or fully nourished by the New Testament, or half-nourished by both. To accept both Testaments means to be only half-nourished by the New Testament; it is like diluting honey with a half-portion of vinegar. To change the metaphor, the Church should receive only Christ's Testament. The Testament of the Jews, with its promises of long life in Canaan, has no place in the Church, because the Church is already fully enriched by the bridal gift of Christ's own Testament. Indeed, Faustus holds that the God of the Jews has proven himself unable to fulfill his promises to the Jews, whereas the risen Christ has shown that he can fulfill his promises. Again changing the metaphor, Faustus argues that to accept both Testaments is to turn the Christian faith into a monstrous entity, like a centaur that is half-horse and half-man but fully neither. In defense of his position, he quotes Romans 7:2–3, where Paul suggests that continuing in the observance of the law, now that the law is dead and we have been united to Christ, is like adultery. We must now worship only the God of the New Testament.

Augustine's response begins with the metaphor of diluting the honey with vinegar. If Faustus is right, then Paul himself must be guilty of diluting the gospel, because Paul begins by calling himself "the servant of Christ Jesus, who was called to be an apostle" (Rom. 1:1) and in the same sentence brings in God's promises "through his prophets in the holy scriptures concerning his Son, who was born as a descendant of David according to the flesh" (Rom. 1:2–3). If employing the Old Testament necessarily dilutes the New, then Paul has done it and should be rejected. But as Jesus suggests, the proper way to understand the two Testaments is to think of the householder "who brings forth from his storeroom new and old things" (Matt. 13:52). Augustine argues that the Old and New Testaments are not two completely different things, laid side-by-side as it were. Rather, since the words and deeds of the Old Testament prefigure the deeds of the New, the Old Testament is interiorly related to the New. The patriarchs and prophets of the Old

Testament looked forward in faith to a future fulfillment that goes beyond anything that they had experienced. They desired an intimacy with God far greater than could be accomplished simply by long life in Canaan. In figures, they spoke of the Messianic fulfillment that they loved. Their writings, as prophetic, relate interiorly to the reality revealed in the New Testament. Failure to appreciate this interior relationship of figure and reality leads to imagining that the Old and New Testaments are related like two separate substances, honey and vinegar, so that one has the law on this side and Christ on the other. Augustine's point is that this is a false separation. Thus, for example, the conversion of the gentiles is not solely a New Testament reality; it is prophesied and prefigured in the Old Testament. The Old Testament cannot be put to the side like an alien substance that competes for space with the New.

In this vein Augustine observes that a favorite Manichean text in which Paul teaches that the Corinthians are "a letter from Christ delivered by us, written not with ink but with the Spirit of the living God, not on tablets of stone but on tablets of human hearts" (2 Cor. 3:3), in fact builds upon Jeremiah 31:33 and Ezekiel 11:19. The Decalogue is not foreign to Christians, but rather describes the loving relationship to God and neighbor that the grace of the Holy Spirit enables us to fulfill.

Augustine answers Faustus's charge of adultery with another god by quoting Deuteronomy 6:4, which teaches the one God in whom Christians believe, and by contrasting this faith with Manichean belief in many spirit-beings who are begotten of God's own substance and in Mani as the perfect teacher of divine realities. Going through the list of the Ten Commandments, Augustine shows how Manichean doctrine undermines each one of them. With respect to 2 Corinthians 3:6, "The letter kills, but the spirit gives life," he argues that Paul here no more intends to condemn the law than Paul intends to condemn knowledge when he writes, "Knowledge puffs up, but love builds up" (1 Cor. 8:1). The problem is not with the letter of the law, or with knowledge, but with the pride of sinners: "The law is good if anyone uses it lawfully" (1 Tim. 1:8), but as Paul also says, "It was sin, working death in me through what is good, in order that sin might be shown to be sin, and through the commandment might become sinful beyond measure" (Rom. 7:13). Even the Manicheans, Augustine notes at the end of Book XV, have been expressly foretold in Scripture. Thus Paul warns that "in the last times some will withdraw from the faith, paying attention to deceitful spirits and to the teaching of demons lying in their hypocrisy. Having their conscience seared and forbidding marriage, they will abstain from the food that God created for those who believe and know the truth to receive with thanksgiving. For every creature of God is good" (1 Tim. 4:1–4).

Book 16: Did Moses Only "Accidentally" Write About the Christ?

In Book 16 Faustus turns to the claim of Christ in John 5:46, "If you believed Moses, you would believe me, for he wrote of me." Faustus notes that it would be possible to affirm that Moses wrote of Christ, without thereby receiving the Old Testament. Moses might have inadvertently written about Christ. After all, even the demons testified to Christ. Yet, not finding any evidence that Moses wrote of Christ, Faustus prefers to think that this passage was not really said by Jesus but instead is a later interpolation. The evidence that is often adduced in favor of Moses writing about Christ—for instance Deuteronomy 18:18, "I will raise up for them from among their brothers a prophet like you"—Faustus finds to be unpersuasive, since Christ was God rather than being a sinful prophet like Moses. Faustus denies that believing Moses would lead to believing Christ, because the two teach quite opposite things (for example, about the Sabbath and food laws). Even had Moses written of Christ, Christians should avoid the Old Testament because the law of Moses would only enslave Christians.

Augustine responds by insisting that everything that Moses wrote prefigures Christ or praises Christ's grace and glory. For example, the temple, animal sacrifice, the altar, and the Mosaic priesthood are all mentioned positively by Christ in the Gospels,[13] and their figurative meaning is shown when Christ compares his body to the temple (Jn. 2:19) and when Paul calls believers the temple of God (1 Cor. 3:17). Augustine challenges Faustus's claim that Jesus did not say the words attributed to him in John 5:46. There is no basis for denying the authenticity of the verses that contradict one's position, especially if one then builds one's case on other seemingly more amenable verses. He then takes up the verse mentioned by Faustus, Deuteronomy 18:18. The differences between Christ and Moses are obvious, but these differences do not mean that Christ is not a prophet like Moses. Christ does not need to be like Moses in every way in order to be like him. After all, Christ is described as like a "lamb" and a "rock" in the New Testament. Likeness does not require equivalence. Because Christ is God, Christ is not like Moses; but at the same time because Christ is a man, Christ is like Moses. Christ is not a sinner, but he is like a sinner in the sense that God sent him "in the likeness of sinful flesh" (Rom. 8:3). Jesus speaks of himself as a prophet in Matthew 13:57. Jesus leads us into the kingdom of heaven, just as Moses was called to lead the people of Israel into the promised land. Moses' literal successor was named Jesus (Joshua), thereby prefiguring his true successor.

Furthermore, Moses is not as bad as Faustus suggests. At the Transfiguration, after all, Moses and Elijah merited to stand with Jesus. Jesus makes clear that the God proclaimed by Moses—the God of Abraham, Isaac, and Jacob (see Matt. 8:11; 22:32)—is the true God, despite Manichean claims to the contrary. Jesus

13 On Augustine's positive reading of the Temple sacrifices, see Fredriksen, *Augustine and the Jews*, 246–250.

was not a prophet who sought to lead the Jews away from their God in violation of Deuteronomy 13:1–2.[14] Indeed, this very passage from Moses foreshadows Mani's leading people away from Christ. Insofar as they teach Moses' law, Jesus honors those who "sit upon the chair of Moses" (Matt. 23:2), although he warns against their hypocrisy.

Augustine's point is that there is plenty of reason to believe that Deuteronomy 18:18 applies to Christ. Once this is recognized, one comes to appreciate why Jesus taught that Moses, in all his writings, "wrote about me" (Jn. 5:46). Moses and his writings signify Christ in diverse ways. For instance, when Moses, striking the rock that according to Paul signifies Christ, doubts the power of God, Moses foreshadows those who nailed Christ to the cross (and the water that flows from the rock foreshadows the grace that flows from the cross). Moses' death on the mountain, similarly, signifies the death of pride that occurs when Christ's glory is recognized. Moreover, even wicked men in the Old Testament, as in the New, are able to speak symbolically of Jesus. With respect to Moses' teachings about the Sabbath and unclean foods, Faustus does not take into account the difference in times. The literal observance of the Sabbath foreshadowed the eternal Sabbath into which the risen Christ leads us. Circumcision of the flesh foreshadowed the circumcision of the heart won by Christ's cross. The commandment that circumcision be undertaken on the eighth day corresponds to Christ's rising on the eighth day after the Sabbath. The clean and unclean animals symbolize behaviors that place us within or outside the Church. In each case, the figure taken literally cannot accomplish intimacy with God, but the figure promotes faith that God will accomplish this reality for us through Christ. Catholics receive Moses' commandments by observing "them all no longer in figures but in the realities that those figures foretold by their signification."[15]

Books 17, 18, and 19: Matthew 5:17 and the Fulfillment of the Law

Book 17 addresses Faustus's claim that Matthew 5:17, "Think not that I have come to abolish the law and the prophets; I have come not to abolish them but to fulfill them," was invented by Matthew or interpolated into the Gospel by a later writer. Faustus emphasizes that the reason why many Jews of Jesus' time thought that he was abolishing the law and the prophets is because he was indeed doing so, as can be seen by his numerous additions to and subtractions from the law of Moses. On this view, Jesus deliberately violated the warning of Deuteronomy 5:32, where Moses says, "You shall observe these commandments that I am giving to you today,

14 On the development in Augustine's thought on this point, see Fredriksen, *Augustine and the Jews*, 255. In his *Commentary on Galatians* and *On Christian Doctrine*, Augustine held that Jesus violated the Jewish law, whereas Augustine denies this in *Answer to Faustus, a Manichean*.

15 Augustine, *Answer to Faustus*, Bk. 16, Chap. 32, p. 225.

O Israel. Be careful not to turn aside from them either to the left or to the right, and do not add anything to them or take anything away."

Since one of Faustus's arguments is that Matthew was not actually present on the mountain when Jesus gave this sermon, Augustine points out that neither were Mani and Faustus. If Matthew is not to be believed for this reason, then neither are Mani and Faustus. But Augustine gladly grants that Jesus did indeed seem to be a destroyer of the law and prophets to those Jews who did not understand him. Quoting Paul, Augustine notes that "the fulfillment of the law is love" (Rom. 13:10). Jesus fulfills the law in two ways: by loving God and neighbor, and by bringing about what the law had prefigured. He thereby fulfills the law, as John says, in "grace and truth" (Jn. 1:17). He does not add or subtract from the law, but instead he carries out the law through the grace of charity and the truth of fulfilled prophecy.

Matthew 5:17 is also the subject of Book 18, where Faustus again presses his claim that both Manicheans and Christians obviously reject Moses' commandments by refusing to circumcise, to obey the laws about unclean foods, and to sacrifice animals. Augustine replies by directing Faustus's attention to Jeremiah 31:31–33:

> Behold, the days are coming, says the Lord, when I will make a new covenant with the house of Israel and the house of Judah, not like the covenant which I made with their fathers when I took them by the hand to bring them out of the land of Egypt, my covenant which they broke, though I was their husband, says the Lord. But this is the covenant which I will make with the house of Israel after those days, says the Lord: I will put my law within them, and I will write it upon their hearts; and I will be their God, and they shall be my people.

Augustine's point is that the Old Testament explicitly looks forward to a New Testament. As such, it is to be expected that the Old Testament is not yet God's final word for his people, but rather contains symbolic words and deeds that prepare the people for God's final word. When God gives his new covenant, the reality toward which the symbols pointed will be revealed, and the full meaning of the symbols will also thereby be revealed. This has happened in Jesus Christ, just as Paul shows in 2 Corinthians 3. Christians now observe the symbols in the reality, which is different from supposing that the symbols themselves have been rejected. By contrast, the pagan rites were rejected by the Jewish people and are rejected by Christians. The Jewish Sabbath took place on the same day that pagans dedicated to Saturn, but the Sabbath's purpose, far from being similar to pagan worship of creatures, was to foreshadow our rest in the risen Christ. As Paul says of the Sabbath and other Jewish festivals, "These are only a shadow of what is to come;

but the substance belongs to Christ" (Col. 2:17). The Jewish animal sacrifices did not imagine that God is placated for sin by the blood of animals; instead they prefigured our redemption by Christ's blood.[16] Christ fulfills what the law of Moses symbolized. Just as the symbols are fulfilled in Christ and the Church, so also the commandments are fulfilled by love of God and love of neighbor: "On these two commandments depend all the law and the prophets" (Matt. 22:40).

In Book 19, Faustus is willing to grant that Jesus said what Matthew 5:17 reports him to have said. Faustus argues, however, that Jesus said it to placate his enemies at the time, and Jesus did not actually mean the Jewish law or the Jewish prophets. Faustus identifies three kinds of law: the Jewish law, the natural law of the gentiles, and the law of the truth (the law of Christians). He also states that not only the Jews, but also the gentiles and the Christians have prophets. According to Faustus, the commandments that Jesus goes on to mention, such as "You shall not kill" (Matt. 5:21), are found long ago among the gentiles. It is these gentile laws that will be fulfilled by the law of truth. The law of the Jews, by contrast, is rejected by Jesus in a series of statements where he tells his audience, "You have heard that it was said" (Matt. 5:38), and then goes on to teach the opposite. Faustus emphasizes once more that he and Catholics should agree on this point, because both Manicheans and Catholics reject circumcision, the food laws, animal sacrifice, and so forth. If Christ had come to fulfill and not to destroy the Jewish law, then both Manicheans and Catholics would need to become Jews so as to observe these commandments. If Catholics imagine that Christ does not destroy the Jewish law, then by their own rejection of the Jewish law they are destroying the Jewish law and simultaneously disobeying Christ.

Augustine, in reply, begins by once more quoting 1 Corinthians 10:6, "All these things were symbols of us," and in confirmation of Christ's mission of fulfillment he adds 2 Corinthians 1:19–20, "He was not 'yes' and 'no,' but there was only 'yes' in him, for all the promises of God were 'yes' in him." He then dismisses Faustus's notion that there are three kinds of law (and prophets) to which Jesus might be referring. John 1:17 and 5:46 are clear that Jesus has in view the law of Moses. Paul says of the law of Moses, "The law, therefore, is holy, and the commandment is holy, just, and good" (Rom. 7:12). The law of Moses humbled its recipients by showing them how easily they failed, thereby making ready for faith in Christ. The law served as a "schoolmaster" (Gal. 3:25) preparing for the freedom that faith in Christ gives through the grace of the Holy Spirit. Christ fulfills the righteousness of the law, and, by faith, transformed by the grace of the Holy Spirit, we share in his fulfillment. Even in grace we fail to fulfill it perfectly, and so we rely on Christ to intercede for us and mediate God's forgiveness to us (see 1 John 2:1–2). In this way, Christ fulfills the prophecies and the divine promises. The fact that the prophecies and promises have been fulfilled is the reason why Christians no

16 See Fredriksen, *Augustine and the Jews*, 250.

longer obey the commandments that symbolized this fulfillment. Christians are not circumcised in the flesh, for example, because Christ's resurrection fulfilled the spiritual birth symbolized by circumcision. Yet this does not mean that Christians are now bereft of sacraments. On the contrary, since the resurrection of the dead has happened to Christ but not to us, Christ has given us the sacrament of baptism to symbolize our participation in Christ's death and resurrection.

Augustine develops further this theology of sacramental signs. Every religion, he argues, requires visible signs in order to unite people. Giving the example of Simon Magus, Augustine points out that these visible signs are misused by those who latch on to their outward aspect and fail to see that their purpose is holiness, charity, and faith, but even so the signs should not be rejected. God gave his chosen people visible signs that symbolized the coming of Christ, and many of his chosen people performed these sacraments in faith, hoping for God's salvation rather than trusting in the outward form. When Christ came, he fulfilled the sacraments that symbolized him. He instituted more powerful (and fewer) sacraments that unite his people in him and, when performed in faith, lead us to the resurrection life that he now possesses.[17] Just as those living before Christ obeyed their sacramental signs often at great personal cost because of their faith in what was to come, so also, living after Christ, we too should not hesitate to endure all hardships for baptism and the Eucharist, in faith that we will receive the resurrection and eternal life won by Christ. What we believe in by faith has already been accomplished in Christ.

The sacraments of the Old Testament and of the New testify to the same faith, namely faith in Christ who redeems his people and leads his people to everlasting life with God.[18] The change in sacraments does not indicate a change in the realities of faith, as if there were no unity between Old and New Testaments. Rather, the old sacraments signify the Christ who is to come, and the new sacraments signify the Christ who has come. The God who ordains the sacraments, and the purpose for which he ordains them, remains the same, despite the necessary change in the bodily actions and words of the sacramental signs. Again, the change in sacraments was necessary to ensure that Christians did not signify, by obeying the sacraments of the Mosaic law, that Christ was still to come. Christ has indeed come and fulfilled the sacraments that symbolized his coming.

Why, then, did St. Paul circumcise Timothy (see Acts 16:1–3)? If Christ fulfilled the old sacraments that symbolized his coming, then how is it that we

---

17 For Augustine's treatment of the sacraments in Book 19, see Phillip Cary, *Outward Signs: The Powerlessness of External Things in Augustine's Thought* (Oxford: Oxford University, 2008), 236–237. Mistakenly I think, Cary argues that for Augustine the "virtus sacramenti" is simply our piety.

18 See Cary, *Outward Signs*, 240–243. Insisting on "the ontological powerlessness of external things in Augustine's thought" (244), Cary holds that Augustine thinks of Christ as exemplifying and signifying, but not causing or accomplishing, our salvation. With regard both to the sacraments and to Christ, however, Cary overstates his case.

find Paul, after Christ has died and risen, still performing the old sacraments as if Christ had not in fact come? Augustine explains that the old sacraments, since they were truly from God, could not simply be rejected as if they were things that had no value. Rather, it had to be shown that they had been fulfilled, not merely negated. Their divine ordination meant that the apostles had to treat them with respect, especially given the unity of faith between the Old and New Testaments. A change in sacramental signs had to be undertaken slowly or else it could have been misunderstood as a rejection of the Old Testament and the God of the Old Testament—the very thing the Manicheans had done. Those who had been raised under the Old Testament's sacramental signs were not forced to give them up, but at the same time those gentiles who came to faith were not forced to adopt the Old Testament sacraments.[19]

Augustine recognizes, of course, that there nonetheless arose a serious controversy among the first Christians regarding whether or not the gentiles needed to obey the Old Testament sacraments. This was the theme of the council of Jerusalem described in Acts 15, and it also appears in Paul's letters (for example, Gal. 2). It was difficult for those who had been born prior to Jesus' death and resurrection, and who had thus grown up under the Old Testament sacraments, to accept that the prophetic sacraments had served their purpose now that Christ had in fact come. The apostles walked a fine line between seeming to reject the value of these divinely ordained sacraments and failing to acknowledge that their prophetic role had now ended. Augustine argues that the apostles, led in this regard by Paul, made the right pastoral decision in permitting those who had grown up under the law to keep the sacraments of the law, while insisting that new believers recognize Christ's fulfillment of the Mosaic sacraments. The apostles' insistence that the Mosaic law and its sacraments had been fulfilled by Christ, so that observance of these sacraments now had to cease lest Christian sacramental practice falsely testify that Christ has not yet come, resulted in break-away groups such as the Symmachians (Nazareans) that continued to require all believers in Christ to obey the Mosaic law. These groups were known to both Augustine and Faustus.

Augustine also distinguishes between commandments that have to do with conduct and laws that are in some way symbolic. Christians continue to obey the commandments that have to do with conduct, such as "You shall not make an idol for yourself" (Lev. 26:1). Christians worship the God who gave these commandments, so Christians obey them through the grace of the Holy Spirit given by Christ. With respect to the symbolic laws, Christians obey them not in themselves but in their fulfillment in Christ. The commandments are fulfilled by a person who has faith working through love (see Gal. 5:6). The symbolic laws (the sacraments) are fulfilled by the coming of what they symbolized. Regarding the latter, Augustine notes that "they were not destroyed but fulfilled, because Christ

19 For discussion see Fredriksen, *Augustine and the Jews*, 256–257.

showed that they were neither invalid nor deceptive when he made known what their significance promised."[20]

Returning to Faustus's claim that Christ fulfilled the law of the gentiles and destroyed the law of Moses, Augustine emphasizes that Christ fulfilled Moses' law and strengthened it by attending to the inner dispositions from which flow our actions. Some commandments, however, were indeed shown by Christ to be suited for the people of Israel but not for Christians. Augustine argues that God gave some commandments that fit the particular time but not all times. For example, Exodus 21:24, "An eye for an eye, a tooth for a tooth," helped to form the people of Israel in their time and place, but was abolished by Jesus, in a certain sense at least. Yet even in this case, Jesus abolished it only because his coming fulfilled the time, so that a new time has begun. Fulfillment, not abolition, is the core reality. With respect to Faustus's notion that Christ fulfilled the law of the gentiles by adding (for example) restraints on anger and lust (see Matt. 5:22, 28), Augustine points out that if the gentiles did not know to restrain their anger and lust, none of them could have been righteous, whereas in fact through faith some of them were righteous, among them Enoch, who "walked with God" (Gen. 5:24). Regarding Christ's commandment that people not swear at all (see Matt. 5:34), Augustine observes that both Paul and the Manicheans swear oaths. Christ here is warning against perjury and against the danger, caused by a habit of swearing oaths, of unintentionally falling into perjury. Not swearing at all frees us from the danger of perjury, but in certain circumstances oaths are permitted. Thus Christ does not negate, but instead strengthens the Mosaic law regarding oaths (see Lev. 19:12).

Faustus had pressed the point that Christ rejected the Mosaic law that required the Jews to love their neighbors but did not require them to love outsiders (for example, Lev. 19:18). Augustine responds that Paul, too, teaches that some persons are hateful to God and deserve to die (see Rom. 1:30–32). The key here is to distinguish the way in which charitable persons love their enemies from the way in which charitable persons hate their enemies. The enemies of charitable persons should be loved as human beings, but their sin should be hated. We should love a person's human nature but hate the sinful distortion of human nature in that person. It is a mark of true love toward the sinner to want the sinner to be freed from sin. Similarly, the Mosaic law about "an eye for an eye" served to restrain uncontrolled vengeance. Jesus did not reject vengeance altogether: someone who has suffered an injury still deserves repayment. It is not wrong for a Christian to ask for the payment of a debt. Even so, Jesus makes clear that the fine line between desiring repayment in a just manner and desiring repayment in an uncontrolled, angry, and bitter manner is not easy to walk, and so it is safest, spiritually speaking, not to demand repayment at all. In this sense, rather than abolishing the Mosaic law, Christ's teaching ensures that what the Mosaic law sought—the avoidance of

20 Augustine, *Answer to Faustus*, Bk. 19, Chap. 19, p. 250.

uncontrolled vengeance—will be more easily attained. Augustine's interpretation here fits with his interpretation of Christ's commandment against swearing oaths. In the same way, he argues that Christ's rejection of divorce fits with the intention of Deuteronomy 24:1, which was to restrain people from dismissing their wives. Moreover, by making us charitable through the grace of the Holy Spirit, Christ not only teaches about the law but enables us to fulfill it, so that we can love God and neighbor and attain to the kingdom of heaven.

Augustine also adduces texts from the Old Testament (especially the wisdom literature) that teach, as Christ does, against anger and lust and in favor of love of enemy and mercy. Similarly, when Christ teaches against divorce, he appeals in his argument to Genesis 2:24. Not only does Christ not negate the law of Moses, he agrees with Moses against the Manicheans in appreciating the good of marriage.

Augustine again observes that the goals of being made holy and living in everlasting union with God are present in both Testaments. Although these goals and the path by which we attain them are often hidden in the Old Testament and are clearly revealed only in the New, the holy people of the Old Testament lived by faith and thus were already united to these goals. By faith, guided by the many symbols of the Old Testament, they already believed in the one who would come, filled with the Holy Spirit, to take away sin and to unite us with God in resurrection and eternal life. The coming of Christ thus fulfills God's promises and, by the outpouring of grace, enables us to fulfill God's law of love.

Book 22: Were the Old Testament Authors Liars?

Book 22 is the longest of all the Books in *Answer to Faustus, a Manichean*. Faustus argues that neither he, nor the Manicheans, are enemies of the law and the prophets. On the contrary, he is willing to believe that what was written in the Old Testament books about the patriarchs and prophets is false. If the Old Testament books are true, however, then it is clear that the patriarchs and prophets lived unrighteous lives.

The law of the gentiles, Faustus maintains, was good. This law, shared by the best men of all nations, can be found in such commandments as "You shall not commit adultery" (Exod. 20:14). But the Jewish writers took this law and intermingled it with all sorts of nonsense about circumcision, animal sacrifices, and so forth. To be holy, we need to obey the true law, but the intermingled nonsensical laws have nothing to do with holiness, as Catholics show by not obeying them. In rejecting the Jewish laws (and Judaism), Faustus does not thereby reject the law, properly understood. The prophets and patriarchs wrote and did abominable things. Perhaps the prophets, in writing about the patriarchs, lied about them, in which case the reputation of the patriarchs could be salvaged. Faustus bemoans the Old Testament's portrait of God. The true God would not have worried about the first man and woman eating from a particular tree, for example. Nor would he have been jealous, angry, and bloodthirsty against various peoples, including his own. He would not have destroyed thousands of men because a few among them had committed a small sin. He would not have threatened to obliterate the whole human race. Faustus can only hope that the prophet or prophets who wrote such things were lying. Certainly such authors were not holy.

Abraham's copulation with his wife's maidservant, with his wife's knowledge, strikes Faustus as disgusting, as does Abraham's lying to Abimelech and to Pharaoh. What kind of husband would cause, by his own lies, his wife to become a king's concubine? Abraham's brother Lot is a drunk who has incestuous intercourse with his two daughters. Isaac too is a liar, and Jacob a philanderer with his two wives and their maidservants. Judah has intercourse with his daughter-in-law, who deceives him by posing as a prostitute. Moses is a murderer and robber, and takes many wives. David has countless wives and still commits adultery with Bathsheba because of his rapacious lust, after which he orders that Bathsheba's husband be killed. Solomon too has countless wives and concubines. Hosea even blames God for commanding him to marry a prostitute. Far from being holy, these men are criminals, and the God that they depict is hardly better—unless the whole Old Testament is a lie, which would be much better than supposing it to be true.

Augustine here is led to offer an extended defense and explanation of the behavior and writings of the Old Testament prophets and patriarchs, as well as the God whom they portray. After briefly distinguishing once more between the commandments—fulfilled by love of God and neighbor—and the promises/symbols of the law, he begins with the portrait of God and creation in Genesis 1. First John 1:5 states that "God is light," and this divine light (wisdom) makes all created light, whether spiritual or bodily. God did not, therefore, previously dwell in the "darkness" that "was over the abyss" (Gen. 1:2). Nor, when God "saw that the light was good" (Gen. 1:4), did that surprise God. Nor are we to suppose that God's question, "Where are you?" (Gen. 3:9), means that God did not know where Adam was.

Augustine then points out that if Faustus is committed to reading the Old Testament in a flat-footed manner, by supposing that the Old Testament teaches that God dwelt in darkness or that God was surprised to see that his work was good, then Faustus will also have to apply the same defective exegetical technique to the New Testament. Christ, after all, chose Judas among the twelve; does this mean that Christ lacked foresight? In his parable of the wise and foolish virgins, Christ speaks of shutting the door on the five foolish virgins; does this mean that Christ is eager to lock us out? When Christ teaches that we must lose our lives for his sake, does this mean that Christ is bloodthirsty? When Christ warns sternly about judgment and punishment, does this mean that Christ is an arbitrary and wrathful God? In a parable, for example, Christ says that those who lack a wedding garment will be thrown "into the outer darkness" (Matt. 21:13). Is Christ, then, arbitrary and wrathful? The same question pertains to the Father who hands over his innocent Son to death (Rom. 8:32) or to the God who permits his saints to endure terrible tribulations.

Having shown that Faustus's mode of exegesis would distort the New Testament (which Faustus accepts) in the same way that it distorts the Old Testament, Augustine observes that pagans could teach Faustus something about reading Scripture. Pagans, Augustine thinks, could understand that God is creator of the world and that God rejoices in the world's goodness. Pagans could understand that God is not to be blamed if he gives a good law and people do not follow it, even if God foreknows that many will fail to follow it. Pagans have some sense of divine providence and of the symbolic role of animal sacrifices, even if pagans have abused sacrificial worship by offering it to demons. Pagans might be open to learning the truth of prophetic discourse. Pagans certainly can understand different modes of speech, and they will recognize that the term "jealous," for instance, can have a much wider range of meaning than Faustus allows. Pagans would be able to understand that God, in sparing neither the wicked nor the just, does so to punish the wicked and to purify and perfect the just.

Faustus's notion of a dark, ignorant, bloodthirsty, jealous, and arbitrarily wrathful Old Testament God thus gives way, on a fair reading, to the God who is light, who foreknows all things, who jealously guards his people against idolatry, who punishes justly, and who purifies those who are on the way to salvation. By contrast, the Manichean God, whom Augustine goes on to describe, truly is monstrous in his relation to the things that he begets from his own substance. After all, the Manicheans believe that God is trapped, as spirit, within animals and foods that are offered in sacrifice to idols. Manicheans believe that God weakly gives up his own members, begotten of his own substance, to the realm of darkness without their free consent, and that God's members are punished in this realm of darkness by being caught up into the darkness.

What about Faustus's charge that the patriarchs and prophets were vicious rather than virtuous? No matter how vicious they were, Augustine argues, they were not as vicious as the Manichean God. In his view, no further answer would be needed if he were responding only to the Manicheans, but the purpose of his response is also to instruct Christians. The principle on which Augustine builds his answer is that "not only the language but also the life of those persons was prophetic, and that the whole kingdom of the nation of the Hebrews was a great prophet because it was prophetic of someone great."[21] To this principle, Augustine adds the point that sin is a violation of God's eternal law. The Holy Spirit heals fallen humans so that, through faith, we can know what God's eternal law is and obey his law by works of love.

---

21 Augustine, *Answer to Faustus*, Bk. 22, Chap. 24, p. 316.

On these foundations, the first question that Augustine takes up is whether Abraham violated the eternal law by having sexual intercourse with Hagar, Sarah's maidservant. Here he argues that Abraham sought this sexual intercourse solely for the purpose of having children, a purpose that accords with God's law for sexual intercourse. Sarah, too, acted from the desire to have children. Although God had promised that Abraham would have a child, he had not told him how this would come about. Since Sarah was barren, it was reasonable for Sarah to call upon her maidservant to serve as the mother of Abraham's child; and Abraham was reasonable to obey Sarah's wishes. Since Hagar was Sarah's maidservant, Augustine considers that Sarah could justly command Hagar in this regard.

Regarding Abraham's supposedly deceiving Abimelech and Pharaoh, Augustine points out that Sarah truly was Abraham's half-sister. Abraham did not lie; he simply did not tell the whole truth. He withheld part of the truth for good reason, namely fear that he would be killed by these kings so that they could take Sarah by force. In stating only that Sarah was his sister, he trusted that God would ensure that Sarah would not be abused, and his trust was shown to be well-founded. Augustine also suggests that Sarah is a figure of the Church, which, in a hidden way, is the chaste bride of Christ in the midst of the earthly kingdoms of the world, symbolized by Abimelech and Pharaoh. He also interprets Lot symbolically, not only with respect to Lot's life in Sodom (which can symbolize the life of the saints among the wicked), but also with respect to his drunken sexual intercourse with his daughters (which can symbolize the illegitimate use of the Mosaic law made by those Israelites whose understanding of the law was darkened).

Augustine does not thereby justify the vicious behavior of Lot in getting drunk, or of Lot's daughters in their incestuous actions. Rather, he argues that their evil actions were permitted by God and were recorded in Scripture for our prophetic instruction. As for Lot and his daughters, God justly judged their evil actions. Yet Augustine observes that Lot's daughters undertook this behavior for the sake of having children after the destruction of the men of Sodom and Gomorrah, and not simply out of lust. Above all, he makes clear that Scripture narrates these actions without approving them, although Scripture narrates them for a reason.

Augustine considers that having many wives need not be a violation of God's eternal law. It is custom, not the eternal law, that determines how many wives are permissible at a given time and place. Since the fundamental purpose of marriage within God's providential order is the propagation of the human race, the number of wives permissible to one man depends on the need for the begetting of children. So long as the man does not seek wives on account of lust, having more than one wife does not necessarily violate God's law. As for the role of the maidservants, Augustine interprets it in the same way as he did for Abraham and Sarah. Jacob was obedient to his wives in the matter of sexual intercourse, and the purpose was consistently the begetting of children for the good of the household. Augustine also draws symbolic meanings from the two wives, the two maidservants, and various events in their lives. For example, Leah symbolizes action, Rachel contemplation. Jacob's active life of moral virtue (Leah) is fulfilled by contemplative wisdom (Rachel). The active life of virtue is loved for its fruits, just as Leah is honored for her children. The contemplative life needs the time that we all too often give to the active life, just as Rachel is sometimes jealous of Leah.

Scripture does not defend the actions of Judah, who sinned by having sexual intercourse with his daughter-in-law and by selling his brother into slavery. Yet Scripture counts Judah among the twelve patriarchs of Israel, and Judah is honored because David and Christ descend from him. How could God have permitted this? Augustine replies that even Judas served as one of the twelve apostles. Since Judah is a sinner, furthermore, Jacob's prophecy regarding Judah (Gen. 49:10) clearly describes not Judah but one who will come from his line, thereby preparing the people for Christ. When David sinned most egregiously, the prophet Nathan rebuked him. David's sins are not honored, although David's good deeds are, especially his humble repentance. Repentant sinners who bear much spiritual fruit in God's eyes excel those who do not commit egregious sins but who nonetheless lack interior humility. Augustine observes that in accord with his humanity, Christ descended not only from good people, but from wicked people; in accord with his divinity, Christ was miraculously born of a virgin.

Faustus despises Moses, but Augustine ardently praises him. Chosen by God to lead Israel, Moses was humble, obedient, vigorous, vigilant, and patient with his often wayward people. Even so, Moses violated God's eternal law by killing the Egyptian. At that time, Moses' zeal for God was powerful but not yet rightly ordered; he had not yet been trained for obedience by God's revelation of himself on Mount Sinai. Similarly, Saul showed a powerful zeal for God in persecuting the Church, but when Christ converted him on the Damascus Road, Paul's zeal became rightly ordered and effective. Again, Peter's defense of Jesus by cutting off the ear of the servant of the high priest was disordered, but Peter's zeal, when rightly ordered by Christ's resurrection, enabled him to shepherd the Church. Scripture praises not the vice but the zealous heart that, when disciplined, has the potential for great good.

What about Abraham's near-sacrifice of Isaac, Moses' despoiling of the Egyptians, and Moses' and Joshua's wars? Did Abraham, Moses, and Joshua sin in these actions, and did God violate his own eternal law by commanding them? Augustine explains that God is the lawgiver whose authority governs human lives and possessions. The Egyptians were oppressing the Israelites by forcing them to work for next to nothing. On their own authority, the Israelites could not have rightly stolen from the Egyptians. But God, who has authority over all things, commanded the redistribution, and Moses was just to implement it. Regarding the taking of life, God likewise has authority over all lives. If God had deemed that Isaac should die at that time, his will in this regard would have been just, and given God's rightful authority, Abraham would have been just in carrying out God's command. Wars undertaken even by legitimate human authority can be just, so long as their true goal is peace rather than vengeance or the desire to dominate others. It is not only the Old Testament that permits soldiering, but also the New (see Lk. 3:14, Matt. 8:9; 22:21). Just wars do not violate God's law, and so God can act directly to punish pride and achieve peace by commanding war. All lives are in the hand of God, and Moses and Joshua would have sinned had they disobeyed God's commands.

Yet Augustine does not end there, as if killing and war were unqualified goods. In the Old Testament, God shows that human kingdoms and military victories are under his power and judgment. God's sovereignty over temporal kingdoms, however, is a figure of what is revealed in the New Testament, namely the true eternal kingdom of God. In the New Testament, Christ conquers by renouncing this life, and he leads his followers into a kingdom not of this world. The martyrs follow Christ by laying down their lives for this eternal kingdom, rather than by conquering earthly kingdoms. Believers worship God not in hope of a temporal kingdom—as might seem to be the case when the Old Testament's witness to the kingdom of Israel is not read as a figure—but in hope of an eternal kingdom. Assured of the resurrection of the body, believers give their lives for this eternal kingdom willingly, like sheep among wolves (see Matt. 10:16). In spreading the kingdom of God, we must imitate Christ's Cross rather than Moses' and Joshua's wars. This does not negate the Old Testament's demonstration that earthly kingdoms are under the power and judgment of God, a lesson that Christian rulers must continue to take to heart. In God's providence, his commands differ for different times.

Augustine concludes that we should not, like Faustus, criticize what God has willed for others. The will of God is just. We are just when we love God and love everything else for God's sake, that is to say, when we love the will of God as we see it worked out and accomplished in others. We cannot know, however, precisely how God is working in others. If God permits someone to die at a young age, for example, we cannot know whether this was a punishment or a blessing. An early death could be a just punishment, or it could be a divine blessing that saves the person from trials that would have caused the person to fall spiritually. This ignorance should instruct us when we see how God differently commands his followers in the Old and New Testaments. We know that Christ's followers are called by God to die at the hands of sinners rather than to seek to defend the kingdom of God by military means, but this knowledge should not set us up to condemn the Israelites who were commanded by God to punish pride and establish peace through military conquests. Likewise, Paul's command that a sinner be excommunicated (1 Cor. 5:5) has Moses' capital punishment of Israel's rebels (Exod.

32, Num. 16) as its figure, but this prophetic meaning does not thereby signify that Moses sinned. On the contrary, Moses rightly obeyed God, just as Paul did. The outward action differed, but the inward disposition of love toward God and neighbor was the same. Neither Moses nor Paul offered the other cheek when he was attacked—Paul called his attacker a "whitewashed wall" (Acts 23:3)—but in both cases their inward disposition was in accord with Christ's command to love one's enemies.

Faustus singled out Hosea, who married a prostitute by God's command, and Solomon for special scorn. In response, Augustine points out that surely a prostitute can repent and become a chaste wife. Christ, after all, teaches that "prostitutes and publicans will enter the kingdom of heaven ahead of you" (Matt. 5:39). Solomon, for his part, receives the condemnation of Scripture, not only for his lust but also for his idolatry. Solomon is an exemplar of virtue in some ways, but a warning against vice in other ways.

Augustine devotes the remainder of Book 22 to showing how the lives of the men criticized by Faustus also have a prophetic role in Scripture. Even their evil deeds, he argues, can prefigure goods that God will bring about. Evildoers do not of course mean for this to be the case, nor does God approve their wicked actions. Nonetheless, God can use their evil deeds for his purposes. An example of this is Caiaphas's speech, which he meant for Jesus' destruction but which unwittingly prophesied Jesus' saving work (Jn. 11:50–51). In his figural interpretation of Judah's sexual intercourse with his daughter-in-law, Augustine makes much of the meaning of the names "Tamar" and "Judah" (including its Latin meaning), as well as the meaning of the name of the town to which Judah came, "Timnah." Sitting at the gate, Tamar symbolizes the Church, called from the nations and desiring the seed of Abraham; she receives in secret the marks of holiness, symbolized by the ring, necklace, and staff. The names "David," "Uriah," and "Hittite" come in for similar figural exposition. Solomon's foreign wives symbolize, perhaps, the churches in gentile nations. Solomon's surpassing wisdom, followed by his terrible fall, symbolize the mingling of good and bad people in the Church. The prophetic significance of Hosea's marriage to Gomer, a prostitute, is explained by the prophet himself in Hosea 1–2, and its fulfillment is made clear by Paul and Peter (see Rom. 9 and 1 Pet. 2). Moses' despoiling of the Egyptians symbolizes the fruitful use that the Church can make of some pagan philosophy. Moses' command that the idolaters who worshipped the golden calf be killed (Exod. 32) foreshadows the destruction of vices. What Moses did to the golden calf symbolizes the spiritual power of righteous zeal, the word of God, and the water of baptism.

Augustine gives many more examples, but the key point is clear: everything in the Old Testament has a figural meaning. Every word and deed in the Old Testament can be fruitfully reread in light of Christ so as to discern prophetic meaning. This is because the Old Testament tells the story of God's formation of his people, and Christ fully reveals how and for what goal God forms his people. At the same time, Augustine defends the holiness of the patriarchs and prophets, as we have seen: the books of the Old Testament are not to be rejected on the grounds that their authors were not worthy of the New Testament. He finds that the Old Testament contains examples of humans in all spiritual conditions, so that we can imitate the good (especially in their repentance) and reject the bad. If we find something in the Old Testament that does not seem to have a figural meaning or seems superfluous, this is an invitation to seek more deeply the figural or mystical meaning. God gives us the Old Testament, like the New, for our salvation. Finally, Augustine observes that even if the patriarchs were as bad as Faustus says, they were not nearly as bad as the Manichean God, whose very substance is embedded in the bodies of sinners and who yielded his members, at some past point in time, to the forces of darkness. In arguing that the patriarchs were unworthy of imitation, Faustus fails to see that it is his own false God who is unworthy of imitation. Indeed, Faustus himself, merely by the goodness of his existence, is much better than the Manichean God he worships.

Book 30: 1 Timothy 4:1–3

In Book 30, Faustus replies to how Catholics apply 1 Timothy 4:1–3 to the Manicheans. 1 Timothy 4:1–3 states, "Certain persons will withdraw from the faith, paying attention to deceitful spirits, to the teachings of demons. They will speak lies in their hypocrisy, having a seared conscience, forbidding marriage, and abstaining from foods that God created to be received with thanksgiving by those who believe." Faustus does not believe that Paul actually wrote this, but he is willing to suppose for the sake of argument that Paul did. If Paul did write it, then Paul must be saying that Moses and the prophets taught demonic teachings. After all, it is Moses and the prophets who claim that God deems some foods unclean, thereby "abstaining from foods that God created to be received with thanksgiving by those who believe." Such foods include the flesh of pigs, rabbits, shellfish, and so forth. The prophet Daniel records that he himself, as well as Hananiah, Azariah, and Mishael, abstained from meat and fasted in obedience to God's law, a further instance of the behavior that Paul rejects in 1 Timothy. Even if Paul said such a thing, therefore, Paul was speaking against the Old Testament (and in favor of the Manicheans). Faustus adds that Catholics encourage consecrated virginity and abstain from meat during Lent, and so Catholics, too, come under Paul's condemnation, if the passage was in fact written by Paul. Further, if Paul were the author of 1 Timothy 4:1–3, he would be condemning both himself and Christ, because Paul favored virginity and Christ encouraged those who "have made themselves eunuchs for the sake of the kingdom of heaven" (Matt. 19:12). Faustus also claims that the apostle John was a virgin.

Against Faustus's attempt to show that if Catholics accept 1 Timothy 4:1–3 they will also have to reject the Old Testament, Augustine remarks that Faustus has failed to recognize why Catholics quote this passage in opposition to Manichean teachings. Certainly Catholics sometimes abstain from meat, and Catholics also encourage virginity. To abstain from meat or to encourage virginity is not to fall into "the teachings of demons." Nor does the Mosaic law teach demonic doctrine with respect to its food laws, because these laws were symbolic as Augustine has previously explained. Rather, the Manicheans take the crucial extra step by arguing both that certain foods are evil by their nature, and that marital intercourse is evil by its nature. It is this exaggeration that constitutes "the teachings of demons," because these Manichean doctrines vilify the work of the Creator God. By denying that the true God created certain foods and by rejecting marriage because it propagates the human race and thus continues the cycle of embodiment, the Manicheans spread the view that God is not the Creator and that matter is evil by nature.

Book 31: Titus 1:15 and Acts 10:12–16

Another text often quoted against the Manicheans is Titus 1:15, "For the clean all things are clean, but for the unclean and those who are defiled nothing is clean, but both their mind and their conscience are defiled." Book 31 takes this verse as its subject. As he did with 1 Timothy 4:1–3, Faustus argues that Titus 1:15 applies much better to Moses and the prophets than it does to the Manicheans. After all, Moses and the prophets reject the view that "all things are clean." They must therefore be "defiled" in "their mind and their conscience." Such men could have known nothing of God. In the same vein, Catholics who purport to obey the New Testament also abstain from foods. If Titus 1:15 is correct, this abstinence shows that Catholics too are "defiled." Having turned Titus 1:15 against Catholics, Faustus takes up another text often quoted against Manicheans, namely Acts 10:12–16, where Peter in a trance sees a sheet with "all kinds of animals and reptiles and birds of the air" let down from heaven, and where God declares all these foods clean. Faustus considers that this text commits Catholics to eating such disgusting foods as snakes and other vermin.

Augustine responds, as in the previous chapter, by noting that the issue has to do not with the Old Testament food laws or with other abstinence from foods, but rather with the Manichean claim that some things are evil by nature. Moses affirms that God, upon creating all things, pronounced them "very good" (Gen. 1:31). This is the very point that Manicheans deny, because they consider that matter comes from Satan rather than from God. The supposition that material things are evil by nature is what Paul has in view when he tells Titus that "for the unclean and those who are defiled nothing is clean."

Book 32: The Manicheans' Selective Reading of the New Testament

In Book 32, Faustus defends his selective reading of the New Testament. As we have seen, he does not accept certain parts of the New Testament as authentic. Rather, when verses seem to conflict, he accepts only the verses that fit with Manichean doctrine and assumes that the other verses have been interpolated. He points out that Catholics read the Old Testament in this same way. Indeed, Catholics ignore almost the entirety of the Old Testament, whereas they obey the entirety of the New Testament. It would be much more logical, Faustus thinks, for Catholics to agree that both the Old Testament and the New Testament have interpolated material, especially since Jesus and his apostles did not write the New Testament but instead it was written much later. Faustus blames the later writers for pretending that their writings were authored by the apostles or by the earliest followers of the apostles.

On this basis, Faustus reiterates his earlier observations that Catholics reject most of the Old Testament laws and that Catholics prefer to ignore the unsavory doings of the patriarchs and prophets. He also brings up, as clearly unacceptable and absurd, the law that requires a surviving brother to marry the wife of his dead brother, if his brother died without having children, and to father children with her. If this law and the others like it are bad, then the Old Testament, as the source of many such laws, should be rejected. At the very least, Catholics should stop hypocritically blaming Manicheans for being selective in what to accept from the New Testament. He lists various laws from the Old Testament that, if they were accepted by Catholics, would decisively undermine Catholic faith, including laws that curse those who hang upon a tree (Deut. 21:23), that curse men who do not raise up offspring in Israel, that curse uncircumcised males (Gen. 17:14), and that condemn to death Sabbath violators (Num. 15:35).

Faustus is aware of the Catholic answer that the Old Testament foretells the coming of Christ and that the laws bind God's people only up to the time of Christ's coming, at which point Christ teaches what laws still apply. This answer should, however, explain to Catholics why the Manicheans accept the New Testament selectively. After all, the Manicheans affirm the New Testament's promise that Christ will send the Paraclete, and the Paraclete teaches the Manicheans what to accept from the New Testament. Just as Catholics think that Christ allows them to reject many (or most) Old Testament laws, so also Manicheans think that the Paraclete allows them to accept as authentic only those sayings in the New Testament that truly honor the Son of the Father. Among the New Testament sayings that do not honor the Son are those that connect him to the flesh or to Judaism, for example, that he was born of a woman, that he was circumcised, that he offered the prescribed Temple sacrifices, that he was baptized, and that he was tempted by the devil in the wilderness. The Manicheans accept his crucifixion, mystically understood, and they also accept as authentic most of his teachings.

Augustine replies that, in contrast to Faustus's view of the New Testament, Catholics do not consider the Old Testament to be corrupted. He repeats that God's commandments were appropriate to the time and place, and truthfully symbolized Christ. The Old Testament predicted its own fulfillment, as in Jeremiah 31's prophecy of a new covenant. This fulfillment is repeatedly attested by Paul, whose authority the Manicheans accept. Paul teaches that Christians, including gentiles, "are the seed of Abraham" (Gal. 3:29); that the laws regarding food, festivals, and the Sabbath were "shadows of things to come" (Col. 2:17); and that "[t]hese things happened to them in figures, but they were written down for the correction of us upon whom the end of the ages has come" (1 Cor. 10:11). If Faustus had understood Paul's words, says Augustine, he would have understood that (for example) the law commanding the surviving brother to marry the wife of his dead brother, if his brother died childless, not only does not command a crime, but also has a symbolic meaning with regard to Christ. The symbolic meaning has to do with preaching the Gospel in order to raise up children for Christ, who has died, rather than for oneself. Faustus would also have observed that the Christian celebration of the Eucharist fulfills the Jewish celebration of the Pasch. The Jewish sacrament points to the one who is to come, while the Christian sacrament remembers the one who has come. Augustine also repeats his argument that while the first Christians distanced themselves only slowly from the Jewish sacraments, in order to show respect for the law of Moses, later Christians rightly did not observe the law of Moses, since Christ has fulfilled it. Due to the difference in times, sacraments that foreshadowed the coming of Christ are no longer fitting sacraments for those who know that Christ has come. The fulfillment is not a negation: "We praise, accept, and approve all the things that were written in those books of the Old Testament as having been written with the greatest truth and the greatest usefulness for eternal life."[22]

Augustine goes on to defend the New Testament against Faustus's charge that it contains internal contradictions and was not written by the apostles. He challenges the basis upon which the Manicheans identify the Paraclete with Mani. He underscores that the Paraclete is the Holy Spirit, who was given to the apostolic community when Jesus was glorified. The authority of Mani cannot suffice for determining which of the teachings of the New Testament about Christ are true. Manichean doctrine has no real basis other than personal opinion for determining which New Testament teachings are acceptable. Indeed, only by accepting the truth of the Old Testament can Manicheans learn to recognize the truth of the New Testament witness to Christ, and give up Mani's inventions about Christ.[23]

---

22 Augustine, *Answer to Faustus*, Bk. 30, Chap. 14, p. 417.

23 See Augustine, *Answer to Faustus*, Bk. 32, Chap. 22, p. 423.

Conclusion

The first set of Books—4, 6, 9, and 10—centers Augustine's reply to Faustus around Paul's typological teaching that "[t]hese things happened to them in figures, but they were written down for the correction of us upon whom the end of the ages has come" (1 Cor. 10:11) and that "[t]hese are only a shadow of what is to come; but the substance belongs to Christ" (Col. 2:17). In the second set of Books—12–19—Augustine focuses on the fact that even though the Old Testament foreshadows the New, the advent of Christ does not negate the Old Testament. The Old Testament remains necessary for attesting to the truth of the realities. For example, we learn the meaning of the name "Christ" from the Old Testament, which prepares us to appreciate the Christ of the New. Having rejected the Old Testament, the Manicheans are unable to understand accurately the New Testament's portrait of Christ. The Old Testament does not claim to contain its goal within itself, but instead promises that it will be fulfilled by Christ. Augustine's view of the Old Testament as figurative, then, does not undermine the value of the Old Testament.

The third set of Books—22 and 30–32—affirms the value of the Old Testament from a different angle. Augustine criticizes Faustus for a flat-footed reading of the Old Testament. If one insists on a rigidly anthropomorphic interpretation of God's wrath in the Old Testament, then one will be compelled to find in the New Testament a divine Father who thirsts for the blood of his innocent Son. Since the patriarchs and prophets encountered God and wrote about him, their testimony to God would be impaired if it could be shown that they were egregious, untrustworthy sinners. Augustine both defends the patriarchs and prophets, and shows that the sins of the patriarchs, such as David's adultery with Bathsheba, are condemned rather than commended. Augustine also differentiates New Testament fasting and Old Testament abstinence from certain foods from Manichean rejection of matter as evil by nature. Here again a more appreciative reading of the Old Testament would have enabled Faustus to understand the teachings of Christ and the Church. Once the prophetic character of the Old Testament laws has been recognized and the enduring value of Old Testament affirmed, the truth about the Creator God becomes clear.

As the Creator of all, this God is opposed by no eternal principle of evil. Rather, he uses scriptural and sacramental signs to lead his people typologically, both before and after the coming of Christ, to union with himself.

Letter & Spirit 7 (2011): 119-131

Scripture, Worship, and Liturgy in the Thought of St. Basil the Great

~: **Stephen M. Hildebrand** :~

Franciscan University of Steubenville

The theme of worship permeates the life and writings of St. Basil, from his first conversion to the ascetic life to the sermons on creation that he wrote just before his death.[1] The source of Basil's thinking about worship and liturgy is Sacred Scripture. Scripture forms the inspirational center of his theology and, indeed, of his whole life. In the course of his life, Basil's understanding of worship shifted in two crucial ways: first, he realized the centrality of the Bible in the act of worshipping God; and, secondly, he recognized the centrality of the liturgy in rightly understanding the Bible.

Basil's Early Life and Conversion

Although Basil had come from a Christian family distinguished for its piety—his paternal grandparents, for example, were confessors in the Diocletian persecution[2]—Basil had set a course for himself to become a rhetor. To this end he studied in Caesarea and then Athens. There is no reason to think that Basil lived a debauched life, and yet, by his own account, his pursuit of a career in rhetoric ran counter to his true calling. In retrospect, he saw his earlier life as vain, futile, and foolish: he had been in a deep sleep.[3] Gregory of Nyssa remarks that when his brother Basil returned from school, "he was monstrously conceited about his skill in rhetoric, contemptuous of every high reputation and exalted beyond the leading lights of the province by his self-importance."[4]

What woke St. Basil up? Anna Silvas presents a very compelling account of the story of Basil's awakening and the persons who lay behind it. In the first place is his sister, St. Macrina, and his brother Naucratius. Macrina had been engaged to be married late in the 330s when her fiancé died. Upon his death Macrina invoked

1 See, for example, the many passages of Philip Rousseau's biography that concentrate on this theme (*Basil of Caesarea* [Berkely: University of California Press, 1994]).

2 See Gregory of Nazianzus' funeral oration for Basil, *Oration* 43.5 (trans. Charles G. Brown and James E. Swallow in *Cyril of Jerusalem, Gregory of Nazianzus*, Nicene and Post-Nicene Fathers 2, 7 [orig. pub. 1894; repr. Peabody, Mass.: Hendrickson, 1995], 396–397). Moreover, his grandmother, Macrina the Elder, his parents, Basil and Emmelia, and three of his siblings, Peter, Gregory of Nyssa, and Macrina are venerated as saints.

3 See Epistle 223.2 in *Saint Basil, The Letters*, trans. Roy J. Deferrari, 4 vols., Loeb Classical Library (Cambridge, Mass.: Harvard University Press, 1926–34), 3:293.

4 Gregory of Nyssa, *The Life of Saint Macrina*, trans. Kevin Corrigan (Toronto: Peregrina, 1998), 24.

her right not to marry again and determined to be a consecrated widow and, in her case, a consecrated virgin. Gregory of Nyssa presents Macrina as the religious center of the family, in whose midst she continued to live as a leaven. It was at Macrina's urging, for example, that her mother took up "the philosophical, immaterial way of life," for Macrina "led her to her own standard of humility, prepared her to put herself on an equal footing with the community of maidens, so as to share on equal terms with them one table, bed and all the needs of life, with every difference of rank eliminated from their lives."[5]

Gregory of Nyssa tells us the story of Basil's next younger brother, Naucratius. Though a talented rhetorician, Naucratius devoted himself to the ascetic life of "solitude and poverty."[6] Naucratius lived in the woods with Chrysaphius, a former servant and now friend, and the two of them provided food for a community of poor and sick old people. Naucratius and Chrysaphius tragically died in a hunting accident that shook Basil's whole family.

Silvas plausibly suggests that it was the death of Naucratius that brought Basil home from Athens.[7] Soon thereafter Macrina converted him to the ascetic life. Gregory of Nyssa writes that Macrina won Basil "so swiftly ... to the ideal of philosophy that he renounced worldly appearance, showed contempt for the admiration of rhetorical ability and went over of his own accord to this active life of manual labor, preparing for himself by means of his complete poverty a way of life which would tend without impediment towards virtue."[8]

"This was not a *new* call," Silvas writes, "but a *re*-call":

> Makrina was not proposing something new to Basil, but recalling him to the piety of their childhood upbringing and to the intention he had formed even in Athens to seek a life of "philosophy." ... She persuaded her brother to make a break once and for all with the conventional life of a catechumen highly educated in the secular curriculum. Now that he was at a new juncture, let him not resume by default the life their father had left off, that of the devout Christian aristocrat and professional man, excellent as far as it went, but seize the moment to embrace baptism and with the life of Christian "philosophy"—virginity and asceticism. ...[9]

In addition to the counsel of Macrina and the example of Naucratius, the mentorship of Eustathius of Sebaste proved formative for Basil. Eustathius modeled for

5 Gregory of Nyssa, *The Life of Saint Macrina*, 28.

6 Gregory of Nyssa, *The Life of Saint Macrina*, 26.

7 Anna Silvas, *The Asketikon of St. Basil the Great* (New York: Oxford University Press, 2005), 68.

8 Gregory of Nyssa, *Life of Macrina*, 25.

9 Silvas, *The Asketikon of St. Basil the Great*, 70.

Basil the path on which he should himself embark. Looking back on his youth and interpreting his own experiences, Basil writes:

> Having lavished much time on vanity, and having consumed almost all my youth in futility, which were mine while I occupied myself with the acquirement of the precepts of that wisdom made foolish by God, when one day arising as from a deep sleep I looked out upon the marvelous light of the truth of the gospel, and beheld the uselessness of the wisdom "of the princes of this world that come to nought" [1 Cor 2:6], bemoaning much my piteous life, I prayed that there be given me a guidance to the introduction to the teachings of religion.[10]

This guidance in the religious life that Basil sought was given him by Eustathius of Sebaste. Eustathius was both a bishop and an ascetic, combining pastoral responsibility with ascetic discipline. He was a man of the church but not of the world, a man "who wished to make the Church as much a force for social change as for cultic enthusiasm, and who certainly wished to inject into Christian experience a degree of moral seriousness that would affect public life as well as personal development."[11] Basil, following Eustathius, traveled to Coele-Syria, Palestine, Mesopotamia, and Egypt to acquaint himself with the ascetic practices of the regions.[12] Upon returning from this trip ca. 357, Basil was baptized by his bishop, Dianius, in Caesarea, and retired to Pontus where he was joined by Gregory of Nazianzus in his pursuit of the ascetic life.

The Importance of the Scriptures in Basil's Life and Thought

It is at this point in Basil's life that we see the first crucial shift, his realization that he could not properly worship God except through studying and praying the Scriptures. The evidence for this shift consists of a few early letters (Ep. 1, 2, 4, 14, and 22). If we accept Silvas' chronological ordering of these letters (thus, 1, 14, 4, 2, and 22), it is manifest "that Basil's ascetic discourse progresses from a philosophical discourse, virtually indistinguishable from that of the pagan ascetic traditions (Letters 1 and 4), through letters which increasingly combine such discourse with more overtly Christian content (Letters 14 and 2) to one which is thoroughly Christian and scriptural in tone (Letter 22)."[13] Silvas notes that in ep. 1, 14, and 4, Basil's ascetic life seems rather classical. In all these letters he heavily

10 Epistle 223.2, *Saint Basil, The Letters*, 3:291–293.

11 Rousseau, *Basil of Caesarea*, 75.

12 See Epistle 223.2, *Saint Basil, The Letters*, 3:293–295.

13 Silvas, *The Asketikon of St. Basil the Great*, 86–87.

uses classical allusions to pagan authors and in ep. 4 indicates that he has taken up the philosopher's mantle.[14]

In Epistle 2 (358), a letter to Gregory of Nazianzus, Basil has actually been practicing his new lifestyle for some time, a year or more. The first thing to notice is Basil's realization that the ascetic life is not exactly what he imagined:

> But I am ashamed to write what I myself do night and day in this out-of-the-way place. For I have indeed left my life in the city, as giving rise to countless evils, but I have not yet been able to leave myself behind. On the contrary, I am like those who go to sea, and because they have had no experience in sailing are very distressed and sea-sick, and complain of the size of the boat as causing the violent tossing; and then when they leave the ship and take to the dinghy or the cock-boat, they continue to be sea-sick and distressed wherever they are; for their nausea and bile go with them when they change. Our experience is something like this. For we carry our indwelling disorders about with us, and so are nowhere free from the same sort of disturbances. Consequently we have derived no great benefit from our present solitude.[15]

There are other important changes, Silvas notes, in this letter. The use of Scripture appears for the first time and distinctively Christian themes emerge. She comments that:

> Basil appears to be straddling two types of discourse and has not quite sorted them out yet. Perhaps the most important new note in ep. 2 is that now, several months into his new life, "prayer" has come to assume a great importance for Basil and the "memory of God" and "yearning" it engenders. Prayer was hardly conceded by the philosophers as a means to divine knowledge; indeed, Plotinus seems to have disdained it.[16]

Basil's shift to a more overtly Christian and scripturally-based asceticism is complete with ep. 22, "On the perfection of the monastic life." "All talk of 'philosophy' and every classical allusion has fallen away."[17] In Epistle 22, Basil writes that "since in the divinely inspired Scriptures many directions are set forth which must be strictly observed by all who earnestly wish to please God, I desire to say … a few

14 See Silvas, *The Asketikon of St. Basil the Great*, 87.

15 Epistle 1, *Saint Basil, The Letters*, 1:7–9.

16 Silvas, *The Asketikon of St. Basil the Great*, 88.

17 Silvas, *The Asketikon of St. Basil the Great*, 88.

words based upon the knowledge which I have derived from the divinely inspired Scriptures themselves."[18] There follows a catalogue with copious allusions and quotations to the New Testament of moral guidelines for the Christian.

Basil's early ascetic work, the *Moralia,* well indicates how far he has progressed in the scriptural ascetic life. On the surface, the text appears simple and even primitive when compared with Basil's ascetic works in their final form. As he says in one of the prefaces to the *Moralia,* he wishes "to bring forward as a reminder ... to those engaged in the combat of the devout life, the passages ... from the Holy Scriptures regarding what is displeasing to God and with what he is well pleased."[19] Thus, the *Moralia* seems little more than select passages from the New Testament (with very little commentary by Basil himself) that outline the way of life of an earnest Christian.

Beneath this superficial simplicity, however, lay at least two profound truths about the Christian life as Basil understands it. The first truth is that worship, in the broadest sense, must be informed by the Scriptures and expressed in the language of the Scriptures. The second, as evidenced in the *Moralia,* is that Basil's understanding of the ascetic life is not only scriptural, but also highly structured and overtly liturgical. "The *Moralia,*" Rousseau writes, "provides us with the essence of Basil's ecclesiology."[20] One can see the liturgical side of the ascetic life in what Basil says about baptism and Eucharist.[21] "What," he asks, "is the nature or the function of baptism? The changing of the person baptized in thought and word and action and his transformation according to the power bestowed on him into that of which he has been born."[22] Basil then writes that "the receiving of the Body and Blood of Christ is also necessary for life everlasting,"[23] and that "he who partakes of the Sacred Species should praise the Lord with hymns."[24] As a final indication of the liturgical and ecclesial context of the ascetic life, we might add

18 Epistle 22.1, *Saint Basil, The Letters,* 1:129.

19 Basil, *On the Judgment of God* 8; trans. M. Monica Wagner, *St. Basil Ascetical Works,* Fathers of the Church, 9 (Washington, D.C.: Catholic University of America Press, 1962), 54. This passage bears similarities to the opening of ep. 22.

20 Rousseau, *Basil of Caesarea,* 232.

21 Rousseau highlights the importance of baptism in the *Moralia*: "[the broad themes of Basil's ascetic teaching] acquire their cohesion in the *Moralia* by their relationship to the section on baptism (§20), which stresses in familiar terms that the sacrament should follow upon belief, leading to a restoration of one's true nature. The impression given is that the previous sections have commented on various principles that governed the lead up to baptism—conversion, belief, the search for the company of others, the consciousness of sin, the discovery of Scripture, the longing for enlightenment. After the reference to baptism, Basil returned, in the sections that follow, to some of those same principles, suggesting how they might be carried to a new level by the baptismal experience itself; that is to say, by one's formal incorporation into the body of the Church" (ibid., 229–230).

22 Basil, *Moralia,* reg. 20, cap. 1; trans. Wagner, 100.

23 Basil, *Moralia,* reg. 21; trans. Wagner, 101.

24 Basil, *Moralia,* reg. 21, cap. 3; trans. Wagner, 103.

that Basil devotes much space to hierarchical ministry and to the proper preaching of the Word.[25]

We can sum up Basil's understanding of the role of Scripture in worship by borrowing the words of Philip Rousseau: Scripture "was itself a Temple, into which the reader as worshipper penetrated."[26] Here Rousseau refers to a passage from Basil's *Hexaëmeron* wherein he compares his exploration of the meaning of the Scriptures in the previous sermon to entering the Temple. Basil had spent the whole of the first sermon on creation, explaining just a few words. The Scriptures are so rich in meaning that his first sermon was like entering the court of the sanctuary. "If the court of the sanctuary is so beautiful," Basil writes, "and the vestibule of the temple is so august and magnificent, dazzling the eyes of our soul with its surpassing beauty, what must be the holy of holies?"[27]

Basil's Thought on the Role of the Liturgy in Understanding the Bible[28]

Late in the trinitarian controversy that consumed the fourth century, there emerged a group of men who denied not the divinity of the Son but that of the Holy Spirit. These men, called Spirit-fighters by their opponents, criticized St. Basil's teaching on the Holy Spirit. In particular, they objected to a doxology that Basil had used in the liturgy on the grounds that it was unscriptural. Basil glorified the Father with the Son together with the Holy Spirit, and Basil's opponents thought that neither this doxology nor the belief in the divinity of the Holy Spirit that it expressed had any foundation in Scripture.[29]

This criticism of Basil's belief and practice was deeply personal, for it came from a man whom Basil had considered a dear friend, the same Eustathius of Sebaste whom we met earlier. Indeed, they had spent much time together and had spoken often about matters of faith. Their relationship, though, fell apart over the question of the divinity of the Spirit. Hermann Dörries long ago showed that many of the objections and replies of Basil's *On the Holy Spirit* recapitulate the argument that Basil had with Eustathius.[30]

---

25 See, for example, Basil, *Moralia*, reg. 70–72.

26 Rousseau, *Basil of Caesarea*, 329.

27 Basil, *Hexaëmeron* 2.1; trans. Way, 21.

28 I have drawn much of what follows from my *The Trinitarian Theology of Basil of Caesarea: A Synthesis of Greek Thought and Biblical Truth* (Washington, D.C.: Catholic University of America Press, 2007), 102–149.

29 On the historical context here, see Jean Gribomont, "Esoterisme et Tradition dans le Traité du Saint-Esprit de Saint Basile" [Esoterism and Tradition in St. Basil's Treatise on the Holy Spirit] in *Oecumenica, an annual symposium of ecumenical research*, 22–58 (Minneapolis: Augsburg Pub House, 1967), 26–40; and Michael A. Kane, "St. Basil's On the Holy Spirit: a secret tradition or the rule of faith?" *Diakonia* 35 (2002): 24–26.

30 See Hermann Dörries, De Spiritu Sancto. *Der Beitrag des Basilius zum Abschluß des trinitarischen Dogmas* [On the Holy Spirit. *St. Basil's Contribution to the Settlement of the*

At the beginning of *On the Holy Spirit*, Basil explains why he is writing the work: some have charged him with liturgical innovation—in the ancient Church, no small accusation—for worshipping God with the doxology ("Glory to the Father, with [*meta*] the Son, with [*syn*] the Holy Spirit").[31] His opponents attack it as unscriptural, and Basil must mount a defense. "They do not stop babbling up and down," Basil writes, "that to give glory with the Holy Spirit is unattested and non-scriptural, and the like."[32] "They cry out for proofs from the Scriptures," he writes in another place, "and dismiss the non-scriptural witness of the fathers as worthless."[33] Against "this 'Puritan' or 'Protestant', so to speak, mentality of Eustathius, this acute 'biblicism,'"[34] Basil argues that the Scriptures cannot be rightly understood apart from apostolic and patristic tradition, and in this case the tradition is liturgical. Thus, the criticism of Eusthatius and the Spirit-fighters provoked Basil to articulate the relationship between the liturgy and the right understanding of Scripture.

One of the key texts for Basil's understanding of Scripture and tradition is *On the Holy Spirit* 27, 66. Basil's text introduces two technical terms, *dogma* and *kerygma*, and gives us two different views on their nature and relation, one to the other. He differentiates *dogma* from *kêrygma*, the latter designating what the Church publicly proclaims, the former what she reserves for the initiated. The distinction, however, between *dogma* and *kerygma* can be confusing. On one reading, *kerygma* designates the public proclamation of a teaching, whether in Scripture or tradition, and *dogma*, the right understanding of the public proclamation. Of the *kêrygmata* and *dogmata* "that are guarded in the Church, we hold some from the teaching of the Scriptures, and others we have received in mystery as the teachings of the tradition of the apostles."[35] In other words, the deposit would be made up of scriptural *kêrygmata* and scriptural *dogmata* as well as non-scriptural *kêrygmata* and *dogmata*. On this reading the *kêrygmata* are the bare words and the *dogmata* comprise the right understanding of these words. The Scriptures are public, but the knowledge whereby they are properly understood is reserved to the initiated. This is why the Scriptures are obscure: obscurity conceals the *dogmata*, the right

---

Doctrine of the Trinity], Abhandlungen der Akademie der Wissenschaften in Göttingen (Göttingen: Vandenhoeck & Ruprecht, 1956).

31 See *On the Holy Spirit* 1.3; trans. Stephen Hildebrand (Yonkers, N.Y.: St. Vladimir's Seminary Press, 2011), 29–30.

32 *On the Holy Spirit* 27.68; trans. Hildebrand, 107.

33 *On the Holy Spirit* 10.25; trans. Hildebrand, 56.

34 Emmanuel Amand de Mendietta, "*The 'unwritten' and 'secret' Apostolic Traditions in the Theological Thought of St. Basil of Caesarea*, Scottish Journal of Theology Occasional Papers, no. 13 (London: Oliver and Boyd: 1965), 23.

35 *On the Holy Spirit* 27.66; trans. Hildebrand, 104. I take *eggraphos* as "scriptural" rather than "written," and will translate *agraphos* as "non-scriptural" rather than "unwritten" because the context shows that this is what Basil means. De Mendieta has collected and analyzed the instances of *agraphos* to show this; see *The 'Unwritten' and 'Secret' Apostolic Ttraditions*, 25–38.

understanding of its teaching, lest it be despised for being familiar.[36] There are also, as de Mendieta has indicated, kergymatic and dogmatic unwritten traditions; things publicly known whose real meaning is not:

> We all look to the East, Basil writes, when we are praying (*kerygma*). But few of us know that we are seeking after our own old country, the Paradise, which *God planted in Eden, in the East* (*dogma*). It is in the standing posture that we are offering our prayers, on the first day of the week (namely on Sunday or Lord's day) (*kerygma*). But the reason of this (posture) we do not know, at least not all of us (*dogma*).[37]

Basil offers more examples, but the point is clear from the parenthetical comments that de Mendieta inserts into his translation: non-scriptural tradition contains both *kerygma* and *dogma*.

This would be plain enough, were it not for the fact that other texts yield a different picture wherein *dogma* is one and the same with unwritten tradition. All of the things that de Mendieta has identified as kerygmatic unwritten tradition are, says Basil, transmitted in fact by unwritten and secret tradition; they are not public. Along these lines the distinction between *kêrygma* and *dogma* is nearly the same as that between Scripture and tradition. Scripture, then, would not contain *dogmata* and tradition would not contain *kêrygmata*. Indeed, though Basil implies that there can be scriptural *dogmata*, he gives no clear examples.[38] All of the examples of *dogmata* are tied to the liturgy. De Mendieta himself writes that *dogma* is basically the Church's liturgical tradition and doctrines implied therein, "the whole structure of liturgical and sacramental life, covered and protected at this time by the *disciplina arcani*."[39] It is easy to forgive the tension between de Mendieta's two works on this matter—in one place calling unwritten traditions kerygmatic, in another dogmatic—for he did not introduce it; Basil did.

---

36 Basil writes: "doctrine is one thing, and proclamation is another. One is kept in silence, but proclamations are made public. Now obscurity is a form of silence used in Scripture, which makes the meaning of dogmas difficult to see for the benefit of the readers" (*On the Holy Spirit* 27.66; trans. Hildebrand, 105–106).

37 *On the Holy Spirit* 27.66; trans. Amand de Mendieta, *The 'Unwritten' and 'Secret' Apostolic Traditions*, 6–8.

38 There may actually be one example. In *On the Holy Spirit* 27.66, explaining why we stand for prayer on Sunday, Basil writes that we so stand because Sunday "seems somehow to be an image of the age to come. On account of this, although it is the beginning of days, Moses names it not 'first' but 'one.' For it is written, 'There was evening, and there was morning, one day' (Gen 1.15), as if the same one often repeated" (trans. Hildebrand, 106).

39 See Emmanuel Amand de Mendieta, "The Pair ΚΗΡΥΓΜΑ and ΔΟΓΜΑ in the Theological Thought of St. Basil of Caesarea," *Journal of Theological Studies* 16 (1965): 135.

Basil's letters yield a similar difficulty.[40] In Epistle 125, the confession of faith for Eustathius of Sebaste, he says that the creed of Nicaea contains saving *dogma*.[41] In Epistle 90, however, Basil exhorts, "let us also pronounce with boldness that good *kêrygma* of the Fathers, which overwhelms the accursed heresy of Arius, and builds the churches on the sound doctrine, wherein the Son is confessed to be *homoousios* with the Father."[42] Obviously, he is talking about the creed of Nicaea.

While Basil is unclear on whether *dogmata* are only non-scriptural or also scriptural, he very clearly asserts that *dogmata* are communicated secretly or "mystically" and are understood only by the initiated or by an elite, not by all. The nature of this secrecy and the identity of the elite are related. R. P. C. Hanson thinks that Basil's unwritten tradition is secret and esoteric and thus that the elite who possess them are very much like the Gnostics.[43] Basil has turned Christianity into "a mystery religion or an ecclesiastical freemasonry" so that he could invest his doxological customs and, hence, his theology of the Spirit, with greater authority.[44] Hanson sees Basil as breaking from his own earlier thinking about tradition and from Athanasius and his predecessors.

Georges Florovsky sees it differently. He eloquently stresses the liturgical and mystical nature of the transmission rather than its secrecy.[45] Thus, the "'silent' and 'mystical' tradition, 'which has not been made public,' is not an esoteric doctrine, reserved for some particular elite. The 'elite' was the Church."[46] Basil, then, though using peculiar language, has not broken with early Fathers in his thinking about tradition but has perpetuated their insight that Scripture cannot be understood apart from the rule of faith which contained the "creedal core" of the Scriptures and epitomized them.[47]

De Mendieta proposes a position between Florovsky's and Hanson's. He agrees with Hanson that tradition is secret and not "mystical," but he thinks that

---

40 See Gribomont, "Esoterisme et Tradition," at 44.

41 Epistle 125.1, *Saint Basil, The Letters*, 2:265.

42 Epistle 90.2, *Saint Basil, The Letters*, 2:127, trans. altered.

43 See R. P. C. Hanson, "Basil's Doctrine of Tradition in Relation to the Holy Spirit," *Vigiliae Christianae* 22 (1968): 249–252.

44 R. P. C. Hanson, *Tradition in the Early Church* (London: S.C.M. Press, 1962), 184; cited in Gribomont, "Esoterisme et Tradition," at 24, n. 15.

45 Florovsky thinks to render *en mystêriô (On the Holy Spirit* 27.66) as "in secret" is a "flagrant mistranslation." Georges Florovsky, "The Function of Tradition in the Ancient Church," *Greek Orthodox Theological Review* 9 (1963): 194. De Mendieta disagrees because *mystêriô* is singular and no article is used (The *'unwritten'* and *'secret' apostolic traditions*, 31 and n. 1). Gribomont sympathizes with Florovsky and judges that de Mendieta has not reckoned with "une certaine contrainte faite aux habitudes de la langue" [a certain concession made to the customs of the language] that the biblical allusion justifies (en mystêriô here harkens back to 1 Cor. 2:7) ("Esoterisme et Tradition," at 52–53).

46 Georges Florovsky, "The Function of Tradition in the Ancient Church," at 195.

47 Georges Florovsky, "The Function of Tradition in the Ancient Church," at 193.

this secrecy does not make Basil into a Gnostic.[48] De Mendieta distinguishes three levels of *dogma*, each of which is understood by a particular group. The baptized know customs, but not all know what the customs mean. Beyond these two levels are a theologically trained monastic elite who can understand the more profound *dogmata*.[49]

Who, then, is right? When we look at the crucial text (*On the Holy Spirit* 27, 66) and the examples that Basil gives we can make the following judgments. Florovsky is right to emphasize the liturgical character of the tradition, but of course not all of the baptized will understand all of the *dogmata*. De Mendieta is right to make distinctions here; some *dogmata* are more profound than others, and some require more education and illumination. Gribomont accentuates Basil's debt here to Origen's homily 5 on Numbers where he "combines the allusions to the *disciplina arcana*, where initiation involves all the baptized, and those with a superior knowledge, where the initiated are fewer and the doctrinal formulation less definite."[50] As did Origen, Basil sees the spiritual life as having stages.[51]

In addition, Hanson's argument that Basil deviated from his own earlier views and from the larger tradition does not persuade. In *Against Eunomius*, the argument runs, Basil, like Athanasius, "thinks that Scripture is doctrinally sufficient," for he refuses Eunomius's technical language precisely because the words cannot be found in the Scriptures.[52] Basil, then, in his letters uses tradition more flexibly, largely through his realization of the importance of the Nicene Creed.[53] Further, in *On the Holy Spirit*, Basil forsakes the sufficiency of the Scriptures interpreted by tradition and posits the necessity of a secret, extra-scriptural, apostolic tradition. There are a couple of problems with this (Hanson's) view of Basil's supposed "devolution." First, while Basil refuses Eunomius's non-Scriptural technical language, he uses his own. His reprimand of Eunomius is not evidence of a kind of thorough-going biblicism that would reject the use of words not found in the Scriptures. Eunomius's words are unscriptural more because they contradict the meaning of Scripture than because they cannot materially be found there. Second, Basil sees his opponents in *On the Holy Spirit* as contradicting Scripture and himself as following it.[54] Hanson writes that Basil was motivated to make his innovations because "he could not meet Eustathius's demand for a full documentation

48 See de Mendieta, "The Pair ΚΗΡΥΓΜΑ and ΔΟΓΜΑ," at 136.

49 de Mendieta, "The Pair ΚΗΡΥΓΜΑ and ΔΟΓΜΑ," at 136–139. See also Kane, "A secret tradition or the rule of faith?" at 30–33.

50 Gribomont, "Esoterisme et Tradition," at 51.

51 In fact he saw the progression in his own; see Epistle 223.3, *Saint Basil, The Letters*, 3:299.

52 Hanson, "Basil's doctrine of tradition in relation to the Holy Spirit," at 244–245.

53 Hanson, "Basil's doctrine of tradition in relation to the Holy Spirit," at 246–248.

54 See *On the Holy Spirit* 10.24; trans. Hildebrand, 55.

from Scripture of his doctrine of the Holy Spirit."[55] It is rather that Eustathius could not see the force and meaning, the *dogma*, of the many scriptural proofs that Basil offered, precisely because he (Eusthathius) rejected the liturgical tradition in which the meaning of the Scriptures became patent. For Basil, this rejection itself was rather unscriptural. He would never have conceded that Eustathius was truer to the Scriptures than he; rather, Eustathius had the words of Scripture but not their sense.

Hanson also accuses Basil of falsely, but not necessarily intentionally, calling his doxology apostolic.[56] He invented a "legend of apostolic origin for rite and custom" that was not justified by the Scriptures, and in his hands "tradition, instead of being left as the word to describe doctrinal development and exploration in continuity with the original Gospel, becomes an historical fiction."[57] Basil's statement in fact is quite strong. After tracing his doxology in patristic authors as far back as Irenaeus and Clement,[58] he affirms that it has been welcomed by all the Churches "from the time when the Gospel was proclaimed."[59] What, then, does Basil mean when he says that his doxology is apostolic? Jean Gribomont answers this well.[60] First of all, Basil maintains that it is apostolic—that is, consistent with the wishes and practice of the apostles—to accept unwritten traditions, for Paul commends the Corinthians and the Thessalonians to do so.[61] Second, Gribomont points out that Basil is not naïve. He has shown, e.g. in his canonical letters to Amphilochius, that he is "very knowledgeable of the variety and flexibility of customs."[62] Basil "loves to join in one voice 'the Apostles and Fathers'"; thus he expresses the continuity so important to tradition and his vision of the Church's unity in history.[63] "Apostolic" means consistent with the teaching of the Apostles preserved in the Fathers.

We have seen that Basil's writing on the relationship between the liturgical tradition and the Scriptures leaves us with some ambiguities and difficulties. These, however, should not obscure what is plainly clear: Basil realized that his opponents had focused too narrowly on the authority of the Scriptures, and he wished to

55 Hanson, "Basil's doctrine of tradition in relation to the Holy Spirit," 252. Kane, following de Mendieta, holds that Basil so stressed the secrecy of the tradition for rhetorical effect (Kane, "A Secret Tradition or the Rule of Faith?" at 36; de Mendieta, *The 'unwritten' and 'secret' apostolic traditions*, 40).

56 See Hanson, "Basil's doctrine of tradition in relation to the Holy Spirit," at 252.

57 Hanson, *Tradition in the Early Church*, 184; cited in de Mendieta, *The 'unwritten' and 'secret' apostolic traditions*, x.

58 See *On the Holy Spirit* 29.72.

59 *On the Holy Spirit* 29.75; trans. Hildebrand, 116.

60 See Gribomont, "Esoterisme et Tradition," at 54–55.

61 See 1 Cor. 11:2 and 2 Thess. 2:15.

62 Gribomont, "Esoterisme et Tradition," at 54.

63 Gribomont, "Esoterisme et Tradition," at 55.

unite what they divide. Their demand for explicit scriptural proof for all teachings compromised the integrity of the faith. He tersely summarizes the consequences of their logic: "let them teach us not to baptize as we have received, or not to believe as we have been baptized, or not to give glory as we have believed."[64] As did Fathers before him, Basil learned that the Scriptures do not interpret themselves, and as they did, he thinks that the rule of faith enshrined in the liturgy has a special place here. In the end he realized that the problem of authority in the Church is not a simple one, and tradition itself can be quite complex and varied. It is not as though the Scriptures are obscure but tradition patent. William Tieck has worked out the Basilian view of authentic tradition. Authentic tradition must be of long usage, universal ecclesial recognition, and most important of all, "bearing a sense in accord with piety and true faith."[65] This is to say that authentic tradition must be consistent with apostolic (in the broad sense) liturgy and worship.

Conclusion

We have seen that, for Basil, worship provides the crucial context in which the Scriptures are best understood. On the one hand, one cannot worship rightly without them. The best prayer is prayer that uses the Scriptures, as Basil's ascetic experience taught him. Moreover, the Scriptures give moral direction, and in their obscurity, invite contemplation, reflection, and awe. If we think of the homily as an extension, so to speak, of the Scriptures, Rousseau's description of Basil's homiletic endeavors illuminates the role of the Scriptures too. In his preaching, "Basil had embarked," he writes, "on something more complex than Christianized oratory: the whole 'atmosphere' of the homiletic occasion was coloured by its cultic context, and by the broader programme of moral transformation of which it formed but a part."[66]

On the other hand, the right understanding of the Scriptures cannot be had apart from Christian worship. The liturgy, in particular, the Trinitarian doxology, unlocks the true Scriptural teaching on the divinity of the Spirit. For Basil, we must give glory to God according to our belief in him; we must believe in him as we have been baptized; and we must baptize as the liturgical tradition has taught us to do.[67]

It is fitting to close with a beautiful, though long, quotation from Rousseau's thoughtful and thought-provoking book on St. Basil:

> [Basil] emphasized a human awareness of the power and the activity of God and stressed the way in which the very vocabulary

64 *On the Holy Spirit* 27.68; trans. Hildebrand, 107.

65 Tieck, "Basil of Caesarea and the Bible," 145.

66 Rousseau, *Basil of Caesarea*, 47.

67 See *On the Holy Spirit* 27.68.

of Scripture brought the creature into a relationship with God. That was why access to truth, to put it simply, could occur only in the context of worship, which orchestrated the human response to revelation. To recognize religious authority, therefore, was not a matter of assenting to statements but rather of seeing oneself bound as a believer to a revealing God. … Adoration brought an understanding of its own.[68]

68 Rouseau, *Basil of Caesarea*, 128–129.

Letter & Spirit 7 (2011): 133-155

Patristic Exegesis and the Liturgy
Medieval *Ressourcement* and the Development of Baptism[1]

~: Owen M. Phelan :~

Introduction

Contemporary interest in patristic exegesis grew steadily over the course of the twentieth century as both critical editions and studies proliferated. Through careful study of the early church, scholars and theologians quickly established the profound influence of patristic exegesis on the liturgy. They also recovered hints to the enduring value of that exegesis for today. In this essay, I will explore an example of early Christian exegesis which exemplifies the impact patristic interpretation of the Bible had on Christian liturgy and suggests the importance of engaging our Christian tradition as we move forward in our own day on important questions of catechesis and conversion. Specifically, I will show how and why Jerome's brief observations about Jesus' language at the Great Commission became normative for medieval baptismal catechesis. But first, a few more words of introduction.

It is well-known that patristic exegesis enriched—and enriches—the theology of the sacraments. For instance, in 1950 Jean Daniélou SJ (1905–1974) published *From Shadows to Reality: Studies in the Biblical Typology of the Fathers.*[2] Famously, Daniélou explored patristic interpretation of several well-known biblical stories including Noah and the Flood and Moses and the Exodus. He illumined the wonderful theological depth and nuance teased out of these stories by patristic thinkers as they interpreted the stories typologically. In his study, he noticed the rich sacramental theology suggested to the fathers by these stories, such as how the Flood or the Israelites' crossing of the Red Sea could teach about the theology of baptism. He almost immediately continued to unpack his findings with some detail in *The Bible and the Liturgy*, in which he focused on how the first theologies of the Church's sacramental life were biblically derived.[3] Daniélou noted how most theologians agreed that sacraments are "efficacious signs," but that most theology focused on the "efficacious" and not on the "sign." In the biblical typology of the Fathers, he argued, the meaning and importance of the sacramental rites becomes fuller and more evident through attention to their nature as signs.[4] Our example

---

1 I would like to thank Neil Dhingra, Meg Garnett, Tom Noble, and Michael Roach for careful reading and advice on various drafts of this article. All remaining errors are my own.

2 Jean Daniélou, *From Shadows to Reality: Studies in the Biblical Typology of the Fathers* (Westminster: Newman Press, 1960).

3 Jean Daniélou, *The Bible and the Liturgy* (Notre Dame, IN: University of Notre Dame Press, 1956).

4 Daniélou, *Bible and the Liturgy*, 3.

of Jerome's comments on the Great Commission builds on the connection of the Bible to the liturgy not in the sense that Jerome deepens our appreciation of the mystery of baptism, but in that Jerome's observations determined how Christians instructed people coming to baptism. The intimate connection of the Bible to the liturgy is not limited to theological meaning, but also includes execution of rites like baptism.

Jerome's example also speaks to a larger concern of theologians like Daniélou, the so-called "*nouvelle theologie*" and its interest in *ressourcement*.[5] Essentially a reaction against what some viewed as a vapid neo-Scholastic stranglehold on Roman Catholic theology in the early twentieth century, theologians like Daniélou, Yves Congar, and Henri DeLubac advocated a return to the sources of the Christian tradition, especially the careful study of the Bible and the Fathers of the Church. They strongly felt that faithful engagement with these ancient sources would put tradition to work for the modern church. Thinking with the best of the Christian tradition would suggest solutions to contemporary problems at the same time creative and traditional. The example of early medieval theologians turning to Jerome and putting Jerome's ideas to work in a new context serves as a medieval example of *ressourcement*. We will see that the practice of turning to patristic exegesis in search of innovation is a powerful theological tool that long pre-dates more recent controversies. The example may also serve as exhortation to us. As the Church faces numerous challenges at the beginning of the twenty-first century, perhaps the way forward lies in faithful and prayerful engagement with sage advice from the past.

Matthew 28: The Great Commission

The Gospel of Matthew has been perhaps the single most influential book for Christians. So important was its putative author and its content that early Christians placed it first among the Gospels and then of the entire New Testament.[6] The Great Commission (Matt. 28:16–20) appears at the very end of Matthew's Gospel, a kind of epilogue or key to a series of five discourses, which focus on Jesus as the Christ and the approach of the Kingdom, interspersed between five narrative sections which move Jesus from Galilee to Jerusalem.[7] The number five

5 For a brief apologetic introduction to *la nouvelle théologie* see Marcellino D'Ambrosio, "Ressourcement Theology, Aggiornamento, and the Hermeneutics of Tradition," *Communio* 18:4 (1991): 530–555. For a sympathetic review in the slightly larger context of twentieth century theology, see the biographies Fergus Kerr, *Twentieth-Century Catholic Theologians* (Oxford: Blackwell, 2007).

6 On the Gospel of Matthew generally see the Dennis C. Duling, "The Gospel of Matthew," *The Blackwell Companion to the New Testament*, ed. David E. Aune (Oxford: Wiley-Blackwell, 2010), 296–318. See also the fuller discussions in William Albright and C.S. Mann, *Matthew*, Anchor Bible 26 (Garden City, NY: Doubleday, 1971) and in John P. Meier, *Matthew* (Wilmington, DE: Michael Glazer, 1980).

7 See Duling, "The Gospel of Matthew," 306–311. Compare Benedict Viviano, "The Gospel

harkens back to the five books of the Torah. In the final chapter of the Gospel, after Jesus' resurrection, Matthew describes the angel at Jesus' empty tomb speaking to Mary Magdalene and the "other Mary." The angel tells the women to have the Apostles gather in Galilee. Jesus then appears to the women and reiterates the order. In this final scene, the eleven are on a mountain in Galilee when Jesus appears to them and issues a last instruction. In the Latin of Jerome's *Vulgate*, the Gospel's final verses run:

> Go, therefore, and teach all nations, baptizing them in the name of the Father and of the Son and of the Holy Spirit, teaching them to observe all that I have commanded you; and behold, I am with you all days, even unto the consummation of the world.[8]

In the context of the Gospel, these words underscore the profound missionary concerns of the author, particularly the importance of transmitting Jesus' teachings contained in the discourses throughout the Gospel, especially as seen in the monumental first discourse, the Sermon on the Mount (Matt. 5–7).[9]

Jerome's Exegesis

In March 398, Jerome (347–420) wrote a commentary on the Gospel according to Matthew at his library retreat in Bethlehem.[10] His treatment encompasses the entire Gospel and is organized as a line-by-line commentary for his friend Eusebius of Cremona, who had requested something edifying to pass the time during an upcoming trip to Italy. Jerome finished the work in only two weeks! The consequent symptoms of haste in the commentary include erroneous citations and extreme brevity.[11] As Jerome reached the end of the Gospel, he paused to consider Jesus' "Great Commission" to the Apostles. He concentrated on the order of Jesus' instruction rather than the general missionary impulse of Jesus' words. He broke

---

According to Matthew," *The New Jerome Biblical Commentary*, eds. Raymond Brown, Joseph Fitzmyer, and Roland Murphy (Englewood Cliffs, NJ: Prentice Hall, 1990): 631–633 and Meier, *Matthew*, 366–374.

8 For a discussion primarily about Western Christianity and the Western liturgy, I cite not the Greek, but the Latin version of the Gospel familiar to all the writers under discussion here. See the *Biblia Sacra iuxta Vulgatam Versionem*, 4th Edition (Stuttgart: Deutsche Bibelgesellschaft, 1994), 1574. The translation here is adapted from the revised Douay-Rheims Bible.

9 Viviano, "Matthew," 674.

10 For a detailed biography see J.N.D. Kelly, *Jerome: His Life, Writings, and Controversies* (London: Gerald Duckworth & Co. Ltd., 1975). See also the more recent portrait with updated bibliography in Stefan Rebenich, *Jerome* (New York: Routledge, 2002). On Jerome as an author, especially his contribution to how the Latin West receives and interacts with the Bible, see Mark Vessey, "Jerome and Rufinus" *The Cambridge History of Early Christian Literature*, eds. Frances Young, Lewis Ayres, and Andrew Louth (Cambridge: Cambridge University Press, 2004), 218–327.

11 Saint Jerome, *Commentary on Matthew*, trans. Thomas P. Scheck (Washington, D.C.: The Catholic University of America Press, 2008), 16.

the command into two sections for analysis. In the first, he focused on the sequence and vocabulary of Jesus' words to the apostles, explaining:

> "Go, therefore, teach all nations, baptizing them in the name of the Father and of the Son and of the Holy Spirit" (Mt. 28:19). First they teach all the nations, then they dip those they taught in water. For it is not possible that a body receive the sacrament of baptism, unless the soul first receives the truth of the faith. They are, however, baptized in the name of the Father and of the Son and of the Holy Spirit so that whose divinity is one, is one dispensation. And the name of the Trinity is one God.[12]

In the sequence of Jesus' words Jerome intuited a catechetical strategy; in the language he discerned the doctrine of a monotheistic Trinity. Further, he assumed a sacramental dimension to mission and understood the teaching required by Jesus to revolve around baptism. He then considered the second part of the instruction, from which he distilled a three step approach to Christian teaching, writing:

> "... teaching them to preserve everything which I commanded you" (Mt. 28:20). The order is particular. He orders the apostles first to teach all the nations, then to dip them in the sacrament of faith and after faith and baptism to instruct them what things ought to be observed. And lest we think what was ordered to be trivial, he added a few things: "everything which I commanded you," so that those who believe, who were baptized in the Trinity, do everything which was taught.[13]

Jerome focuses his readers' attention on two issues: Christian education and the doctrine of the Trinity. Moreover the centrality of baptism is not merely systematic, but instrumental. He twice emphasized the significance of a specific approach to catechesis. Faith is the initial step. Faith, then, provides a foundation for fruitful baptism. Only with a sound faith and after a right baptism can moral instruction finally be delivered. Jerome's brief remarks, his juxtaposition of education and the baptismal liturgy, would capture the interest of influential medieval Christians beginning with the Venerable Bede.

Bede's Development

Some 300 years later and on the far side of Continental Europe, an Anglo-Saxon monk brought Jerome's teachings into the context of the liturgy to which it ap-

12 Hieronymus, *Commentariorum in Matheum libri iv*, CCSL 77, eds. D. Hurst and M. Adriaen (Turnhout: Brepols, 1969), 282. For an English translation see the corresponding section in Saint Jerome, *Commentary on Matthew*.

13 Hieronymus, *Commentariorum in Matheum*, 282–283.

plied. Sometime in the 720s, Bede (673–735) composed a homily on the Great Commission for his brother monks at Wearmouth-Jarrow, where this particular passage was read at Easter.[14] The Easter liturgy, of course, along with Pentecost, had long been the preferred setting for baptism.[15] Bede's homily, delivered within a liturgy already strongly tied to baptism, reflects not only the close connection of the Bible to the liturgy in the mind of this celebrated Anglo-Saxon monk, but also an instance of looking to patristic exegesis for advice on current matters. Bede, ever the teacher, adopted Jerome's perspective on order in baptismal instruction and clarified it so as to make it more compelling as an argument for contemporary preachers, and not simply an observation.

Bede's sermon focused on the Lord's triumph and its implications for Christians. Throughout his homily he cited writings from Augustine, Gregory the Great, and Jerome. At the heart of his address Bede recalled the three-stage instruction outlined by Jerome, while adding important developments of his own. Bede identified a contemporary context for Jesus' instruction: modern preaching. From within his own homily, he addressed preachers and insisted upon the importance of proper order in their preaching. Bede took up and added to Jerome's thoughts.

Drawing from his own experience as a teacher, Bede explained why Jerome's order was so important. Specifically, he considered the pedagogical challenge of sound moral instruction. Bede's own skill and experience as a teacher enabled him to identify for his audience when a student would be ready to accept teaching and under what conditions. A skilled preacher must take into account both a person's mind-set and his general circumstances. Bede described a ready student as free. One should not be forced into moral behavior, but after proper preparation one should want to be moral. He added that moral teaching should be offered at an opportune moment, when the student is free from distraction:

> "Go," he [Jesus] said, "teach all nations baptizing them in the name of the Father and of the Son and of the Holy Spirit, teaching them to observe everything I have commanded you (Mt. 28:19-20)." This, indeed, is the most correct order of preaching and to be followed most diligently also by modern church

14 For an overview of Bede's importance in his own time and his subsequent influence see the essays (and bibliography) in *The Cambridge Companion to Bede*, ed. Scott DeGregorio (Cambridge: Cambridge University Press, 2010). On the liturgical calendar see Hurst's introduction to Bede's homilies, Beda Venerabilis, *Homeliarum evangelii libri ii*, CCSL 122, ed. D. Hurst (Turnhout: Brepols, 1955), xiv.

15 The tradition of holding baptisms on Easter (or Pentecost) has been observed in the Western Church at least since the time of Tertullian. For a summary of this tradition see *The Study of the Liturgy*, eds. Cheslyn Jones et al. (New York: Oxford University Press, 1978), 97–99 and W.J. Conway, *The Time and Place of Baptism. A Historical Synopsis and a Commentary* (Washington: Catholic University of America Press, 1954), 4–20.

> preachers so that first the hearer is taught, then imbued with the sacraments of faith, then unconstrained and at the right time he should be instructed in keeping the Lord's commands. This is because one uninstructed and ignorant of the Christian faith is not able to be washed in the sacrament of the very same faith. It does not suffice to be purified from sins by the bath of baptism, if he does not strive after baptism to persevere in good works.[16]

Bede continued by teasing out theological implications of the order proposed by Jerome. With the juxtaposition of two scriptural passages, he explored how Jerome's notion of order hints both at the efficacy of the sacrament and at the final end of those to be baptized. First, he viewed order in terms of metaphysical causation. A passage from the letter to the Hebrews—in this context—frames moral life as a consequence of faith. Faith enables one to obey God's commands. This is related to but distinguishable from the proper understanding of faith that leads people to want to obey Christian moral teachings. Second, he identified the ultimate goal toward which Christian teaching must be oriented, namely, eternal life.[17] A passage from the Gospel of John illumines why in Bede's mind Christians must get baptism right. Baptism is more than just water. The Holy Spirit is at work in and through the sacrament. His agency guarantees its effect. Bede foregrounded what he saw as being at stake in the whole discussion of preaching:

> First, therefore, teach the nations, that is, establish a knowledge of truth, and thus he orders them to baptize because "without faith it is impossible to please God" (Heb. 11:6) and "unless one is born again of water and of the Holy Spirit, he is not able to enter the kingdom of heaven" (Jn. 3:5).[18]

Bede concluded his thoughts on the "Great Commission" by reiterating the importance of having faith well taught and baptism rightly executed. Again, his genius as an instructor appears. He recognized that Jerome's explanation lacked an explicit compelling conclusion. Why does formation matter? Sliding another passage into his analysis of Matthew, this time a verse from the Letter of James, Bede reiterated that a rewarding afterlife follows from a moral life enlivened by faith. He dropped Jerome's Trinitarian insight and replaced it with a reason for conversion.

---

16 Beda, *Homeliarum*, 235. For an English translation see Bede the Venerable, *Homilies on the Gospels, Volume 2*, trans. L. Martin and D. Hurst (Kalamazoo, MI: Cistercian, 1991).

17 On the importance of the afterlife to early medieval missionary strategies, including those of Bede and Alcuin, see Owen M. Phelan, "Catechising the Wild: The Continuity and Innovation of Missionary Catechesis under the Carolingians" *Journal of Ecclesiastical History* 61:3 (2010): 455–474.

18 Beda, *Homeliarum*, 235.

Christians toiling in the present needed to know that eternal reward awaited those who in faith lived a holy life:

> "... teaching them to observe everything which I commanded you (Mt. 28:20).' 'Because just as the body without spirit is dead, thus faith without works is dead" (Ja. 2:26). He [Jesus] subsequently suggests how great are the rewards of a devout way of life and the kind of pledge of future beatitude remaining for the faithful in the present saying: "Behold I am with you all days, even to the consummation of the world" (Mt. 28:20).[19]

Even as he appropriated Jerome, Bede added to Jerome's thoughts for a contemporary audience at a baptismal liturgy. Bede deepened Jerome's contribution through a consideration of formation's purpose. His great sensitivity as a teacher led him to concentrate not on the meaning of the liturgy, but rather on enriching his discussion of the Gospel with pedagogical flourishes directed to contemporary preachers seeking to instruct others.

Alcuin's Augmentation

Late in the eighth century, Jerome's interpretation resurfaced. This time the Latin doctor's comments on the Great Commission were marshalled to address a burning issue for a nascent Christendom: high stress, high stakes Frankish missionary endeavors.[20] Throughout the 790s, the Carolingians were dealing with a political, military, and religious challenge from the Saxons, who nearly annually rose up against the Franks in violent efforts to reject conquest and conversion.[21] In the mid-790s Carolingian expansion continued with the conquest of the pagan Avars of east-central Europe, and Carolingian theologians thought hard about mission and about how to avoid the dreadful mistakes committed among the Saxons.[22]

Alcuin of York (ca. 740–804), an Anglo-Saxon deacon recruited by Charlemagne to lead religious and intellectual reform in Frankish Europe, found a solution to this contemporary conundrum in the wisdom of Jerome, as trans-

19 Beda, *Homeliarum*, 235.

20 For an introduction to Christianity during the early medieval period with an emphasis on mission see Richard Fletcher, *The Barbarian Conversions: From Paganism to Christianity* (Berkeley: University of California Press, 1997); Ian Wood, *The Missionary Life: Saints and the Evangelization of Europe, 400–1050* (New York: Longman, 2001); and Peter Brown, *The Rise of Western Christendom: Triumph and Diversity, AD 200–1000*, 2nd Edition (Oxford: Blackwell, 2003).

21 For a general treatment of the Saxons and the Carolingians see Roger Collins, *Charlemagne* (Toronto: University of Toronto Press, 1998), 43–57. See also the provocative study Yitzhak Hen, 'Charlemagne's jihad' *Viator* 37 (2006): 33–51.

22 On the Avars and the Carolingians consult Collins, *Charlemagne*, 89–101. For a more thorough treatment of the Avars, see Walter Pohl, *Die Awaren: Ein Steppenvolk im Mitteleuropa, 567–822 n. Chr.* (Munich: Beck, 1988).

mitted by Bede.[23] Alcuin evidences the close connection between the Bible and the liturgy, and exemplifies *ressourcement* as he sought to apply faithfully in a new context traditions handed down from Jerome through Bede via biblical exegesis. Alcuin distilled from Jerome's observation concrete liturgical advice. He developed not a new theology of baptism, but rather refined a useful approach to baptism's execution. He then dispersed it across Western Europe through his numerous contacts, friends, and students.

In 796 Alcuin drafted three letters on the mission to the Avars. He considered not only how best to avoid the disappointing Saxon cycle of subjugation and revolt, but also how best to communicate his ideas to the right people. The first letter was written to Arn, the bishop of Salzburg, who Alcuin felt should run the mission to the Avars. A second letter was dispatched to Meginfrid, the Carolingian court chamberlain, who had influence over financial matters and a widely known special advisory role with the Frankish king.[24] A third letter Alcuin directed to King Charlemagne himself. In each letter, Alcuin used Jerome's interpretation to apply Matthew's passage to a very complicated contemporary problem, and did so for three individuals with differing concerns about the Avars.

While the core of his position remained Jerome's order, Alcuin tailored his explanation for each recipient. For Arn, he placed Jerome's model amid a treatment of how a sound catechetical program would yield reliable Christians, emphasizing the religious themes of faith and salvation and accenting the duty of preaching to his friend and bishop. Alcuin wrote:

> Therefore, our Lord Jesus Christ commanded his disciples saying: "Go, teach all the nations, baptizing them in the name of the Father and of the Son and of the Holy Spirit, teaching them to preserve everything I have commanded you" (Mt. 28:19-20). In those very few words, he set out the order of all holy preaching. He said to teach twice and to baptize once. First, he instructed them to teach the catholic faith to all and he ordered after the faith is received to baptize in the name of the Holy Trinity; then, given instruction in the faith and washed with holy baptism, he commanded to instruct with evangelical precepts.[25]

---

23 The most recent biography of Alcuin is Donald Bullough, *Alcuin: Achievement and Reputation* (Leiden: Brill, 2004). For a brief introduction to education, learning, and Carolingian Renewal—especially Alcuin's role—see Rosamond McKitterick, "The Carolingian Renaissance of Culture and Learning" *Charlemagne: Empire and Society*, ed. Joanna Story (Manchester: Manchester University Press, 2005), 151–166.

24 A brief discussion of Meginfrid's widely acknowledged special influence with Charlemagne is in Bullough, *Alcuin*, 441.

25 Alcuin, *Epistola* 113, *MGH Epistolae IV*, ed. Ernst Dümmler (Berlin: Weidmannschen Verlagsbuchhandlung, 1895), 164.

Alcuin made virtually the same case to Meginfrid. This time, however, Jerome's insight is set in a discussion of how well-formed Christians would enrich the Carolingian treasury. Alcuin developed his argument by exploiting the semantic range of "glory" and "wealth." Unlike for Arn, whom Alcuin advised to instruct the Avars with Christian moral precepts, for Meginfrid the precepts should be doled out to the Avars:

> For our Lord Jesus Christ, returning to his Father's seat in the triumph of his glory, instructed his apostles, saying: 'Go, teach all the nations, baptizing them in the name of the Father and of the Son and of the Holy Spirit, teaching them to preserve everything that I have commanded you (Mt. 28:19-20).' First the faith ought to be taught, and then the sacrament of baptism ought to be received, then the evangelical precepts ought to be handed over.[26]

Finally, Alcuin laid out his interpretation for Charlemagne. He described how baptism in the context of his formation program would yield good Carolingian subjects. And, rather than recasting Jerome's argument for Charlemagne, Alcuin merely recopied the words of the famous church father, with special emphasis on the sequence of instruction:

> And the Lord himself in the Gospel teaching his disciples said: "Go, teach all the nations, baptizing them in the name of the Father and of the Son and of the Holy Spirit" (Mt. 28:19). Saint Jerome explains the order of this teaching thus in the commentary which he wrote on the Gospel of Matthew. First they teach all the nations, then they dip those they taught in water. For it is not possible that a body receive the sacrament of baptism, unless first the soul first receives the truth of faith. They are, however, baptized in the name of the Father and of the Son and of the Holy Spirit so that whose divinity is one, is one dispensation. And the name of the Trinity is one God. "... teaching them to observe everything that I have commanded you" (Mt. 28:20). The order is particular. He orders the apostles first to teach all the nations, then to dip them in the sacrament of faith, and after faith and baptism to instruct them with what things ought to be observed. And lest we think what was ordered to be trivial, he added a few things: "Everything which I commanded you"

26 Alcuin, *Epistola* 111, 160.

> (Mt. 28:20), so that those who believe, who were baptized in the Trinity, do everything which was taught.[27]

Alcuin's fidelity to Jerome is evident in each of his letters; however, Alcuin's study of tradition was not reserved to a single Latin church father.[28] He also, clearly, was indebted to Bede. In this way, he demonstrates the very best process of *ressourcement*, returning not to one source but consulting the full tradition as it was available to him. Bede's thoughts appear through Alcuin's choice of biblical citations. Both the Letter to the Hebrews and John's Gospel shaped his analysis. For example, in his letter to Arn, immediately following his exposition of Matthew's Great Commission, Alcuin reiterated that the order of teaching should be observed for all adults. In the case of infants, however, even though they cannot be taught as adults are, they must nevertheless be baptized because of the stain of original sin. The passage from Hebrews cited by Bede supports his defense of infant baptism. As with his use of Jerome, Alcuin used Bede's work to address a contemporary concern. Following a long-held view in Christian theology, Alcuin tied together his Christian anthropological assumptions with ideas of legal representation first laid out in Late Antiquity by theologians both eastern and western.[29] He dealt with the baptism of infants by a reference to the idea of a *fideiussor*, one who swears an oath on behalf of another. Because infants presented for baptism are stained with the sin of another (Adam), it is appropriate for others, in this case the godparents, to answer for infants at baptism. Making the then common assumption that Hebrews was written by Paul, he explained to Arn:

> You, most holy teacher, firmly maintain this order of catechizing everywhere in men of adult age, to those of a more frail age the Holy Mother Church grants that he who is bound to sin in paternal transgression by another, another may release him by profession in the mystery of baptism. But if this may not be, how many children passed away from whose number now the heavenly Jerusalem is built daily? Without faith what profit is

---

27 Alcuin, *Epistola* 110, 158.

28 Alcuin is well-known for walking "in the footsteps of the fathers." See, for example, John C. Cavadini, "A Carolingian Hilary," in *The Study of the Bible in the Carolingian Era*, eds. Celia Chazelle and Burton Van Name Edwards (Turnhout: Brepols, 2003) 133–140; idem, "The sources and theology of Alcuin's 'De fide sanctae et individuae trinitatis,'" *Traditio* 46 (1991): 123–146; and, idem, "Alcuin and Augustine: *De Trinitate*," *Augustinian Studies 12* (1981): 11–18. Moreover, in the context of these letters themselves, Alcuin advises his audience to consult Augustine's *De catechizandis rudibus* and Gregory the Great's *Regula pastoralis*. Gregory the Great's *Regula pastoralis* is mentioned to Arn at Alcuin, *Epistola* 113, 166. Augustine's *De catechizandis rudibus* is recommended to Charlemagne at Alcuin, *Epistola* 110, 158.

29 Joseph Lynch, *Godparents and Kinship in Early Medieval Europe* (Princeton: Princeton University Press, 1986), 106–109 and 123–124.

> baptism? Since the Apostle says: "Without faith it is impossible to please God (Heb. 11:6)."[30]

The necessity for infant baptism and importance of godparents vouching faith is cemented in Alcuin's mind by the remark from the letter to the Hebrews on the necessity of faith.

In the very next section of his letter to Arn, Alcuin grounded his treatment of baptism's efficacy with the other quotation supplied by Bede:

> He [the catechumen] equally ought to understand that the Holy Trinity works the salvation of man. The Lord himself says in another place: "No one is able to come to the Father except through me (Jn. 14:6).' Likewise concerning the Holy Spirit he says: 'Unless anyone is reborn from water and the Spirit, he is not able to enter the kingdom of God" (Jn. 3:5). For what the priest at baptism visibly works in the body through water, the Holy Spirit does this invisibly in the soul through faith.[31]

Again Alcuin applied Bede's work to late eighth century Europe. He took up Bede's thread and used John's Gospel to confirm that it is not the priest, nor the baptizand (be one adult or infant) who works the sacrament. Rather, the power of the sacrament to reform one's soul flows from the Holy Spirit. Unlike Bede, whose use of John accented the baptized entering the kingdom of God, Alcuin focused on the agency of the Spirit who guarantees baptism's effect. Alcuin's primary concern remained mission. Whether addressing the conversion of pagan adults or children, he consistently defended the necessity of an orderly baptismal program.

Importantly, Alcuin did not confine his efforts to these letters. He aggressively advocated his ideas through liturgical commentaries and hagiography. At the end of the eighth century Alcuin composed a commentary on the rite of baptism which provided a concrete form to his plan for Christian formation.[32] He applied Jerome's three steps to the liturgy of baptism, at once adapting the baptismal liturgy to fit Jerome's order and presenting the liturgy as a pedagogical tool for communicating faith and morals to others. The commentary, identified by its opening words *Primo paganus*, survives in two separate letters from the year 798, likely indicating a circular letter-type distribution, not dissimilar from his advocacy of Jerome's (and Bede's) interpretation of Matthew's Great Commission.[33]

30 Alcuin, *Epistola* 113, 164.

31 Alcuin, *Epistola* 113, 164.

32 The authorship of the commentary has been the subject of scholarly disagreement. I have argued that Alcuin composed the work himself in Owen M. Phelan, "Textual Transmission and Authorship in Carolingian Europe: *Primo Paganus*, Baptism, and Alcuin of York," *Revue Bénédictine* 118 (2008): 262–288.

33 Not surprisingly, the letters are transmitted in otherwise unrelated collections of Alcuin's

Wide distribution of the text is further evidenced by its unquestionable popularity across the Carolingian world. It was the most copied and cited commentary on baptism in early Medieval Europe.[34]

The first surviving instance is a letter to an otherwise unknown priest named Oduinus.[35] The note contains little more than a brief introduction and the commentary itself. The second instance is a longer missive addressed as an open letter to a community of monks in southern Gaul, whom Alcuin knew through Leidrad, bishop of the important and influential see of Lyon.[36] The letter includes the commentary amid a larger treatment of the dangers of Spanish Adoptionism and advice on how to combat its spread.[37] *Primo paganus* enumerates the various elements of the baptismal ceremony and offers a spiritual interpretation of each. In typically Alcuinian fashion, the text draws heavily on earlier authors, reworking older materials to new ends.

For explanations of the liturgy Alcuin plundered two earlier texts, a long letter on baptism written by the sixth-century Roman, John the Deacon, to a man named Senarius, and a sermon spuriously attributed to Saint Augustine.[38] Echoing Jerome's three steps, the text considers pre-baptismal instruction, baptism itself, and post-baptismal instruction. Put simply, Alcuin explained that doctrine ought to be taught before baptism, especially through instruction in the Creed and the Paternoster. Baptism itself is presented as a refashioning of a person in the image of the Trinity, so that after baptism the new Christian could gradually take on the moral responsibilities of Christianity. Post-baptismal moral teachings

letters. For an introduction to Alcuin's letters, see Ernst Dümmler, *Epistolae karolini aevi II, Epistolae IV* (Berlin: MGH, 1895), 1–17. See also the discussion of major collections of Alcuin's letters in Bullough, *Alcuin*, 43–102.

34 See Susan A. Keefe, *Water and the Word: Baptism and the Education of the Clergy in the Carolingian Empire*, Vol. I (Notre Dame, IN: University of Notre Dame Press, 2002), 80.

35 Alcuin, *Epistola* 134, 202–203. An English translation of this letter is supplied in Gerald Ellard, *Master Alcuin, Liturgist: A Partner of our Piety* (Chicago: Loyola University Press, 1956), 76–78.

36 Alcuin, *Epistola* 137, 210–216. That the letter was written for circulation among clerical and monastic communities of Gothia and Provence is discussed at Bullough, *Alcuin*, 7.

37 On Spanish Adoptionism generally, see John C. Cavadini, *The Last Christology of the West, Adoptionism in Spain and Gaul 785-820* (Philadelphia: University of Pennsylvania Press, 1993).

38 John the Deacon, *Letter to Senarius*, PL 59.399–408. For further treatment of John the Deacon's material in *Primo paganus* consult: "Epistola de Iohannis Diaconi ad Senarium" in "Un florilège carolingien sur la symbolisme des ceremonies du baptême, avec un Appendice sur la lettre de Jean Diacre," ed. André Wilmart, in *Analecta Reginensia* (1933): 170–179. The sermon is printed in Migne PL 47.1151A-1152C. The text is identified as spurious in *Clavis Patristica Pseudepigraphorum Medii Aevi*, vol. 1 (Turnhout: Brepols, 1990): 273–274. On the myriad problems still surrounding pseudo-augustinian material, see *Augustine Through the Ages: An Encyclopedia*, ed. Allan D. Fitzgerald (Grand Rapids: William B. Eerdmans, 1999), 530–533. On Alcuin's blending of John the Deacon and pseudo-Augustine, see Phelan "Textual Transmission," 262–288.

revolved around instruction in the virtues and vices, their benefits and dangers to the immortal soul.

Alcuin's efforts to spread his approach spilled beyond letters and into saints' lives. In mid-796, at the same time he wrote his letters, he composed a *Life of Saint Willibrord* in two versions, both dedicated to Beornrad, the powerful archbishop of Sens and abbot of Echternach. Alcuin expected him to promote the vision of baptismal formation featured in the works on Willibrord, one in prose and the other in verse. He anticipated that the former would be read "publically by the brothers in church" and that each of Beornrad's monks would read the latter "privately in his room."[39] The works recount the miraculous birth of St. Willibrord in 658, his early education in Northumbria, his quest for personal holiness in an Irish monastery, and his mission to the Continent—including authorization by the papacy, his death in 739, and some posthumous miracles.[40]

An example of Jerome's order flowed from the mouth of the saint in the midst of a particularly audacious speech before the notoriously violent Frisian king, Radbod. The speech addressed the king's charge that Willibrord's mission had insulted the Frisian deity. In the middle of the speech, the missionary invited the king to convert. In a passage filled with references to the sacrament of baptism, Alcuin identified conversion with the three stages identified by Jerome: faith, baptism, moral life. The sophistication of Alcuin's presentation is accented by an echo of the Creed in the invitation to assent and the references to cardinal virtues in the characterization of moral life:

> As his [God's] servant I [Willibrord] call upon you this day to renounce the empty and inveterate errors to which your forebears have given their assent and to believe in the one Almighty God, our Lord Jesus Christ. Be baptized in the fountain of life and wash away all your sins, so that, forsaking all wickedness and unrighteousness, you may henceforth live as a new man in temperance, justice, and holiness.[41]

39 Alcuin, *Vita Willibrordi archepiscopi Traiectensis*, ed. Wilhelm Levison, MGH SRM 7 (Hannover: Hahnshe, 1920), 113.

40 For a further information on Willibrord see Arnold Angendt, "Willibrord im Dienste der Karolinger," *Annalen des historischen Vereins für den Niederrhein: insbesondere das alte Erzbistum Köln* clxxv (1973): 63–113; and *Der hl. Willibald-Klosterbischof oder Bistumsgründer?*, eds. Harald Dickerhof, Ernst Reiter, and Stefan Weinfurter (Regensburg: Pustet, 1990). On Alcuin's *Life of Willibrord* more specficially see Kate Rambridge, "Alcuin's narrative of evangelism: The life of St. Willibrord and the Northumbrian hagiographical tradition," *The cross goes north: processes of conversion in northern Europe, AD 300-1300*, ed. Martin Carver (Rochester, NY: Boydell and Brewer, 2003), 371–381 and Wood, *The missionary life*, 81–85. An English translation of the *Life of Willibrord* may be found in *Soldiers of Christ: Saints and Saints' Lives from Late Antiquity and the Early Middle Ages*, eds. Thomas F.X. Noble and Thomas Head (University Park, PA: Pennsylvania State University Press, 1995).

41 Alcuin, *Vita Willibrordi*, 125.

This stirring depiction of the work of Christian formation under the most difficult circumstances emphasizes the value seen by Alcuin in right catechetical order for missionary work. Thus is the *Life of Willibrord* another key component in Alcuin's circulation of Jerome's insight into Matthew, its ramifications for the practice of baptism, and its importance to Christian mission.

Subsequent Reception and Development

Alcuin's flurry of literary activity quickly gained traction among influential Carolingians. His friends, contacts, and students across Carolingian Europe integrated Jerome's approach to baptism into their own teachings. Almost immediately after Alcuin's letters on the Avar mission were dispatched a synod held on account of the Avars gave canonical teeth to Alcuin's missionary strategy. By the fall of 796, Patriarch Paulinus of Aquileia, and likely Arn, organized a council on the banks of the Danube in order to present a policy on the appropriate understanding and execution of the sacrament of baptism for the conversion of the Avars, a record of which survives from Paulinus' own hand.[42]

Both in its general approach and in the particulars of its explanation, the council applied the advice of Jerome as recommended by Alcuin. As if reading an epitome of Alcuin's principal concerns, the Patriarch of Aquileia wrote:

> The Lord ordered his disciples saying "Go, teach all the nations baptizing them in the name of the Father and of the Son and of the Holy Spirit, teaching them to observe all things whatsoever I commanded you" (Mt. 28:19–20), and again, "who believes and is baptized will be saved" (Mk. 16:16). Indeed it is agreeable to look at the Lord's words with watchful zeal and to pay close attention to the most sacred order in those commands. For he does not say "Go, baptizing all the nations teaching them," but first he brings in "teach" and then he adds "baptize." And not who was baptized and believes, but "who believes and was baptized will be saved." And after baptism again "teach them to observe all things whatsoever I commanded you," so that manifestly it was given to be understood and the faith was to be taught before baptism, and so the new one understands what the grace of baptism is, because through it sins are forgiven and a new man is regenerated. Certainly with the old man with his

42 *Conventus episcoporum ad ripas danubii, MGH Concilia 2:1,* ed. Albert Werminghoff (Hannover: Hahnsche, 1906), 176. On this meeting in the context of Carolingian councils see Wilfried Hartmann, *Die Synoden der Karolingerzeit im Frankenreich und in Italien* (Paderborn: Ferdinand Schöningh, 1989), 116–117. For the council in the context of the Avar conquest see Pohl, *Die Awaren*, 319–320. On Paulinus' importance to Carolingian control of Lombard Italy see Nick Everett, "Paulinus, the Carolingians, and Famosissima Aquileia," *Paolino d'Aquileia e il contributo italiano all'Europa carolingia*, ed. Paolo Chiesa (Udine: Forum, 2003): 115–154.

> acts having passed away among the waves of redemption, who was a son of sin may begin to be a son of God through adoption and a sharer in the kingdom of heaven and after this mortal life may obtain a blessedness of life. After baptism they ought to be taught to observe all the commands of God by which, mercifully and rightly, they ought to live in this age.[43]

The continuity with Jerome's approach as mediated through Bede and Alcuin is evident. Moreover, the influence of biblical interpretation on the liturgical activity is quite direct. Rather than an academic exercise of one stripe or another, here Jerome's interpretation of Matthew appears in a document suggesting imminent application to liturgical practice "out in the field."

Alcuin's vigorous advocacy of Jerome's idea resonated with Carolingian intellectuals in an enduring way. Across the ninth century, several theologians with connections to Alcuin incorporated Jerome's teaching on Matthew's Great Commission into their efforts. For example, one of Alcuin's most celebrated students, Hrabanus Maurus (780–856) incorporated the explanation into several texts including his own *Exposition of Matthew* and his widely transmitted manual on clerical formation, *On the Training of Clergy*.[44]

Hrabanus served as the Abbot of Fulda and Archbishop of Mainz. One of the greatest intellectuals of his age, he is remembered as man of deep prayer and immense learning. His *Exposition* was written between 814 and 822 while he was schoolmaster at the famous monastery of Fulda. Hrabanus for the most part copied Bede's homily in explaining the end of Matthew's Gospel, but with an addition. Hrabanus underscored that prebaptismal formation is essential to the success of baptism, writing in his *Exposition*:

> This, indeed, is the most correct order of preaching and to be followed most diligently also by modern church preachers, so that first indeed the hearer is taught, then imbued with the sacraments of faith, then unconstrained and at the right time he should be instructed to preserve the Lord's commands, *because it is not possible for the body to receive the sacrament of baptism, unless first the soul receives the truth of the faith. Since* one uninstructed or ignorant of the Christian faith is not able to be washed in the sacraments of the very same faith, and the washing of baptism does not suffice to cleanse from sins, if after baptism one does not strive to persevere in good works. First, therefore, teach the nations, that is establish a knowledge of truth, and thus he

43 *Conventus episcoporum*, 174–175.

44 For an introduction to Hrabanus see *Hrabanus Maurus: Lehrer, Abt und Bischof*, eds. Raymund Kottje and Harald Zimmermann (Wiesbaden: Steiner, 1982).

> orders them to baptize, because "without faith it is impossible to please God" and "unless he is reborn from water and the Holy Spirit, he is not able to enter the kingdom of God."[45]

Hrabanus did not merely regurgitate Bede, but remixed Bede's interpretation of Jerome with Jerome's own work, likely reflecting his work with Alcuin. Hrabanus' concluding observation broke from Bede and added a sentiment from Jerome, but not Bede, before concluding with the quotation from James, again from Bede. Although most of the text was drawn from Bede, interest in a happy afterlife is noticeably de-emphasized. Hrabanus' tinkering delivered a slightly more ominous reflection on the theological stakes of moral action for the Christian, no doubt underscoring the importance of *successful* missionary conversion so important to his teacher:

> And to the end indeed he added "teaching them to preserve everything whatsoever I commanded you." And lest we think this is trifling and small, what he commanded, he added "everything whatsoever I commanded you" so that whoever believes, who was baptized in the Trinity, does everything which was ordered, because "just as the body without the spirit is dead, so faith also without works is dead."[46]

In his widely-esteemed work on clerical formation, *On the Training of Clergy*, Hrabanus testifies to how quickly Jerome's order became tied to the administration of the sacrament of baptism. In his section explaining baptism, Hrabanus anchored pre-baptismal instruction in the Great Commission. Written sometime between 816 and 819, he dedicated the work to Haistulf, the archbishop of Mainz (813–825). The work had a long influence on theological reflection concerning priestly life, cited throughout the Middle Ages by people like Gratian, Thomas Aquinas, and Gabriel Biel. The work comprises three books, which treat holy orders and the sacraments, clerical life, and clerical education.

In the middle of the first book, when considering the priest's obligations at baptism, Hrabanus addressed the formation of catechumens. He presented baptism as following a beginning of faith laid down during pre-baptismal instruction. Referring to Matthew and to Jesus' instructions to the Apostles, he interpreted Jesus' message as assigning order to formation where catechumens would be taught the faith first and then baptized. Hrabanus explicitly mentioned pre-baptismal instruction and baptism itself. He did not include an exhortation to moral in-

45 Hrabanus Maurus, *Expositio in Matthaeum*, ed. Bengt Löfstedt, CCCM 174A (Turnhout: Brepols, 2000), 787 (my emphasis, highlighting Hrabanus' addition to Bede).

46 Hrabanus Maurus, *Expositio in Matthaeum*, 787.

struction because he did not consider post-baptismal teaching, which appears in another section of his text:

> But before baptism of the one to be catechized, his [the priest's] duty to the person ought to come first so that the catechumen first receives the beginning of the faith. For it is read in the Gospel according to Matthew that after the resurrection the Lord ordered the apostles to teach in the name of the Father and of the Son and of the Holy Spirit and to baptize all peoples, that is, first to teach the faith of God to them and then to baptize the ones believing into the remission of sins. Hence it is because according to the Gospel of Mark the same Lord is read to have placed the faith of baptism first when he said thus: "He who believes and is baptized shall be saved, but he who does not believe shall be condemned" (Mark 16:16). And according to John Jesus himself smeared over the eyes of the man born blind mud that he made from his spit and then sent him to the waters at Siloe because first the one to be baptized ought to be instructed in the faith of the incarnation of Christ and then, now a believer, be admitted to baptism, so that he knows in whose grace he is a partaker, and to whom now from this moment he becomes a debtor.[47]

Throughout his discussion of baptism, though not in this section, Hrabanus betrayed a dependence on his teacher Alcuin. For example, once Jerome's order was established as normative, Alcuin's liturgical commentary *Primo paganus* was raided for its interpretation of the baptismal rites.[48] Perhaps Alcuin's influence can also be detected in the reference to Mark, cited earlier by Paulinus, which helped Hrabanus establish the stakes involved in baptismal formation. As befitting a text on teaching, he emphasized sound instruction as the fundamental responsibility of the priest and a critical element for fruitful baptism. In both his commentary and his training manual, Hrabanus advanced Alcuin's approach to the Bible and the liturgy as well as his inclination to *ressourcement*.

Paschasius Radbertus (785/795–865), an instructor and abbot at the celebrated monastery of Corbie across the tumultuous middle decades of the Ninth Century, shows an impulse similar to Hrabanus'.[49] A learned and devout monk,

---

47 Hrabanus Maurus, *De institutione clericorum libri tres*, ed. Detlev Zimpel (Frankfurt: Peter Lang, 1996), 318.

48 See Hrabanus Maurus, *De institutione clericorum*, 320–323.

49 For more on Paschasius' life, see Henri Peltier, *Pascase Radbert, Abbé de Corbie, contribution à l'étude de la vie monastique et de la pensée chrétienne aux temps carolingiens* (Amiens: L.H. Duthoit, 1938).

Paschasius was a widely respected exegete and theologian. In addition to learned commentaries on scripture, he wrote one of the first Latin treatises on the Eucharist and the oldest surviving Latin treatise on the Assumption of the Blessed Virgin Mary. In his massive twelve-book *Exposition of Matthew,* Paschasius' explanation of the Great Commission is textually dependent upon both Jerome and Bede, but with changes that reflect his own interests—especially his personal investment in Christian mission—and, I think, a debt to Alcuin of York.

Paschasius' predecessor as abbot of Corbie, Adalhard, had been a regular correspondent of Alcuin and consequently the library at Corbie was well-stocked with Alcuin's works.[50] Moreover, Paschasius was sensitive to the demands of mission and conversion. During his lifetime, Corbie established daughterhouses such as Corvey, erected in Saxony, and sponsored missions among the Danes.[51] Throughout his comments on Matthew's Great Commission, Paschasius emphasized how integral both education and preaching were to the rite of baptism, showing that Alcuin's efforts had been absorbed into ninth century liturgical customs:

> "Go," he says, "teach all nations baptizing them in the name of the Father and of the Son and of the Holy Spirit, teaching them to obey everything whatsoever I commanded you." The most correct order of preaching is therefore handed down and most carefully preserved. It should be preached by all modern preachers of the churches of God so that, indeed, first they teach their hearers and then hand over to them the sacraments of the faith. From the newness of their birth to the last they should observe everything which was commanded to them for one renewed, because neither is baptism without faith beneficial nor is faith without the works of the commands of God. And, therefore, first is to be taught faith by which God is rightly believed and that faith is given so that all things are possible for those believing, and also, indeed, is given the power of adoption so that we are called and are sons of God. Thence to these ones who have thus been instructed the sacraments of faith are to be handed over and thus they are to be dipped in baptism so that they are reborn whole in the same sacrament. Then finally it is fitting that the preacher and doctor press so that now thereafter in that

50 See David Ganz, *Corbie in the Carolingian Renaissance* (Sigmaringen: Jan Thorbecke, 1990), 43–45, 137.

51 Paschasius' famous treatise on the Eucharist was in fact first written for the instruction of unlettered novices at Corvey. See Paschasius Radbertus, *De corpore et sanguine domini*, ed. Beda Paulus, CCCM 16 (Turnhout: Brepols, 1969), 4–5.

> new birth the works of faith follow and the commands in which charity is fulfilled are preserved.[52]

Thanks largely to Alcuin and his network, the Hieronymian interpretation dominated reflection on the Great Commission and on baptism across the ninth century, though far removed from its late antique context and applied to the missionary and organizational concerns at the dawn of Christendom.

A High Medieval Assumption

The impetus for considering baptism fundamentally as an issue of formation diminished in the twelfth century when theological reflection began to shift somewhat from issues of mission and the execution of baptism toward questions of sacramental efficacy.[53] For baptism, philosophical and intellectual problems supplanted social and missionary ones. Still, Jerome's order for Christian formation had been so integrated into the practice of baptism that it was simply assumed, even as interest in baptism moved in new directions.

For example, the issue of baptismal formation appeared in Peter Lombard's (c. 1100–1160) *Sententiae*, the basic textbook of high medieval theology.[54] In his fourth book, which deals with sacraments, Peter took up catechetics. That the issue was of some importance is established by its inclusion. Yet the relative (un) importance of the matter is suggested not only by the fact that Peter addressed formation in the thirty-first and final paragraph on baptism, but also that the topic is conceptually joined with and subordinated to exorcism. The resulting picture preserved the sense of order to catechetical formation, but not the purpose. Questions of mission became invisible. Teaching was very deliberately separated from baptism and not treated as essential to the rite. Catechesis was sacramental, but not sacrament. Peter emphasized the theology of baptism over the transmission and understanding of faith.

---

52 Paschasius Radbertus, *Expositio in Matheo libri xii*, ed. Beda Paulus, CCCM 56B (Turnhout: Brepols, 1984), 1432–1433.

53 The Twelfth Century has long been seen as a period of dramatic change in Western Europe, for an introduction consult the essays in *Renaissance and Renewal in the Twelfth Century*, eds. Robert Benson, Giles Constable, and Carol Lanham (Cambridge, MA: Harvard University Press, 1982). On the vibrance of the theological tradition in the twelfth century see M.D. Chenu, *Nature, Man, and Society in the Twelfth Century*, trans. Jerome Taylor and Lester Little (Chicago: University of Chicago Press, 1968), originally published in a more substantial form as M.D. Chenu, *La théologie du douzième siècle* (Paris: J. Vrin, 1957). For a darker perspective on the period see R.I. Moore, *The Formation of a Persecuting Society: Power and Deviance in Western Europe, 950–1250* (Oxford: Blackwell, 1987).

54 On Peter Lombard see the exhaustive treatment in Marcia Colish, *Peter Lombard* (Leiden: Brill, 1994). On Book Four in particular, see the translation and introduction in Peter Lombard, *The Sentences, Book 4: On the Doctrine of Signs*, trans. Giulio Silano (Toronto: Pontifical Institute of Medieval Studies, 2010).

His textual dependence on Hrabanus Maurus underscores the new and different interest of the Parisian thinker. He drew from Hrabanus' *On the Training of Clergy*, from the very section where Hrabanus interpreted Matthew's Great Commission. However, Peter selected text from around the abbot of Fulda's interpretation and then juxtaposed his selections with passages from Augustine's *On the Symbol*. Peter used Hrabanus' language, but did not communicate Hrabanus' concern when he wrote:

> Catechism and exorcism pertain to neophytes, and are to be called sacramentals rather than sacraments. ... And so these precede baptism: not that there cannot be true baptism without them, but so that the one to be baptized may be instructed concerning the faith, and that he may know whose debtor he will afterwards become, and that the power of the devil may be diminished in him. Hence Hrabanus: "The office of catechizing the candidate is to precede baptism, so that the catechumen may receive the rudiments of the faith and know whose debtor he will afterwards become."[55] Also Augustine: "Children are breathed over and exorcized, so that the devil's power may be expelled from them;"[56] "lest he strive to subvert them so that they do not attain baptism."[57] "And so in children it is not God's creature which is blown over and exorcized, but"[58] the devil, so that he may go out of the person.[59]

The catechetical imperative imposed by missionary anxiety at the end of the eighth century has faded and concerns about sacramental efficacy raised by changing philosophical interests has moved to the fore. Nevertheless, Alcuin's application of Jerome remains.

Another example of the same transition is found in the writings of Hugh of St. Victor's (1096–1141). While little is known about Hugh's life, his surviving works encompass an intimidating breadth of topics from grammar to geometry to hermeneutics to theology. Among the most influential of the Victorines, his works remained hugely popular throughout the Middle Ages. *On the Sacraments of the*

55 Hrabanus Maurus, *De institutione clericorum*, 318.

56 Augustine, *De symbolo ad catechumenos*, ed. R. Vander Plaetse, CCSL 46 (Turnhout: Brepols, 1969), 186.

57 Hrabanus Maurus, *De institutione clericorum*, 321.

58 Augustine, *De symbolo*, 186.

59 Peter Lombard, *Sententiae in iv libris distinctae*, ed. Ignatius Brady, OFM, Vol. 2 (Grottaferrata: Editiones Collegii S. Bonaventurae Ad Claras Aquas, 1981), 276.

Christian Faith is his rather sizeable compendium of Christian theology.[60] Hugh took up the sacrament of baptism in book two, part six of *On the Sacraments*.[61] As with Peter Lombard, the order of topics reflect Hugh's interests: pre-baptismal catechesis is the ninth entry in the section on baptism.

Clues to the concerns guiding Hugh's interests survive in the writings of Bernard of Clairvaux (1090–1153). Around 1125, Hugh wrote to Bernard asking for his opinion on four questions concerning baptism. While Hugh's letter is lost, Bernard's reply survives, and lengthy excerpts were incorporated into Hugh's treatment of baptism in *On the Sacraments*. Bernard's letter addressed the four questions in order and at some length.[62] The first three are clearly derived from the opinions of the famous philosopher Peter Abelard.[63] The first is whether one can be saved without baptism. The second revolved around the extent of faith possible before the time of Christ. The third considered the culpability of one who sins out of ignorance. The fourth question addressed Bernard's novel opinions on the Blessed Virgin Mary.

Bernard's antipathy toward Peter Abelard is well-known. Hugh's concern may derive from Abelard's strident philosophical and theological opinions, or perhaps from Abelard's coarse treatment of his teacher and then adversary, William of Champeaux (d. 1121), who established the canons of St. Victor in 1108. Whatever the reason, Hugh's interest in the sacrament differed from that of the early medieval theologians insofar as he prioritized the theology of baptism over its application. Nevertheless, Hugh's explanations retained the Hieronymian analysis of the Great Commission. He evaluated Jesus' instruction as imposing order on catechetics, but not to the extent emphasized under the Carolingians. After a definition of catechumen well-known from the early Middle Ages, the Victorine offers a streamlined recapitulation of Jerome's order, sans moral instruction.[64]

---

60 For an overview of Hugh and his work see Paul Rorem, *Hugh of St Victor* (Oxford: Oxford University Press, 2009).

61 See Hugh Feiss, "St Bernard's Theology of Baptism and the Monastic Life," *Cistercian Studies* 25:2 (1990): 79–91 and *idem*, "Bernardus Scholasticus: The Correspondence of Bernard of Clairvaux and Hugh of St. Victor on Baptism," *Bernardus Magister*, ed. John R. Sommerfeldt (Kalamazoo, MI: Cistercian Publications, 1992), 349–378.

62 Bernard of Clairvaux, *Epistola 77*, *Sancti Bernardi Opera 7*, eds. J. Leclercq and H.M. Rochais (Rome: Editiones Cistercienses, 1974,) 184–200. See also the introduction and translation in Bernard of Clairvaux, *On Baptism and the Office of Bishops*, trans. Pauline Matarasso, intro. Martha G. Newman and Emero Stiegman (Kalamazoo, MI: Cistercian Publications, 2004).

63 For an orientation on Peter Abelard see Michael Clanchy, *Abelard: A Medieval Life* (Oxford: Blackwell, 1997); and John Marenbon, *The Philosophy of Peter Abelard* (Oxford: Oxford University Press, 1997).

64 This definition is repeated in many early medieval discussions of baptism. For example, see the letter by Magnus of Sens (d. 818) in Keefe, *Water and the Word, Vol. II*, 266.

Interestingly, he included the quotation from Mark first seen in Paulinus' record from the Synod on the Danube. He wrote:

> A catechumen is interpreted as one instructed or as one hearing; for to catechize is to instruct, since those to be baptized are first instructed and are taught what the form of the Christian faith is in which they must be made safe and receive the sacrament of salvation, as it is written: "Go, teach all nations, baptizing them in the name of the Father and of the Son and of the Holy Spirit" (Mt. 28:19). First teach, afterwards baptize. Teach unto instruction, baptize unto cleanness. Teach unto faith, baptize unto remission of sins. Therefore, teach since you baptize him who has believed because "he that is baptized, shall be saved" (Mk. 16:16). So, this form of catechization was instructed from the earliest period of the Christian faith.[65]

Hugh's analysis transmits much of what had come before, even as its priority was somewhat diminished in his overall presentation of the sacrament.

Conclusion

Jerome's hurried observations on Matthew's Gospel in the late fourth century sprouted in the Christian tradition and burst into full bloom in the early Middle Ages, especially in the mind of Alcuin of York. Through careful attention to the transmission of Jerome's comments on the Great Commission, we can learn a lot about medieval Christianity and—I hope—a little about contemporary Catholicism.

First, we can see how Jerome's thoughts were transformed by Bede and then synthesized and popularized by Alcuin. This action underscores the close connection in the Church between the Bible and the liturgy. When liturgical development is called for, the Bible remains a principal source for inspiration. Moreover, we learn about the nature of the connection between the Bible and the liturgy. More than just connected in meaning, which Danielou demonstrated more than half a century ago, the Bible informs the practice or execution of the liturgy, and not via some sort of reductionist originalism. It is active in responding to contemporary pastoral concerns, but not unbounded or detached from the traditions of the Church.

---

65 Hugh of St. Victor, *De sacramentis christianae fidei*, PL 176.455D-456C. For an English translation, see Hugh of St. Victor, *On the Sacraments of the Christian Faith*, trans. Roy Defarrari (Cambridge, MA: The Medieval Academy of America, 1951).

Second, we have discovered the "pre-history" of *ressourcement*. Rather than "a new theology" dreamed up *ex nihilo* in the first half of the twentieth century, *ressourcement* may be the recovery of a theological instinct long important to the Church and deeply embedded in the history of theology, liturgy, et al. Across the church's deep tradition, Christians looked for answers to pressing contemporary problems and sometimes found them in unusual places or prompted by unrelated concerns. When Alcuin of York diagnosed a problem with mission and baptism among his contemporaries, he turned to the long tradition of the Church for an answer. And he found one. In this case, the solution to a critical early medieval missionary crisis lay—of all places—in a hasty explanation of Matthew occasioned by the fear of boredom.

Letter & Spirit 7 (2011): 157-172

Psalm 22 in Syriac Tradition[1]

~: **Stephen D. Ryan, O.P.** :~

Dominican House of Studies

I. Introduction

That "the Church is not afraid of scientific criticism" of the Bible, as John Paul II put it, is due largely to the patient labors of Catholic exegetes of previous generations.[2] Contemporary Catholic exegetes owe them a debt of gratitude. What is at issue currently is not fear, but relevance or promise. Brian Daley, S.J., has recently observed that there is a growing sense among Biblical scholars and theologians that

> the dominant post-Enlightenment approach to identifying the meaning of Biblical texts has begun to lose some of its energy, that it has less of substance to say than once it did to those who want to spend their time reading the Christian Bible: the members, by and large, of the Christian Churches.[3]

Biblical scholarship that uses the text of the Bible primarily as a source for recovering the culture and religion of ancient Israel is useful in itself as an academic discipline, but is of limited usefulness to theology. It simply fails to go far enough or to ask many important questions. Biblical exegetes too often adopt the model of the technician, explaining a text's pre-history and its meaning for its original audience, resolving its historical problems, but failing to penetrate beyond the words to the realities mediated by the text. In other words, we fail to treat the

---

1 An earlier version of this paper, prepared for the symposium on "Syriac and Antiochene Exegesis and Biblical Interpretation in the Church" held at Mount St. Mary's Seminary in Emmitsburg, Maryland on June 15, 2004, was published in Robert D. Miller, ed., *Syriac and Antiochian Exegesis and Biblical Theology for the 3rd Millennium* (Piscataway, NJ: Gorgias, 2008), 189–221.

2 Pope John Paul II, "Address on the Interpretation of the Bible in the Church," (April 23, 1993), 4, in *The Pontifical Biblical Commission, The Interpretation of the Bible in the Church* (Boston: St. Paul Books & Media, 1993), 11–24, at 14. The Holy Father goes on to add: "She distrusts only preconceived opinions that claim to be based on science, but which in reality surreptitiously cause science to depart from its domain."

3 Brian E. Daley, S.J., "Is Patristic Exegesis Still Usable?: Reflections on Early Christian Interpretation of the Psalms," *Communio* 29 (2002): 185–216, at 186. A slightly different form of Daley's paper appeared with the same title in *The Art of Reading Scripture*, eds. Ellen Davis and Richard Hays (Grand Rapids: Eerdmans, 2003), 69–88. See also his recent reflections on this topic in Brian Daley, S.J., "Christ, the Church, and the Shape of Scripture: What We Can Learn from Patristic Exegesis," in *From Judaism to Christianity: Tradition and Transition, A Festschrift for Thomas H. Tobin, S.J., on the Occasion of His Sixty-fifth Birthday*, Supplements to Novum Testamentum 136, ed. Patricia Walters (Leiden: Brill, 2010), 267–288.

text theologically, as Scripture, as the living Word of God.[4] Andrew Louth has correctly observed that when dealing with Scripture we deal not "with a technique for solving problems but with an art for discerning mystery."[5]

On another level, the historical-critical method is sometimes alleged by its ardent proponents to be able to determine the meaning of a biblical text in such a way that other, figural readings are necessarily excluded.[6] The hegemony of this method can at times be as limiting and as theologically restrictive as some of the rigidly Christological programs of the patristic and medieval periods that denied to the Old Testament any literal or contextual meaning apart from Christ. That biblical texts can have more than one level of meaning is a basic tenet of Christian interpretation. Saint Augustine puts it this way: "So, while one may say, 'Moses meant what I think,' and another, 'No, he meant what I think,' I think, for myself, it is more religious to say this: why did he not mean both, if both are true?"[7] The historical-critical methods go a long way in helping to determine if an interpretation is true, but they are not the sole arbiters of the truth of Scripture.

In 1988 Cardinal Ratzinger called for the development of a new exegetical method that would be of greater relevance to the Church.[8] Tentatively labeled "Method C" exegesis, it would take advantage of the strengths of both the patristic-medieval exegetical approach, Method A, and the modern historical-critical approach, Method B, while remaining cognizant of the shortcomings of both.[9] In a study of Psalm 22 published in *The Thomist* in 2002, Gregory Vall offered a

---

4 For a discussion of the theological task of exegesis see Augustine Di Noia, O.P. and Bernard Mulcahy, O.P., "The Authority of Scripture in Sacramental Theology: Some Methodological Observations," *Pro Ecclesia* 10 (2001): 329–345, especially 339–340.

5 Andrew Louth, *Discerning the Mystery, An Essay on the Nature of Theology* (Oxford: Clarendon, 1983), 113.

6 See Daley's discussion of Joseph Fitzmyer's position in Daley, "Is Patristic Exegesis Still Usable?" 192–194.

7 Augustine, *Confessions*, xxxi. 42, as translated and cited in Daley, "Is Patristic Exegesis Still Usable?" 199. Similarly Luke Timothy Johnson and William Kurz, S.J. (*The Future of Catholic Biblical Scholarship, A Constructive Conversation* [Grand Rapids: Eerdmans, 2002]) identify inclusive both/and thinking to be characteristic of Catholic biblical interpretation.

8 See Joseph Cardinal Ratzinger, "Biblical Interpretation in Crisis: On the Question of the Foundations and Approaches of Exegesis Today," in *Biblical Interpretation in Crisis: The Ratzinger Conference on Bible and Church*, ed., Richard J. Neuhaus (Grand Rapids, Mich.: Eerdmans, 1989), 1–23, here 6. This essay was first presented as the Erasmus Lecture delivered by Cardinal Ratzinger at St. Peter's Lutheran Church, New York City, on January 27, 1988.

9 The source of this terminology is a roundtable discussion with Cardinal Ratzinger summarized in Paul T. Stallsworth, "The Story of an Encounter," in *Biblical Interpretation in Crisis: The Ratzinger Conference on Bible and Church*, ed., Richard J. Neuhaus (Grand Rapids, Mich.: Eerdmans, 1989), 102–190, here 107–108. See also the more recent discussion in Gregory Vall, "Psalm 22: Vox Christi or Israelite Temple Liturgy?" *The Thomist* 66 (2002): 175–200, here 175–176. The terms Exegesis A, B, and C, were suggested only provisionally for the purposes of discussion and have not gained currency in theological scholarship nor, to the best of my knowledge, has Pope Benedict XVI used them in his later writings.

test case for Method C exegesis.[10] I am sympathetic to the aims of this project and to Vall's specific contribution using Psalm 22 as a test case. Method C, as Vall envisioned it, would also take into consideration approaches that do not fall neatly under Methods A or B, namely Jewish interpretation and newer literary methodologies such as narrative criticism.

In this paper I would like to build on Vall's study and ask if the tradition of Syriac Old Testament commentary has anything to add to Method C exegesis as described by Ratzinger and developed by Vall. In formulating the topic in this way I hope to offer a preliminary and modest contribution toward answering the question whether Syriac biblical commentary can contribute to the apparent impasse in biblical scholarship between historical criticism and a desire for theological relevance. After a brief survey of the reception of Psalm 22 in the Syrian Orient, focusing primarily on the tradition of Syriac Old Testament commentary, I will suggest several areas in which this tradition might contribute to the project described by Cardinal Ratzinger.

II. Psalm 22 in Syriac Translation and in Syriac Tradition

Psalm 22 in Syriac Translation

The two most important Syriac translations of the Psalter are the Peshitta and the Syro-Hexapla. According to Michael Weitzman, the Peshitta Psalter was translated from Hebrew into Syriac by a small Jewish community in the late second century AD with only occasional reference to the Greek.[11] The Syro-Hexapla, a translation from Greek into Syriac, is ascribed to Paul of Tella and dated to A.D. 615–617.[12]

Although a full catalog of the ways in which these translations differ from the Hebrew Masoretic text and from our modern English translations is not possible in this context, I shall note a few of the readings that are important in understanding the later Syriac commentary tradition.[13]

---

10 Vall, "Psalm 22."

11 Michael Weitzman, *The Syriac Version of the Old Testament, An Introduction* (Cambridge, 1999). See also idem, "The Peshitta Psalter and its Hebrew Vorlage," *Vetus Testamentum* 35 (1985): 341–354. Similar conclusions are reached by Jerome Lund, "Grecisms in the Peshitta Psalms," in *The Peshitta as a Translation: Papers read at the II Peshitta Symposium, Leiden, 19–21 August 1993*, eds. Piet B. Dirksen and Arie van der Kooij, Monographs of the Peshitta Institute 8 (Leiden: E.J. Brill, 1995), 85–102.

12 On the Syro-Hexapla see Robert J.V. Hiebert, "The 'Syrohexaplaric' Psalter: Its Text and Textual History," in *Der Septuaginta-Psalter und seine Tochterübersetzungen*, [The Septuagint Psalter and its Daughter Versions] eds. Anneli Aejmelaeus and Udo Quast, Mitteilungen des Septuaginta-Unternehmens XXIV (Göttingen, 2000), 123–146.

13 For a full discussion of the differences between the Greek and Hebrew versions of Psalm 22 see Gilles Dorival "La Bible grecque des Septante et le texte massorétique," [The Greek Bible of the Seventy and the Masoretic Text] in *David, Jésus et la reine Esther, Recherches sur le Psaume 21 (22 TM)*, [David, Jesus, and Queen Esther, Research on Psalm 21 (22 Masoretic Text)] ed. Gilles Dorival (Paris-Louvain: Peeters, 2002), 13–25.

While the Hebrew title to Psalm 22 reads, "For the leader; according to "The deer of the dawn." A psalm of David," (NABRE) the Syriac tradition has several alternative titles. A representative title used in the East Syrian tradition reads: "It is said by David by way of a prayer when he was persecuted by Absalom."[14] This title, which may stem from Theodore of Mopsuestia, indicates the basic historical approach of the traditional East Syrian interpretive tradition. It should be noted, however, that an alternative East Syrian title found in the Denha commentary adds that "others" understand the psalm to speak "about Christ our Lord."[15]

The Syro-Hexapla Psalter tended to include the Greek titles. The Syriac commentary attributed to Athanasius of Alexandria directly translates the Greek title: "To the end for morning help, a psalm of David."[16] West Syrian commentary follows Greek tradition in interpreting this title Christologically to refer to both the epiphany, when the morning light of the redeemer shone forth, and to the morning of the resurrection, when Christ rose from the dead at the break of dawn. Another West Syrian title combines both the historical and Christological interpretive traditions in reading: "Of David. When his persecutors mocked him, and about the passion of our Lord and the cry of the nations."[17]

There are three readings in the Syriac that are significant for our purposes. The first is found in Psalm 22:1b where the Hebrew Masoretic Text reads "my cries of anguish," (NABRE) while the Peshitta follows the Greek in reading "the words of my wrongdoing." This reading caused difficulties for the Christological interpretation.[18] Dionysius bar Salibi, for example, follows the Greek patristic tradition in asking, "If he had not taken hold of the person of mankind, how do these (words) fit the Son? For 'he did no sin, neither was deceit found in his mouth.'" (1 Pet. 2:22)[19]

---

14 Willem Bloemendaal, *The Headings of the Psalms in the East Syrian Church* (Leiden, 1960), 42. Unless otherwise indicated all translations from the Syriac are my own.

15 Denha, Mingana Collection Manuscript 58, folio 57 recto and Bloemendaal, *The Headings of the Psalms*, 42.

16 Robert W. Thomson, *Athanasiana Syriaca, Part IV: Expositio in Psalmos* [Syriac Athanasius, Part IV: Exposition on the Psalms] (CSCO, 387; Scriptores syri, 167. Louvain: Sécretariat du CorpusSCO, 1977), 14.

17 Alain G. Martin, "La Peshitta et la Syro-Hexaplaire," [The Peshitta and Syro-Hexapla] in *David, Jésus et la reine Esther, Recherches sur le Psaume 21 (22 TM)* [David, Jesus, and Queen Esther, Research on Psalm 21 (22 Masoretic Text)], ed. Gilles Dorival (Paris-Louvain: Peeters, 2002), 38.

18 For a survey of patristic commentary on this difficult verse see Gilles Dorival, "L'interprétation ancienne du Psaume 21 (TM 22)," [Ancient Interpretation of Psalm 21 (22 Masoretic Text)] in *David, Jésus et la reine Esther, Recherches sur le Psaume 21 (22 TM)* [David, Jesus, and Queen Esther, Research on Psalm 21 (22 Masoretic Text)], ed. Gilles Dorival (Paris-Louvain: Peeters, 2002), 225–314, here 271–272.

19 All citations from Dionysius bar Salibi are based on the critical text in Marjorie Helen Simpkin, "The Psalm Commentary of Dionysius Bar Salibi," (2 vols; Ph.D. diss., University of Melbourne, 1974). I have occasionally employed readings in the manuscripts Paris Syriaque 66 (A.D. 1354)

The second significant variant for our purposes is found in Psalm 22:30a where the Peshitta departs from the Hebrew and Greek (and Syro-Hexapla) by rendering the Hebrew Masoretic text "fat ones" (differently NABRE: "who sleep") with the Syriac word "hungry." The Syriac of Psalm 22:30 thus reads: "They will eat and prostrate themselves before the Lord, all of the hungry of the earth." The expanded (rubricated) portion of the East Syrian commentary of Denha applies the word "the hungry" to believers: "Those who hunger for mercy and for knowledge of God or for contrition."[20] Daniel of Tella, in the West Syrian tradition, glosses the Peshitta with a citation from the Beatitudes: "*They shall eat and prostrate themselves before the Lord, all the hungry of the earth*, i.e., as our Lord said, 'Blessed are those who hunger and etc.'"[21] Bar Salibi, by way of contrast, comments on the Greek text (Syro-Hexapla) which, with the Hebrew, reads "fat ones": "*They shall eat and they shall worship*, i.e., the mystical provisions, that is, the divine doctrines, and when their mind has grown fat, they worship him."

Finally we may note that in the difficult text of Psalm 22:30b the Peshitta reads the first person possessive pronoun "my soul is alive for him," with the Greek and the Syro-Hexapla but against the Hebrew, which has the third person and a particle of negation: "he who cannot keep himself alive" (RSV). Bar Salibi comments: "*It is to him that my soul lives*, that is, in death my soul lives in Sheol, and there it proclaims and preaches him."

Psalm 22 in Syriac Liturgies

Psalm 22 is used in the traditional Syriac liturgies of the Syrian Orthodox and of the Maronites principally during the celebration of the Lord's Passion on Good Friday.[22] In the Church of the East Psalm 22:26 is used as part of an anthem at the beginning of the offertory of the Mass.[23] Psalm 22 is also used in the office of the Church of the East, where it is found in the first Marmyatha of the third Hulala.[24]

---

and Harvard Syriac 130 (A.D. 1888). The translation generally follows Simpkin, with some revisions. I have also consulted the translation by Walter Robert Roehrs, "Bar Salibi on the Psalms," (Ph.D. dissertation, University of Chicago, 1937). Roehrs based his translation on Mingana 152 (A.D. 1891).

20 Denha, Mingana 58, folio 59 recto. As will be explained below, the "expanded (rubricated) portion" of this commentary consists of later additions that provide spiritual interpretation.

21 Daniel of Tella, Mingana 147 folio 21 recto, from a photograph in Simpkin, "The Psalm-Commentary of Dionysius Bar Salibi," 2:617.

22 Edouard Courte, *Le psaume vingt-deuxième au point de vue ecdotique et de la forme ainsi qu'au point de vue messianique et dans la liturgie* [Psalm Twenty-Two from Textual and Formal Points of View as well as from a Messianic Point of View and in the Liturgy] (Paris: P. Geuthner, 1932), 143.

23 John Alexander Lamb, *The Psalms in Christian Worship* (London, 1962), 53.

24 Lamb, *The Psalms in Christian Worship*, 66.

III. Ps 22 in Syriac Biblical Commentaries

Here I shall offer a brief review of the major extant Syriac commentaries on the Psalms.

Athanasiana Syriaca

A commentary attributed to Athanasius of Alexandria is extant in two Syriac forms, long and short.[25] The longer version (B.L. Add. 14568) is preserved in a damaged manuscript of A.D. 587. The shorter version (B.L. Add. 12168) dates from the 9th century. The exegesis in both forms of the commentary is very similar. Athanasius begins by relating the psalm title, which refers to "morning help," to the incarnation, which freed humanity from darkness. It is Christ who sings this psalm in the person of all humanity. In the psalm Christ describes what happened to him at his crucifixion, prays on our behalf, and teaches us that we should pray in a similar manner. The commentaries do not make reference to David or offer an historical interpretation of the psalm's original setting. Though originally composed in Greek, this commentary attributed to Athanasius was influential in the Syriac tradition and was used by later commentators such as Dionysius bar Salibi.[26]

Daniel of Salah (6th century) and Daniel of Tella

The earliest extant commentary on the Psalms composed in Syriac is by the 6th century author, Daniel of Salah. The form of this work is homiletical but the biblical text is cited and commented on in a full and systematic way.[27]

Daniel of Salah gives Psalm 22 a traditional Christian interpretation, seeing it largely as a prophecy of Christ's passion, death, and resurrection by King David under the influence of the Holy Spirit. With regard to Psalm 22:19 ("they divided my garments ..."), for example, Daniel of Salah observes that the words of this

25 Robert W. Thomson, *Athanasiana Syriaca, Part IV: Expositio in Psalmos* [Syriac Athanasius, Part IV: Exposition on the Psalms] (CSCO, 387; Scriptores syri, 167. Louvain: Sécretariat du CorpusSCO, 1977).

26 On the use of Athanasius by Bar Salibi see Stephen D. Ryan, *Dionysius Bar Salibi's Factual and Spiritual Commentary on Psalms 73–82* (Cahiers de la Revue Biblique 57; Paris: Gabalda, 2004), 71–75.

27 David Taylor is currently editing the Syriac text of the commentary. I have read it only in part and in a partially legible British Library manuscript, AD 17187. A full analysis and comparison with the other commentaries discussed here will have to await the publication of the critical edition and translation of Taylor. Even a preliminary study of this text indicates that the later Syriac commentator Bar Salibi is heavily dependent on a form of Daniel's commentary or on one of Daniel's principle sources. See David G. K. Taylor, "The Manuscript Tradition of Daniel of Salah's Psalm Commentary," in *Symposium Syriacum VII*, ed. R. Lavenant (Orientalia Christiana Analecta, 256; Rome: Pontificio Istituto Orientale, 1998), 61–69.

verse need no commentary, for it is clear that God spoke them in advance as a prophecy of the passion.[28]

Taylor has noted that one of Daniel of Salah's concerns is to combat the Phantasiast heresy which denied the corruptibility of Christ's body. With regard to Daniel's commentary on Psalm 22 Taylor writes, "Daniel is adamant that Christ's great suffering is proof that he died a natural death with all the usual consequences."[29]

A shorter edition of this commentary, revised by an unknown author, is extant in several manuscripts, the earliest of which dates to the 16th century. This new edition not only abbreviates the original but adds new material. Several manuscripts ascribe this work to Daniel of Tella, and it is not clear whether this is intended to be a reference to Daniel of Salah or to another Daniel who was later confused with Daniel of Salah.[30]

The form of the Daniel of Tella commentary is that of a brief lemma followed by a brief gloss. Most but not all of the verses are treated, with the longest discussion being given to v. 7 ("I am a worm and no man"). Psalm 22 is read Christologically as a prophecy about the coming redemption of Christ. Following Greek tradition, passages that do not seem appropriate for Christ are said to refer to sinful humanity. The psalm is not related to the life of David and little room is given to historical interpretation. At both the formal and thematic levels the commentary has much in common with Bar Salibi's spiritual commentary on the Peshitta. A comparison of this text with that of Daniel of Salah will have to await the publication of Taylor's edition.

Ishodad (9th century)

The East Syrian commentary of Ishodad of Merv comments on less than half of the verses of Psalm 22, with most lemmas followed by only brief glosses.[31] The commentary follows the tradition of Theodore of Mopsuestia in reading Psalm 22 historically as a psalm about David persecuted by Absalom. In an extended introductory paragraph Ishodad cites the position of those who read the psalm Christologically and then offers two objections. The first is that some verses of the psalm are not appropriately applied to Christ. The second objection challenges the contention that in these same cases Christ speaks in the name of humanity. Ishodad responds that some verses are clearly spoken by an individual speaking

28 British Library Add. 17187 folio 63 recto-63 verso.

29 David G. K. Taylor, "The Great Psalm Commentary of Daniel of Salah," *The Harp* 11–12 (1998–1999): 38.

30 I have consulted the Daniel of Tella commentary in a copy of Mingana 147 (A.D. 1899) reproduced in Simpkin, "The Psalm-Commentary of Dionysius Bar Salibi," 2:617.

31 Ishodad of Merv, *Commentaire d'Ishodad de Merv sur l'Ancien Testament, VI. Psaumes* [Commentary of Ishodad of Merv son the Old Testament, VI. Psalms], ed. Ceslas van den Eynde, O.P. (CSCO 434; Scriptores syri 81).

in his own name, and not as a representative of humanity in general. His basic argument then is that the prosopography must remain uniform throughout the psalm. Ishodad goes on to offer an explanation of why Christ cited this psalm from the cross. In short his position is that Christ cited the psalm for didactic purposes, to convince the Jews and to offer us an example of how we should pray in our sufferings.

What complicates the picture slightly is the final sentence: "But others (say): numerous prophecies were spoken of our Lord, even if in the meantime they were applied to others, as in the example of the cup and the building, which we have explained above."[32] Here Ishodad refers to his theory of prophecy of double application. This seems at first glance to offer an opening to a strong figural reading in which the psalm would be taken originally to have referred to Christ, but to have been applied to others as well in the meantime, in this case to David. Thus the psalm would be read on both historical and figurative or Christological levels. Fortunately, Ishodad elaborates on his position elsewhere. In his commentary on Deuteronomy 18:15, the verse about raising up a prophet like Moses, Ishodad notes that some others hold that this text is a prophecy accomplished preliminarily in Joshua but perfectly in Christ. He then discusses Old Testament texts traditionally applied to Christ because they share a certain similitude. In this context he quotes five Old Testament texts, three of which are from Psalm 22 (vv. 2, 15, 18). He concludes: "Yet these texts do not envision our Lord alone, but as words they are appropriate to him and since they contain a similitude as to the events, their witness was applied to the economy of the incarnation."[33] Here we see more clearly that Ishodad follows Theodore of Mopsuestia in seeing in Psalm 22 a simple, accommodated sense. He does not envision a stronger figural reading in which the psalm could be said to be properly Christological.[34] Like Theodore, Ishodad limits the properly Christological psalms to four: Psalms 2, 8, 45, and 110.

---

32 Ishodad of Merv, *VI. Psaumes*, 51. The cryptic reference to the cup and the building refers to his discussion of Ps. 16:10, in which he follows Theodore of Mopsuestia in seeing here a prophecy of double application. The verse refers first to Israel, but "receives its true fulfillment in Christ, as Peter [Acts 2:25–31] also testified." See Ishodad of Merv, *VI. Psaumes*, 41.

33 Ishodad of Merv, *Commentaire d'Ishodad de Merv sur l'Ancien Testament, II. Exode-Deutéronome* [Commentary of Ishodad of Merv on the Old Testament, II. Exodus-Deuteronomy] ed. Ceslas van den Eynde, O.P. (CSCO 179; Scriptores syri 81), 16.7

34 I follow here Van den Eynde's analysis, Ishodad of Merv, *II. Exode-Deutéronome*, iv–v.

Denha (9th century)

The East Syrian commentary ascribed to Denha and Gregory is dated to the 9th century.[35] Mingana's catalog notes that the commentary is twofold.[36] The longer of the two commentaries, which follows the tradition of Theodore of Mopsuestia, is in black ink, and the shorter, interspersed, is in red ink. The material in red, which tends to include spiritual interpretation, seems to represent a later expansion of the commentary.[37] The treatment of Psalm 22 is lengthy and accounts for nearly every verse. As was noted above, the psalm title offers both an historical or Davidic setting in life and a Christological reading: "A prayer of David when he was being pursued by Absalom on account of his sins. Others, about Christ our Lord." The commentary itself is largely historical, applying the psalm verses to the life of David and his persecution by his son Absalom. Reference is made to Christ in the expansions, but mainly to indicate how the psalm was used by Christ and corresponds to the events of the passion, not to indicate that the psalm is itself explicitly prophetic. In sum, the commentary appears to be in line with East Syrian literal interpretation, while acknowledging a restricted and quite limited accommodated usage of and by Christ.

Dionysius Bar Salibi (12th century)

Dionysius bar Salibi, a bishop of the Syrian Orthodox Church who died in 1171, wrote three complete commentaries on Psalm 22. These were presented in parallel synoptic columns. The first is labeled literal or factual, and is based on the Peshitta. The other two are labeled spiritual.[38] Of these the longer of the two is based on the Syro-Hexapla version of the Psalms (from the Greek) and the shorter one on the Peshitta (from the Hebrew).

Bar Salibi's short factual commentary is similar to Ishodad's commentary in format and in thematic content, but shows clear verbal dependence in only one verse.[39] With the East Syrian tradition, he understands the psalm to refer to David pursued by Absalom. The commentary makes no mention of Christian doctrine and avoids making any direct application to the life of the reader. David is portrayed as a faithful man of prayer unjustly persecuted.

---

35 I consulted the commentary in a microfilm copy of Mingana 58, which was written in A.D. 1895. I am grateful to Professors Luk Van Rompay and Clemens Leonhard for providing me with this text.

36 Alphonse Mingana, *Catalogue of the Mingana Collection of Manuscripts, Vol 1: Syriac and Garshuni Manuscripts* (Cambridge, 1933), 158–60.

37 Bloemendaal, *The Headings of the Psalms*, 7.

38 On the terminology see Ryan, *Dionysius Bar Salibi's Factual and Spiritual Commentary*, xviii n. 14 and 27–28.

39 For a discussion of Bar Salibi's sources in his commentaries on Psalm 22 see Simpkin, "The Psalm-Commentary of Dionysius Bar Salibi," 1:76–77.

Bar Salibi's spiritual commentary on the Syro-Hexapla is the longest of the three. Nearly every verse is given a comment, with some verses given several alternative interpretations. Here Bar Salibi uses a number of sources of Greek origin, chief among them Athanasius and Eusebius of Caesarea. It is not clear in what form he had access to these sources, but my own supposition is that he had access to a Palestinian catena of Greek origin in Syriac translation. It is Bar Salibi's use of sources deriving from Greek which explains the fact that his commentary is based on the Greek text.[40] Even within this commentary, however, some of the lemmas agree with the Peshitta against the Syro-Hexapla. The psalm is read Christologically from start to finish with no mention made of the life of David. Passages that are not fittingly applied to Christ are said to be spoken in the name of humanity.

What is most striking about the rhetorical form of the commentary is the constant appeal to the reader as a member of the Body of Christ. Repeatedly we read that Christ came for us, suffered for us, and rose for our sake. Equally striking are the numerous references to the mysteries of the Christian faith: Trinity, Incarnation, Virgin Birth, Redemption, the Cross, Resurrection, the Descent into Hell, Original Sin, Satan, the holiness of the Church, prayer, and the call of the Gentiles. While the treatment that each of these themes receives is fleeting, the overall effect is to relate the biblical text to the truths of the faith such that one is given a strong impression of the overall coherence of the divine plan. In Catholic tradition this coherence is known as the analogy of faith (*analogia fidei*), and Church documents on Scripture indicate that the recognition of this fundamental coherence is one of the essential elements of Catholic Biblical interpretation.

Bar Salibi's spiritual commentary on the Peshitta is considerably shorter. As in the spiritual commentary on the Syro-Hexapla, the psalm is given a thoroughly Christological reading with no mention being made of David. Scripture is cited more often in this commentary than in the other two, though the citations are in the form of brief glosses. Rhetorically this commentary contains less of the direct appeal to the reader that so marks the commentary on the Syro-Hexapla.

Bar Salibi's commentaries were often transmitted in abbreviated versions. Berlin 188 [Sachau 218], dated to A.D. 1847, contains such a shortened version.[41] In this commentary only a few of the verses are cited, and the commentary takes the form of extremely brief glosses. The approach is spiritual, but the text is so abbreviated that it bears little resemblance to either of Bar Salibi's spiritual commentaries.

40 Ryan, *Dionysius Bar Salibi's Factual and Spiritual Commentary*, 52.

41 On this text see Eduard Sachau, *Die Handschriften-Verzeichnisse der königlichen Bibliothek zu Berlin* [Manuscript Catalog of the Royal Library of Berlin] (Berlin, 1899), 2:609–12; see also Ryan, *Dionysius Bar Salibi's Factual and Spiritual Commentary*, 104–105.

Bar Salibi also wrote a fairly complete commentary on the New Testament. Though my investigation thus far has been limited to the genre of Psalm commentaries, I shall briefly consider Bar Salibi's commentary on Matthew in so far as it offers a commentary on Psalm 22. In commenting on Matthew 27:35 Bar Salibi notes that the dividing of the garments took place "to fulfill the prophecy of David," that is, the prophecy contained in Psalm 22.[42] His commentary on Matthew 27:46 is more extensive and includes a lengthy discussion of the dereliction on the cross and of the varying Christologies of the Arians, those he refers to as the Nestorians, the Chalcedonians, and his own community, the Syrian Orthodox. In the course of this discussion he cites Psalm 22 several times. The rhetorical style is reminiscent of his Syro-Hexapla commentary, with frequent reference to Christ's action for us, on our behalf, for our sakes. In the following excerpt he comments on the opening words of the psalm and deftly links them with a verse from the end of the psalm by way of composing a response to Christ's prayer to the Father:

> He cries out for us, for he saw to what ruin our generation would come. Again, because of this the Son asks the Father, "My God, my God, why have you forsaken me?" (v. 1) Let us listen to what is written in this psalm. It speaks as if from the person (*prosopon*) of the Father when it says, "For this reason I forsook you, that you should suffer and that you should be crucified, in order that 'they shall remember and shall turn toward the Lord, all the ends of the earth.' (v. 27)"[43]

This analysis is quite different than anything found in Bar Salibi's Old Testament commentaries on Psalm 22. In this commentary on Matthew he sees the psalm at once as giving voice to Christ's prayer and at the same time providing the Father's response to that prayer. Bar Salibi uses Psalm 22 itself to provide the words of the Father's response to the Son.

IV. Conclusion

In conclusion, I will briefly suggest several areas in which the tradition of Syriac Old Testament commentary might contribute to the project of a more theologically relevant exegesis. But first, I would add this caution. If part of my findings are negative, that is that the Syriac tradition of Psalm commentary appears to have little that is unique, that cannot be found elsewhere in the Greek, Latin, Coptic, Ethiopic, or Armenian traditions, this may reflect the limitations of the present study rather than the objective reality. It is entirely possible, for example, that there are genuine elements of the kind of rich typological interpretation so characteristic

42 Dionysius Bar Salibi, *Dionysii bar Salibi commentarii in evangelia II/1* [Dionysius bar Salibi Commentaries on the Gospels II/1], ed. Arthur A. Vaschalde and Jean-Baptiste Chabot (CSCO 95, 98; Louvain, 2d ed. 1953), 95.

43 Bar Salibi, *Dionysii bar Salibi commentarii in evangelia II/1*, 134.

of Ephrem, Aphrahat, Jacob of Saroug, or Jacob of Edessa that are preserved in Syriac Psalm commentary that have escaped my attention.

Syriac Old Testament Commentary and Vall's "Method C" Approach

Gregory Vall's 2002 article in *The Thomist* contained what he called "a Method C attempt to describe the organic connection between the psalm in its Old Testament context and Jesus' quotation of it from the cross (Matthew 27:46; Mark 15:34)."[44] He reads Psalm 22 as a prayer of the afflicted (in Hebrew: *anawim*), that prepares Israel, by God's providential role in the development of *anawim* piety within Israel, for the eschatological kingdom of God. In using this psalm Israel participated, by prophetic anticipation, in Christ's passion. Christ prayed this psalm, in an ultimate act of *anawim* piety, as the true Israel who embodied Israel's unique filial relationship to God.[45] Vall suggests the possibility that Jesus prayed this prayer not only for himself but as a proclamation of his identity and of the significance of his death on the cross.[46] That is, he prayed it entrusting himself completely to God with all his Israelite brethren and the clans of the nations in mind. As Bar Salibi would say, he offered himself completely to the Father for our sake.

My survey of Syriac Psalm commentary has found nothing that would make a substantive contribution to Vall's central thesis. I would note simply that Vall's attempt to articulate what the *Catechism of the Catholic Church* calls "the unity of God's plan, of which Christ Jesus is the center and heart," accomplishes in a modern and historically sophisticated way many of the same things that patristic commentaries did in a very different way.[47]

Where I think the Syriac tradition can aid Vall's Method C interpretation is in giving a fuller and more balanced picture of Method A (that is, of patristic and medieval interpretation). Vall states, for example, that the Method A approach reads Psalm 22 in a way that was exclusively Christological. It demonstrated no desire to locate the psalm in an Old Testament context. He notes briefly the Antiochene tradition but states that Diodore and Theodore were condemned as heretics. Perhaps Bar Salibi's widely circulated and influential commentary containing one factual and two spiritual commentaries in parallel columns, which in its very format proclaims that this and all the psalms are patient of both an historical and a Christological reading, would help to give a slightly more accurate sketch of Method A, the patristic approach. Early Christian attempts to preserve a Davidic life-setting for Psalm 22 were not quite as fleeting or as marginal as Vall suggests, at least when the Syriac tradition is included in the discussion. This

44 Vall, "Psalm 22," 178.

45 Vall, "Psalm 22," 196.

46 Vall, "Psalm 22," 197.

47 *Catechism of the Catholic Church*, 2d. ed. (Vatican City: Libreria Editrice Vaticana, 1997), no. 112.

being said, we must also add that Christian historical interpretations of Psalm 22 are by no means limited to the Syriac tradition.[48] We may say only that in Denha, Ishodad, and Bar Salibi the tradition was alive and well and is preserved to our day.

In *Fides et Ratio* [Faith and Reason] John Paul II recalled that the Church reflects on Revelation "in the light of the teaching of Scripture and of the entire Patristic tradition."[49] While consideration of the *entire* Patristic tradition is not always possible or practical, the fact that the Syriac patristic tradition is becoming increasingly accessible and familiar to theologians will help ensure that the Church's reflection on Revelation is not limited to the Greek and Latin traditions.

A final area in which the Syriac tradition could make a contribution is in the example Bar Salibi and others give in commenting not only on the Masoretic text of the Hebrew but on the Septuagint and Peshitta as well. Contemporary critics generally use the versional evidence only to establish the earliest Hebrew text. For Bar Salibi, the Greek, the Hebrew, and the Syriac Old Testament versions were treated equally as authentic texts, each worthy of commentary.[50] The contemporary hegemony of the Masoretic or a critically established Hebrew text of the Old Testament is a relatively new and, in my opinion, somewhat problematic development in Catholic theology. The sources of this modern development can be traced to renaissance Humanism, to Reformation doctrines of inspiration, and to the Protestant sensibilities with which the historical-critical method has traditionally been practiced. The late Dominique Barthélemy, O.P., who devoted most of his scholarly life to the establishment of the critical Hebrew text of the Old Testament, called repeatedly for the recognition of a Christian Old Testament in two columns: one containing the Septuagint of the first centuries of our era, the second the Hebrew text canonized by the scribes of Israel.[51] While it is not

48 Dorival ("L'interprétation ancienne du Psaume 21 (TM 22)," [Ancient Interpretation of Psalm 21 (22 Masoretic Text] 268) cites evidence from Didymus the Blind on Ps 22:30c indicating "that the tradition that centered itself on Christ gave a certain value to the purely historical interpretation of the Antiochene tradition."

49 Pope John Paul II, *Fides et Ratio* [Faith and Reason], Encyclical Letter on the Relationship of Faith and Reason (September 14, 1998), 8, available at http://www.vatican.va/holy_father/john_paul_ii/encyclicals/documents/hf_jp-ii_enc_15101998_fides-et-ratio_en.html.

50 I do not mean to suggest that Bar Salibi is by any means unique. Jerome, for example, commented on both Greek and Hebrew lemmas in his Old Testament commentaries as well; on Jerome's practice see Adrian Schenker, O.P., "Septuaginta und christliche Bibel," [The Septuagint and the Christian Bible] *Theologische Revue* 91 (1995): 461.

51 Dominique Barthélemy, O.P., "La place de la Septante dans l'Église," [The Place of the Septuagint in the Church] reprinted in D. Barthélemy, *Études d'histoire du texte de l'Ancien Testament* [Studies in the History of the Text of the Old Testament] (OBO 21; Fribourg, 1978), 126; see also Adrian Schenker, O.P., "L'Ecriture Sainte subsiste en plusieurs formes canoniques simultanées," [Holy Scripture Subsists Simultaneously in Several Canonical Forms] in *L'interpretazione della Bibbia nella Chiesa, Atti del Simposio promosso dalla Congregazione per la Dottrina della Fede* [Interpretation of the Bible in the Church, Acts of a Symposium Sponsored by the Congregation for the Doctrine of the Faith (Città del Vaticano: Libraria Editrice Vaticana, 2001), 178–186, and the expanded German version of Schenker's article,

possible to develop this suggestion in the present context, Catholic exegesis should take seriously the role that these early translations have had in forming Christian culture and should not exclude their unique readings or commentary on the basis of a narrow doctrine of inspiration.[52] An encouraging sign in this direction are the several translation projects now underway to provide fresh English translations of the Septuagint and the Peshitta. Equally encouraging is the decision in the first volume of "The Church's Bible" to provide complete English translations of the Vulgate and Septuagint texts for each verse discussed.[53] A fine example of how the treasures of the biblical versions and the patristic tradition can be exploited in popular commentary can be seen in Pope John Paul's recent commentaries on the psalms and canticles of Morning Prayer. There the Pope occasionally cites interpretation of the Psalter based on the text of the Vulgate and the Septuagint alongside of his comments on the Hebrew text.[54]

"Die Heilige Schrift subsistiert gleichzeitig in mehreren kanonischen Formen," [The Holy Scriptures Subsists Simultaneously in Several Canonical Forms] in *Studien zu Propheten und Religionsgeschichte* [Studies on the Prophets and the History of Religion] ed., Adrian Schenker (Stuttgarter Biblische Aufsatzbände 36; Stuttgart: Verlag Katholisches Bibelwerk, 2003), 192–200.

52 There is ample support in ecclesial documents to defend the use of the ancient versions, even when it is clear that for modern biblical translations the original texts are to be used. *Dei Verbum* [The Word of God], Dogmatic Constitution on Divine Revelation, (November 18, 1965), 22 (in *Vatican Council II: The Conciliar and Post Conciliar Documents*, ed. Austin Flannery, O.P. Northport, NY: Costello, 1987, 762–763), for example, refers to the honor with which the Church holds these versions even while going on in the next sentence to call for translations to be based on the original texts: "For this reason the Church, from the very beginning, made her own the ancient translation of the Old Testament called the Septuagint; she honors also the other Eastern translations, and the Latin translations, especially that which is called the Vulgate." The recent instruction *Liturgiam authenticam* [Authentic Liturgy] Fifth Instruction on Vernacular Translation of the Roman Liturgy, (March 28, 2001), 41 (in Liturgiam Authenticam, Fifth Instruction on Vernacular Translation of the Roman Liturgy, Latin-English Edition, Washington, D.C.: United States Conference of Catholic Bishops, 2001), suggests a similar concern for preserving the riches of the biblical versions: "... other ancient versions of the Sacred Scriptures should also be consulted, such as the Greek version of the Old Testament commonly known as the "Septuagint", which has been used by the Christian faithful from the earliest days of the Church. ... Finally, translators are strongly encouraged to pay close attention to the history of interpretation that may be drawn from citations of biblical texts in the writings of the Fathers of the Church, and also from those biblical images more frequently found in Christian art and hymnody."

53 Ricahrd A. Norris, *The Song of Songs: Interpreted by Early Christian and Medieval Commentators*, The Church's Bible (Grand Rapids, MI: Eerdmans, 2003).

54 Pope John Paul II, *Psalms & Canticles of Morning Prayer* (Chicago: Liturgical Training Publications, 2004). Examples of the Pope's use of spiritual readings based on the Vulgate and Septuagint can be found on p. 94 (Ps. 150:1), p. 108 (Ps 43:4), pp. 177–178 (Ps. 96:10), and pp. 189–190 (Ps. 86:2).

Brian Daley on Early Christian Interpretation of the Psalms

In the same year that Vall's article appeared, Brian Daley, S.J., published an article entitled, "Is Patristic Exegesis Still Usable?: Reflections of Early Christian Interpretation of the Psalms."[55]

Daley listed six characteristics of early Christian interpretation of the Psalms: (1) the conviction of the present reality of God; (2) the presumption of a unified narrative (3) the use of the rule of faith; (4) the view of Scripture as a diverse, yet unified whole; (5) the conviction that scriptural texts have their own historical meaning, yet are meant for us; and (6) the understanding of the Scriptural text as mystery.[56]

While Daley cites examples from the Greek and Latin tradition, these same characteristic features are shared by the Syriac tradition, in part because the Syriac tradition was in contact with and indebted particularly to the Greek Christian tradition. This being said, we can ask whether the Syriac tradition can add anything unique. My brief survey does not find any distinctive elements of Syriac exegesis that cannot be found elsewhere, other than the unique format of Bar Salibi's commentary. His is the only Christian commentary to present factual and spiritual interpretations in parallel synoptic columns. This format suggests a hermeneutic that could be useful for Method C exegesis[57], but nowhere does Bar Salibi articulate such a hermeneutic in explicit terms.[58]

Although Daley does not refer to Method C exegesis as such, he does suggest the need for a new branch of biblical studies, one that would be explicitly theological.[59] His vision for that new branch of biblical studies is decidedly ecumenical:

55 Brian E. Daley, "Is Patristic Exegesis Still Usable?," in *The Art of Reading Scripture*, eds. Ellen Davis and Richard Hays (Grand Rapids: Eerdmans, 2003).

56 Daley, "Is Patristic Exegesis Still Usable?" 194–204.

57 Again, Method C draws on the strengths of both the patristic-medieval exegetical approach (Method A), and the modern historical-critical approach (Method B), while remaining cognizant of the shortcomings of both.

58 On Bar Salibi's understanding of the purpose and rationale for composing three commentaries and the relationship between the factual and spiritual commentaries, see Ryan, *Dionysius Bar Salibi's Factual and Spiritual Commentary*, 26–46. Bar Salibi's commentary contains a preface to the Psalter written by Moshe Bar Kepha, and this text comes close to an explicit articulation of the relationship between the factual and spiritual approaches.

59 While in sympathy with Daley on this point, it is important to avoid giving the impression that such a new discipline would retreat from the academic and scientific study of the Bible. It is useful in this context to recall John Paul II's words ("Allocution de sa sainteté le pape Jean-Paul II sur l'interprétation de la Bible dans l'Église," [Allocution of His Holiness Pope John Paul II on the Interpretation of the Bible in the Church] 5, p. 7) about the dangers of "une sorte de dichotomie entre l'exégèse scientifique, destinée a l'usage externe, et l'interprétation spirituelle, réservée à l'usage interne" [a type of dichotomy between scientific exegesis destined for eternal use, and spiritual interpretation reserved for internal use]. That Daley himself does not envision such a dichotomy is clear, for he speaks about such a new branch of biblical studies being created by the academic establishment and having "parallel authority in the 'guild.'" (Daley, "Is Patristic Exegesis Still Usable?" 215).

"Christian exegesis must not only become more theological but more theologically ecumenical, if it is to nourish the Church."[60] The rich ecclesial diversity of the Syrian exegetical tradition could certainly make a contribution to achieving this goal of a more theologically ecumenical exegesis. Bar Salibi's use of Ishodad of Merv as a source for his factual commentary is but one example of the ecumenical nature of the Syriac tradition. In this case Bar Salibi, a Syrian Orthodox bishop, incorporated much of the commentary of Ishodad, a member of the Church of the East, thereby, in a small way, helping to heal ancient divisions.

Daley concludes his article by noting that it is not clear to what extent increased familiarity with patristic biblical commentary can aid modern exegetes to develop a more theological reading of Scripture. He does suggest, however, that renewed contact with ancient Christian Psalm commentary is a promising place to begin. I have tried to show in this brief contribution that the Syriac tradition of Psalm commentary, though by no means unique, has distinctive and important features that should not escape the attention of scholars seeking to develop a more theologically relevant exegesis.

60 Daley, "Is Patristic Exegesis Still Usable?" 213.

Letter & Spirit 7 (2011): 173-190

Interiority and Extroversion in Biblical Trinitarian Faith in Augustine's *De Trinitate*[1]

~: Khaled Anatolios :~

Introduction

Perhaps one of the main fault-lines in the landscape of modern theology lies between two radically different interpretations of the notion of "faith." On the one side, "faith" is understood to be primarily an experience in the domain of individual interiority and is characterized in terms of transcendental subjectivity, such as in Schleiermacher's *Abhängingkeitsgefühl* (the feeling of absolute dependence) or Tillich's "ultimate concern."[2] In this model, doctrine (or, the *fides quae*) as well as the biblical word, which is its basis, tend to be relegated to a secondary status, as derivative objectifications and symbolizations of the original experience, inevitably amounting to a dilution of that experience.[3] Moreover, this putative original

1 An earlier version of this paper was presented at the Academy of Catholic Theology meeting on May 26, 2011. I would like to thank my colleagues Boyd Coolman and Robert Imbelli for their comments on an earlier draft.

2 On the notion of "absolute dependence," see Friedrich Schleiermacher, *The Christian Faith*, trans. H. R. Mackintosh and J. S. Stewart, from 2nd German ed. [1830] (Edinburgh: T & T Clark, 1968), 12–18. In this work, absolute dependence is equated with "God-consciousness (*GottesbewuBtsein*)," "piety (*Frömmigkeit*)," and "faith (*Glauben*)". In §14 he speaks of "faith in God, which [is] nothing but the certainty concerning the feeling of absolute dependence..." (idem, 68). The experience of a "state of absolute facility and constancy" in the feeling of absolute dependence as caused by Christ is the content of "faith in Christ" (idem., 68). Paul Tillich defines faith as "ultimate concern" in Tillich, *Dynamics of Faith* (New York: Harper Torchbooks, 1958), 1–4. In his earlier *Systematic Theology*, he had acknowledged that "Schleiermacher's 'feeling of absolute dependence' was rather near to what is called in the present system 'ultimate concern' about the ground and meaning of our being." (Paul Tillich, *Systematic Theology*, 3 vols. (Chicago: University of Chicago Press, 1951-1963), 1:42. On the other hand, Tillich criticizes Schleiermacher for his over-reliance on the experience of religious consciousness: "The event on which Christianity is based...is not derived from experience; it is *given* in history." (idem., 1:42).

3 Thus, Roger Haight (*Dynamics of Theology* [New York: Paulist Press, 1990]), who relies explicitly on Tillich's conception of faith as "ultimate concern," defines faith as "a universal human phenomenon" that can be gleaned through "a transcendental analysis" (idem., 5) and distinguishes between "faith" and "beliefs": "Faith is not reducible to belief; faith is more than believing; rather beliefs may be considered expressions of faith that are distinct from faith itself." (idem, 26). Beliefs are "imaginative portrayals" of the object of faith, "interpretations of it, conceptualizations and propositions characterizing transcendent reality or interpreting the finite world in the light or on the basis of transcendence." (idem, 27). Faith, as transcendental interior experience, has a clear priority over such symbolic objectifications: "In other words, within the phenomenon of faith coupled with beliefs the significance of beliefs emerges out of what is deeper than beliefs, namely, the experience of, and the surrender and commitment of, loyalty in faith to transcendence." (idem, 27).

experience functions as a foundational criterion by which the adequacy of doctrinal objectifications may be judged. In this way, Schleiermacher consistently subjects traditional doctrinal formulations to the test of whether they adequately express the feeling of absolute dependence.

On the other side, "faith" is understood as an assent to external words and happenings, a response to God's acting out a "theo-drama" on the stage of human history, to use the language of Hans Urs von Balthasar.[4] A large part of the impact of George Lindbeck's work is due to his identification and critique of the first model, which he calls the "experiential-expressivist" model, even if not all practitioners of the second model would fit neatly into the exact specifications of his own proposed alternative of the "cultural-linguistic" model.[5]

It is tempting but ultimately misleading to characterize the essential difference between these two approaches in terms of the presence and absence or extent of the element of human subjectivity in the act of faith. Rather, at stake are distinct *characterizations* of the subject of the act of faith or, more precisely, distinct emphases on the particular aspect of subjectivity that is implicated in the act of faith. One stresses the aspect of wordless interiority as the point of correspondence between divine revelation and the human subject of faith, while the other identifies the subject of faith as radically extroverted toward the external manifestations of revelation and *thus* interiorly informed by that act of extroversion.[6]

These tensions between what we can call "interior" and "exterior" conceptions of faith correlate in interesting and sometimes subtle ways with modern treatments of Trinitarian doctrine. An enduring signpost remains Schleiermacher's claim that the interior feeling of absolute dependence, which posits a transcendent unitary "whence" of the manifold experiences of creaturely dependence, does not require, but rather mitigates against, the conception of a Triune God.[7] On the other hand, the insistence that the doctrine of the immanent Trinity must be anchored in the Trinitarian economy of salvation can be seen as an effort to externalize Trinitarian doctrine. This insistence is primarily associated with Karl Rahner and his celebrated, but also controverted dictum, "The 'economic' Trinity is the 'immanent' Trinity, and the 'immanent' Trinity is the 'economic' Trinity."[8] Rahner's own exposition of Trinitarian doctrine balances interior and exterior orientations in a

4 Hans Urs von Balthasar, *Theo-Drama: Theological Dramatic Theory*, 5 vols., trans. Graham Harrison (San Francisco: Ignatius Press, 1989-1998).

5 See his comparison of the two approaches in George Lindbeck, *The Nature of Doctrine: Religion and Theology in a Postliberal Age* (Philadelphia: Westminster, 1984), 30–45.

6 Lindbeck, *Nature of Doctrine*, 36.

7 See Schleiermacher's exposition of the claim that Trinitarian doctrine, "as ecclesiastically framed, is not an immediate utterance concerning the Christian self-consciousness" in *The Christian Faith*, §170, 738–742.

8 Karl Rahner, "The Method and Structure of the Treatise 'On the Triune God,'" trans. Joseph Donceel, reprinted in *The Trinity* (New York: Crossroad, 2004), 22.

way typical of his whole theological system and its somewhat Hegelian dialectic of Spirit and history. Thus, the economy of the Word is associated with history while that of the Spirit with interiority and the life of the human being as transcendental spirit.[9] There is perhaps also a complex, if not convoluted tension between interior and exterior orientations in the debate between proponents of the so-called "psychological analogy" and those who favor a social analogy of the Trinity. The latter accuse the former of positing the subject of faith, and human personhood in general, in the domain of Cartesian interiority and propose to relocate them in the realm of outward relationality.[10] Yet, perhaps both tendencies, to the extent that they locate the intelligibility of Trinitarian doctrine primarily in analogical sites rather in the givenness of revelation, are in danger of abstracting from the particular exteriority of the biblically proclaimed economy of salvation.[11]

As these various tensions are played out, the ancient figure of the North African bishop, Augustine of Hippo, is invoked with some regularity. An initially strident wave of critique faulted Augustine and his alleged "psychological analogy" for bypassing the Trinitarian economy and positing the subject of faith as radically individual and introspective.[12] The English theologian, Colin Gunton, can stand in for the chorus of such complaints when he says, "The conclusion is inescapable: *The crucial analogy for Augustine is between the inner structure of the human mind and the inner being of God, because it is in the former that the latter is made known, this side of eternity at any rate, more really than in the 'outer' economy of grace.*"[13] But Augustine's more recent defenders have retrieved the Scriptural basis of his

9 In this way, Rahner (*The Trinity*, 47) sees the Trinity as the ultimate ground of the dialectic of history-transcendence: "[T]he incomprehensible, primordial, and forever mysterious unity of transcendence through history and of history into transcendence holds its ultimate depths and most profound roots in the Trinity, in which the Father is the incomprehensible origin and the original unity, the "Word" his utterance into history, and the "Spirit" the opening up of history into the immediacy of its fatherly origin and end." Compare his essay, Karl Rahner, "Oneness and Threefoldness of God in Discussion with Islam," *Theological Investigations* Vol. XVIII, trans., Edward Quinn (New York, Crossroad, 1983), 114–115: "This one and incomprehensible God is unsurpassably close to man historically in Jesus Christ ... [who is] the final and unsurpassable self-promise of this one God in history. And this one and the same God imparts himself to man in the innermost centre of human existence as Holy Spirit for salvation and for the consummation which is God himself. For Christian faith then there are two utterly radical and definitive and unsurpassable factualities, modes of existence of the one God in the world, factualities which are the final salvation freely granted by God to the world, in history and transcendence."

10 See, for example, Colin E. Gunton, *The Promise of Trinitarian Theology*, 2nd ed. (Edinburgh: T&T Clark, 1997), especially 30–55.

11 On the over-reliance of modern Trinitarian theology on analogy, see my more extended treatment in Khaled Anatolios, *Retrieving Nicaea: The Development and Meaning of Trinitarian Doctrine* (Grand Rapids: Baker Academic, 2011), 6–7.

12 For a survey of modern critiques of Augustine, see especially Michel René Barnes, "Augustine in Contemporary Trinitarian Theology," *Theological Studies* 56:2 (1995): 237–250.

13 Gunton, *The Promise of Trinitarian Theology*, 45, italics original.

Trinitarian theology, downplayed the significance of the "psychological analogy" and countered the claim that Augustine privileges human individuality and divine unity over personhood actualized in communion.[14]

Presuming and building on these recent defenses of Augustine, my intent in this essay is to look at his classic work, *De Trinitate*, from the perspective of the dialectic of interiority and exteriority in the appropriation of Trinitarian faith—and thus, in Christian faith in general. I hope to show that Augustine offers enduring resources for mediating and transcending this polarity. Concretely, I would like to derive three principles for treating this dialectic on the basis of a reading of *De Trinitate*: first, that the originating moment and enduring content of Christian faith is the inter-section of divine and human *extroversion* which is distinctly configured by the Christocentric-Trinitarian economy of revelation and salvation; second, that a crucial negative moment in the assent of faith is the repudiation of an interiorist foundationalism that allows the subject to judge the contents of faith by reference to the standards of his own interiority; and, thirdly, that Nicene Trinitarian faith views the human person as radically and irreducibly extroverted and defines the life of faith as a Christological reformation of this extroversion. In the form I just presented, these principles are admittedly quite abstract and suspiciously alien to the surface level of the linguistic and conceptual field of *De Trinitate*. My task, then, is to show how they are concretely anchored in Augustine's classic text itself.

I. Christian Faith: The Inter-section of Divine and Human Extroversion

I proposed that the first principle to be derived from *De Trinitate* is that the originating moment and defining content of Christian faith is the inter-section of divine and human extroversion in a distinctly Christological and Trinitarian mode. While recent defenders of this work have emphasized its Christological framework, which comes to the fore in Books 4 and 13, there has not been adequate attention to how this Christological framework intersects with Augustine's opening remarks on the fundamental structure of Christian faith and the distinctly Christian con-

14 A representative sample of the more notable recent rebuttals of criticism against Augustine's Trinitarian theology would include Lewis Ayres, *Nicaea and its Legacy: An Approach to Fourth-Century Trinitarian Theology* (New York: Oxford University Press, 2004), 364–383; Michel René Barnes, "Re-Reading Augustine's Theology of the Trinity," in *The Trinity: An Interdisciplinary Symposium on the Trinity*, eds. S. T. Davis, D. Kendall and G. O'Collins (Oxford: Oxford University Press, 1999), 145–176; John Cavadini, "The Structure and Intention of Augustine's *De Trinitate*," *Augustinian Studies* 23 (1992): 103–123; Luigi Gioia, *The Theological Epistemology of Augustine's* De Trinitate (New York: Oxford University Press, 2008); Basil Studer, *Augustins De Trinitate: Eine Einführung [Augustine's On the Trinity: An Introduction]* (Paderborn: Ferdinand Schöningh, 2005); Rowan Williams, "*Sapientia* and the Trinity. Reflections on *De Trinitate*," in *Collectanea Augustiniana: Mélanges* [Essays on Augustine in Honor of T.J. van Bavel] (Leuven: Leuven University Press, 1990), 317–332. For a fuller exposition of my own interpretation of *De Trinitate*, see Anatolios, *Retrieving Nicaea*, 241–280.

figuration of reason and revelation.[15] In the very first words of Book 1, Augustine announces that he will part ways with those who reject the "starting point of faith" (*initium fidei*) through a "misguided love of reason" (*perverso rationis amore*).[16] Augustine's explication of what he means by "reason" anticipates Feuerbach's objection that all religion is projection.[17] For Augustine, all merely "reasoned" approaches to God are inevitably projections onto God of either creaturely corporeal features or creaturely spiritual features or fanciful ideas about God that apply neither to God nor to creatures.[18]

On the other hand, the way of faith provides a way out of this impasse not by shunning the application of creaturely categories to God but by God's co-opting of human self-projection by his own self-symbolization through creaturely signs. Rather than being the inert object of human projection, God thus becomes its active subject, without changing its essential modality:

> It was therefore to purify (*purgaretur*) the human spirit of such falsehoods that holy Scripture, adapting (*congruens*) itself to babes, did not shun any words, proper to any kind of thing whatever, that might nourish our understanding and enable it to rise to the sublimities of divine things. Thus it would use words taken from corporeal things to speak about God . . . and from the sphere of created spirit it has transposed many words to signify (*significaret*) what was in fact not like that but had to be expressed like that. ... The divine Scriptures then are in the habit of making something like children's toys out of things that occur in creation, by which to entice our sickly gaze and get us step by step to seek as best as we can the things that are above and to forsake the things that are below.[19]

---

15 A notable exception is Basil Studer's *Augustins De Trinitate: Eine Einführung* [*Augustine's On the Trinity: An Introduction*]. Studer discusses the Christological structure of Christian faith as an ascent from the humanity of Jesus Christ to his divinity, focusing especially on Books 1 and 13 (see especially, 219–225). He does not deal with the specific problematic I treat here, namely Augustine's opening reflections on the inevitability of human projection in signifying the things of God and how that is overcome by the Christological economy of salvation. I have also highlighted the importance of this theme in *De Trinitate* in my "Divine Semiotics and the Way to the Triune God" in *God in Early Christian Thought: Essays in Memory of Lloyd G. Patterson*, eds. Andrew McGowan, Brian E. Daley, and Timothy Gaden (Boston: Brill, 2009), 163–193.

16 *De Trinitate* 1.1.1; English translation after: Augustine, *The Trinity*, trans. Edmund Hill (New York: New City Press, 1991) [henceforward: Augustine, *The Trinity*], 65.

17 See Ludwig Feuerbach, *The Essence of Christianity*, trans. George Eliot (Amherst, NY: Prometheus, 1989).

18 *De Trinitate* 1.1.1.

19 *De Trinitate*, 1.1.2; Augustine, *The Trinity*, 66.

It is instructive to compare this passage with the reflections on virtue by the Egyptian Neo-Platonist philosopher, Plotinus, which are woven around a strikingly similar constellation of themes and vocabulary. Plotinus is discussing the ultimate orientation and aspiration of the human being to become "like God." The way to this likeness is through "virtue" (*aretē*), which can be divided into two kinds, the lower virtue, which constitutes a "purification," and the higher virtue of direct contemplation. Despite many overlapping motifs shared by the Alexandrian philosopher and the African bishop, the key difference has to do with how "purification" is understood. While for Plotinus purification is strictly a matter of abstraction from the body, for Augustine it consists in God's communication of his own reality precisely through bodily and creaturely being.[20] Augustine refers to this scriptural mode of revelation as a divine "adaptation" (*congruentia*). For our present purposes, I think it is legitimate to speak of a divine "extroversion" in which God is not manifest merely in the unfathomable interiority of his being-as-mystery but rather by turning towards creatures for the terms of his own self-expression. Augustine's fundamental insight is that without such an extroversion on God's part, humanity would be unable to transcend its own self-referencing, the otherwise ineluctable pattern by which we always gesture toward ourselves when we intend to speak of God.

The Divine Extroversion is Christological and Trinitarian

Taken together, Books 1-4 of *De Trinitate* collectively demonstrate the pervasively Christological and Trinitarian character of this divine extroversion. After describing the fundamental dialectic of faith in Book 1, as the overcoming of human self-projection by divine adaptation, Augustine goes on in Books 2 and 3 to present the various theophanies of the Old Testament precisely as examples of such divine self-manifestations in creaturely forms. On one level, this presentation has the polemical purpose of countering an anti-Nicene exegesis that sought to identify all the Old Testament theophanies as appearances of the Son and thus as indications of the natural visibility of his inferior divinity.[21] Augustine is seeking to demonstrate that there is no scriptural warrant for attributing these theophanies particularly to the Son; they are merely creaturely symbolizations of divine presence and activity. But on the level of Augustine's positive account of the epistemology of faith, the

20 Thus, Plotinus: "What then do we mean when we call these other virtues 'purifications,' and how are we made really like by being purified? Since the soul is evil when it is thoroughly mixed with the body and shares its experiences and has all the same passions, it will be good and possess virtue when it no longer has the same opinions but acts alone—this is intelligence and wisdom—and does not share the body's experiences. ... One would not be wrong in calling this state of the soul likeness to God, in which its activity is intellectual, and it is free in this way from bodily affections." *Enneads* I.2.2 ; English version: Plotinus, *Enneads*, trans. H. Armstrong, Loeb Classical Library, 440 (Cambridge, MA: Harvard University Press, 1966), 135.

21 See Michel René Barnes, "The Visible Christ and the Invisible Trinity: Mt. 5.8 in Augustine's Trinitarian Theology of 400," *Modern Theology* 19:3 (July 2003): 329–355.

presentation of Old Testament theophanies serves as a prelude to showing how the economy of divine self-symbolization comes to a climax in Jesus Christ.

Prior to the Incarnation of the Word, there is a structural incompleteness or deficiency in the modality by which divine revelation co-opts human self-projection into its own self-symbolization. The problem is that there continues to be a pervasive otherness between the creaturely symbol that signifies divine presence and its referent. Such otherness is depicted by Augustine as a "dissonance" that, apart from Christ, is internal even to the scriptural mode of the *initium fidei*, "the starting point of faith". In the semiotic vocabulary that Augustine himself uses, the creaturely symbols (*signa, similitudines*) of divine revelation orient faith but are ultimately at variance with the truth of the divine being which they symbolize. This dissonance is only overcome in the perfect symbol of the Incarnate Word, in whose personal unity the otherness between creaturely sign and divine signified is overcome. Only in this way is the project of divine self-symbolization stabilized and consummated:

> Now just as the rational mind is meant, once purified, to contemplate eternal things, so it is meant while still needing purification to give faith to temporal things. ... So now we accord faith to the things done in time for our sakes, and are purified by it; in order that when we come to sight and truth succeeds to faith, eternity might likewise succeed to mortality ... Now until this happens and in order that it may happen, and to prevent the faith which we accord with all trust in this mortal life to things "that have originated" from clashing (*dissonaret*) with the truth of contemplating eternal things which we hope for in eternal life, truth itself, co-eternal with the Father, *originated from the earth* (Ps. 85:12) when the Son of God came in order to become the Son of man and to capture our faith and draw it to himself, and by means of it to lead us on to his truth; for he took our mortality in such a way that he did not lose his own eternity. ... So it was proper for us to be purified in such a way that he who remained eternal should become for us "originated"; it would not do for there to be one person for us in faith, another in truth.[22]

In this passage we have a condensed summary of Augustine's theological epistemology as outlined in the first four books of *De Trinitate*. Human beings are incapable of an unmediated apprehension of the reality of the divine, a fact that Augustine

22 *De Trinitate*, 4.18.24; Augustine, *The Trinity*, 169–170. I have treated elsewhere the centrality of this passage for the Christological structure of *De Trinitate*. See my "Oppositional Pairs and Christological Synthesis: Rereading Augustine's *De Trinitate*" *Theological Studies* 68:2 (June 2007): 231–253, especially 243–244; also, *Retrieving Nicaea*, 252–255.

ascribes not merely to creaturely finitude but also to the sinfulness of attachment to lower realities. Divine revelation heals this attachment by a purification and adaptation that uses the lower realities with which humans are attached as symbolizations and upward nudges toward the divine. But the difference between the creaturely features of even divine self-symbolizations and their divine referent persists as a dissonance within the dynamic of faith until the divine self-symbolization is consummated in the creature who is God, Jesus Christ. Augustine concludes his account of the economy of divine self-symbolization in Books 1–4 by depicting the mission of the Son precisely as the objective consummation of this economy and the mission of the Spirit as consisting in enabling the human recognition of this consummation.[23]

Rahner's Contribution

The significance of this fundamentally Trinitarian account of the character of Christian faith can be further illumined by comparison to a passage from a very different provenance to which it has no textual connection. I am referring to an article by Karl Rahner, originally published in German in 1978, and hence translated as "Oneness and Threefoldness of God in Discussion with Islam."[24] Rahner makes no mention of Augustine and there are no traces of Augustinian influence. But this lack of dependence makes all the more intriguing a similarity of argument. Rahner acknowledges that Christian theologians need to give an account to their Jewish and Muslim counterparts of why the doctrine of the Trinity does not amount to tri-theism. Such an account would need to present Trinitarian doctrine as the expression of a radical and "concrete" monotheism. Conversely, it would also offer its own challenge as to "whether these two world religions have not failed to achieve that elucidation and radicalization of monotheism which finds expression precisely in the doctrine of the Trinity."[25]

The essence of Rahner's argument is that both Judaism and Islam, indeed all monotheistic religions that assert divine sovereignty over creation, cannot do so without positing created mediations that render access to the divine and express God's sovereignty in the immanent sphere. Rahner suggests that the integrity of a concrete monotheism hinges on how one negotiates the relation between these created mediations and the God to whom they refer. Either one must demythologize these created mediations "as radically creaturely and finite and lying on this side of the abyss between God and creature," which then leads to "a merely theoretical," or abstract monotheism.[26] Or, one can strive for a concrete affirmation of the absolute closeness of the absolute God by accepting these creaturely mediations

23 *De Trinitate* 4.20.29.

24 Rahner, "Oneness and Threefoldness of God in Discussion with Islam."

25 Rahner, "Oneness and Threefoldness of God in Discussion with Islam," 105.

26 Rahner, "Oneness and Threefoldness of God in Discussion with Islam," 117.

as themselves divine and end up in implicit polytheism. The only way out of this impasse, concludes Rahner, the only possible form of a *concrete* monotheism, is one in which the creaturely mediation of God is itself divine and thus a form of divine self-communication. Because Trinitarian faith posits precisely this self-mediation of the one God in the Son and the Spirit, it represents a uniquely concrete form of monotheism.[27]

As I said, I find no signs of textual or conceptual dependence of Rahner on Augustine here but the similarity of argument that persists despite very different contexts is mutually illuminating and sheds significant light on our theme of the dialectic of interiority and exteriority in the act of faith. Rahner is engaged in a fundamentally apologetic discourse which seeks to defend Trinitarian faith on the basis of the notion of "concrete monotheism". While Islam and Judaism can challenge Christianity to explain why its Trinitarian faith is not tri-theism, Christianity poses its own challenge to forms of monotheism in which the concrete mediations of divine sovereignty inevitably de-stabilize precisely the monotheistic character of this faith to the extent that they must either detract from the concrete immediacy of divine sovereignty or acquire an aura of absoluteness alongside the one God. The essential point for our purposes is that Rahner associates the Trinitarian relation of God to the world, which is grounded in the Trinitarian being of God in himself, with a maximally concrete monotheism in which our access to the one God is through God's own self-mediation through the activity in the world of the Son and Spirit.

In the opening books of *De Trinitate*, Augustine is also engaged in a fundamental apologetic discourse, against both "Arians" who apply creaturely categories to God (thus, for example, interpreting the derivation of the Son from the Father as inferiority) and Platonists who attempt to abstract from creaturely reality but end up saying things that are true neither of God nor creation but rather products

27 Rahner's argument is vulnerable to one objection that evokes an interesting comparison with Augustine's approach. Rahner seems to treat the "mediations" of the Son and Spirit equivalently, as two modes of concrete divine self-communication which constitute a *self*-communication because they are integral to the divine being. What distinguished Christian Trinitarian faith from Judaism and Islam is that divine self-communication achieves a maximally concrete form inasmuch as this self-communication takes place in the form of a *creaturely* mediation. But the complete coincidence of divine self-communication and creaturely mediation happens only in the hypostatic union of the Word/Son with the humanity of Jesus. No such coincidence happens in the case of the Spirit, who does not become a creature. Thus, Rahner's own argument would seem to require a more Christocentric Pneumatology than the one he presents, at least in this essay. The presentation of the Spirit as a divine self-communication whose concreteness is parallel and as it were equivalent to that of the Incarnation is perhaps symptomatic of Rahner's tendency to parallel in too symmetrical a fashion the categorical/objective/exterior and transcendental/subjective/interior dimensions of Christian faith rather than make the former the *concrete* reference for the latter. By contrast, Augustine presents the mission of the Son as providing the co-incidence of creaturely mediation and divine self-communication and the mission of the Spirit not as a parallel "concrete" mediation but as enabling the recognition of the Christological revelation.

of their own fancy. Augustine's fundamental point is that the biblical style of revelation, what he calls the "*initium fidei*," is one in which God is able to make use of creaturely realities to genuinely represent himself, a project that achieves consummation in the creaturehood of the Son who is consubstantial with the Father, and in the witness of the Spirit to this consummation. As Rahner sought to challenge Jewish and Moslem monotheisms on the basis of the criterion of "concrete monotheism," Augustine's approach can challenge modern interiorist conceptions of faith on the basis of the analogous criterion of the concrete sovereignty of divine revelation. If the scriptural witness of God's "acting out" in human history, with its attendant network of symbols, concepts and doctrinal interpretation, is relegated to the level of a merely human interpretation and objectification of a transcendental experience, then it would seem that the concrete sovereignty of divine revelation is radically undermined. Furthermore, no genuine extroversion occurs in the divine-human encounter of faith so conceived. On the one hand, God does not get to act out in a genuinely self-communicative way but is still abstractly enclosed in his mystery and, on the other, humanity cannot get beyond its own self-projection.

By contrast, Augustine's Christological-Trinitarian conception of biblical faith, while not denying the ineluctably human element in divine revelation, nevertheless affirms that God is pervasively active within that human element and is able to signify himself effectively through it, a self-symbolization that achieves its consummation through the Incarnation of the Son and the witness of the Spirit. For Augustine, the authentic content of faith is found not in merely human objectifications and symbolizations of an inward experience but rather in the biblically proclaimed economy of divine self-symbolization and self-expression through creaturely means. God's self-expression can certainly take place through human "inward experiences" but the outward expression of these experiences is still under the provenance of the sovereignty of God's agency; in Christ and the Spirit, God is always the sovereign agent of his own self-symbolization. The starting point of biblical faith, the *initium fidei*, consists precisely in the adherence to this program of divine self-symbolization which is ultimately encompassed in the ascent from the symbolic humanity of Jesus to the divinity signified by that humanity. In this way, the integrity of both divine and human extroversion, which constitutes the act of faith, is actualized in the Trinitarian economy witnessed to by the Scriptures.

II. The Repudiation of an Interiorist Foundationalism in the Ascent of Faith

The second principle I propose on the basis of a reading of Augustine's *De Trinitate* in the framework of the dialectic of interiority and exteriority is that a crucial negative moment in the assent of faith is the repudiation of an interiorist foundationalism that allows the subject to act as judge over the contents of faith by reference to the standards of his own interiority. This principle can be derived from Augustine's work by an attentiveness to the structural importance of the language of certainty and doubt in the argument of *De Trinitate*, an aspect that I believe to have received insufficient attention in modern interpretations of this work.[28] In Book 1, Augustine announces that he will try to respond to those "garrulous rationalizers (*istis garrulis ratiocinatoribus*) who are skeptical of Nicene Trinitarian faith by helping them to "discover reasons they can have no doubt about."[29] What are these invincible reasons that Augustine provides on behalf of Trinitarian faith? Indeed, is there not something fundamentally self-contradictory about the project of responding to "rationalizers" by providing invincible *reasons* for faith?

But, from the outset, Augustine's promise of providing invincible reasons comes with a strange twist. He promises to provide reasons that will demonstrate both the aptness of the claims of faith and the inadequacy of the human mind to apprehend that aptness. A strangely paradoxical endeavor! Augustine is in fact promising to provide reasons that will demonstrate the incapacity of reason to judge the contents of Trinitarian faith, reasons that will show the light of Trinitarian faith as superior to but also as nurturing of the light of reason:

> That is why with the help of the Lord our God, we shall undertake to the best of our ability to give them the reasons they clamor for, and to account for the one and only and true God being a trinity, and for the rightness of saying, believing, and understanding that the Father and the Son and the Holy Spirit are of one and same substance or essence. In this way, instead of feeling that they have been mocked by my excuses, they may actually come to realize that that supreme goodness does exist which only the most purified minds can gaze upon and also that they are themselves unable to gaze upon it and grasp it for the good reason that the human mind with its weak eyesight cannot concentrate on so overwhelming a light, unless it has been nursed back to full vigor on the justice of faith.[30]

28 For a fuller exposition of this theme, see my *Retrieving Nicaea*, 262–280. Augustine's preoccupation with the categorical doubt of skepticism runs throughout his writing career, starting with one of his earliest extant writings, the *Contra Academicos* (English version: Augustine, *Against the Academics*, trans. John J. O'Meara, Ancient Christian Writers: the Works of the Fathers in Translation, 12 [Westminster, MD: The Newman Press, 1950]). Note his account of his own struggles with skepticism on the way to his Christian conversion in his *Confessiones* (English version: *Confessions* in *Nicene and Post-Nicene Fathers*, Series I, vol. 1, ed. Philip Schaff [reprint, Grand Rapids: Eerdmans, 1956]), 5.19-24; 6.6. In *De Trinitate*, he deals explicitly with skepticism in 15.12.21. For an overview of Augustine's pervasive concern with skepticism, see John M. Rist, *Augustine: Ancient Thought Baptized* (New York: Cambridge University Press, 1994), 41–91.

29 *De Trinitate* 1.2.4; Augustine, *The Trinity*, 67, translation amended.

30 *De Trinitate*, 1.2.4. Translation amended.

Is Certainty Possible?

Augustine's announcement of his paradoxical project in Book 1 should alert us to track the language of certainty and indubitability in Augustine's account of the triadic structure of human consciousness. If we do this, we discover that Augustine's "inward turn" in the second half of *De Trinitate*, in light of his whole project of providing indubitable reasons for faith, is in fact intended to be a turn toward certainty:

> So let us put aside all consideration of things we know outwardly through the senses of the body, and concentrate our attention on what we have stated that all minds know for certain about themselves. ... Nobody surely doubts, however, that he lives and remembers and understands and wills and thinks and knows and judges. At least, even if he doubts, he lives; if he doubts, he remembers why he is doubting; if he doubts, he understands he is doubting; if he doubts, he has a will to be certain; if he doubts, he thinks; if he doubts, he knows he does not know; if he doubts, he judges he ought not to give a hasty assent. You may have your doubt about anything else, but you should have no doubts about these; if they were not certain, you would not be able to doubt anything.[31]

Augustine's resolution of the analysis of consciousness into the triad of memory, intellect, and will retains this initial emphasis on the quest for certainty: "Now let us put aside for the moment the other things which the mind is certain about as regards itself, and just discuss these three, memory (*memoria*), understanding (*intellegentia*), and will (*voluntas*). . . ."[32] Augustine's crucial move here is that, instead of subjecting Trinitarian faith to the standards of rational certainty, he redefines rational certainty in Trinitarian terms. The ultimate foundation for certainty itself is the triadic self-presencing of human consciousness as memory, intellect, and will. It is only because of this innate certainty of the mind's own triadic self-presencing that we can be certain of anything else.

But has Augustine now proved Trinitarian faith by recourse to a so-called "psychological analogy"? We can only come to that conclusion if we ignore as an essentially pointless digression Augustine's prolonged meditations in Book 10 on what Rowan Williams has called "the paradoxes of self-knowledge" in Augustine's phenomenology of human consciousness.[33] After demonstrating that the structure

31 *De Trinitate* 10.10.14; Augustine, *The Trinity*, 296–297.

32 *De Trinitate* 10.11.17; Augustine, *The Trinity*, 298.

33 Rowan Williams, "The Paradoxes of Self-Knowledge in the *De Trinitate*," in *Augustine: Presbyter Factus Sum, Collectanea Augustiniana*, [Augustine: I was made a Priest: Essays on Augustine], eds. Joseph T. Lienhard, et al. (New York: Peter Lang, 1993), 121–134.

of human certainty is radically constituted by the mind's triadic self-presencing in the inner processions of self-knowing and self-loving, Augustine spends much time probing the mysterious reality that we tend *not* to know ourselves, and the mind needs to be literally *re-minded* to do that which it cannot but do in order to be itself.[34]

The logical resolution to this conundrum is provided by making a distinction between self-knowledge and self-awareness (*se nosse - se cogitare*). The mind cannot but know itself and love itself and yet the mind can be estranged from itself such that it is not consciously aware of its self-knowledge. But this distinction simply describes the paradox rather than resolving it. And Augustine's point does not at all depend on resolving the paradox but precisely in letting it stand as a demonstration that human certainty is structurally broken.

That in fact is his paradoxical reply to the rationalizers of Book 1 and their imperious demands for reasons they can have no doubt about. On the one hand, the very structure of human certainty is triadic in a way that suggests the aptness of Trinitarian faith; on the other hand, our access to Trinitarian faith cannot depend on human certainty since human certainty itself is existentially broken.

At the beginning of Book 4, wherein Augustine brings his depiction of the scriptural economy of salvation to its Christological climax, he offers both a self-portrait and an account of the essential standpoint of the Christian theologian. Such a person has come to value self-knowledge above the "knowledge of earthly and celestial things."[35] Stirred by the Holy Spirit and awakened unto God, this person comes to know himself "in God's light" and discovers the real disproportion between his own sickness and God's purity. For this person, self-knowledge is primarily a knowledge of one's own weakness and one's situation of exile from the homeland of divine life. And this person is Augustine himself: "As one of this sort of men, O Lord my God, I sigh among your poor ones in the family of your Christ…I am struggling to return from this *far country* (Luke 15:13) by the road he has made in the humanity of the divinity of his only Son."[36] As Luigi Gioia has suggested, such an account of self-knowledge is in fact the best characterization of the real intent and significance of Augustine's "inward turn" in the second half of *De Trinitate*.[37] Designed to respond to those who want to judge Nicene Trinitarian faith by the standards of human certainty, it tries to demonstrate both the inherent weakness of the human capacity for certainty as well as the Trinitarian imprint

34 It is because of this radical post-lapsarian incapacity of the mind that the Platonic ascent is doomed to failure on its own terms. For an acute analysis of this aspect of Augustine's argument, see John Cavadini, "The Structure and Intention of Augustine's *De trinitate*" in *Christianity in Relation to Jews, Greeks, and Romans*, Recent Studies in Early Christianity 2, ed. E. Ferguson (New York: Garland, 1999), 231–252.

35 *De Trinitate* 4.Pref.1.

36 *De Trinitate* 4.Pref.1; Augustine, *The Trinity*, 152–153, italics original.

37 Gioia, *Theological Epistemology of Augustine's* De Trinitate, 220.

in what endures of that capacity. True self-knowledge issues in a self-assessment which eschews the standpoint of rationality standing in judgment over faith in favor of rationality coming to terms with its own exile status, guided by faith to discern the imprint in itself both of its divine homeland and its estrangement from that homeland.

III: Nicene Trinitarian Faith: Radically and Irreducibly Extroverted

The third principle which I propose can be derived from Augustine's *De Trinitate* is that Nicene Trinitarian faith leads to a view of the human person as radically and irreducibly extroverted and to a conception of the life of faith as a Christological reformation of this extroversion. Modern critics of Augustine, beginning with Olivier du Roy's strident critique in *L'Intelligence de la Foi*, have typically characterized his attempts to find a Trinitarian likeness in the human *mens* as solipsistic and modalist.[38] His modern defenders emphasize Augustine's clarification in Book 14 that the Trinitarian image in the human person is not actualized through the mind's remembering, understanding, and loving itself but rather through its remembering, understanding, and loving its Creator.[39] However, in order to appreciate that this qualification is not a mere afterthought or a notional *deus ex machina*, it is helpful to trace the route by which Augustine's creative contemplation of the givenness of Nicene Trinitarian faith leads him to this conception of the human person as constituted by a triadic extroversion toward the Trinitarian God. The key hermeneutical principle to which we must adhere is that Augustine's analysis of human consciousness as memory, intellect, and will should not be read in a static and reified way as simply an objective map of what human consciousness looks like, on the inside, as it were. Rather, it is crucial to see how this analysis functions within the overarching program announced in Book 1 of *De Trinitate*, that of travelling along the way of faith by adhering to the divine economy of self-symbolization.

We have already seen that one important function of this analysis is to confront the demand for rational certainty about Nicene Trinitarian faith by showing how this faith uncovers both the triadic structure of the self-presencing that is foundational to certainty and its existential faltering. But Augustine implicitly concedes that the triadic analysis of the mind as memory, intellect, and will is not the only way to analyze the mind's self-presence as the foundation of its innate capacity for certainty: "Now let us put aside for the moment *the other things*

38 Olivier du Roy, *L'intelligence de la foi en la Trinitaté selon s. Augustin: genèse de sa théologie trinitaire jusqu'en 391* [The Understanding of Faith in the Trinity according to St. Augustine: The Genesis of his Trinitarian Faith up to 391] (Paris: Études augustiniennes, 1966), 462–463.

39 *De Trinitate* 14.12.15. See the magisterial essay of Rowan Williams, "*Sapientia* and the Trinity: Reflections on *De Trinitate*," 317–332. Williams (*Sapientia* and the Trinity, 321) argues that the inward turn of the latter half of *De Trinitate* is in fact "a movement into God's own life as turned outwards."

which the mind is certain about as regards itself, and just discuss these three, memory, understanding, and will."[40] We can ask, "Why just those three?" Why not, for example, the Neoplatonic triad of being-life-mind/thought which Augustine uses elsewhere?[41] After all, one can say that the mind is certain of itself as existing, as living, and as knowing. But the principal reason why the latter triad would not suit Augustine's purposes is precisely that he is deliberately looking for relational categories, whereas "being," "life," and "mind" delineate substances rather than relations.

Augustine does in fact use the triad of being-life-thought but he applies these terms to the unity of the self as a whole, not to the relational distinctions within that whole: "These three then, memory, understanding, and will, are not three lives but one life, nor three minds but one mind. So it follows of course that they are not three beings but one being."[42] In Book 5 of *De Trinitate*, Augustine had organized the grammar of Nicene Trinitarian faith into language that speaks of the divine being with reference to itself, *ad se*, by way of substance, and language that speaks of the divine being by reference to another, *ad alterum*, by way of the mutuality of relation.[43] Because Augustine is carefully applying this Nicene grammar, which itself represents a way of reading Scripture, to his analysis of the human *mens*, he is led to posit alterity and relatedness within human interiority. Within this framework, there is a clear path from the scriptural designations of the Son as *Logos* and Wisdom and the Spirit as the love of God poured into our hearts[44] to the analysis of the interior alterity and relatedness of the human person in terms of knowledge and love.

Of course, to say that the human person is comprised of a dynamic inter-relatedness does not of itself rebut the charge of solipsism. It seems rather to devalue the notion of relation from the milieu of persons-in-relation to that of a merely structural inter-relatedness of an individual person. That, of course, is a common objection made by proponents of the "social analogy" against Augustine. But the appropriate rejoinder to this charge is to note the continuity in Augustine's theological anthropology in *De Trinitate* between what we can call exterior (*ad extra*) relationality and interior (*ad intra*) relationality, a continuity which arguably posits a more integral vision of being-as-communion than that proposed by

40 *De Trinitate* 10.11.17; Augustine, *The Trinity*, 298 (my emphasis).

41 On the Neoplatonic triad of being-life-mind/thought, see Pierre Hadot, "Être, Vie, Pensée chez Plotin et avant Plotin" [Being, Life, Thought in Plotinus and Before Plotinus] in *Les Sources de Plotin* [*Plotinus's Sources*], ed. E.R. Dodds, Entretiens sur l'Antiquité Classique V (Geneva: Fondation Hardt, 1960), 107–157.

42 *De Trinitate* 10.11.18; Augustine, *The Trinity*, 298, translation amended; see also *Confessiones* 13.11, where Augustine speaks of the triad of being-knowing-willing as "one life, one mind, one being (*una vita et una mens et una essentia*)."

43 *De Trinitate* 5.2.9.

44 See Rom. 5:5.

those who only see relationality as occurring between persons in a way that does not determine the interiority of individual persons. If relationality only occurs between persons without any foundations in the subjectivity belonging to the person as such, personhood would only pertain to the collectivity or state and would not be a feature *intrinsic* to particular persons. This is a key point neglected by "personalist" readings of the anthropological implications of Trinitarian doctrine, but fully acknowledged in the Christian personalist philosophy from which such an anthropology derives.[45]

A full account of Augustine's presentation of the continuity between inward and outward aspects of relationality would be beyond the scope of this essay. For our present purposes, it is sufficient to note well the order of presentation in Books 8 to 10.

Augustine begins with a contemplation of the ineluctable presence of God to the human mind as Truth, Justice, and Goodness and from there proceeds to an analysis of what happens when we love a just person, such as the apostle Paul, on the basis of knowing the form of justice which he exhibits in his person, to a parsing of human consciousness as the inter-relationality of knowledge and love. So we start with the innate transitive relatedness of the mind to the divine presence through knowledge of God's Truth and Justice and love of his Goodness; and from there proceed to the mind's relatedness to another human person through love and knowledge; and finally to the mind's innate self-knowledge and self-love. Thus, even on a surface literary level, the mind's self-relatedness is not presented by Augustine in abstraction from external relatedness but is in fact derived from this external relatedness.

Far from intimating that that there is any level of human existence that is hermetically sealed by the activity of remembering, understanding, and loving oneself, Augustine presents the self-relatedness of *mens* as both foundational to and determined by the mind's *ad extra* relatedness. In this way, Augustine describes human interiority as radically extroverted and as oriented toward outward relation through its innate dynamism of knowledge and love. In the last analysis, we can say that Augustine's description of *mens* as memory, understanding, and love is really an account of the triadic structure of human extroversion.[46]

To say that *De Trinitate* presents the human person as radically extroverted—and indeed radically extroverted unto God—might seem to align Augustine with the approach that sees the foundations of faith in humanity's radical and transcendental openness to the Absolute. Indeed, I would contend that such an anthropological foundationalism for faith is not absent from Augustine's vision.

45 See, for example, Jacques Maritain, *The Person and the Common Good*, trans. John J. Fitzgerald (Notre Dame: University of Notre Dame Press, 1946).

46 For a similar assessment, see John Milbank, "Sacred Triads: Augustine and the Indo-European Soul," in *Augustine and His Critics: Essays in Honour of Gerald Bonner*, eds. Robert Dodaro and George Lawless (London and New York: Routledge, 2000), 91.

But it is balanced by a dialectical reading of this openness. Augustine is quite clear that the radical exteriority of the human person is existentially manifest in two opposed outward orientations: covetousness and love.[47] The former, *cupiditas*, manifests the irreducible extroversion of the human person in a way that inverts the hierarchy of being between creatures and Creator, while the latter manifests this extroversion in harmony with this hierarchy.

The idolatrous extroversion of concupiscence distorts the mind's own internal relatedness such that it loses hold of its own self-presencing and becomes radically uncertain and incapable of perceiving the analogy between its own self-presencing and the self-disclosure of the Triune God. On the other hand, the extroversion of *caritas* illumines the mind's own internal relatedness and actualizes it as a triadic extroversion unto the divine Trinity: remembering, understanding, and loving its Triune Creator. Thus, the Christological reprise in Book 13, which follows Augustine's account of the triadic structure of the human subject, makes the crucial point that what determines the direction of human extroversion ultimately is not good will or dialectical exercises of any kind but the Christological economy, "the blood of the just man" that heals human concupiscence and the outpouring of the love of God in our hearts through the Holy Spirit.[48] Augustine's sketch of the trinitarian image in humanity is only completed in Book 13, wherein he depicts the healing of human knowing through adherence to the *scientia* of the Christological economy and the healing of human willing through receiving the Holy Spirit.[49]

Conclusion

The unfortunate tendency to reduce *De trinitate* to the "psychological analogy" as a description of how individual interiority is like the Trinity has largely hidden from view its genuine and enduring contribution to the exposition of the Nicene interpretation of biblical Trinitarian doctrine as determinative to the life of faith, globally considered. Largely abstracting from issues of external influence and development, I have focused on a synchronic reading of *De Trinitate* for the sake of presenting three principles that can be derived from such a reading for contemplat-

47 *De Trinitate* 9.7.13.

48 See Rom. 5:5.

49 An excellent account of this process as one of "cultural transformation" in which the "inner word" is healed by the Incarnation and enabled to become a transformative power within the outwardness of cultural engagement is found in John Cavadini, "The Quest for Truth in Augustine's *De Trinitate*," *Theological Studies* 58:3 (September 1997): 429–440. Cavadini (*De Trinitate*, 339–340) comments, "This is not in the first place an exhortation to look within but to look without, for paradoxically that is how the inner image becomes healed and transformed ... God's entry into the realm of signs and signification does not mean that *we* leave it behind ... but rather that in our use of cultural forms (at least those not classified as hopelessly demonic), they become more and more transparent to the justice the divine *doctrina* is teaching us to love, themselves ever more able to participate in imaging God."

ing the distinctiveness of Nicene biblical faith, especially in light of the dialectic of interiority and exteriority.[50]

First, if we consider faith as most basically an encounter between the human person and the living God, a primary question is how that encounter can take place given humanity's inescapable tendency to project its own features onto God. How can humanity truly go outside of itself in order to authentically encounter God? Augustine's response is that the human tendency to merely see itself even when it attempts to see God is only overcome when it is in fact co-opted by the biblical Christological economy of divine self-projection through creaturely symbols. Only in the humanity of the one who shares the substance of the Father can the extroversion of faith be actualized beyond the otherwise inescapable self-referencing of human religiosity.

Second, faith is inevitably challenged by the demand to justify itself before the tribunal of reason. Augustine's response to this challenge is to allow Nicene Trinitarian faith to probe the fragility of reason, its existential incapacity for self-authentication, as well as to let Nicene faith illuminate the mysteriously triadic self-relatedness of the mind, which is the foundation of its capacity for certainty.

Third, Nicene Trinitarian faith lights up a path that proceeds from the innate relatedness of the human person to God and the interior relatedness of the Triune God to the interior self-relatedness of the human person, which is the foundation for relationship to other creatures through knowing and loving.

But Christian faith also discloses the pervasively conflicted nature of humanity's innate extroversion. Only the scripturally proclaimed Christological and Pneumatological economy of salvation heals human extroversion unto knowing and loving oneself and other creatures through knowing and loving the Triune God. The most fitting expression of this healed extroversion is the worship of God, which is simultaneously the summit of human wisdom: "For God himself is supreme wisdom, while the worship of God is human wisdom."[51]

50 For a thorough treatment of issues of external influence and development in Augustine's Trinitarian theology, see now Lewis Ayres, *Augustine and the Trinity* (New York: Oxford University Press, 2010).

51 *De Trinitate* 14.1.1; see also 14.12.15.

Letter & Spirit 7 (2011): 191-207

Patristic Biblical Hermeneutics in Joseph Ratzinger's *Jesus of Nazareth*

~: **William M. Wright IV** :~

Duquesne University

Introduction

In the concluding chapter of his extensive study of Origen's exegesis, Henri de Lubac advocates the careful study of premodern Christian biblical interpretation both as an important component in the historical development of Christianity and as a theological practice, which "reaches ... to the permanent foundations of Christian thought."[1] For de Lubac, who wrote so extensively on the history and theology of Christian biblical interpretation, premodern exegesis, amidst its variety and periodic excesses, embodies a profound theological synthesis which is essential and thus permanently valuable to Christianity. This theological synthesis, expressed in the doctrine of the fourfold sense of Scripture, is an integration of Christian faith, practice, and spirituality, all of which are centered in Christ and grounded in the reading of Scripture. De Lubac encourages the *ressourcement* study of premodern exegesis in order to understand more deeply its "spirit" and integrate its theological principles with modern biblical criticism.[2]

One of the more prominent attempts in recent years to synthesize the theological principles of premodern Christian exegesis with modern biblical criticism for the theological interpretation of Scripture is Pope Benedict XVI/Joseph Ratzinger's *Jesus of Nazareth*.[3] Throughout *Jesus of Nazareth*, Ratzinger often

1 Henri de Lubac, *History and Spirit: The Understanding of Scripture according to Origen*, trans. Anne Englund Nash and Juvenal Merriell (San Francisco: Ignatius Press, 2007 [1950]), 431. De Lubac here references Johann Adam Möhler, *L'Unité dans l'Église*, appendix 7, *Unam Sanctam* (1938): 260–261.

2 De Lubac writes (*History and Spirit*, 450), "Without either a return to archaic forms or servile mimicry, often by totally different methods, it is a spiritual movement that we must reproduce above all." Compare Henri de Lubac, *Medieval Exegesis: The Four Senses of Scripture*, 3 vols., trans. Marc Sebanc and E. M. Macierowski (Grand Rapids: Eerdmans, 1998–2009), 1.xix–xxi. The original French text is Henri de Lubac, *Exégèse Médiévale: Les Quatre Sense de l'Écriture, I and II* [*Medieval Exegesis: The Four Senses of Scripture*,"], Théologie 41–42 (Paris: Aubier, 1959–1964).

3 Joseph Ratzinger (Pope Benedict XVI), *Jesus of Nazareth: From the Baptism in the Jordan to the Transfiguration*, trans. Adrian J. Walker (New York: Doubleday, 2007); Idem, *Jesus of Nazareth: Part Two—Holy Week: From the Entrance into Jerusalem to the Resurrection*, trans. Philip J. Whitmore (San Francisco: Ignatius, 2011). The author makes clear (*Jesus of Nazareth*, 1.xxiii–xxiv) that this book is not a work of papal authority. Accordingly, I will refer to the author as Joseph Ratzinger rather than by his papal name Benedict XVI.

appeals to the biblical interpretation of various Church Fathers as a resource for drawing out the abiding theological significance of the Gospels. While he regards patristic exegesis as making a valuable theological contribution, his appropriation of it is neither uncritical nor nostalgic. This essay will offer some reflections on Ratzinger's retrieval of patristic biblical hermeneutics by focusing in detail on his interpretation of a specific biblical text: the Good Shepherd discourse in John 10:1–18.[4]

Ratzinger does not rely on patristic exegesis in his interpretation of this text in the same way that he does, for instance, in his treatment of the Our Father, which makes heavy and explicit use of Cyprian's *De dominica oratione* ["*On the Lord's Prayer*"].[5] However, a close analysis of Ratzinger's treatment of John 10:1–18 brings to light the ways in which principles and habits of patristic biblical hermeneutics inform his theological interpretation of the Good Shepherd discourse as Scripture. Moreover, even though Ratzinger is often critical of the methods of early Christian biblical interpretation, I will argue that in some instances, he actually provides helpful examples of retrieving patristic interpretive strategies for use in a contemporary context. Before turning to Ratzinger's biblical interpretation, I will first offer some brief remarks about the Good Shepherd discourse itself.

I. An Overview of the Good Shepherd Discourse (John 10:1–18)

The Good Shepherd discourse (John 10:1–18) immediately follows the healing of the man born blind in John 9. The sequence of John 9 is a narrative demonstration of Jesus' identity and work as the Light of the World, whose actions as the Light include revelation, giving life, and judgment.[6] As the Light of the World, Jesus effects judgment in one respect by laying bare the distinction between believers and unbelievers. This work of judgment appears in the contrast between the Pharisees and the formerly blind man, which becomes increasingly sharp over the course of 9:8–34. While some Pharisees entertain a degree of openness to Jesus during the forensic proceedings (see 9:16b), those who do not figure most prominently in the narrative. Their resistance grows more adamant over the course of the chapter. By contrast, the man who begins the story with congenital blindness not only receives physical sight from Jesus, but he comes to acquire the spiritual sight of faith when he professes his belief in Jesus as the Son of Man, the One Who has come down

4 Ratzinger's interpretation of the Good Shepherd discourse appears in *Jesus of Nazareth*, 1.272–286. Unless otherwise noted, all translations of the biblical text are my own from the Hebrew or Greek text.

5 Ratzinger, *Jesus of Nazareth*, 1.128–168, especially pp. 131–132, 151–168.

6 See William M. Wright IV, *Rhetoric and Theology: Figural Reading of John 9*, Beihefte zur Zeitschrift für die neutestamentliche Wissenschaft 165 (Berlin and New York: Walter de Gruyter, 2009), 156–198; Josef Blank, *Krisis: Untersuchungen zur johanneischen Christologie und Eschatologie* [*Judgment: Investigations into Johannine Christology and Eschatology*] (Freiburg: Lambertus, 1964), 252–263.

from heaven to reveal the Father (9:38).[7] The narrative sequence concludes with Jesus declaring the Pharisees who do not believe in Him to be spiritually blind and remaining in sin. Jesus continues to address these Pharisees in the shepherd discourse, but he shifts the predominant imagery from sight and blindness to the pastoral.[8] Aside from the shift in imagery, the Gospel narrative gives no indication that Jesus' audience in John 10 differs from that in 9:39–41.

The Good Shepherd discourse is often divided into two movements, and some scholars even classify these two movements as constituting two different literary genres.[9] The first movement (10:1–6) introduces the basic pastoral images of the discourse: the shepherd, his sheep, the sheepfold, the shepherd's opponents, as well as the theme of the mutual knowledge between shepherd and sheep. Jesus develops the distinction between Himself and His Pharisee opponents, as rival religious leaders of disciples (suggested in 9:27–29), with the figures of the "shepherd" and the "thieves and bandits" (10:1–2). In 9:34, the Pharisees "drove out" the formerly blind man (Greek: *exebalon ... exō*) for boldly proposing to teach them, and the same Greek verb denotes the action of the Shepherd, who leads His sheep after He has "driven [them] out" (Greek: *ekbalē*) from the sheepfold (10:4).[10] The first part of the discourse concludes with the narrator's observation that Jesus' audience did not understand the meaning of His figurative speech (10:6).

Consequently, Jesus elaborates on many of the pastoral images and distinctions in the second movement of the discourse (10:7–18), while maintaining the same mode of figurative speech. Jesus develops the motif of the fold being opened for the sheep to be called out (10:2) with His self-identification as the "Door for the sheep" (10:7), for it is through Him that the sheep go out to the pasture of eternal life (10:9, 28; compare 14:6). Jesus also contrasts Himself as the "Good Shepherd" (10:11), who gives life to the sheep by laying down His own life, with a series of opponents—the thief (10:10), the hired man (10:12–13), and the wolf (10:14)—who are destructive, self-interested, or neglectful of the sheep. Moreover, Jesus relates the mutual knowledge between shepherd and sheep (10:3–5) to the

---

7 Wright, *Rhetoric and Theology*, 183–187. For the association of the Son of Man with the Incarnation in John 9:38, see Francis J. Moloney, S.D.B., *The Johannine Son of Man*, Biblioteca di Scienze religiose 14 (Rome: Libreria Ateneo Salesiano, 1976), 155.

8 Wright, *Rhetoric and Theology*, 191–192.

9 Raymond Brown classifies 10:1–5 as parable and 10:6–18 as the allegorical interpretation of the parable. See his *The Gospel according to John*, 2 vols., Anchor Bible 29–29A (New York: Doubleday, 1966–1970), 1.390–399. This generic distinction rests on taking the mention of Jesus' "figure of speech" (Greek: *paroimia*) in 10:6 as a specific literary genre rather than a generic mode of figurative language. Against this generic division, see Robert Kysar, "The Meaning and Function of Johannine Metaphor (John 10:1–18)," in *Voyages with John: Charting the Fourth Gospel* (Waco, TX: Baylor University Press, 2005), 161–182; reprint from *Semeia* 53 (1991): 81–112; William M. Wright IV, "Hearing the Shepherd's Voice: The *Paroimia* of the Good Shepherd Discourse and Augustine's Figural Reading," *Journal of Theological Interpretation* (forthcoming).

10 Wright, *Rhetoric and Theology*, 192.

mutual knowing between the Father and the Son (10:14–15). Although the narrative setting of the Gospel shifts to the Festival of Dedication in 10:22, the pastoral imagery reappears briefly in 10:26–30.

As readers of John 10:1–18 can observe, the discourse employs a mode of figurative language which John designates in 10:6 by the word *paroimia* ("figure of speech"). Elsewhere in the Gospel, John uses the term *paroimia* to refer to Jesus' veiled speech which His audience (whether His disciples or others in the narrative) does not readily understand at that present moment (see 16:25, 29). Accordingly, the Good Shepherd discourse does not provide its audience with the clear meaning of many of the pastoral images. While the Gospel is clearer about the meaning of some images, for example, the door (10:2, 7, 9), the shepherd (10:2, 11, 14), the sheep (10:3, 14, 26–27) and the pasture (10:3, 9, 28), John's audience is never told the specific meaning of the doorkeeper (10:3), the thief and robber (10:1, 10), the hired man (10:12–13), or the wolf (10:12). The discourse's figurative language and elusive imagery call for its audience to interpret it in more-than-literal ways. This rhetorical invitation makes the Good Shepherd discourse a helpful test case for examining Ratzinger's retrieval of patristic exegesis.[11]

With this overview in place, I will now turn to Ratzinger's *Jesus of Nazareth*. First, I will discuss Ratzinger's programmatic remarks about patristic exegesis and its hermeneutical value, and then I will focus more narrowly on his interpretation of the Good Shepherd discourse.

II. Ratzinger's Interpretation of John 10:1–18

Patristic Methods and Patristic Interpretations in **Jesus of Nazareth**

Ratzinger's *Jesus of Nazareth* displays a methodologically complex approach to biblical interpretation. In the Foreword to volume 1, he acknowledges the basic need for a historical-critical reading of Scripture.[12] He justifies this claim on theological grounds. The appropriateness of historical criticism for the interpretation of Scripture corresponds to the essential role played by real historical events, such as the life of Christ, in Christian faith.[13] But Ratzinger is also quick to point out methodological shortcomings of a historical-critical approach: its concern for

---

11 I discuss the matters of this paragraph, including Augustine's figural interpretation of the discourse's rhetoric, more fully in "Hearing the Shepherd's Voice."

12 Ratzinger, *Jesus of Nazareth*, 1.xv–xvi. Denis Farkasfalvy suggests, "The book's success among students of the Bible and theologians will depend on the way its introductory twenty-four pages (i–xxiv) are received and evaluated" in Denis Farkasfalvy, "*Jesus of Nazareth* and the Renewal of New Testament Theology," *Communio* 34 (2007): 438–453, at 439.

13 Ratzinger makes similar claims in volume 2: "The New Testament message is not simply an idea; essential to it is the fact that these events actually occurred in the history of the world: biblical faith does not recount stories as symbols of meta-historical truths; rather, it bases itself upon history that unfolded upon this earth" (2.103–104). That being said, Ratzinger goes on to discuss the limits of the historical knowledge of these events afforded by critical historiography (2.104–105, 111–112).

the Bible as a past artifact; the treatment of history as a closed system without reference to the transcendent; its inability to let the voice of Scripture speak to the present; the neglect of the canon's unity as an interpretive principle; the hypothetical nature of many historical-critical findings.[14]

Referring to the Second Vatican Council's *Dei Verbum* [*The Word of God*] §12, Ratzinger argues that a truly theological interpretation of the Bible as Scripture must attend to it "in the same Spirit in which it was written," a phrase which comes from Origen and his spiritual exegesis.[15] Accordingly, Ratzinger adopts several theological principles for his interpretation of Scripture, many of which are consistent with patristic exegetical habits.[16] First, Ratzinger argues that the theological interpreter reads Scripture as a canonical whole with Christ as the principle of its unity—a hermeneutical principle which Ratzinger elsewhere calls "the fundamental concept of patristic exegesis."[17] Second, Ratzinger acknowledges that speech has the capacity to transcend its original circumstances. New meaning comes to light by subsequent consideration of those words over time. He relates this transcendent aspect of speech to biblical inspiration and the classic doctrine of the fourfold sense. He writes, "The four senses of Scripture are not individual meanings arrayed side by side, but dimensions of the one word that reaches beyond the moment."[18] Third, Ratzinger reads the Bible in relation to the believing community, for the Bible's status as Scripture is derived from its relation to the people of God. The biblical books were produced within the context of the believing community (involving both Israel and the Church as the people of God), and it is within the historically continuous faith community that these books are received and proclaimed as God's Word in the present.

When he turns to the biblical interpretation of the Church Fathers, Ratzinger often distinguishes between their theological claims and the interpretive methods which they used to articulate those claims. This distinction comes to light in his interpretation of parable of the Good Samaritan (Luke 10:29–37). Ratzinger cites the patristic reading of this parable in terms of Christ's redemptive work to heal a wounded humanity. He calls this interpretation "an allegorical reading ...

---

14 Ratzinger, *Jesus of Nazareth*, 1.xvi–xvii.

15 Ratzinger, *Jesus of Nazareth*, 2.xiv; cf. *Jesus of Nazareth*, 1.xviii. Quotation from *Dei Verbum* §12 is mine from the Latin text available at http://www.vatican.va/archive/hist_councils/ii_vatican_council/ documents/vat-ii_const_19651118_dei-verbum_lt.html. Accessed June 7, 2011. On the Origenian background of this phrase see de Lubac, *History and Spirit*, 361–374; Ignace de la Potterie, S. J., "Interpretation of Holy Scripture in the Spirit in Which It Was Written (*Dei Verbum* 12c)," in *Vatican II: Assessments and Perspectives—Twenty Five Years After (1962–1987)*, 3 vols., ed. René Latourelle (Paulist, 1988–1989), 1.220–266, at 223–233.

16 Ratzinger, *Jesus of Nazareth*, 1.xviii–xxi.

17 Joseph Cardinal Ratzinger, *Principles of Catholic Theology: Building Stones for a Fundamental Theology*, trans. Mary Frances McCarthy, S.N.D. (San Francisco: Ignatius Press, 1987), 136.

18 Ratzinger, *Jesus of Nazareth*, 1.xx.

an interpretation that bypasses the text."[19] Ratzinger likewise characterizes the Scholastic interpretation of the traveler's injuries in terms of the twofold character of humanity's fallenness as "allegory, and it certainly goes far beyond the literal sense."[20]

Even though Ratzinger speaks of such interpretations as going beyond the text, he finds much that is theologically valuable in them. Consistent with his statements about the capacity of language to transcend its original circumstances, Ratzinger states that the patristic interpretation "reflects an inner potentiality in the text and can be a fruit growing out of it as from a seed."[21] He later adds that the "great vision" of this interpretation ascertains "a deeper dimension of the parable."[22] For Ratzinger, the more-than-literal patristic interpretation may go beyond the plain sense of the parable, but it develops a certain dynamic in the parable into a larger theological interpretation. It picks up on the narrative dynamic of the Samaritan's generous action to heal the helpless, wounded traveler, and develops it theologically in terms of Christ's gracious work to redeem humanity wounded by sin. For Ratzinger, this more-than-literal reading has interpretive viability in part because it develops something present in the text. This narrative dynamic, available in the plain sense reading of the text, provides a basis and tether for more-than-literal interpretation.

Placing the Good Shepherd Discourse in Context

Ratzinger wants his study of Jesus to have a historical grounding. When he turns to the Good Shepherd discourse, he first places the shepherd image in its ancient Near Eastern and biblical contexts. He observes that in the ancient Near East the shepherd image was often associated with kingship, and that this imagery appears in biblical texts such as Psalm 23. The most prominent biblical precursor for the Good Shepherd discourse is Ezekiel 34, which speaks of God coming to shepherd

---

19 Ratzinger, *Jesus of Nazareth*, 1.199. Instances of this patristic reading can be found in Origen, *Homilies on Luke*, 34.3; Ambrose, *Exposition of the Gospel according to Luke*, 7.71–84. See Arthur A. Just, Jr., *Luke*, Ancient Christian Commentary on Scripture NT 3, general ed. Thomas C. Oden (Downers Grove: InterVarsity Press, 2003), 177–181.

20 Ratzinger, *Jesus of Nazareth*, 1.200. As these statements suggest, Ratzinger operates with a conventional notion of allegory as a reading which abandons the plain sense for a textually unrelated and unfounded meaning. For a critique of this conventional notion of allegory as not actually corresponding to patristic interpretive practice see Henri de Lubac, S.J., "Typology and Allegorization" in *Theological Fragments*, trans. Rebecca Howell Balinski (San Francisco: Ignatius Press, 1989), 129–164; Henri Crouzel, "La distinction de la 'typologie' et de l''allégorie'," ["The Distinction of Typology and Allegory"] *Bulletin de Littérature Ecclésiastique* 65 (1964): 161–174; Elizabeth A. Clark, *Reading Renunciation: Asceticism and Scripture in Early Christianity* (Princeton: Princeton University Press, 1999), 70–78; Peter W. Martens, "Revisiting the Allegory/Typology Distinction: The Case of Origen," *Journal of Early Christian Studies* 16 (2008): 283–317.

21 Ratzinger, *Jesus of Nazareth*, 1.199.

22 Ratzinger, *Jesus of Nazareth*, 1.201.

His people in place of Judah's corrupt leadership. Ratzinger then links Ezekiel 34 to the chronologically later shepherd imagery in Zechariah 12–13, which speaks of the shepherd figure being killed—a text which Ratzinger also sees as resembling the vicarious death of Isaiah's Servant of YHWH. Ratzinger remarks that the distinctive use of shepherd imagery in Zechariah 12–13 is a "surprising and thought-provoking turn that leads directly to the mystery of Jesus."[23] Ratzinger understands Jesus as standing within this unfolding trajectory of the shepherd image across Israel's Scripture. Situated within this theological trajectory, Jesus "takes upon himself all the historical associations of the shepherd image, which he then purifies, and brings to its full meaning."[24]

Ratzinger uses Ezekiel 34 and Zechariah 12–13 to chart an interpretive trajectory across the canon, which provides the biblical context for Jesus' use of the shepherd imagery. He sees the re-readings of the shepherd image across the biblical books as exemplifying an unfolding theological current, which finds its *telos* in Christ. This claim is not a historical-critical one, but it is informed by Ratzinger's adoption of the patristic hermeneutical tenet that Christ is the principle of the canon's unity. Ratzinger reads Ezekiel and Zechariah as having historical and literary integrity in their own rights (a historical-critical tenet) as well as pointing forward, in various ways, to Christ (a patristic-theological tenet). Ratzinger's interpretation of the prophets in this regard closely resembles the kind of Christological reading of the Old Testament discussed in the 2001 Pontifical Biblical Commission document *The Jewish People and Their Sacred Scriptures in the Christian Bible*.[25]

"I am the Door for the Sheep"

Ratzinger divides his interpretation of John 10:1–18 into two sections. Whereas most Johannine scholars divide the text between 10:1–6 and 7–18, Ratzinger structures his interpretation around the discourse's two "I am + predicate" statements. He begins with the Jesus' self-identification, "I am the Door for the Sheep" (10:7). He connects this statement in 10:7 with the previous contrast in 10:1–2 between the thief and robber, who climb up into the fold, and the shepherd, who enters through the door. Ratzinger interprets the identification of Christ as both the Door and the Shepherd, who enters through the door, as instructions for those in the Church who lead Christ's sheep. He writes, "The proof of a true shepherd is that he enters through Jesus as the door."[26] While Ratzinger does not reference any

23 Ratzinger, *Jesus of Nazareth*, 1.274.

24 Ratzinger, *Jesus of Nazareth*, 1.278.

25 Pontifical Biblical Commission, *The Jewish People and Their Sacred Scriptures in the Christian Bible* (Vatican City: Libreria Editrice Vaticana, 2001), §21. The English edition is available at http://www.vatican.va/roman_curia/congregations/cfaith/pcb_documents/rc_con_cfaith_doc_20020212_popolo-ebraico_en.html. See the quotation in note 51 below.

26 Ratzinger, *Jesus of Nazareth*, 1.276.

patristic writer here, his interpretation of John 10:1–18 in terms of instruction for bishops and pastors is redolent of the Augustinian exegesis of this text.[27]

Ratzinger cites the dialogue between the Risen Jesus and Peter (21:15–19) as exemplifying what it is for a pastor to enter through Christ as the Door. He observes that Jesus calls Simon personally, by name, and Peter's installation as pastor of Christ's sheep is grounded in his three-fold profession of love for Jesus. As a faithful shepherd, Peter tends the sheep, knowing that they belong to Christ and are not his own private property. Peter's personal love for Christ and his selfless reception of Christ's sheep dispose him to serve as an instrument through whom Christ continues to lead His sheep. But Peter also remains one of the flock as indicated by Christ's command, "follow Me" (21:19). Peter is both a shepherd and one of Christ's sheep.

"I am the Good Shepherd"

Ratzinger organizes his interpretation of Jesus' second self-identification, "I am the Good Shepherd" (10:11), around four thematic elements in the discourse. First, Ratzinger attends to the contrast between the shepherd and the thief (10:1, 8, 10). The contrast between these two figures turns on the dispositions and actions that each one takes towards the sheep. Jesus states that the thief "does not come except to steal, slaughter, and destroy" (John 10:10). Ratzinger interprets the thief's activity in terms of his exploitation of the sheep for his own personal profit. He does not make the connection explicit, but his characterization of the thief reflects those attributes which the pastor of Christ's sheep should not have: exploitative self-interest and possessiveness of the sheep.[28]

Unlike the thief, the Shepherd does not use the sheep as objects for His personal gain. Instead, the Shepherd does the very opposite of the thief: He gives up His own life for the sheep's benefit. Ratzinger then asks, rhetorically, what life would be like "When *we* live like the thief and the robber, taking everything for *ourselves* alone?"[29] Ratzinger positions himself and his present readers so as to identify themselves with the individuals in the Gospel narrative and to interpret their own situations in its light. This kind of *mimetic* exegesis (interpretation having the exhortative purpose of *imitation*) is highly evocative of the patristic characterization of Scripture as a mirror (*speculum*) in which readers see their own situations reflected in and interpreted by the biblical text—an interpretive technique which I shall discuss in greater detail below.[30]

27 See Augustine, *Tractates on the Gospel according to John*, 46.5–8 (Patrologia Latina 35: 1728–1730). See also Gregory the Great, *Homily* 15; Walafridus Strabo, *Glossa Ordinaria* (Patrologia Latina 114: 396–398); Thomas Aquinas, *Commentary on John*, §1398–1408.

28 Compare Augustine, *Tractates on the Gospel according to John*, 46.5.

29 Ratzinger, *Jesus of Nazareth*, 1.278 (my emphasis).

30 For example, see Athanasius, "A Letter to Marcellinus," in *Athanasius: The Life of Antony and the Letter to Marcellinus*, trans. Robert C. Gregg, Classics of Western Spirituality (Mahwah:

Ratzinger links the abundant life with the "pasture" (10:9), which he in turn associates with the pasture in Ezekiel 34:14, "With good pasture I will tend them, and on the mountainous heights of Israel—there will be their grazing area." Commenting on this text, Ratzinger cites the Augustinian interpretation of the good pasture and mountains in Ezekiel 34 as God's Word.[31] This interpretation, Ratzinger states, "is not the historical sense of the text, [but] in the end the Fathers saw correctly and, above all, they understood Jesus himself correctly."[32] Once again, Ratzinger values the theological substance of the patristic interpretation, while acknowledging that it does not correspond to the historical sense of Ezekiel. The theological point that Ratzinger draws from the patristic interpretation is that in feeding on the good pasture of God's Word, "Man lives on truth and on being loved: on being loved by the truth."[33] The basic sustenance for human beings is the truth and love which is God Himself. In leading His sheep to pasture and giving them abundant life, Christ gives nothing less than Himself as divine truth and love.

The second element which Ratzinger treats (albeit briefly) in connection with Jesus as the Good Shepherd is the Shepherd laying down His life for the sheep. Ratzinger discusses this motif as constituting the exact opposite of the thief's selfish and exploitative behavior. The Shepherd's laying down of His life for the sheep is central to both the Shepherd's own identity and the discourse proper. Ratzinger claims that the characterization of the Shepherd's death as a free laying down of His life offers a new perspective on the cross. By speaking of His death in this way, Jesus reveals the cross as the radical, free gift of Jesus' own life for the good of the sheep.

The third element concerns the Shepherd's knowing. For Ratzinger, this knowing involves two connected aspects. First, the Shepherd's knowing the sheep is related to their being His sheep: "I know mine and mine know Me" (10:14). In keeping with the selfless attitudes of the Shepherd(s) toward the sheep, Ratzinger defines the relationship between Shepherd and sheep as one of personal commitment, not the ownership of property. The thief and the robber view the sheep as things to be used for their personal gain. Ratzinger again brings the biblical text to bear on contemporary socio-political situations by identifying the thief and the

---

Paulist, 1980), §12 (p. 111); Augustine, *Enarrationes in Psalmos* 119.6; Idem, *Sermon* 49.5. For secondary discussion, see John J. O'Keefe and R. R. Reno, *Sanctified Vision: An Introduction to Early Christian Interpretation of the Bible* (Baltimore: Johns Hopkins, 2005), 82–84; Sister Ritamary Bradley, C.H.M., "Backgrounds of the Title *Speculum* in Mediaeval Literature," *Speculum* 29 (1954): 100–115.

31 See Augustine, *Sermon* 46.24: "Gather yourselves to the mountains of holy scripture. There you will find your heart's desire ... they are the richest pastures." Citation from Saint Augustine, "Sermon 46" in *Sermons II (20–50): On the Old Testament*, ed. John E. Rotelle, O.S.A., trans. Edmund Hill, O.P., Works of St. Augustine 3.2 (Hyde Park: New City Press, 1990), 263–297, at 279. Ratzinger does not explicitly label this patristic reading as Augustinian.

32 Ratzinger, *Jesus of Nazareth*, 1.279.

33 Ratzinger, *Jesus of Nazareth*, 1.279.

robber as "the ideologues and the dictators [for whom] … human beings are merely a thing that they possess."[34]

The second aspect of the Shepherd's knowing is the relationship between His knowing the sheep and the mutual knowing between the Father and the Son: "I know mine and mine know me just as the Father knows Me and I know the Father" (10:14–15). With this statement, Ratzinger connects the Trinity and ecclesiology via the category of communion. He writes, "The knowing that links Jesus with 'his own' exists within the space opened up by his 'knowing' oneness with the Father."[35] The Shepherd knows His sheep and wants them to find genuine freedom, rooted in the truth (that is, "the pasture"). The fullness of this freedom and truth are only available in communion with the Triune God into which Jesus leads His sheep. Ratzinger presents this vision of truth and freedom, which are rooted in God, in opposition to modern materialism. He writes, "Any 'self-knowledge' that restricts man to the empirical and the tangible fails to engage with man's true depth."[36] Ratzinger again allows the Gospel to speak to present situations by interpreting them within the terms and horizon of the Gospel narrative.

The fourth thematic element of the discourse which Ratzinger treats is unity. He first turns to Ezekiel 37:15–17. Reading this text together with Ezekiel 34, Ratzinger accents God's action as Shepherd to gather together His scattered people, that is, the restoration of Israel. The ingathering of God's people provides the biblical context for the unity motif in John 10. As with the canonical shepherd image, Ratzinger sees Jesus embracing this component of biblical eschatology while also expanding it.[37] While Ezekiel 34–37 focuses specifically on the ingathering of Israel, Jesus extends the ingathering motif to include all of humanity. Ratzinger justifies this claim by linking Jesus' remark about His "sheep, who are not of this fold" (10:16) with the narrator's remark in 11:52: Jesus would die "not only on behalf of the nation, but so that He may gather together into one God's scattered children." Jesus' extension of the ingathering component does not negate Ezekiel's claims, but rather presupposes and expands on them.[38] Theologically, Ratzinger grounds the relationship of unity and universalism in Christ's identity as the Logos (Word). Christ is able to gather all people into one because as the Logos, all people (and indeed all creation) were made through Him (1:3). Ratzinger writes,

34 Ratzinger, *Jesus of Nazareth*, 1.281.

35 Ratzinger, *Jesus of Nazareth*, 1.282.

36 Ratzinger, *Jesus of Nazareth*, 1.282.

37 Ratzinger (*Jesus of Nazareth*, 1.284) writes, Jesus "takes up this vision, while very decidedly enlarging the scope of the promise."

38 In his discussion of Jesus as interpreter of Scripture, Ratzinger (*Jesus of Nazareth*, 1.116–122) argues that the universalism of the Gospel builds upon the prophetic trajectory which envisions God's salvation extended to the Gentiles through Israel as a "light to the nations" (compare Isa. 49:6).

"however scattered they may be, yet as coming from him and bound toward him they are one."[39]

Having connected the Shepherd's gathering activity with Christ's identity as the Logos, Ratzinger closes his interpretation of John 10:1–18 by referring this equation to his readers' personal relationships with Christ. Citing Clement of Alexandria (*Paedagogus* [*The Pedagogue*] 3.12.101), Ratzinger states that early Christians occasionally used the biblical shepherd imagery for interpreting their life in the world. Texts such as Psalm 23 and the Parable of the Lost Sheep (Matthew 18:12–14; Luke 15:4–7) depict the shepherd bearing his sheep through difficult situations to safety. Ratzinger then puts himself and his readers in the place of the sheep, whom the shepherd carries upon his shoulders in the Gospel parable (see Luke 15:5). He writes: Christ, as the Shepherd and Logos, "brings home the stray sheep, humanity; he brings *me* home, too. ... Carried on his shoulders, *we* come home."[40] In this way, Ratzinger, who at the time of publication serves as the successor to Peter, places himself among Christ's sheep.

III. Ratzinger's Appropriation of Patristic Biblical Hermeneutics

A Synthesis of Modern and Premodern Interpretation

Ratzinger's appropriation of *patristic* biblical interpretation is neither wholesale nor straightforward because it is conditioned by his commitments to modern historical criticism. Like Henri de Lubac, Ratzinger does not advocate a nostalgic retreat to the Fathers as a mythical golden age of exegesis.[41] Not only is this a practical impossibility but Ratzinger also genuinely values the contributions of modern biblical exegesis. At the same time, Ratzinger maintains that contemporary theological interpretation has much to gain by drawing on patristic exegesis. A statement from his famous 1988 Erasmus Lecture articulates his attitude well: Christian exegesis "cannot withdraw to the Middle Ages or the Fathers and use them as a shield against the spirit of modernity. That said, it also cannot take the opposite tack of dispensing with the insights of the great believers of all ages and of acting as if the history of thought begins in earnest only with Kant."[42] The kind of

39 Ratzinger, *Jesus of Nazareth*, 1.284.

40 Ratzinger, *Jesus of Nazareth*, 1.286 (my emphasis).

41 Ratzinger (*Principles of Catholic Theology*, 145) explicitly rejects any return to the Fathers that is based on nostalgia or a myth of origins: "We have drawn a fundamental distinction here between the mythical concept of tradition and the Christian concept of patrology. ... The Fathers, we must now say, are not marked out simply because they belong to "antiquity"; the fact that they stand near *in time* to the origin of the New Testament does not necessarily prove that they are *inwardly* close to it. But that inner closeness is what matters." See also de Lubac, *Medieval Exegesis*, 1.xix–xxi.

42 Ratzinger, "On the Foundations and the Itinerary of Exegesis Today," 19.

theological interpretation proposed by Ratzinger must genuinely be a synthesis of the wisdom found in both patristic and modern exegesis.[43]

As has been shown, Ratzinger often formally distinguishes the theological claims of patristic *interpretations* (which he values) from their interpretive *methods* (which he often criticizes or dismisses). He often focuses on the theological substance of patristic interpretations and uses them to develop his own theological interpretations. Thus, he develops the Augustinian association of "the pasture" in Ezekiel 34:13–14 with God's Word to articulate the human desire for the truth and freedom which is satisfied only in Trinitarian communion through Christ. At one level, Ratzinger values patristic exegesis as a kind of extended "chronicle of research": a collection of theologically and exegetically interesting observations, which he consults and develops in his own interpretation.

Even though Ratzinger is often cool towards patristic interpretive *methods*, I propose that he actually appropriates in a creative way a key patristic interpretive strategy: regarding Scripture as a *mirror* for the readers' situations. A succinct formulation of this patristic interpretive strategy is given by Athanasius in his *Letter to Marcellinus*:

> These words [of the Psalms] become like a mirror to the person singing them, so that he might perceive himself and the emotions of his soul. ... For in fact, he who hears the one reading receives the song that is recited as being about him, and either, when he is convicted by his conscience, ... he will repent, or hearing of the hope that resides in God, and of the succor available to believers—how this kind of grace exists for him—he exults and begins to give thanks to God.[44]

Athanasius invites the Christian audience to hear the Psalms speaking personally to their present lives and situations. So contemporized and personalized, the biblical text speaks to the faithful reader, encourages him or her to repent, grow in holiness, and offer praise to God. Similarly, I have noted several instances in which Ratzinger uses the shepherd discourse to interpret realities in his readers' present. He employs the "thief and robber" to interpret both peoples' self-interested greed and also those political despots who exploit their own people. He contrasts the "pasture" of divine truth and freedom with the false vision provided by modern materialism. He also identifies all Christians, himself included, as "the lost sheep," whom Christ carries home.[45] Like Athanasius, Ratzinger invites his readers to interpret their lives and present situations in the world in light of the Gospel nar-

43 See William M. Wright IV, "A 'New Synthesis': Joseph Ratzinger's *Jesus of Nazareth*," *Nova et Vetera*, English Edition 7 (2009): 35–66, especially pp. 35–51.

44 Athanasius, *Letter to Marcellinus*, §12 (p. 111).

45 See Ratzinger, *Jesus of Nazareth*, 1.278, 281, 282, 286 respectively.

rative. He reads the discourse in a more-than-literal way to configure the readers' present situations in light of the biblical text.[46] Scripture thus provides the master horizon in which the readers are to interpret and understand themselves and their situations. By providing the interpretive framework for all reality, the biblical text (to use George Lindbeck's expression), "absorbs the world."[47]

Retrieving a Patristic Theological Style

More significant is Ratzinger's vision for the whole program of theological interpretation. As others have observed, Ratzinger's basic approach to Scripture and theology in *Jesus of Nazareth* resembles the kinds of theological thinking characteristic of early Christians.[48] Ratzinger not only uses patristic exegesis as a collection of interpretive possibilities from the Christian past, but he also embraces it as a template for the very practice of theology. This may be the most compelling aspect of Ratzinger's retrieval of patristic hermeneutics for the theological interpretation of Scripture. I will focus on four specific ways in which Ratzinger's approach to biblical interpretation incorporate principles of patristic biblical hermeneutics.

First, Ratzinger's theological presentation in *Jesus of Nazareth* is identical with his biblical exegesis. Rather than subjective experience or theory, Scripture provides the starting point and the substance for Ratzinger's theological thinking. Theology and exegesis are so integrated in *Jesus of Nazareth* that it is exceedingly difficult, if not impossible, to make any real distinction between them. This indistinguishablility of theology and exegesis characterizes much premodern Christian biblical interpretation. As de Lubac writes, for premodern exegetes "theological science and the explication of Scripture cannot but be one and the same thing."[49]

Second, Ratzinger reads the Gospels in light of the whole canon of Scripture with Christ as the principle of its unity. He places Christ within the horizon of the Old Testament, but his Christian reading of the Old Testament departs in some ways from the classical Christian hermeneutic. Much of this can be attributed to the new context of biblical interpretation created by modern historical exegesis. Ratzinger first situates the canonical compositions in their historical contexts of origin and then discerns a theological dynamic developing across the canon. He

---

46 See Lewis Ayres, "On the Practice and Teaching of Christian Doctrine," *Gregorianum* 80 (1999): 33–94, especially 53–59, 71; Wright, "Hearing the Shepherd's Voice." [Forthcoming]

47 George A. Lindbeck, *The Nature of Doctrine: Religion and Theology in a Postliberal Age* (Philadelphia: Westminster Press, 1984), 118. See also Bruce D. Marshall, "Absorbing the World: Christianity and the Universe of Truths" in *Theology and Dialogue: Essays in Conversation with George Lindbeck*, ed. Bruce D. Marshall (Notre Dame: University of Notre Dame Press, 1990), 69–102. This resemblance to Lindbeck is also noted by Anthony C. Sciglitano, Jr., "Pope Benedict XVI's *Jesus of Nazareth*: Agape and Logos," *Pro Ecclesia* 17 (2008): 181.

48 See Roch Kereszty, "The Challenge of *Jesus of Nazareth* for Theologians," *Communio* 34 (2007): 456–458, 473; Sciglitano, "Pope Benedict XVI's *Jesus of Nazareth*: Agape and Logos," 177.

49 De Lubac, *Medieval Exegesis*, 1.27.

then situates Christ within this unfolding dynamic, which He brings to its fullness. In this way, Ratzinger maintains that the Old Testament books both have a historical and abiding theological sense in their own right, and, within the context of the Christian canon, they also have other, more-than-literal meanings which are not apparent apart from faith in Christ.[50] For Ratzinger, a more-than-literal reading of Scripture expands or develops something present in the text. These more-than-literal meanings may go beyond the original sense of the text, but they maintain some degree of congruence and correspondence to it. In this way, the literal, historical meaning functions as a point of departure and control for more-than-literal meanings. Ratzinger relates the Old Testament and Jesus on the basis of textual meanings, language, and cross-compositional theological ideas.

Like much modern biblical criticism, Ratzinger tends to identify the literal sense with a text's claim understood within its original historical circumstances. By parsing the literal and spiritual senses in terms of words and texts, Ratzinger differs somewhat from the classic Christian hermeneutic, which (at least according to de Lubac) associates the spiritual sense with *the things* or *realities* presented by the text rather than the language of the text itself.[51]

Consider, for example, the formulation of the fourfold sense given by Thomas Aquinas in *Summa Theologiae* pt. 1, q. 1, a. 10. Aquinas defines as proper to the literal sense of Scripture "that first signification whereby words signify things."[52] It

50 Compare Ratzinger's reading of the Old Testament in light of Christ with the 2001 PBC text *Jewish People and Their Sacred Scriptures in the Christian Bible* §21: "for Christians, all the Old Testament economy is in movement towards Christ; if then the Old Testament is read in the light of Christ, one can, retrospectively, perceive something of this movement. But since it is a movement, a slow and difficult progression throughout the course of history, each event and each text is situated at a particular point along the way. … Although the Christian reader is aware that the internal dynamism of the Old Testament finds its goal in Jesus, this is a retrospective perception whose point of departure is not in the text as such, but in the events of the New Testament proclaimed by the apostolic preaching." Cited from http://www.vatican.va/roman_curia/congregations/cfaith/pcb_documents/rc_con_cfaith_doc_20020212_popolo-ebraico_en.html #4.%20Return%20to%20the%20Literal%20Sense. Accessed June 14, 2011.

51 For De Lubac, the spiritual sense (or Christian allegory) is the spiritual participation of historical realities, presented by Scripture, in the mystery of Christ. He distinguishes Christian allegory from Hellenistic allegory on the grounds that the former deals with the spiritual participation of real things in Christ, whereas the latter abandons history for abstract speculation. He states that Christian allegory "is not in the service of some naturalist thought or philosophical abstraction. It goes from history to history—although not to history alone or only to the exterior elements of history. It relates the unique facts with another unique fact, divine interventions that have already taken place with another kind of divine intervention, equally real and incomparably more profound. … It is, we repeat, the fact of Christ, both unique and universal. It is the Christian mystery in all its dimensions" in Henri de Lubac, "Hellenistic Allegory and Christian Allegory," in *Theological Fragments*, trans. Rebecca Howell Balinski (San Francisco: Ignatius, 1989), 165–196, at 195. See also de Lubac, *Medieval Exegesis*, 2.1–19. A recent attempt to articulate this "participatory dimension of historical realities" in divine providence in Thomistic terms is Matthew Levering, *Participatory Biblical Exegesis: A Theology of Biblical Interpretation* (Notre Dame: University of Notre Dame Press, 2008).

52 Thomas Aquinas, *Summa Theologiae*, pt. 1, q. 1, a. 10. Quotations from Aquinas' *Summa*

is the simple sense of the words which signify things or realities—or as Aquinas puts it in *De potentia Dei* [*On the Power of God*] 4.1 "the ways the words go."[53] For Aquinas, the spiritual senses do not pertain to the biblical words or texts as such, but the realities, which the words present, as they signify the Mystery of Christ: "That signification whereby things signified by words have themselves also a signification is called the spiritual sense, which is based on the literal, and presupposes it."[54] Through this Augustinian distinction of words and things, Aquinas discerns the relationships between the Old Testament and Jesus as existing properly between *things* or *realities*, not words or textual meanings. Hence, de Lubac writes:

> To discover this allegory [i.e. the spiritual senses], one will not find it properly speaking in the text, but in the realities of which the text speaks; ... the text acts only as spokesman to lead to the historical realities; the latter are themselves the figures, they themselves contain the mysteries that the exercise of allegory is supposed to extract.[55]

Or, as Francis Martin succinctly puts it, "the spiritual sense of Scripture is based, not on a theory of text, but on a theology of history."[56]

These differences between Ratzinger and Aquinas highlight the well-known complexities that attend defining "the literal sense" and parsing its relationship with the more-than-literal senses of Scripture. The models of Ratzinger and Aquinas are not irreconcilable, but they do diverge in their locating of the more-than-literal senses of Scripture, whether entirely in the text's surplus of meaning or in the concrete historical realities of the divine economy as given in Scripture. These divergences underscore that any retrieval of patristic exegesis must reckon with the various definitions of "literal sense" in Christian history, what exegetical techniques are appropriate for apprehending it, and its role in relating the Testaments.[57]

Theologiae are taken from St. Thomas Aquinas, *Summa Theologica*, trans. Fathers of the English Dominican Province, 3 vols. (New York: Benziger Brothers, Inc., 1947–1948).

53 The phrase in quotation marks is Bruce Marshall's translation of Thomas Aquinas' characterization of the literal sense as *salva circumstantia litterae* in *De potentia Dei* 4.1, cited in Marshall, "Absorbing the World," 93. See also Eugene F. Rogers, Jr., "How the Virtues of an Interpreter Presuppose and Perfect Hermeneutics: The Case of Thomas Aquinas," *Journal of Religion* 76 (1996): 64–81, especially p. 74; Mark F. Johnson, "Another Look at the Plurality of the Literal Sense," in *Medieval Philosophy & Theology* 2 (1992): 117–141, especially pp. 126–136.

54 Aquinas, *Summa Theologiae*, pt. I., q. 1, a. 10.

55 De Lubac, *Medieval Exegesis*, 2.86.

56 Francis Martin, "Election, Covenant, and Law," *Nova et Vetera*, English Edition 4 (2006): 867.

57 For a survey of the different ways in which "literal sense" has been defined in Christian history, see Brevard S. Childs, "The Sensus Literalis of Scripture: An Ancient and Modern Problem," in *Beiträge zur Alttestamentlichen Theologie: Festschrift für Walther Zimmerli zum 70. Geburtstag* [*Contributions to Old Testament Theology: Festschrift for Walther Zimmerli for His 70th Birthday*],

Third, Ratzinger not only reads Scripture theologically, but he also operates with an implied theology of Scripture. That is, he understands the nature and function of Scripture within a larger doctrinal framework.[58] Ratzinger does not write extensively about this in *Jesus of Nazareth*, but he does make some suggestive comments in the Foreword to volume 1 when discussing the relationship between Scripture and the Church. He understands Scripture as embedded within the larger context of God's relationship with His people: "The Scripture emerged from within the heart of a living subject—the pilgrim people of God—and lives within this same subject."[59] The people of God exist in close relationship with Scripture because the Scripture came to be within it and the historically-continuous faith community continues to hear God's voice sounding through the Scriptures. For Scripture to be read as God's Word, it must be read within the context of the believing community—a community which is constituted by its relationship with God. As Lewis Ayres has observed, "the very notion of 'canonical' Scriptures implies the existence of the community that sees those scriptures as the focus for their attempt to articulate an account of God, of God's actions, and of the most appropriate shape of Christian life in response to those actions."[60] In other words, according to Ayres, the existence of a biblical canon necessarily presupposes a community for whom that canon is normative. Since he reads Scripture in terms of its relationship with the Church, Ratzinger brings what he knows and practices by faith to bear on his biblical interpretation. Hence, he justifies the importance of historical biblical study to Christian exegesis by making a theological appeal to the historical reality of the Incarnation. For Ratzinger, theology provides and secures the space for historical research in Christian exegesis.[61]

Finally, Ratzinger's theological interpretation ultimately aims at the spiritual transformation of Christians. Ratzinger makes clear from the beginning that his goal in writing this book is to help readers come to know and love Christ more. While he presents his work in contrast to certain historical Jesus studies that have obstructed or impeded the possibility of knowing Him personally through the Gospels, Ratzinger does not present his work as an exercise in modern critical

---

eds. Herbert Donner, Robert Hanhard, and Rudolf Smend (Göttingen: Vandenhoeck & Ruprecht, 1977), 80–93.

58 My thinking here is indebted to Ayres, "On the Practice and Teaching of Christian Doctrine," 50–74.

59 Ratzinger, *Jesus of Nazareth*, 1.xx-xxi, quotation from 1.xx. In a 1965 essay, Ratzinger discusses the relationship between Scripture and Tradition, understood as the Church's interpretation of Scripture in light of Christ's abiding presence in the Church. See Joseph Ratzinger, "Revelation and Tradition," in Karl Rahner and Joseph Ratzinger, *Revelation and Tradition*, trans. W. J. O'Hara, Quaestiones Disputatae 17 (New York: Herder and Herder, 1966), 26–49.

60 Ayres, "Practice and Teaching of Christian Doctrine," 50.

61 Compare Pope Benedict XVI, *Deus Caritas Est* §28–29. Benedict makes a similar argument to secure the autonomy of reason and temporal space by placing them within the Christian account of the world.

exegesis.[62] Rather, Ratzinger offers his interpretation of the Gospels as an aid by means of which his readers may come to know Christ and grow in their relationships with him. He writes, "it struck me as the most urgent priority to present the figure and message of Jesus in his public ministry, and so to help foster the growth of a living relationship with him."[63]

This concern—that biblical interpretation should ultimately serve a transformative end—places Ratzinger squarely in line with the main goals of patristic exegesis. His appropriation of mimetic exegesis, in which the audience is invited to interpret their lives and situations in terms of the biblical text, illustrates this well. By bringing the Scriptures to bear on the readers' present situations and interpreting them accordingly, Ratzinger enables the Scriptures to speak to the present. Ratzinger uses this patristic exegetical strategy in part to overcome the historical-critical method's inability to let the Scripture speak with present and personal relevance.

IV. Conclusion

Reinhard Hütter has characterized the effort to integrate modern historical criticism with traditional Christian exegesis as a "quandary" which corresponds to an unresolved tension in recent Catholic pronouncements about the interpretation of Scripture.[64] When viewed in light of post-conciliar Catholic biblical exegesis, Ratzinger's *Jesus of Nazareth* appears as one of the most substantive efforts to work out that tension in practice. The individual claims and interpretations in *Jesus of Nazareth* can and will be debated (as Ratzinger himself invites). But in a larger sense, *Jesus of Nazareth* offers a model for the theological interpretation of the Gospels, which combines both "the new and the old" (Matt. 13:52), in service of the readers' spiritual transformation by Christ. Ratzinger's retrieval of patristic biblical hermeneutics allows God's Word to sound in the Church and the world today, a task most appropriate to the man who serves as chief shepherd of Christ's sheep.

---

62 Ratzinger (*Jesus of Nazareth*, 1.xxiii) explicitly makes this claim: "my intention in writing this book is not to counter modern exegesis."

63 Ratzinger, *Jesus of Nazareth*, 1.xxiv.

64 Reinhard Hütter, "A Symposium on 'The Jewish People and Their Sacred Scriptures in the Christian Bible' from the Pontifical Biblical Commission, 2001," *Pro Ecclesia* 13 (2004): 19–21. Both Hütter and Ratzinger cite *Dei Verbum* §12 as exhibiting an uneasy association of both modern and traditional modes of exegesis. See Hütter, "Symposium," especially 21, n.18; Ratzinger, *Principles of Catholic Theology*, 134–137.

Letter & Spirit 7 (2011): 209-220

Vicarious Representation[1]

~: **Joseph Ratzinger / Pope Benedict XVI** :~

Jared Wicks, S.J., translator

Introduction

What follows is the translation of an essay by Joseph Ratzinger which appeared in a collaborative manual of basic theological concepts.[2] The text was written during the years 1959–63, when J. Ratzinger was professor of Fundamental Theology in the Catholic Theology Faculty of the University of Bonn. Among the motives for a translation at this late date are (1) the exemplary character of the text as a Christology worked out from biblical sources, (2) the presentation here of central convictions about Christ and the Church which Pope Benedict XVI has held throughout his theological career, but which several recent English-language accounts of the Pope's theology have not mentioned, and (3) the foundational role played by this Christology in the two volumes of *Jesus of Nazareth*, in which the Pope speaks often of Jesus' representative role as his "pro-existence" and repeatedly takes the Servant of Deutero-Isaiah as the key to Jesus' understanding of his mission.[3]

Text

Vicarious representation is a fundamental category of biblical revelation, which however, most likely because it lacks a corresponding philosophical model, plays only a meager role in theology. The concept has instead been largely relegated to the literature of edification and spirituality.

In the history of religions, vicarious representation occurs most frequently in magical actions on a substitute reality, in which one sees what is most basic to magical performance. What is done to the substitute reality is expected to happen, for good or ill, to the person or thing represented. In the ancient Near Eastern

---

1 The translation is published with permission of the Liberia Editrice Vaticana, which holds the copyright to all works of Joseph Ratzinger / Pope Benedict XVI. The translation omits several cross-references made in the original text to other entries in *Handbuch theologischer Grundbegriffe*.

2 "Stellvertretung," *Handbuch theologischer Grundbegriffe*, ed. Heinrich Fries, 2 vols. (Munich: Kösel Verlag, 1962–63), 2:566–575.

3 *Jesus of Nazareth: From the Baptism in the Jordan to the Transfiguration* (New York: Doubleday: 2007; reprint with an Index, San Francisco: Ignatius, 2008), 18, 21, 331–332 ("pro-existence"); *Jesus of Nazareth, Holy Week: From the Entrance into Jerusalem to the Resurrection* (San Francisco: Ignatius, 2011), 16–17, 100–101, 120, 131, 133, 134 ("pro-existence"), 136, 172–173, and 174 ("pro-existence").

cultures surrounding the Bible, this elementary phenomenon of the history of religions found its most significant expression in the so-called *šar-pûh i* (substitute king) and *salam-pûh i* (substitute image) texts, whether from the Hittites of the 14th or 13th centuries BC, the Babylonians, or especially the Assyrian texts from the era of Asarhaddon (681–669 BC). In a magical rite, a substitute representative or a substitute image was exposed to the angry gods in place of the real king or another person who was the object of their anger. It could happen that the substitute, in magical identity with the one threatened, would even suffer a vicariously representative death, which was supposed to ward off the havoc threatening the real king.[4]

I. Biblical Accounts of Vicarious Representation

1. When the notion of vicarious representation makes its first appearance in the Bible, it has already left all traces of magical thinking far behind. What was proper to the magical rite performed on a substitute was that a human being would, for his own benefit, designate something or someone as his representative, so that the havoc meant for him would come over the substitute. But the ancient narrative given by the Jahwist in Genesis 18:20ff portrays the exact opposite. As Abraham bargains with Jahweh over the fate of Sodom, he ultimately offers himself and his own friendship with God, in order to snatch the threatened city away from the havoc toward which it is reeling. This righteous man senses his own solidarity with sinners and seeks to have his own dignity replace what they lack and thus represent them before God. More of a substitutionary performance appears in the rite of the scapegoat on which the sins of the people are laid.[5] But this remains ultimately a symbolic performance which impresses on the people the urgency of their own conversion, while it manifests the gracious mercy of Jahweh from whom alone one hopes for forgiveness and salvation. Clearly, Israelite piety was even in its cultic expressions thoroughly personalistic, and this most likely caused the maturing and ongoing purification of the concept of vicarious representation as free and personal, as in Genesis 18:20ff, and not as magical and objectified.

Portrayals of the king's role as representative of his people and so as cultic dispenser of blessing,[6] as well as intercessor,[7] all remain for the most part within contexts common to ancient Near Eastern thinking. But the idea of vicarious representation reaches its highpoint in the image of Moses in Deuteronomy and in the Songs of the Lord's Servant in Deutero-Isaiah.

4 See Josef Scharbert, "Stellvertretendes Sühneleiden in den Ebed-Jahwe-Liedern und in altorientalischen Ritualtexten" [Vicarious Sufferings of Atonement in the Songs of the Lord's Servant and in Ancient Near Eastern Ritual Texts], *Biblische Zeitschrift* 2 (1958): 190–213, at 204–210.

5 Lev. 16:22; see also Ezek. 4:4.

6 2 Sam. 6:18; 1 Kings 8:14, 55f; 1 Chron. 16:2; 2 Chron. 6:3.

7 1 Kings 8:22–53; 2 Kings 19:15–19; 2 Chron. 6:12–42, 30:18f.

While Jeremiah accepts his suffering as a mysterious undoing which he cannot explain, other prophetic figures appear who stand in the breach for their people,[8] or offer themselves to be representatively erased from the book of life,[9] and who in fact bear the fated disaster meant for their people. Thus, Moses dies outside the promised land as the one struck vicariously by God's wrath and made an outcast.[10] He anticipates in this the fate of the Servant of God of Second Isaiah, who in the same way dies the death of the guilty and outcast and for this receives "the many," that is, humankind itself, as his portion.[11] The same line of thought turns up again in "the one they have pierced" in Zechariah 12:10ff, whose fated death opens the way to the people's salvation.

The lament over the one pierced bears clear traces of the contemporary Tammuz-liturgies,[12] which may have also marked Isaiah 53, in ways possibly related to the Babylonian New Year's ritual.[13] But the biblical notion of vicarious suffering differs radically from pagan rites of suffering. Tammuz is said to be like a wilted rice plant, without splendor or form as he descends to the underworld, as wounded and a man of tears, as beaten and degraded, like a sacrificial lamb led to slaughter, like a chained criminal whose lot is with murders, who though will rise like a heroic victor. All this is like the ritual passion undergone by the Babylonian king in the night of the new year, that is, a thoroughly naturalistic parable. Tammuz represents the death and rising of nature and the Tammuz liturgy is a substitutionary performance of the type sketched above. Its focus is the desired renewal in the real world of vegetation, which is anticipated in the cultic realm of substitution in order to influence the course of nature for the good. Similarly the king is symbolically degraded and exalted at the turn from one year to the next, in a kind of new creation of time with assurance of weal in both nature and political life in the year then beginning.

In the biblical application of terms from such liturgies to the suffering prophet, the vocabulary comes to have a completely new personalized meaning. The issue is not the death and rising of vegetation and no longer a magical consolidation of the political regime. At the center a human being really suffers and loves, in a service of vicarious representation from which salvation comes to the whole community. The true liturgy of suffering is not a ritual lamentation over Tammuz, but it consists in the patient endurance of the prophet, by which one hopes that the world will be renewed and permeated by the force of real life.

---

8 Compare Ps. 106:23; Ezek. 13:5.

9 This appears already in Exod. 32:32.

10 Deut. 3:23–28, 4:21f.

11 Isa. 53:8–12.

12 Zech. 12:11. Compare Ezek. 8:14. [Tammuz was a Mesopotamian deity, associated with vegetation, who was ritually lamented as dying at the summer solstice. (Translator's note).]

13 See Scharbert, "Stellvertretendes Sühneleiden," 196–204.

The biblical account also shows that the conferral of salvation on "the many" does not follow magically and automatically. Instead, those who are saved must be converted and give their interior compliance, as do the "we" in the dramatic structure of Isaiah 53. They change from despising the Servant and so open themselves to salvation coming from him. In this respect the vicarious representation of Isaiah 53 coheres closely with the Old Testament conception of community, to which Joseph Scharbert applies the term "solidarity." For a person neither stands individually only for himself, nor is one, for good or ill, absorbed into the collective. Everyone meets his or her fate amid an oscillation between one's own action and one's receiving from the community.

The notion of the service of vicarious suffering lived on in the post-exilic era and clearly entered repeatedly the concrete existence of devout individuals. Texts such as Daniel 3:40 and Second Maccabees 7:38 give evidence of a new and profound theology of martyrdom. The first text depicts the suffering that the world lays on the faithful, as they remain constant in the furnace of temptation and become an atoning burnt-offering. This is the holy worship that the exiled people of God set against idol-worship. In the second case the devout give witness by shedding their blood to the hope that by their suffering God's wrath will cease. The bold power of these grand visions of suffering Israel served to interpret what happened to the three young men in the furnace of blazing fire and to the seven brothers martyred for God's Law. Thus devout believers of post-exilic Israel continued to find in their painful distress amid righteous living a profound meaning inspired by the figure of the Servant of the Lord.

Through all this Second Isaiah's sketch of the Servant remains the culmination of Old Testament thinking. It breaks open Israel's nationalistic narrowness and at the same time lets God's Servant become a light to the nations. From the Servant salvation reaches to the end of the world.[14] The texts that formulate these ideas make a close connection between the figure of the Servant and the mission of all Israel. Consequently Israel has to recognize in the Servant's fate an account of its own mission and thereby experience the mystery of vicarious representation as the true center of its historical existence. As a people cast out, crushed, and despised, Israel gives witness to the one and only God and precisely in the national catastrophe of exile it becomes increasingly the light of the nations bearing God's message to the ends of the earth. Here is an indication that God's election of Israel is at the same time a vocation to the service of suffering and that this election is for the benefit of the others.

2. These themes reach their proper fulfillment in the figure of the New Testament Servant of the Lord, which Jesus Christ clearly and from the beginning understood himself to be. From him New Testament theology is first and foremost a theology of vicarious representation. It seems commonly accepted today

---

14 Isa. 49:6, 51:5, 45:22.

that the earliest christology, that of the Jerusalem community, was a christology of the Servant. The evangelists place the whole life of Jesus symbolically under the same conception, when they relate the word about the Spirit at Jesus' baptism and also cite the introduction to the Songs of the Servant of the Lord, "You are my Son, my Beloved; with you I am well pleased."[15] This is first an interpretation of Jesus' baptism, but also a mirror casting light on the meaning of our Lord's whole existence. The others go under John's baptism to do penance for their sins, but Jesus is sinless and so his baptism has another meaning. He does not receive it for himself, but for the others. He enters the destiny awaiting them and acts out symbolically what will be from then on the content of his whole existence, namely, sharing the destiny of sinners and standing in their place. With his baptism, Jesus takes on the mission of the Servant and from then on his whole life is existence for others, which reaches its completion in the baptism of his death,[16] which fulfills his sharing in the fate of human beings destined to suffer death.

At the end Jesus takes up in a word of his own what the Spirit proclaimed when his mission began. At the Last Supper, he interprets his whole earthly life through the Isaian theme of service "for the many" and takes as his life's meaning the conception of an exchange of destinies.[17] Since this eucharistic meal will become the integrating center of the Christian community and give Christian living its fundamental qualification, both of these have as a consequence their deepest meaning in the mystery of vicarious representation. Christians live first of all and totally from the Lord's service of representation and at the same time they receive it as the basic law of their own being.

The New Testament theology of vicarious representation reaches its highpoint in the Pauline and Johannine writings. In Romans 9–11 Paul works out the expansion by which the idea of representation comes to offer a comprehensive view of history. Earlier, post-exilic theology had to make sense of the suffering of God's elect people, but now Paul faces the task of explaining Israel's rejection, its unbelief, and thus its apparent exclusion from the line of prophetic fulfillment. Was all this a final breakdown of God's thousand-year history of dealing with human beings? To be sure, the prophecy of the Servant of the Lord had reached fulfillment and the light of the Lord had gone out to the nations, but in that very instant Israel appeared to be thrown on the trash heap of both world history and salvation history.

But Paul worked out a further deepening of the notion of election on the basis of vicarious representation. Israel's failure became the occasion for bringing the message of Christ to the gentile pagans. Israel opened a place into which the nations of the world could come streaming in. Israel's downfall made salvation available for the pagans, leading to an exchange of places in the world-historical

15 Mark 1:11 par.; compare Matt. 12:18; Ps. 2:7; and Isa. 42:1.

16 Mark 10:38; Luke 12:50.

17 Mark 14:23 par.; compare Mark 10:45.

roles apportioned to humans. From being far from God, the pagans come into the space of election from which the old people of God had exited. But for Paul this is not the end of the drama of world history. He asks, "If their (= the Jews') rejection brings the reconciliation of the world, what then will their acceptance bring but the resurrection of the dead?"[18] In this audacious sketch of history, the different groups do not live only for themselves but are instead ordered to each other in mutual service. Each lives for the other and from the other. With this, Paul sees the whole past history of Israel in a new light and reinterprets it with reference to its definitive meaning.

One can ascertain peculiar relations between pairs of brothers in Old Testament narratives of election. Isaac displaces Ishmael; in an odd exchange contrary to the right of the elder brother, Jacob displaces Esau; and against the right of the first-born Ephraim is preferred over Manasseh. Jesus took up the theme of two brothers in a new way and gave it an unmistakable meaning corresponding to the historical change that our Lord ascribed to the arrival of his own hour.[19] In the Matthean parable, the rebellious son first defies his father but then still obeys him, while the other son submits verbally but in reality shows no concern for doing his father's will. This brings out what is in fact occurring as Jesus preaches: the tax-collectors and prostitutes truly hear God's call, while the "pious" and "righteous" in the end do their own will.

The Lukan parable of brothers differs in that it depicts what takes place as salvation history reaches its full expanse at the hour of Jesus Christ. The son once lost who returned home represents the nations in their thousand years of error far from the father's house of the one God amid the apparent delights of idol-worship which however lead to final bankruptcy. The son who stayed at home but became envious stands for righteous Israel, which cannot bear seeing the homecoming of the pagans and God's unconditional goodness toward sinners, but instead feels itself defrauded of the reward of its patient faith through the centuries.

These parables make it seem as if the outcasts of long ago, Ishmael and Esau, have returned to favor. But the parables do not answer questions which arise about the strange interconnection of the destinies of the sons and about the lot of the one favored for so long. Instead they are content to be a word of present address and a message of good news about God's mercy toward those seemingly outcast and forgotten.

Paul attempts a synthesis of all this in Romans 9–11, where the overarching affirmation posits God's unsearchable freedom in choosing. Within this the Apostle uncovers the changing linkage of the respective destinies, with the alter-

18 Rom. 11:15.

19 Luke 15:11–32; Matt. 21:28–32.

nating shifts from rejection to election serving in the end the rescue of both groups. "For God has imprisoned all in disobedience so that he may be merciful to all."[20]

This makes it clear that the respective services rendered to each other have their ultimate basis in the vicarious representation of Jesus Christ, from which both groups live. For Paul the decisive contrast is not between Jews and pagans, but between humanity and Jesus Christ, while the decisive change of places is not the Jewish-pagan role-exchange, which we tend to notice first, but the exchange between Christ and humanity, in which for us "he was made to be sin" and to bear the curse of those disobedient to the law, which we in truth all are, when for us he hung on a tree.[21]

Paul gave this theology of vicarious representation its theoretical background in his teaching on the two Adams,[22] which also allowed him to apply it to the life in history of those who live from Christ. For from birth we are all initially "the first Adam" caught in egotism, living for ourselves over against others and for this destined to suffer death. We are not capable of true life since we seek it in ourselves. But we are all called to become in Christ the second Adam, by passing from lives of self-seeking to living for others, that is, to sharing in Christ's service of representation, by which he recreated us for life by taking our place in death and thereby opening space for us in his own sphere of life. This approach makes it clear that Paul did not only apply the theme of place-exchange, that is vicarious representation, to the general historical structure of the exchange between Jews and pagans, but he made it decisively significant for individual Christian living and especially for that of the Apostle. Thus he took up Moses' self-offering, to be for the sake of his own people cast out from God, that is, from Christ.[23] Thus Paul saw in the sufferings of imprisonment a completion in his own flesh of Christ's afflictions for the sake of Christ's body the church.[24] Clear traits of this conception appear then in the image of the Apostle sketched in Second Corinthians.[25]

The Johannine writings also work out this extension of Christ's service of vicarious representation to the point of applying it to the lives of individual Christians, as we read in First John, "We have known love in this, that he laid down his life for us—and we ought to lay down our lives for one another."[26] We recall above all the great image of the Lord carrying out the role of Servant when

20 Rom. 11:32.

21 1 Cor. 5:21; Gal. 3:13.

22 Rom. 5:12–21 and 1 Cor. 15:45–49.

23 Rom. 9:3.

24 Col. 1:24.

25 Especially 2 Cor. 4:5 and chapter 11.

26 1 John 3:16.

he washed his disciples' feet and thereby gave a living sign of what Christian life should be from then on and forever.[27]

II. The Historical Development of Vicarious Representation

Based on the Pauline conception of the church as Christ's body and on what this posits about the coordination of services, the church understood it to be an essential quality of its own reality that believers were oriented to serve one another. A classic formulation of this image of the church comes from Methodius of Olympus.

> The higher souls, who have a more inward grasp of the truth, cast away, in their perfect purity and perfect faith, the follies of the flesh, and thus become the church and helpmate of Christ; to him they are, according to the words of the Apostle, betrothed and espoused to him as a virgin, in order that they may receive within themselves the pure and fecund seed of doctrine and cooperate as helpers in teaching for the redemption of others. But those who are still imperfect and only beginners in doctrine will be drawn by the more perfect into the pregnant womb of the redemption, and formed as in a mother's body, till they are born and brought to existence ... ; for those, in turn, thanks to their progress, have become the church and cooperate in the birth and training of other children, in that they accomplish the immaculate will of the Logos in the womb of their souls as in a mother's body.[28]

It was especially in early penitential practice, with its various liturgical and other possibilities of intercessory prayer, that this image of the church came to realization, including both those supporting and those being supported, so that the weak lived from the service and burden-bearing of the strong in Christian love. This conception grounds a central notion of Christian worship in Augustine, for whom the *communio sanctorum*, that is, the community of the praying, suffering, and loving church, is properly the one who confers the sacraments. Here Christ's service as mediator comes to realization through the *Christus totus, caput et membra* [the whole Christ, head and members].

---

27 John 13:1–16.

28 Methodius, *Symposium* [The Banquet], Logos 3, par. 8 [including a reference to 2 Cor. 11:2, on the church espoused to Christ], cited from Hans Urs von Balthasar, "Who Is the Church?," trans. A. V. Littledale with Alexander Dru, in *Explorations in Theology*, vol. 2, *Spouse of the Word* (San Francisco: Ignatius, 1991), 143–191, at 175. [Methodius, said to have been bishop in Lycia in the latter part of the third century, wrote influential theological and ascetical treatises in Greek, of which few are extant, and is reported to have suffered martyrdom under Diocletian about 311 AD. (Translator's Note)]

What has been shown so far is the representative bearing of burdens by the faithful along with our Lord in the inner life of the church, that is, in the community of believers in Christ. In contrast, a well-known motif of Alexandrian theology is more ample. Here the church senses itself oriented beyond itself toward the whole of humanity, especially by the parable of the shepherd who brings home the lost sheep, when this is applied allegorically to the Logos who brings humanity back to its origin. The church as well does not stand simply for itself, but "can know herself (in the humble awareness of her election), as representative for mankind before God, in faith, prayer, and sacrifice, in hope for all, and still more in love for all."[29]

The succeeding centuries saw the christological aspect of vicarious representation largely displaced by the theory of satisfaction, which does imply the notion of representation but in fact overlaid it so much with juridical categories that its original power of illumination could hardly have any effect.

One can ascertain the same juridicizing of thought in ecclesiology, in which the doctrine of *thesaurus ecclesiae* [the treasure of the church] came to dominate ongoing thinking about bearing burdens in and by the church. The historical-theological perception of the church's service to all humanity disappeared almost completely from the field of vision. In modern times the idea of vicarious representation came back in the Sacred Heart devotion and then in the Marian devotion of Lourdes and Fatima, in which it was admittedly cut off from the mainstream of theological thinking. The latter had imprisoned itself in its own juridical concepts and thus vicarious representation was condemned at times to a peculiar devotional diminishment and hesitancy.

III. Systematic Theological Consideration of Vicarious Representation

Today the doctrine of vicarious representation is again gaining influence, above all because of Karl Barth's understanding of predestination and in this by his important interpretation of Romans 9–11. In fact this doctrine may well come to have decisive importance for understanding Christian existence in the world of today, in so far as it can help to give new meaning to what we say about the absolute character of Christianity and, closely related to this, about the notion of no salvation outside the church. The concept of vicarious representation can revitalize once again these endangered ideas which at first glance seem hardly tenable today. Our topic can thus enrich the total self-understanding of Christians and can open afresh the very possibility of our being Christian.

Christians of today will surely not hold stubbornly that they alone can attain salvation, nor will they fictitiously interpret non-Christians as being somehow intentional Christians or even Catholics. This would undermine the seriousness of our own Christian status, as often occurs quite simplistically by inventing a

29 Balthasar, "Who is the Church?," 183.

Christianity based on a desire of which people are themselves not aware. Instead, Christians can come to see that in the body of humanity there are works of service, which while not being required of all are nonetheless necessary for all, since all live from them. One will realize that the central service on which this whole body depends is the service rendered by Jesus Christ and one will further grasp that the community of believers in him carries on this service without which humanity cannot live.

One will thereby understand in a fresh way the meaning of the church's absolute value and how it is strictly necessary for salvation. Those who grasp in this way the content of the Christian reality will stop comparing themselves fallaciously with others in questions and calculations about the advantage they have in being Christian, as by helps toward living morally and by a higher sense of spiritual well-being and existential balance. One will realize that being called to the church, at least to judge humanly, quite possibly makes life not easier but more burdensome, simply because one is taken into a service that benefits all humanity. One will realize that being Christian is being-for-the-others and one does not have to deny that in many respects this is a burden, which though is the holy burden of serving humanity as a whole.

Being Christian appeals to human beings in their generosity and in the large-heartedness of being ready, like Simon of Cyrene, to serve under the world-historical cross of Jesus Christ, and so to take on the burden of all of history and thereby to render service to true living. Christians will thus not look aside enviously to compare the weight of the burdens laid on them with what seem to be much lesser burdens laid on the others, whom we do believe will arrive in heaven. Christians will instead happily lay hold of the commission given them and it will be indeed their humbling pride and joy, even in the darkest hours of testing, that God has called them, precisely them, to such a holy service. This service does not have its greatness in our being saved while the others are lost—which would be the attitude of the envious older brother and of the workers of the first hour—but it is great because the others also reach salvation *through* this our service!

Such an understanding of Christian existence then makes possible a new theology of history. Believers need no longer to worry about the Christian era being so extremely brief when compared with the total duration of humankind's history. It is also no longer puzzling that during the Christian era the Christian message has reached only a fraction of humanity. For the church to be the means of salvation for all, it does not have to extend itself visibly to all, but has instead its essential role in following Christ, who is uniquely "the one," and therein the church is the little flock, through which God however intends to save "the many." The church's service is not carried out *by* all human beings, but is indeed carried out *for* all of them.

One hardly needs to mention that understanding vicarious representation as the task of the church has no connection with a conception of *apokatastasis* or universal salvation which would eliminate individual responsibility or the possibility of guilt and damnation. Instead this view really shows the true responsibility of individuals much more clearly and demonstrates how serious this is. This is the deeper seriousness that never arises from a semi-pelagian conception of a *votum ecclesiae* [desire of being in the church], taken as some kind of good faith or sincerity. Vicarious representation makes it clear that in the differentiation of services there is no place for indifference about rendering one's service. In fact, resisting the inalterable commission given the individual makes one guilty of going contrary to God's saving will, which wants to make use of just this service for the benefit of the others.

It is also clear that the salvation arising in virtue of vicarious representation does not arrive mechanically in a person, but requires in the recipient some kind of openness and readiness, as we saw was inherent in the Old Testament theme of solidarity. A Pauline type of *pistis* [faith] must be somehow present, but we do not have to determine in detail what this could be. One might then even speak of this attitude of openness as a *votum ecclesiae* [desire of being in the church], but one must not forget that this is only the subjective side of a totality which only has sense and meaning through the objective reality of the vicarious representation of the *Christus totus* [the whole Christ]. Neglect of this leads to practically declaring that human good will is itself the sufficient principle of salvation for the larger portion of humanity—which is to surrender the whole doctrine of grace.

In conclusion, one may say both that the notion of vicarious representation is one of the fundamental ideas to which Scripture gives witness and that its rediscovery can in the present hour of world-history decisively help Christianity toward renewing and deepening its self-understanding.[30]

Bibliography[31]

Buchsel, Friedrich. "*anti*" [in place of]. In *Theological Dictionary of the New Testament*, eds. Gerhard Kittel and Gerhard Friedrich; trans. and ed., Geoffrey

30 Translator's Note: This essay appeared in translations of the *Handbuch theologischer Grundbegriffe* into Italian (1966), French (1967), and Spanish (1979). Shortly after the original publication, the Swiss Catholic theologian, Johannes Feiner, adopted J. Ratzinger's main argument in an exposition of the mission of the Church in its association with Christ in representative service and worship within the divine economy of saving grace given universally to human beings. Feiner's essay came out in *Gott und Welt*, a collection honoring Karl Rahner in 1964, with an English translation appearing as "Particular and Universal Saving History," in *One, Holy, Catholic, and Apostolic*, ed. Herbert Vorgrimler (London: Sheed & Ward, 1968), 163–206. Karl-Heinz Menke developed J. Ratzinger's main topic in his ambitious work, *Stellvertretung. Schlüsselbegriff christlichen Lebens und theologische Grundkategorie* [Vicarious Representation. Key Concept of Christian Life and Basic Category of Theology] (Einsiedeln: Johannes Verlag, 1991).

31 Translator's Note. Volumes translated into English are given here with reference to the translation, adding an indication of the date of the original work to which J. Ratzinger made reference in his original text of 1963.

W. Bromley. 10 vols. Grand Rapids: Eerdmans, 1964–1976. 1:372–373 (original, 1933).

de Lubac, Henri. *Catholicism. Christ and the Common Destiny of Man*. San Francisco: Ignatius, 1988 (original, 1938).

Balthasar, Hans Urs von. *The Theology of Karl Barth*. New York: Holt, Reinhard and Wilson, 1971 (original, 1951).

de Fraine, Jean. "Individu et societé dans le religion de l'Ancient Testament" [Individual and Society in Old Testament religion]. *Biblica* 33 (1952): 324–355.

Wright, George Ernest. *The Biblical Doctrine of Man in Society*. London: SCM Press, 1954.

Zimmerli, Walter, and Joachim Jeremias. "*pais theou*" [servant of God]. In *Theological Dictionary of the New Testament*. 5:654–717 (original, 1954).

Kremer, Jacob. *Was an den Leiden Christi noch mangelt* [What Is Still Lacking in the Sufferings of Christ]. Bonn: Hanstein, 1956.

Nötscher, Friedrich. *Zur theologische Terminologie der Qumran-Texte* [Theological Terminology in the Texts of Qumran]. Bonn: Hanstein, 1956.

Cullmann, Oscar. *Christology of the New Testament*. Philadelphia: Westminster, 1959 (original, 1958).

Rad, Gerhard von. *Old Testament Theology*. 2 vols. New York: Harper, 1962–1965. 1:394–395 (original, 1958); 2:275–277, 403–404 (original, 1960).

Ratzinger, Joseph. "Die neuen Heiden und die Kirche" [The New Pagans and the Church]. *Hochland* 51 (1958): 1–11.

Scharbert, Josef. *Solidarität in Segen und Fluch im Alten Testament und in seiner Umwelt* [Solidarity in Blessings and Curses in the Old Testament and in Its Surrounding Cultures]. Bonn: Hanstein, 1958.

________. "Stellvertretende Sühneleiden in den Ebed-Jahwe-Liedern und in altorientalischen Ritualtexten" [Vicarious Sufferings of Atonement in the Songs of the Lord's Servant and in Ancient Near Eastern Ritual Texts]. *Biblische Zeitschrift* 2 (1958): 190–213.

Delling, Gerhard. "*antanaplēroō*" [I fill up a lack]. In *Theological Dictionary of the New Testament*. 6:307 (original, 1959).

Scharbert, Josef. "Solidarität" [solidarity]. In *Bibeltheologisches Wörterbuch*, ed. Johannes B. Bauer, 699–706. Graz: Styria Verlag, 1959.

________. "Die Rettung der 'Vielen' durch die 'Wenigen' im Alten Testament" [The Rescue of the "Many" through the "Few" in the Old Testament]. *Trierer theologische Zeitschrift* 68 (1959): 146–159.

Ratzinger, Joseph. *The Open Circle. The Meaning of Christian Brotherhood*. New York: Sheed and Ward, 1966 (original, 1960).

Balthasar, Hans Urs von. "Who is the Church?" In *Spouse of the Word*, trans. A. V. Littledale with Alexander Dru, in *Explorations in Theology*, vol. 2. San Francisco: Ignatius, 1991. 143–191, at 170–184 (original, 1961).

Letter & Spirit 7 (2011): 221-230

Liturgy[1]
The Context of Patristic Exegesis

~: **Patrick McGoldrick** :~

Taking the title of this paper fairly literally, I propose to speak rather about liturgy than about patristic exegesis, examining historically and in more general terms the relationship between the liturgy and Scripture. I hope that this will throw some light, direct and indirect, on the context that the liturgy provided for the patristic understanding of the Scriptures and so on the influence it exercised on this understanding.

The Relationship of Scripture and Liturgy: Beginnings

The relationship between Scripture and liturgy is a rich and complex one, because both are rich and complex realities. We can find a good point from which to start in three episodes from the Gospels, three occasions on which Jesus brought word and ritual action closely together.

If the Last Supper was a paschal meal, there would have been a place for the *haggadah*, presumably spoken by Jesus. Moreover, two of the Gospel accounts attribute a discourse to Jesus: John at considerable length, and Luke more economically. The celebration of the Last Supper seemed to call for a word from Jesus that was additional to the normal prayers and to Jesus' own special ritual words.

In John 6 the discourse on the Bread of Life seems to speak both of the bread that was Jesus' word and of the bread that was His flesh. Word and sacrament, it may be hinted, belong harmoniously together.

In Luke 24, Jesus made Himself known to the two disciples on the road to Emmaus in the word by which He opened the Scripture and in the breaking of the bread. Would the Christian hearer not be reminded of the Eucharist?

These three texts then, involving Jesus Himself, suggest an affinity between word and sacrament such that liturgical action invites the accompaniment of the word and the word somehow tends toward sacrament.

"In the beginning was the Word," John said, not "in the beginning was Scripture." There is no doubt that the liturgy had an important role to play in the emergence of the Christian Scriptures. While historically this must have been a complex matter, and many fine distinctions should be made, it is enough for the purpose of this paper to refer in a broad and general way to some early connections between liturgy and Scripture:

1 This article originally appeared in *Scriptural Interpretation in the Fathers*, eds. Thomas Finan and Vincent Twomey (Dublin: Four Courts Press, 1995), 27–37.

a) From the New Testament we know that passages from the Old Testament were read in a Christian sense.[2]

b) The memory of Jesus, His actions, words, etc. and the experience of His disciples were handed on in Christian assemblies, many of them no doubt liturgical. This transmission of His memory was connected with the early Christians' own situations and own lives, and so the tradition grew. Apostolic preaching and tradition of this sort must have been important for the formation of the Scriptures.

c) The letters of Paul were read at and exchanged between Christian assemblies.[3]

Thus the emergence of the Christian liturgy and the emergence of the corpus of Scripture are closely related, so that the early Church includes the word in this form as part of its service of worship. The ritual has its word, its accompanying narrative. From the beginning the word, Scripture, is at home in the liturgical assembly and is not something extraneous or alien or additional.

A couple of sentences from a mid-second-century text of St. Justin Martyr can sum up the development. He is describing the Sunday Eucharist of the assembled believers: "The memoirs of the apostles or the writings of the prophets are read for as long as time allows. When the reader has stopped, the one presiding speaks, admonishing and inviting all to imitate such fine examples." Prayer follows and then the eucharistic liturgy.[4]

Reading of Scripture in the Liturgical Assembly

So the Church has acquired its Scriptures, written texts, New Testament and Old Testament. How will it use these in the liturgy?

A first answer: by reading them publicly in the assembly. It will arrange them in many different ways; different numbers of readings, different systems will eventually emerge; different rituals too. And yet there will be notable agreement about the importance of the reading, about the appropriateness of certain books and pericopes for certain seasons or occasions; about the use of the Psalms; about Gospel acclamations; about signs of reverence for the word. There will be universal acknowledgment of the place of the reading of the Scriptures in the liturgy.

This raises a further question: how have the scriptural texts functioned in the liturgy? Different roles can be distinguished. I borrow the enumeration that

---

2 See, for example, Luke 4:16–21; Acts 4:24–30; 8:26–40; 13:14–40.

3 In addition to these connections, it is sufficient to note here that the synagogue service had an important influence on the developing Christian liturgy of the word; to note also that some acclamations, hymns, prayers, greetings or other formulas from early Christian liturgy were quoted or echoed in the Scriptures; and to note finally that the regularity of the liturgical assembly, the celebration of the Eucharist, and the practice of Baptism were bound to have had some impact on the contents of the Scriptures.

4 Apol. I 67.

follows from Paul Bradshaw.[5] The functions are not mutually exclusive; the dominance of one in a particular case does not exclude others:

a) A *didactic* or catechetical function can be recognized, one that starts from the Scriptures themselves. The Scriptures are read to make people familiar with them, to deepen the understanding. This practice may have roots in the liturgy of the synagogue and there are some indications that Christian assemblies adopted early a practice of regular, sustained—you might say, systematic—reading week by week and, perhaps in some places later, day by day. The Christian people must know the most important portions of the Scriptures and so they are formed in the Christian spirit and grow in the knowledge and love of God. Indeed, how else will the great assembly become familiar with the Scripture before the age of printing or even before the mass production of bibles and the spread of literacy? Systems of readings will develop; the lectionary will emerge. A homily or address or commentary or explanation will frequently accompany the reading, required by the primarily didactic function of the reading. In this first case envisaged, the liturgy largely provides the occasion or the context of the reading; the relationship of the reading to the sacramental act that follows will be an indirect one, primarily through the internal effect that it achieves in the participants as it forms them in the Christian spirit.

b) The second function is *anamnetic* and takes its start from the liturgical rite. As an example of this Bradshaw cites the practice in the early Jerusalem cathedral office of reading the same text every Sunday morning throughout the year: the account of the passion and resurrection of Christ. Obviously the primary purpose here is not didactic but rather to recall the resurrection at just the spot where and the time when it was believed to have happened. The rite then was an anamnesis, the reading serving to recall God's great deed and to interpret the meaning of the rite and provide warrant for it. This is just one example of what went on very widely from the fourth century. Before then what we know as the liturgical year had scarcely begun to emerge, and its evolution will obviously be the principal influence on the expansion and the development of this way of using Scripture in the liturgy. No doubt this use will have had some Jewish roots—in connection with the Passover especially—and Christians will have had something similar in their early celebration of the paschal vigil.[6]

---

5 Paul F. Bradshaw, "The Use of the Bible in Liturgy: Some Historical Perspectives," in *Studia Liturgica* 22 (1992): 36–43. In another article in the same number of this journal, "Lectionaries—Principles and Problems: A Comparative Analysis," H.T. Allen Jr. in a somewhat similar way identifies six functions of lectionaries (71–77). The greater part of this volume is given over to the papers of the Congress of Societas Liturgica held in Toronto in 1991 on Bible and Liturgy. Much of this material is of interest to our topic.

6 Compare the inclusion of the institution narrative in the celebration of the Eucharist.

Where this is the primary purpose of the scriptural reading, the texts will be specially selected, that is, they will not simply follow the order of regular readings,[7] and they will be more directly related to the sacramental rite that follows them or, better, they will be more obviously part of an integral rite.

Bradshaw warns that didactic and anamnetic functions may both be present together and indeed that over time or for groups at the same time one may yield in priority to the other.

c) The third function, identified by Bradshaw as *paracletic,* starts from the worshippers. What are their needs that are to be met by appropriate Scripture reading? This is primarily a pastoral function. Readings are chosen accordingly for such occasions as funerals, votive Masses, Masses for particular needs, and so on.

d) The final function is *doxological,* to glorify God, a purpose that underlies all public reading of Scripture. The liturgical reading of the Scriptures is always the acknowledgment of the word of God, and hence a confession of God's glory. But this can be the dominant intention—readings have continued to be proclaimed in ancient languages even when these are no longer commonly understood.

In proposing this useful distinction of functions Bradshaw did not intend to confine himself to any particular time but ranged over the whole history of the Christian liturgy. However, all four functions can be recognized within the patristic period. Local and cultural influences will also have come into play, of course, in the way and the circumstances in which these functions were fulfilled and in further determination of them.

What is happening when the Scriptures are read in the liturgy? The word, frequently in origin a spoken word (the prophetic word of the Old Testament, the Gospel word preached by the apostles)—this word, written down and preserved as Scripture is now restored to its original function and its true status as the living word of God spoken to God's people. As has been suggested earlier, the Scripture is nowhere more at home than in the liturgical assembly. It is for the reader and for the preacher to enable the word to speak today, to be a living and active word, a sword that will apply its sharp edge, cutting into the heart of the community gathered to hear it. The Scripture then is to become word once again through the ministries of the reader and the preacher. On reading from the prophet Isaiah, Jesus said: "Today this scripture is fulfilled in your hearing."[8] Something of that remains the aim of the proclamation in the "today" of the liturgy.

According to Paul De Clerck, there is an act of tradition in the liturgical assembly. Through the proclamation of Scripture the word of God is *received* in faith by the participants as the living word of God; it is *assimilated* in a variety of

---

7 In his notable work *The Origins of the Liturgical Year* (New York: Liturgical Press, 1986), T.J. Talley proposes that on occasion the influence may have worked in the opposite direction, that it may have been the course reading of one of the Gospels that occasioned the introduction of elements of the liturgical year.

8 Luke 4:21.

ways by them, made their own, translated into action, done; and it is actualized by preaching.[9] And so it is *transmitted*. It is not enough, after all, simply to have the Bible. Celebrated in faith, this is the story that gives identity to the Christian people and, in being appropriated and passed on in the liturgy, that takes within itself new assemblies and succeeding generations. Thus the history of salvation continues, the divine plan is worked out, the mystery of Christ is accomplished, God's great deeds are somehow prolonged, when the Scriptures are proclaimed in the liturgical assembly.

From all of this there emerges something of the context of patristic exegesis, something of the dynamics at work when the Fathers addressed themselves to the Scriptures and then to their hearers (or, to put the matter differently, when the Fathers were addressed by the Scriptures and then enabled the participants to be addressed by that same living word).

Other Uses of Scripture in the Liturgy

Earlier the question was asked: how does the Church use the Scriptures in the liturgy? A first answer given was by reading them publicly in the assembly. A second answer may be given in two parts:

a) By taking over psalms and biblical canticles for use as Christian prayer and hymns in its liturgical celebrations.

This happened first with individual psalms, then with the Psalter as a whole and with some Old Testament canticles, and, more gradually, with some of the New Testament canticles. There may have been several related reasons for this and some variety in the interpretation of the fact. In the first place, before these psalms and canticles are the prayer of the Church addressed to God, they are part of the word of God spoken to the Church. Thus in the Mass, for example, the psalm was included in the liturgy of the word not simply to afford an opportunity for response to the readings; it was itself a proclamation of the word of God, as the reading from St Paul or one of the Gospels was, and it could be the subject of the homily. A second reason close to this was the fact that these psalms and canticles were viewed differently from non-scriptural compositions, having a quality all their own as part of the word of God. This gave them an authority lacking in popular hymns. It is well known that during the fourth century the Church abandoned almost completely its corpus of early non-biblical hymns because of the use of such compositions in support of heresy, notably Gnosticism and Arianism. As a result the standing of the psalms and other canticles was bound to be enhanced and their use to be increased: they were canonical and therefore trustworthy. A third important and all-pervasive factor at work was the interpretation of the psalms in the light of the mystery of Christ. This is perhaps the most decisive influence in

9 Paul De Clerck, "'In the beginning was the Word': Presidential Address," *Studia Liturgica* 22 (1992): 10f.

making the Jewish psalter the prayerbook of the Christian Church, and it is too well known to need elaboration here.[10]

b) By using biblical events, phrases, images, references, language in its prayers.

This second way was made relatively easy by the fact that a common text was in use in Greek, and later in Latin, and also because by and large the Fathers shared a rich common biblical culture. The use of the Scriptures in this way varied from a shallow and fairly banal employment of a biblical word or expression, an allusion that set off no deep resonances or suggested no fresh insight, all the way to a profoundly developed and sophisticatedly exploited typology.

Typology

Typology requires no explanation in this context. For the purpose of this paper I use the word very broadly here, much as in earlier times. The late Jean Daniélou dealt with this forty years ago in *Bible et liturgie*,[11] a book that still retains its value. Typology has its roots in the Scriptures themselves, which already read some of the events of the Old Testament in the light of Christ and find in them foreshadowings of the good things to come.

The liturgy is shot through with typology. This approach will influence the choice of Old Testament readings to accompany New Testament pericopes and the choice of texts for special occasions. But of more concern here is the way in which many of the prayers of the liturgy reflect this typological approach and develop it skillfully.

A good example can be seen in the Ordination Prayers of the *Apostolic Tradition* of Hippolytus, probably written in Rome about 215.[12] The prayer for the ordination of a bishop looks back to God's appointment of leaders and priests among the Jewish people, to His provision of ministry for His sanctuary, to the choice He exercised from the beginning. Now God is asked to send upon the candidate the power of the governing Spirit given by God to Jesus Christ and given by Jesus to the Apostles, who established the Church in every place as God's sanctuary. The work of the bishop is characterized as an exercise of the high priesthood and is further described with scriptural phrases and allusions.

10 See B. Fischer, *Die Psalmenfrommigkeit der Martyrerkirche* (Freiburg 1949), a work updated and translated several times since; L. G. Walsh, "The Christian Prayer of the Psalms" in *Studies in Pastoral Liturgy*, vol 3, ed. P. Murray O.S.B. (Dublin, 1967), 29–73.

11 See Jean Daniélou, *Bible et liturgie, la théologie biblique des sacrements et des fêtes d'après les Pères de l'Église* (Paris: Éditions du Cerf, 1951). For an English translation, see *The Bible and the Liturgy* (London: Darton, Longman & Todd, 1960). For a recent (positive) retrospective appraisal see G. Wainwright, "'Bible et Liturgie': Daniélou's Work Revisited," *Studia Liturgica* 22 (1992): 154–162.

12 B. Botte, *La tradition apostolique de Saint Hippolyte : essai de reconstitution.* (Münster Westfalen: Aschendorf, 1989) num. 3, 7.8; pp. 6–11,20–23,26–27.

Likewise the prayer for the ordination of a presbyter sets the context of God's favor towards His people and appeals to the choice of elders made by Moses at God's command and filled by God with the Spirit He had given to Moses.

For the ordination of a deacon the prayer bases itself on God's sending of Jesus Christ as servant of the divine will and revealer of the divine plan. The deacon in turn is referred to as servant and as chosen for the service of the Church, and the prayer goes on to speak of his service in the sanctuary and to the offering of the appointed high priest (that is, the bishop).

The point is clear. A line is established that runs from the beginning of time through events, figures and institutions (the sanctuary, the offering, the priesthood) of the Old Testament, the event and the person of Jesus Christ, and the present life of the Church. These figures, events and institutions find their focus in Jesus Christ and they are given actuality in the liturgical rite today. What unties all of them and allows the prayer to see them in a single perspective is belief in the continuing action of God carried out in fulfillment of an unfolding salvific design that was revealed and pre-eminently realized in Jesus Christ.

A similar example is found in the ancient Roman blessing of baptismal water, the consecration of the font.[13] Here the symbol of water carries the divine gift of salvation, of life. The prayer cites the primeval waters over which the Spirit was moving (so that water conceives the power of sanctification); the flood, in which by water sin was brought to an end and virtue began; the four rivers that flow from paradise to water the whole world; the water that gives joy to God's city; the water given in the desert; the water of Cana changed into wine; the water in which Jesus was baptized; the water that poured from His side. The Holy Spirit is invoked to give fecundity to the water of this font in order that it may bring about all the salvific effects of Baptism (which are also developed).

Water has been God's instrument and sign of salvation from the beginning, so that events and texts of the past can be read in the light of the mystery of Christ and in turn can enable us to understand what God does now in the sacrament of Baptism. Scripture and liturgy are brought into a most harmonious relationship, since ultimately it is the same mystery that both celebrate.

A further example is provided by the ancient Roman prayer, which we still use today, for the consecration of chrism.[14] This prayer begins, as it says, "in the beginning," when at God's command the earth brought forth the olive tree and so the oil that provides chrism. With prophetic insight David anticipated the sacraments of God's grace in singing of the joy that the oil would bring us; at the time of the flood the olive branch carried by the dove was the sign of a future gift, announcing

13 Liber Sacramentorum Romanae Aeclesiae Ordinis Anni Circuli, herausgegeben von Leo Cunibert Mohlberg, O.S.B. (Rome, 1960), nn. 445–448, pp. 72–74. This text remained in use virtually unchanged until it was revised after the Second Vatican Council.

14 Liber Sacramentorum Romanae Aeclesiae Ordinis Anni Circuli, nn. 386–388, p. 62.

the restoration of peace. All of this, the prayer continues, is clearly fulfilled now in Baptism with its water and its oil. God commanded the washing and then the anointing by Moses of Aaron as priest; and chrism attained even greater honour in the baptism of Jesus and the descent of the Holy Spirit in the form of a dove upon Him. So God manifestly fulfilled David's prophecy that Christ would be anointed with the oil of gladness beyond His fellows. The prayer then asks the Father to sanctify the oil, to infuse it with the power of the Holy Spirit through Christ, from whose name chrism takes its name. By chrism God anointed priests, kings, prophets and martyrs. For those to be baptized may it be the chrism of salvation for eternal life.

The line and the continuity of this prayer are even clearer. Past events look towards the future; future fulfillment is seen and anticipated in the past. And all of this is brought to a point in this present rite and in the use of the oil in the Baptism (and in the other sacraments) for which this rite prepares.

A final and somewhat different example can be seen in some of the great eastern anaphoras (on which our Roman Eucharistic Prayer IV was modeled). There the theme of our thanksgiving is the whole sweep of history seen in the light of the economy of salvation.

Is the Eucharist merely the occasion for the use of richly-textured biblical prayers of such magnificent scope? More than that, I should think. Rather, these are prayers that proclaim a history, a design that is celebrated in the Eucharist and finds fulfillment and actuality there, in anticipation of the consummation of all things in Christ in God's kingdom.

I should like to select one point as a particular illustration. In the epiclesis of very many prayers, especially Syrian texts and those influenced by the Anaphora of James, the eucharistic action of the Spirit is set in the context of, and in relation to, some of the Spirit's actions recounted in Scripture, in particular His coming on Mary and being active in the Incarnation, the descent on Jesus at the Jordan, the coming on the Apostles at Pentecost. This is done in either of two ways: (a) by referring explicitly to the scriptural episodes in a brief development on the Spirit at this point; (b) by using of the Spirit's coming in the Eucharist such words as "illapse," "descend upon," "rest on," "hover over," "overshadow," "dwell in," "breathe on" (singly or in some combination), which are understood as allusions to the operation of the Spirit in the Scriptures.

So, for example, the Spirit who came upon Mary and formed a body for the Word is to come upon us and upon the mysteries, and by His descent is to make the bread the holy Body of Christ and what is in the cup the Blood of Christ, for the fruit of the Eucharist among the participants. Similarly, as the Spirit rested on the only-begotten Son in the form of a dove in the river Jordan and as He appeared in tongues of fire on the Apostles, so He is to dwell and to rest on us and on the offerings, and by His coming is to make the bread and the wine the Body and

Blood of Christ, for the benefit of those who share in the Eucharist. The connection being established between the two sets of actions is closer than simply their common origin in the same agent, the Holy Spirit. The Eucharist can be seen as the actualization of a divine economy revealed and realized in and by Jesus Christ. In the context of the whole Eucharist the epiclesis seeks the realization by the Spirit in the Church of what was accomplished once for all in the paschal mystery of Jesus Christ. The role that the Holy Spirit played in the mysteries of Christ's earthly life, in the resurrection, and on the Pentecost, He continues to play in the Eucharist and in making the Eucharist effective in the Church's life.[15]

These are some notable examples from the liturgy of both East and West, the liturgy the Fathers would have celebrated. Its vision was one they would have shared, its sacramental world one they were at ease in, and, of course, many of them composed and adapted the classic prayers of the liturgy. They preached the great mystagogies that were part of the liturgy and explained the liturgy. This typological approach then is one they will develop expertly and energetically. They will recognize a continuity and a progression that stretches from creation, from Adam and Eve and the dominant figures of Genesis through God's mighty deeds in favour of the Chosen People, through the figures of the Old Testament that in their own way pointed to and anticipated Christ, to Christ the fulfillment of the promises, and from Christ through the times of the Church to the consummation of all in the fullness of God's kingdom, in which the Church shares even now by anticipation. It is a magnificent vision of faith and it gives the Fathers a perspective in which to read history.[16] The overall continuity which they recognize confirms their sense of the unity in Christ of the two Testaments and of the completion of the Old in the New, a sense elegantly summed up in St. Augustine's phrase, *et in vetere novum latet et in novo vetus patet* ["the New is in the Old concealed, the Old is in the New revealed"—ed.].[17] Within this they can embrace some of the great, enduring anthropological and religious realities (e.g. sacrifice, guilt, expiation, law). Such an understanding is obviously of enormous hermeneutical importance for their exegesis of the Scriptures. I am aware that some or much of this would be challenged today, but it is not the concern of this paper to deal with such contemporary questioning.[18]

---

15 This paragraph and the preceding one are taken largely from my article, "The Holy Spirit and the Eucharist," *Irish Theological Quarterly* 50 (1983/84): 48–66.

16 The liturgy gives expression to this not only in its readings and prayer but also in icons, ritual actions, etc.

17 Quaest. In Hept. II, 73, (CSEL 28/2, 141); in this original context the verbs are in the present subjunctive.

18 A third answer, of less concern to this paper, can be given to the question, how does the Church use the Scriptures in the liturgy?—by developing rites from events and actions described in its Scriptures. This can range from the establishment of liturgical feasts (for example, Christmas, Ascension, the Martyrdom of St. Stephen) to such imitations and adaptations as the fast of

Conclusion

The liturgy will not allow us to treat the Scriptures simply as written texts. The reading must be proclaimed by a minister so as to be heard by all present ("heard" in the biblical sense). The setting of the proclamation must be such as to heighten expectation and engage the hearers actively. Because in the final analysis it is Christ who is present and who addresses them. So too, from the beginning the liturgy has had the tradition of preaching and continues to insist on it. The word must be interpreted for and applied to *this* people, *now.*

This word contained in the Scriptures and proclaimed in the Christian assembly is made alive, given its cutting edge in the celebration of the liturgy. The sacrament actualizes it, makes it effective again and again.

Thus the liturgy will not allow us to hear the Scripture as a message from the past or as a record of events and persons long ago. The liturgy insists on bringing that history, that story, down into the present, today, the liturgical *hodie*. Neither will it permit the hearers to remain within the confines of their immediate present. As the liturgy sees it, the Scriptures proclaim a mystery, a mystery that is continuing and is ever actual, a mystery that transcends the limitations of past and present and future, of here and there. This is the mystery that the liturgy engages; every time we celebrated the Sacrament that mystery is actualized for us and we are carried into reaches that lie beyond space and time. This is the understanding that liturgy has of itself, an understanding that the Fathers shared. It must influence their exegesis.

---

forty days, the washing of the feet, the procession with palms, the ephphetha, some anointings. The development of the liturgy and the popular devotions of Holy Week is interesting and instructive in this regard, as is the tendency through many centuries towards an allegorical or a dramatic interpretation of the Mass with reference to Christ's passion and death. For some expansion of this see Bradshaw, "The Use of the Bible in Liturgy," 49–52.

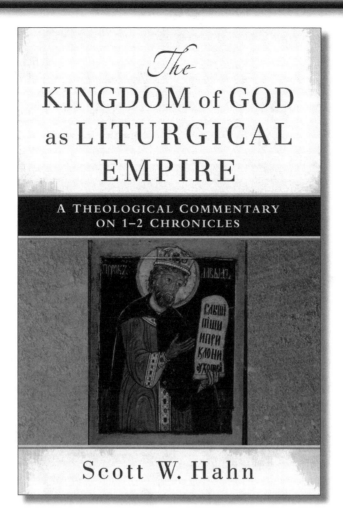

COVENANT AND COMMUNION

THE BIBLICAL THEOLOGY OF POPE BENEDICT XVI

BY SCOTT W. HAHN

"A superb introduction to the way in which the theology of Pope Benedict XVI has been shaped by the Bible. Hahn's crisp and clear analysis puts the reader at the very center of this remarkable pope's thought."

Gary Anderson,

University of Notre Dame

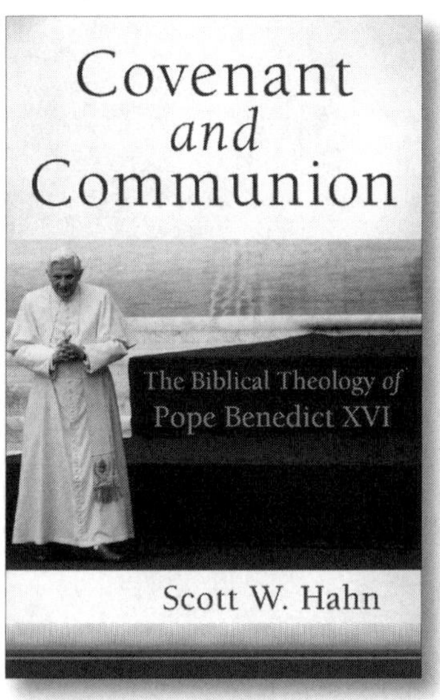

Cardinal Joseph Ratzinger's election as Pope Benedict XVI brought a world-class biblical theologian to the papacy. There is an intensely biblical quality to his pastoral teaching and he has demonstrated a keen concern for the authentic interpretation of sacred Scripture.

Here Scott Hahn, a foremost interpreter of Catholic thought and life, offers a probing look at Benedict's biblical theology and provides a clear and concise introduction to his life and work. Hahn argues that the heart of Benedict's theology is salvation history and the Bible and shows how Benedict accepts historical criticism but recognizes its limits. The author also explains how Benedict reads the overall narrative of Scripture and how he puts it to work in theology, liturgy, and Christian discipleship.

160 pages | Publisher: Baker Brazos Press (October 1, 2009) | $21.99

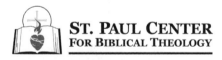

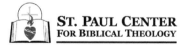